Rethinking Intellectual History

Rethinking Intellectual History

Texts, Contexts, Language

by DOMINICK LACAPRA

Cornell University Press

ITHACA AND LONDON

First published 1983 by Cornell University Press.
First printing, Cornell Paperbacks, 1983.
Fourth printing 1990.

International Standard Book Number (cloth) 0-8014-1587-x
International Standard Book Number (paper) 0-8014-9886-4
Library of Congress Catalog Card Number 83-7218

Printed in the United States of America

*Librarians: Library of Congress cataloging information
appears on the last page of the book.*

*The paper in this book is acid-free and meets the guidelines
for permanence and durability of the Committee on Production
Guidelines for Book Longevity of the Council on Library Resources.*

And what work nobler than transplanting
foreign Thought into the barren domestic soil;
except indeed planting Thought of your own,
which the fewest are privileged to do?

Thomas Carlyle, *Sartor Resartus*

Contents

Acknowledgments

Many people have contributed to the writing of this book, above all, students at Cornell University who participated in courses given on related topics. I am, however, especially grateful to Martin Jay of the University of California at Berkeley and Harry Harootunian of the University of Chicago for reading the manuscript and offering many insightful suggestions.

The last three chapters are published here for the first time. The other chapters, or versions of them, have appeared elsewhere and are reprinted by permission: "Rethinking Intellectual History and Reading Texts," *History and Theory* 19 (1980), © 1980 by Wesleyan University; "A Poetics of Historiography: Hayden White's *Tropics of Discourse*," *Modern Language Notes* 93 (1978), published by John Hopkins University Press; "Reading Exemplars: *Wittgenstein's Vienna* and Wittgenstein's *Tractatus*," *Diacritics* 9 (1979); "Who Rules Metaphor? Paul Ricoeur's Theory of Discourse," *Diacritics* 10 (1980); "Habermas and the Grounding of Critical Theory," *History and Theory* 16 (1977), © 1977 by Wesleyan University; "Sartre and the Question of Biography," *The French Review* 55 (1982), special issue no. 7; and "Marxism in the Textual Maelstrom: Fredric Jameson's *The Political Unconscious*," *History and Theory* 21 (1982), © 1982 by Wesleyan University. "Rethinking Intellectual History and Reading Texts" also appeared in Dominick LaCapra and Steven L. Kaplan, eds., *Modern Euro-*

pean Intellectual History: Reappraisals and New Perspectives (Ithaca, 1982). I reprint it here only because it serves as a useful introduction to the other essays in this volume and may be read differently given its new context.

DOMINICK LACAPRA

Ithaca, New York

Rethinking Intellectual History

Introduction

"Who thinks abstractly?" This leading question serves as the title to a remarkably concise and witty essay in which Hegel seems to depart from stereotypical portraits of him as the cumbersome theorist of totalization.[1] His object of attack is in fact the dogmatic advocacy of common sense with its ready stereotypes and naturalized concepts. In the example Hegel adduces, the murderer is seen in the light of common sense purely and simply as a murderer. This "perception" converts the murderer into an abstract "other" in a manner that denies both his humanity and, more pointedly, one's own degree of complicity with him. Hegel's conclusion is not that the murderer should not be punished but that punishment is a more problematic process than conventional categories and processes of naturalization would allow. And for Hegel it appears that "elevated" theory—conventionally seen as abstract—and the "lowly" understanding of a common old woman paradoxically combine to disclose the abstract and dubious nature of common sense that furnishes one-sided handles on reality. The perspective of the theorist somehow relates to the uncommon understanding of the common person who sees the severed head of the criminal blessed by God's grace in the light of a higher sun.

1. See *Hegel: Texts and Commentary*, tr. and ed. Walter Kaufmann (Garden City, N.Y., 1965), 114–118.

This philosophical parable may be applied to the standard notion of context as it has often functioned in intellectual history. The cliché that something can be understood only in context has long been the historian's daily bread. The attempt to return a thinker to his own times or to place his texts squarely in the past has often served as a mode of abstract categorization that drastically over-simplifies the problem of historical understanding. Indeed, the rhet-oric of contextualization has often encouraged narrowly documen-tary readings in which the text becomes little more than a sign of the times or a straightforward expression of one larger phenomenon or another. At the limit, this indiscriminate approach to reading and interpretation becomes a detour around texts and an excuse for not really reading them at all. It simultaneously avoids the claims texts make on us as readers—claims that impress themselves upon us both at naive and at theoretically sophisticated levels of understand-ing. And it underwrites the facile belief that anything one has to read slowly, or even reread, must be objectionably "abstract."

In literary criticism and philosophy, it was in good measure a reaction against the refusal to read that prompted an insistence upon close reading and careful scrutiny of the tense, ambiguous structure of complex texts. Yet this necessary emphasis upon the distinctive demands posed by difficult texts could readily be conjoined with the idea that a text is its own self-enclosed cosmos and that great art is autotelic. As historians reduced texts to mere documents, literary critics and philosophers reduced history to background information. Today, however, nothing is more prevalent than the injunction to go beyond formalism (except, perhaps, the tendency of historians not to achieve its rigor in analysis and of literary critics to fall back upon its assured victories in classroom teaching). At times this in-junction can induce a return to eclectic contextualism wherein the mere skeleton of formalist criticism is decorated helter-skelter with bits and pieces of contextual information of any and every prove-nance. Yet the interpretative practice of great formalists has often been more intricate and engaging than their polemical rhetoric would lead one to believe, and it at times broached a conception of

14

style that related text and context in a penetrating way. The one crucial context to which formalists were always sensitive was that formed by other written texts, especially those in the same or closely related genres. Indeed, aside from being a rebuke to lax and feuilletonistic contextualism, formalism could in certain contexts function as an avenue of cultural and even political protest. (This still is often true in central and eastern Europe, and it was at times at least partially the case in the late nineteenth and early twentieth centuries elsewhere. Before it became a secure posture inclining toward escapism, the elitist defense of the genteel tradition, and the workaday pedagogy of practical criticism, formalism could be an apotropaic gesture whereby the artist or theorist impudently turned his back on society.) The obvious problem at present is how to learn from formalism without accepting its more extreme claims at face value. This problem has, I think, been confronted more fully in areas of contemporary literary criticism and philosophy than it has in other disciplines, notably intellectual history. Literary criticism and philosophy are in many ways the "heavy sectors" of self-reflexive and self-critical theory at the present time. And it is perhaps by inquiring into these neighboring fields, where theoretical developments bearing upon the reading of texts have emerged in their strongest forms, that intellectual historians can acquire the conceptual means to come to terms with problems in their own field. At the very least, recent developments in these fields disclose the many ways critical self-reflection, theoretical inquiry, and rhetorical mode cannot be reduced, as they so often are in historiography, to debates about the referential content of propositions, the applicability of operational rules of method, and the embellishing or expressive role of a constricted, subjective, and often pear-shaped notion of "style." Instead the plurality of problems linked to the notion of dialogization, which itself cannot be identified with conventional versions of pluralism or with the rounded-off replies of a literal dialogue, become the polytropic order of the day.

Yet polemical animus should not induce rhetorical overkill that blinds one to the openings that have occurred in historiography in the recent past.[2] Indeed, in historiography, the demand for a close reading of contexts themselves has recently become widespread, in part through the impact of Clifford Geertz's elaboration in anthropology of the notion of "thick description."[3] The special value of this notion is the insistence upon the way a context has its own complex particularity that calls for detailed interpretation—indeed the way it may fruitfully be seen on the analogy of the text. Intellectual history shares with disciplines such as literary criticism and the history of philosophy, however, an initial focus upon complex written texts and a need to formulate as a problem what is often taken, deceptively, as a solution: the relationship between texts and their various pertinent contexts. It is only when the precise nature of this relationship is posited as a genuine problem that one will be able to counteract the dogmatic assumption that any given context—the author's intentions, a corpus of texts, a genre, a biography, the economic infrastructure, modes of production, society and culture in some all-consuming and frequently circular sense, codes, conventions, paradigms, or what have you—is *the* context for the adequate interpretation of texts. My explicit goal in these essays is to make "context" less a shibboleth or a *passe-partout* and more a limited, critical concept in historical research.

My specific concern is of course intellectual history as a subdiscipline within the larger field of historiography. The historian has, I think, typically been a professional with at least a dual identity. One identity is clearly that of the scholar or *érudit* who is con-

2. For a sanguine appraisal of these openings, see Michael Kammen's introduction to the volume he edited, *The Past Before Us* (Ithaca, 1980). By contrast, I think that even the early jeremiads of Hayden White still have some point, given the deep-seated conservatism of the historical profession, especially over *la longue durée*. See also Dominick LaCapra and Steven L. Kaplan, eds., *Modern European Intellectual History: Reappraisals and New Perspectives* (Ithaca, 1982).

3. See Clifford Geertz, *The Interpretation of Cultures* (New York, 1973), chap. 1. Geertz, with his notion of symbolic meaning, was clearly the *genius loci* at the conference that gave rise to the volume *New Directions in American Intellectual History*, ed. John Higham and Paul K. Conkin (Baltimore, 1979).

strained by scientific procedures, notably the constraint of thoroughly documenting propositions about the past. But other identifications have complicated the historian's task and have helped to shape his or her rhetoric. A traditional identification is with the judicious statesman or even with the just judge who employs exhaustive documentation to arrive at balanced appraisals of the objects of study. Another, more recent one is of course with the professionalized expert. In the following pages, the role I find more compelling for a practitioner of a subdiscipline such as intellectual history, which straddles the academy and the public marketplace, is that of the intellectual, with the elements of contestation and even of carnivalization inhering in that role, for I think that the combination of scholar and intellectual typifies the role tension (or the internal "dialogue") at work and at play in the intellectual historian.

The perspective that I try to explore on the problems of historiography tends to destabilize a prevalent opposition. On the one hand, there are (presumably) historical agents in the past who do not know how their actions (or texts) will "turn out" in the larger course of events. Thus we have Nietzsche and Hegel writing without awareness of the ways their texts would be used and abused by the Nazis. On the other hand, there are historians who employ narrative as a mode of retrospective reconstruction. They presumably know how things will turn out, and their superior vantage point allows them to plot events in a "followable" story that makes sense of things. Or it may induce them to hazard a more insistently analytic and explanatory account of the whys and wherefores of events instead of a descriptive story about them—a procedure many historians today somewhat oversimplifyingly see as an alternative to narrative rather than as a supplement tensely related to it. Historians may even aspire to a noncommittal or transcendent sense of irony that underwrites their critical distance on the past and enhances the objective authority of their firm narrative voice.

The insistence upon a more "dialogical" relation to the past as a companion and a counterpart to documented knowledge has at least two implications that mitigate the opposition between the historical agent and the historian. First, it attests to the ways historical agents themselves are involved in attempts to make sense—or to explore the limits of sense-making—in their texts or other historical acts. (Narrative structures from the despairingly realistic to the utterly fantastic inform, however problematically, the ways we lead life as well as the ways we tell stories about it.) Second, it questions historians' rights to the position of omniscient narrators—a position that the novel since Flaubert has forcefully challenged—for historians in an important sense do not know how it all turned out. Their knowledge is limited, and their very approach to writing history is itself inserted in an ongoing process where it may make at least a small difference. Indeed the narratives of historians may be opened to some extent by the attempt to explore alternative possibilities in the past that are themselves suggested by the retrospective or deferred effects of later knowledge. These possibilities arise in texts especially at their most intense moments of inner difference and self-contestation—moments that engage the reader in self-questioning that has a bearing on the present and future. These moments, which are repressed through a scapegoat mechanism that projects all difference onto pure oppositions, reveal how the past is not simply a finished story to be narrated but a process linked to each historian's own time of narration. In a word, historians are involved in the effort to understand both what something meant in its own time and what it may mean for us today. The most engaging, if at times perplexing, dimensions of interpretation exist on the margin, where these two meanings are not simply disjoined from one another, for it is at this liminal point that the dialogue with the past becomes internal to the historian.

The foregoing comments should suffice to indicate that the rethinking of intellectual history by way of the text-context problem raises the issue of language, which is the leitmotif of this book. Language is a signifying practice that is connected, from its emphatic use to its studied avoidance, with other signifying practices in human life. It undercuts the dichotomy between text and context and underscores their sometimes ambivalent interaction. If intellectual history is anything, it is a history of the situated uses of language constitutive of significant texts. In this sense, nothing related to the problem of language is alien to it. To say this is neither to accord an incontestable privilege to language nor to degrade the human being, as some alarmists seem to assume; it is to try to understand better that being's possibilities and limits as they appear in and through an important signifying practice whose ramifications are difficult to delimit.

"Text" derives from *texere*, to weave or compose, and in its expanded usage it designates a texture or network of relations interwoven with the problem of language. Its critical role is to problematize conventional distinctions and hierarchies, such as that which presents the text as a simple document or index of a more basic, if not absolute, ground, reality, or context. Yet the use of the notion of the text (or of textuality) to investigate a relational network inevitably raises the specter of "textual imperialism" or "pantextualism." When the notion of the text is itself absolutized, one confronts the paralyzing and truly abstract sort of interpretative bind that the appeal to the notion of textuality was intended to avoid or at least to defer.

To refer to social or individual life as a text (or as "textualized") is in an obvious sense to employ a metaphor. But the metaphor is not a "mere" metaphor. It combines the polemical vehemence of assertion with the critical distance that counteracts dogmatism. The reliance on a metaphor to provide a way of seeing problems nonetheless involves linguistic inflation. If this risk comes with the opportunity to understand problems better than in alternative perspectives—for example, the one that takes "reality" or "context" as an unproblematic ground or gold standard—then the risk is well worth taking. But the metaphor of textuality is in no sense perfect, even as a medium for contesting the standard dichotomy between metaphor and its opposites (the literal, the conceptual, the serious, and so forth). For some phenomena it may be too strong, and for others too weak. There is, for example, a sense in which it would take an extremely anesthetized or overly aestheticized sensibility to refer to the holocaust as a "text," although the value of the textual metaphor might prove itself even here by enabling one to resist the temptation to constitute any phenomenon in history as absolutely unique or incomparable. Nor does the metaphor imply that language is now to be seen as a realm of "liberated signifiers" or of autonomous discursive practices—a view that amounts to a new avatar of formalism. Rather it directs attention to the relationships of various uses of language to one another and to the activities with which they are articulated.

The ten essays in this book approach the problem of the interaction between texts and contexts through a variety of related topics. The first essay functions as a general frame for the problems explored in the others. Of the remaining, five are essays in the more conventional sense, and four are essay-reviews. The reader will notice, however, that the mode of inquiry and argument is strikingly similar in both groups of essays. The theorists discussed in them, moreover, are all significant figures in their respective fields (as far as these can be delimited) and in interdisciplinary studies: Hayden White, Ludwig Wittgenstein, Paul Ricoeur, Jürgen Habermas, Jean-Paul Sartre, Fredric Jameson, Karl Marx, and Mikhail Bakhtin. My treatment of these theorists is itself informed by the work of other figures—notably Jacques Derrida and Martin Heidegger—whom I find especially relevant for rethinking the nature of research in intellectual history.

It is noteworthy that a number of important journals, such as *Diacritics, Modern Language Notes,* and *History and Theory,* are devoted in whole or in part to essay-reviews in which a specific book becomes the occasion for the exploration of a set of problems. I think that the contemporary rise to prominence of the essay-review as a distinct genre is emblematic of several important developments. It is an acknowledgment that we academics think and teach in terms of books—a fact that has a special significance in the humanities. But, less parochially, it is a recognition that critical discourse is dialogical in that it attempts to address itself simultaneously to problems (*die Sache selbst,* in the inimitable German expression) and to the words of others addressing those problems. In this sense, the essay-review takes its place alongside the traditional essay for reasons that are both structural and conjunctural: it is an enactment of the humanistic understanding of research as a conversation with the past through the medium of its significant texts; it is also an especially vital forum in a contested discipline that is undergoing reconceptualization. To say this is to intimate that a conversation or dialogue, including the kind that splits or multiplies the self, can run the gamut from friendly persuasion to impassioned polemic. It is also to indicate that a crucial problem is the nature of the relationship between cognitive and rhetorical (or documentary and performative) uses of language in historiography itself—a problem having political implications both in terms of the historical discipline and in less restricted senses. I think it is safe to assert that an area that will receive increased attention from historians in the near future is the rhetoric of their own discipline and the varied ways it helps to shape their interaction with one another and with the past.

Finally, I would like to note the obvious. This book is a collection of essays which, to the extent that they are successful, are essays in the etymological sense of the word. I have intentionally decided not to try to recast them in the form of a systematic treatise on method in intellectual history. One reason is my belief that the essay is the best "form" in which to explore the interaction between unification and challenges to it in the attempt to define an approach to intellectual history. A series of essays will necessarily harbor tensions, "internal contestations," and even contradictions that are worth preserving insofar as they stimulate further thought about the questions at issue. One recurrent concern in these essays is to relate intellectual history to the work of Derrida, especially his earlier texts whose bearing on intellectual history is for me most evident and accessible. I often offer limited "defenses" of Derrida against what I take to be misinterpretations of his texts and general tendencies. But I do not provide anything like a comprehensive analysis of, or "conversation" with, his texts. My own feeling is that the most fruitful dimension of Derrida's writings may well be their carnivalesque impetus, which has perhaps had the least telling impact upon those working in and around the furrows in thought he has created. But it is clear that to be effective in a desirable way this impetus must be related to a general critique of society, politics, and culture. As the later essays in this book indicate, one crucial issue here is the connection between "carnivalization" and Marxism, which in certain respects remains the most ambitious mode of criticism we have.

[1]

Rethinking Intellectual History
and Reading Texts

> But if we see this circle as a vicious one and look out for ways of
> avoiding it, even if we just "sense" it as an inevitable imperfection,
> then the act of understanding has been misunderstood from the
> ground up.
>
> Heidegger, *Being and Time*

Over the last decade, intellectual historians have come increasingly to believe that their field is undergoing a crisis significant
enough to reopen the question of the field's nature and objectives.
Whatever the presumed causes of this sense of crisis (for example,
the rapid rise of social history), one of its beneficial effects is the
pressure it places upon practitioners to be more articulate about
what they are doing and why. In response to this pressure, I shall
attempt to define and to defend in relatively theoretical terms the
approach to the field, and specifically to modern European intellectual history, that I have come to find most fruitful. In setting forth
this approach, I shall stylize arguments to bring into prominence a
number of controversial issues. At times I shall be forced not to
practice what I preach, for I shall selectively treat the texts of other
historians or theorists in order to highlight problematic positions as
well as possible directions for inquiry.

In the course of its own history in this country, intellectual history has often patterned itself on the approaches of other branches of the discipline, taking a framework of significant questions from somewhere else to orient and organize its research. The desire to adapt to modes of inquiry immediately intelligible to some important set of historians, if not to all historians, has characterized perspectives that are frequently seen as competing or opposed options: the internal or intrinsic history of ideas (exemplified in the works of A. O. Lovejoy); the extrinsic or "contextual" view of intellectual history (exemplified in the works of Merle Curti); and the attempted synthesis of internal and external perspectives that has most often taken the form of a narrative of "men and ideas" (for example, in the works of Crane Brinton or H. S. Hughes). The problems generated by these options have become increasingly evident, and I shall return to some of them. They are exacerbated by intellectual history's tendency either to become narrowly professional and even antiquarian by applying the internal method to increasingly insignificant problems, or to become fixated more or less permanently at a popularizing and introductory level in narrating the adventures of "men and ideas." The more recent elaboration of a social history of ideas has seemed to offer an answer to these problems, for in its rigor and methodological sophistication it goes beyond the older forms of contextualism, and it promises to give intellectual history access to the remarkable achievements of modern social history. Undoubtedly, certain questions that earlier intellectual historians addressed impressionistically can be cogently investigated only through the techniques of modern social history. But intellectual history should not be seen as a mere function of social history. It has other questions to explore, requiring different techniques, and their development may permit a better articulation of its relationship to social history. It may even suggest areas in which the formulations of social history stand in need of further refinement.

In the pages that follow, an obvious "territorial imperative" is at work, modified by an active awareness of both the limits of intellectual history and its relations to other perspectives. Thus my argument is not motivated by the desire to establish a specious autonomy for intellectual history within historiography or within the disciplines in general. On the contrary, it is informed by an understanding of the subdiscipline of intellectual history that is in important respects transdisciplinary, and it defends what may be called the relative specificity of intellectual history. It also urges the intellectual historian to learn of developments in other disciplines addressing the problem of interpretation, notably literary criticism and philosophy. In fact, the argument I shall put forth constitutes a new twist to a rather traditional view of things—but one that involves a sometimes disorienting critique and rethinking of tradition through an insistence upon problems and interests that have been obscured in more traditional approaches. The concern I want to reanimate centers on the importance of reading and interpreting complex texts—the so-called "great" texts of the Western tradition—and of formulating the problem of relating these texts to various pertinent contexts. This is a concern that, I think, does not have the place it deserves in historiography today, including intellectual history, which would seem to be its "natural home." The approach I shall discuss does not, however, aim solely at returning these texts to their rightful place. It also critically raises the question of why these texts are often objects of excessively reductive interpretation even when they are centers of analysis and concern. The primary form of reduction I shall discuss arises from the dominance of a documentary conception of historical understanding, because I believe that it is most prevalent in the historical profession today. But the implications of my argument extend to all extreme derogations of the dialogue between past and present, dialogue that requires a subtle interplay between proximity and distance in the historian's relation to the "object" of study. (This dialogical relation between the historian or the historical text and the "object" of study raises the question of the role of selection, judgment, stylization, irony, parody, self-parody, and polemic in the historian's own use of language—in brief, the question of how the historian's use of language is mediated by critical factors that cannot be reduced to factual predication or direct authorial assertion about historical "reality." Significant in this respect is the manner in which the historian's approach to the "object" of study is informed or "influenced" by the methods and views of other historians or "speakers.") In addition, the approach I shall defend is not motivated exclusively by the attempt to find order in chaos by familiarizing the unfamiliar; it is also sensitive to the ways in which the ordinary format for the acquisition of knowledge may be placed in question as the familiar is made unfamiliar, especially when it is seen anew in significant texts.

What is meant by the term "text"? It may initially be seen as a situated use of language marked by a tense interaction between mutually implicated yet at times contestatory tendencies. On this view, the very opposition between what is inside and what is outside texts is rendered problematic, and nothing is seen as being purely and simply inside or outside texts. Indeed the problem becomes one of rethinking the concepts of "inside" and "outside" in relation to processes of interaction between language and the world. One of the more challenging aspects of recent inquiries into textuality has been the investigation of why textual processes cannot be confined within the bindings of the book. The context or the "real world" is itself "textualized" in a variety of ways, and even if one believes that the point of criticism is to change the world, not merely to interpret it, the process and results of change themselves raise textual problems. Social and individual life may fruitfully be seen on the analogy of the text and as involved in textual processes that are often more complicated than the historical imagination is willing to allow. In addition, the attempt to relate texts to other "symbolic," "representational," or "expressive" media (music, painting, dance, gesture) raises the problem of the interaction among signifying practices— the problem of translating from medium to medium in a process that entails both losses and gains in "meaning." To the extent that the historian or critic employs language to effect this translation, he or she confronts the issue of textuality writ large. More generally, the notion of textuality serves to render less dogmatic the concept of reality by pointing to the fact that one is "always already" implicated in problems of language use as one attempts to gain critical perspective on these problems, and it raises the question of both the possibilities and the limits of meaning. For the historian, the very reconstruction of a "context" or a "reality" takes place on the basis of "textualized" remainders of the past. The historian's position is not unique in that all definitions of reality are implicated in textual processes. But the issue of historical understanding is distinctive. The more general problem is to see how the notion of textuality makes explicit the question of the relationships among uses of language, other signifying practices, and various modes of human activity that are bound up with processes of signification. The more distinctive issue in historiography is that of the relationship between documentary reconstruction of, and dialogue with, the past.[1]

To the extent that the relationship between the documentary and the dialogical is a problem relevant to all historiography, the argument I shall develop is not restricted to intellectual history. I shall generally forgo extended discussion of the larger issues I may evoke, however, in order to focus on the limited topic of the relation of a "textual" problematic to intellectual history, and I shall concentrate on the even more limited topic of written texts and, within this topic, on the problem of reading and interpreting the "great" texts of the tradition. These texts are not absolutely unique, and the processes they disclose are not altogether peculiar to them. But two reasons for focusing intellectual history on these texts are that the study of them tends not to be emphasized in contemporary historiography and that in them the use of language is explored in an

---

1. This essay is best read in conjunction with the works of Hayden V. White, notably *Metahistory* (Baltimore, 1973) and *Tropics of Discourse* (Baltimore, 1978). White's work has been of immense importance in generating the current debate about approaches to historiography. My own discussion agrees with White's critique of conventional narrative and a narrowly documentary approach as inadequate to the tasks of intellectual history. But it is critical of the more "presentist" and "constructivist" tendencies that at times emerge in White's works, and it tries to provide a different way of understanding intellectual history as in part a dialogue with the past. For a discussion of White's *Tropics of Discourse*, see the next essay in this volume. For a discussion of related problems as they arise in the interpretation of the works of Jean-Paul Sartre, the reader is referred to my *Preface to Sartre* (Ithaca, 1978).

especially forceful and critical way—a way that engages us as interpreters in a particularly compelling conversation with the past.[2]

It is important to argue over the question of what works are to be considered great and to reevaluate the "canon" of works to which we devote special attention. I even see value in the argument that our understanding of a canon has been too ethnocentric in its confinement of the text to the book and in its exclusion of texts from other traditions and cultures. Indeed it is important to examine critically the very notion of a canon and certain of the functions it may serve. But I must confess that most often I agree with traditional authorities in identifying works to be included in any necessary but not sufficient list of especially significant texts. What puzzles me at times, however, is the way these works are interpreted, for the interpretations may have little correspondence to the judgment that the work is great or at least of special significance. Here one may wonder whether something is elided in the passage from the judgment that identifies a great work to the discourse that interprets it, for interpretations often treat these texts in terms that domesticate them by emphasizing their commonality with lesser works or with ordinary beliefs, desires, tensions, and values. Such treatment begs a number of crucial questions. Are great texts of special interest not in their confirmation or reflection of common concerns but, to paraphrase Nietzsche, in the exceptional way in which they address commonplace themes?[3] Do they often or even

---

2. The notion of historical understanding as a conversation with the past is developed in the works of Martin Heidegger and in those of his more conservative disciple, Hans-Georg Gadamer. See especially Heidegger's "Onto-theo-logical Constitution of Metaphysics" in *Identity and Difference*, tr. Joan Stambaugh (New York, 1969), and Gadamer's *Truth and Method*, tr. Garrett Barden and John Cumming (New York, 1975), and *Philosophical Hermeneutics*, tr. David E. Linge (Berkeley and Los Angeles, 1976). In his understanding of full consensual truth as the *telos* of dialogue, Gadamer is closer to Habermas than to Heidegger.

3. See especially Nietzsche's *Use and Abuse of History*, tr. Adrian Collins (Indianapolis, 1957), 39. For Nietzsche's argument that the renunciation of interpretation and the restriction of scholarship to pure "truth" in its residual form as "truth to facts" constitute an expression of the ascetic ideal, see *On the Genealogy of Morals*, tr. Walter Kaufmann (New York, 1969), 151. For a more general

typically engage in processes that employ or refer to ordinary assumptions and simultaneously contest them, at times radically? Is the judgment of greatness at times related to the sense that certain works both reinforce tradition and subvert it, perhaps indicating the need for newer traditions that are more open to disconcerting modes of questioning and better able to withstand the recurrent threat of collapse? Do certain works themselves both try to confirm or establish something—a value, a pattern of coherence, a system, a genre—and call it into question? Is there something sensed in judgments that is perhaps not said in reductive interpretations that make certain works all too familiar? Are processes of contestation often or typically more powerful in certain kinds of texts—for example, literary or poetic texts—than in philosophical or historical ones? How watertight are these higher-order forms of classification in relation to the actual use(s) of language in texts? What does a less reductive, normalizing, or harmonizing mode of interpretation require of the reader?

These are the types of question raised in what Heidegger calls "thinking the unthought" of tradition and Derrida, "deconstruction." (What I take to be especially valuable in the approaches to textuality developed by Heidegger and Derrida is critical inquiry that tries to avoid a somnambulistic replication of the excesses of a historical tradition by rehabilitating what is submerged or repressed in it and entering the submerged or repressed elements in a more even-handed "contest" with tendencies that are damaging in their dominant forms.)

I want to begin to address these questions by distinguishing be-

---

discussion of Nietzsche's "genealogical" understanding of history, which combines the documentary and the critically reconstructive in a polemical perspective, see Michel Foucault, "Nietzsche, Genealogy, History," in *Lauguage, Counter-Memory, Practice*, tr. Donald F. Bouchard and Sherry Simon (Ithaca, 1977), 139–164. (The essays collected in this book represent an often critical supplement to the more well-known and somewhat doctrinaire "structuralist" positions that Foucault—despite protestations to the contrary—often develops in his principal works.)

tween documentary and "worklike" aspects of the text.[4] The documentary situates the text in terms of factual or literal dimensions involving reference to empirical reality and conveying information about it. The "worklike" supplements empirical reality by adding to and subtracting from it. It thereby involves dimensions of the text not reducible to the documentary, prominently including the roles of commitment, interpretation, and imagination. The worklike is critical and transformative, for it deconstructs and reconstructs the given, in a sense repeating it but also bringing into the world something that did not exist before in that significant variation, alteration, or transformation. With deceptive simplicity, one might say that while the documentary marks a difference, the worklike makes a difference—one that engages the reader in recreative dialogue with the text and the problems it raises.

I shall return to this distinction and its implications in a somewhat different light. What I stress here is that the documentary and the worklike refer to aspects or components of the text that may be developed to different degrees and related to one another in a variety of ways. We usually refer to *The Brothers Karamazov* and *The Phenomenology of Mind* as works, and to a tax roll, a will, and the register of an inquisition as documents. But the work is situated in history in a way that gives it documentary dimensions, and the document has worklike aspects. In other words, both the "document" and the "work" are texts involving an interaction between documentary and worklike components that should be examined in

4. The notion of the "worklike" is of course indebted to Heidegger's discussion in "The Origin of the Work of Art," in *Poetry, Language, Thought*, tr. Albert Hofstadter (New York, 1975), 15–87. It does not exclude receptivity and should not be interpreted in a narrowly "productivist" sense. The distinction between the documentary and the worklike may also be compared to J. L. Austin's distinction between the "constative"—the descriptive statement that is measured against the criteria of truth and falsehood in "corresponding" to facts—and the "performative"—the doing of things with words that brings about a change in the situational context. On the approach I am suggesting, the constative and the performative are best seen not as generic types or sets of speech acts ("realms of discourse") but as more or less pronounced aspects of speech acts (or texts) that may be conceptually elaborated into analytic distinctions, ideal types, or heuristic fictions.

30

a critical historiography. Often the dimensions of the document that make it a text of a certain sort with its own historicity and its relations to sociopolitical processes (for example, relations of power) are filtered out when it is used purely and simply as a quarry for facts in the reconstruction of the past. (A register of an inquisition, for example, is itself a textual power structure with links to relations of power in the larger society. How it functions as a text is intimately and problematically related to its use for the reconstruction of life in the past.) Conversely, the more documentary aspects of a work are neglected when it is read in a purely formalistic way or as an isolated source for the recovery of past meaning. Clearly, the larger questions at issue turn on the relations between documentary and work-like aspects of the text and between the correlative ways of reading it.

A dialogue with an "other" must have a subject matter and must convey information of some sort. But, as Weber and Collingwood have observed, a fact is a pertinent fact only with respect to a frame of reference involving questions that we pose to the past, and it is the ability to pose the "right" questions that distinguishes productive scholarship. Heidegger has emphasized that these questions are themselves situated in a "context" or a "life-world" that cannot be entirely objectified or fully known. For Heidegger, moreover, it is only by investigating what a thinker did not explicitly or intentionally think but what constitutes his still question-worthy "unthought" that a conversation with the past enters into dimensions of his thinking which bear most forcefully on the present and future. Here anachronism is an obvious danger, but an imaginative and self-reflective kind of comparative history inquiring into the unrealized or even resisted possibilities of the past is nonetheless an important supplement to more empirical kinds of comparison in the dialogue between past and present. (Weber himself, it may be recalled, argued that the attribution of causal weight to an event or phenomenon depended upon its comparison with an imaginative rethinking of the historical process in which it figured. Only by hypothesizing what might have come to pass given the absence or significant variation of an event or phenomenon could one arrive at the understanding of transformational possibilities that enabled one to appreciate the fact that something occurred in the form it actually took.) Indeed, insofar as it is itself "worklike," a dialogue involves the interpreter's attempt to think further what is at issue in a text or a past "reality," and in the process the questioner is himself questioned by the "other." His own horizon is transformed as he confronts still living (but often submerged or silenced) possibilities solicited by an inquiry into the past. In this sense, the historicity of the historian is at issue both in the questions he poses and (*pace* Weber) in the "answers" he gives in a text that itself reticulates the documentary and the worklike. It may, finally, be argued that the interaction between documentary and worklike tendencies generates tension, and this tension is neutralized only through processes of control and exclusion. These processes may operate both in the text being interpreted and in the text interpreting it. In intellectual history, they tend to operate more in our interpretations or uses of the texts of primary interest than in those texts themselves.[5]

A documentary approach to the reading of texts has predominated in general historiography and, in important respects, it has also characterized intellectual history. If the dominance of this approach is open to question in other areas of historiography, it is perhaps even more questionable in intellectual history, given the texts it addresses.[6] For certain texts themselves explore the interaction of various uses of language such as the documentary and the worklike and they do so in ways that raise the issue of the various possibilities in language use attendant upon this interaction. The Menippean satire is a manifest example of a type of text openly

5. This theme has been especially important in the works of Foucault and Derrida. For an application of it to the interpretation of Rousseau, see Jacques Derrida, *Of Grammatology*, tr. Gayatri C. Spivak (Baltimore, 1976; first pub. 1967). In his recent work, Foucault has of course turned to a micrological analysis of the mutual articulations of power and knowledge.

6. A critique of an exclusively or even predominantly documentary conception of historiography in general is developed by Hayden V. White in *Tropics of Discourse*. See especially the introduction and chapters 1–4. Curiously, White in this book does not explore the more specific applications of his arguments to intellectual history.

exploring the interaction or dialogue among uses of language.[7] But this issue may be raised in relation to any text in a manner that both opens it to an investigation of its functioning as discourse and opens the reader to the need for interpretation in his or her dialogue with it. Indeed there would seem to be something intrinsically wrong-headed in the idea of a purely or even predominantly documentary approach to a markedly worklike and internally "dialogized" text making claims on its readers that are not met by documentary understanding alone.

The predominance of a documentary approach in historiography is one crucial reason why complex texts—especially "literary" texts—are either excluded from the relevant historical record or read in an extremely reduced way. Within intellectual history, reduction takes the form of synoptic content analysis in the more narrative method and the form of an unproblematic identification of objects or entities of historical interest in the history of ideas.[8] These en-

---

7. For an illuminating discussion of Fernand Braudel's *Mediterranean and the Mediterranean World in the Age of Philip II* as a Menippean satire, see Hans Kellner, "Disorderly Conduct: Braudel's Mediterranean Satire," *History and Theory* 18 (1979), 197–222. Kellner, however, does not address two important issues: (1) the role of scientific discourse in Braudel's work and the problem of how it relates to other uses of language, and (2) the way the "Menippean satire" is not simply a category that allows one to identify the genre of a work but a multivalent use of language that may test the limits of genre classifications. These issues arise in a pointed way when one attempts to relate Northrop Frye's classical understanding of the menippea to the more carnivalized notion of Mikhail Bakhtin (notably in *Problems of Dostoevsky's Poetics*, tr. R. W. Rotsel [Ann Arbor, 1973], 92–100). On Bakhtin, see Julia Kristeva, "Le mot, le dialogue et le roman," in *Semiotikè* (Paris, 1969), 143–173, and Tzvetan Todorov, *Mikhail Bakhtine: Le principe dialogique* (Paris, 1981).

8. I shall not further discuss synoptic content analysis, which is both necessary and limited as a method of analyzing complex texts. But for one of the most successful and perspicuous narratives relying essentially on synoptic methods, see Martin Jay, *The Dialectical Imagination: A History of the Frankfort School* (Boston, 1973). In an extremely ambitious and intelligent work, Mark Poster, with some misgiving, also practices intellectual history as a narrative relating synopses or paraphrases of the arguments in texts to contextual developments (*Existential Marxism in Postwar France: From Sartre to Althusser* [Princeton, 1976]). For an attempted analysis and critique of the role of the synoptic method in contextualist interpretation, see "Reading Exemplars: *Wittgenstein's Vienna* and Wittgenstein's *Tractatus*," below.

tities are, of course, "ideas" ("unit-ideas" in the work of A. O. Lovejoy) or "structures of consciousness" or of "mind" (for example, in the work of Ernst Cassirer). Ideas or structures of consciousness are abstracted from texts and related to comprehensive, formalized modes of discourse or symbolic forms (philosophy, literature, science, myth, history, religion). How these structures actually function in complex texts is often not asked or is given only marginal attention. The ideas or structures (for example, the idea of nature or the great chain of being) may then be traced over time and used to distinguish between periods. This approach is criticized as excessively detached—a form of history of ideas "in the air"—from a more socially oriented perspective.[9] But, on a very basic level, the social history of ideas often shares the assumptions of the approach it criticizes. For it too may take ideas, structures of consciousness, or "mentalities" as relatively unproblematic entities and not raise the question of how they function in texts or actual uses of language—looking instead into the causes or origins of ideas and their impact or effect in history. In brief, social history often adjusts a history of ideas to a causal framework and a conception of the social matrix without critically investigating what is being caused or having an impact.[10] It may also lead to the idea that the only things

9. See the critique of Cassirer in Peter Gay, "The Social History of Ideas: Ernst Cassirer and After," in *The Critical Spirit: Essays in Honor of Herbert Marcuse*, ed. Kurt H. Wolff and Barrington Moore, Jr. (Boston, 1967), 106–120. Gay nonetheless praises Cassirer for his emphasis upon structure and his ability to find order in seeming chaos. Gay does not raise the question of the extent to which the order thus found is limited or even specious. (The point of this remark is to suggest that the imposition of "order and perspicuity"—in one of Gibbon's favorite phrases—upon the historical record is misleading and that the objective of the historian should rather be to explore critically the ways in which the interaction between order and its contestatory "others" takes place.)

10. For an extremely successful example of this approach, inspired by the methods of the *Annales* school, see Daniel Roche, *Le siècle des lumières en province: Académies et académiciens provinciaux, 1680–1789*, 2 vols. (Paris, 1978). Roche's approach to the texts of Rousseau, of which he does not provide an extended critical analysis, may be contrasted with that of Derrida in *Of Grammatology*. There are, however, signs at present that those affiliated with the *Annales* school are developing an expanded notion of "*le travail du texte*" that reveals

worth studying are those that had a social impact or effect in their own time, thereby depriving historiography of the need to recover significant aspects of the past that may have "lost out."

A different understanding of intellectual history as a history of texts may permit a more cogent formulation of problems broached by established approaches and a more mutually informative interchange with the type of social history that relates discourse and institutions. On this understanding, what was taken as an assumption or elided in the perspectives I have mentioned becomes a problem for inquiry. One such problem at the very crossroads of the documentary and the dialogical is the precise nature of the relation between texts and their various pertinent contexts. I will break this problem down into six partially overlapping areas of investigation and, in discussing them, stress certain points that are often neglected at present.

It may be helpful if I first make my own objective clear. My list is not exhaustive, and my point is that in treating the relation of texts to contexts, what is often taken as a solution to the problem should be reformulated and investigated as a real problem itself. An appeal to the context does not *eo ipso* answer all questions in reading and interpretation. And an appeal to *the* context is deceptive: one never has—at least in the case of complex texts—*the* context. The assumption that one does relies on a hypostatization of "context," often in the service of misleading organic or other overly reductive analogies. For complex texts, one has a set of interacting contexts whose relations to one another are variable and problematic and whose relation to the text being investigated raises difficult issues in interpretation. Indeed, what may be most insistent in a modern text is the way it challenges one or more of its contexts. In addition, the assertion that a specific context or subset of contexts is especially significant in a given case has to be argued and not simply assumed

---

the limitations of narrowly documentary readings. See, for example, Jacques Le Goff and Pierre Nora, *Faire de l'histoire* (Paris, 1974), and Michel de Certeau, *L'écriture de l'histoire* (Paris, 1975) and *L'invention du quotidien* (Paris, 1980).

or surreptitiously built into an explanatory model or framework of analysis. With these caveats in mind, the six "contexts" I shall single out for attention are intentions, motivations, society, culture, the corpus, and structure (or analogous concepts).

1. *The relation between the author's intentions and the text.* I would not deny the importance of intentions and of the attempt to specify their relationship to what occurs in texts or in discourse more generally. But speech-act theory has lent support to the extreme belief that the utterance and, presumably by extension, the text derive their meaning from the author's intentions in making or writing them. Quentin Skinner has argued forcefully that the object of intellectual history should be the study of what authors meant to say in different historical contexts and communicative situations.[11] This view tends to assume a proprietary relation between the author and the text as well as a unitary meaning for an utterance. At best it permits an overly simple idea of divisions or opposing tendencies in a text and of the relationships between texts and analytic classifications of them. By presenting the text solely as an "embodied" or realized "intentionality," it prevents one from formulating as an explicit problem the question of the relationship between intentions, insofar as they can be plausibly reconstructed, and what the text may be argued to do or to disclose. This relationship may involve multiple forms of tension, including self-contestation. Not only may the intention not fill out the text in a coherent or unified way; the intention or intentions of the author may be uncertain or radically ambivalent. Indeed the author may in good part discover

11. See especially Skinner's "Meaning and Understanding in the History of Ideas," *History and Theory* 8 (1969), 3–53. For a defense of authorial intention as providing the criterion of valid interpretation, see E. D. Hirsch, Jr., *Validity in Interpretation* (New Haven, 1967) and *The Aims of Interpretation* (Chicago, 1976). For a critique of Hirsch, see David C. Hoy, *The Critical Circle* (Berkeley and Los Angeles, 1978). Hoy's book is a good introduction to the works of Gadamer, who offers an extensive criticism of the attempt to center interpretation on the *mens auctoris*. A more fundamental critique is provided by Jacques Derrida, notably in "Signature Event Context," tr. Samuel Weber and Jeffrey Mehlman, *Glyph* 1 (1977), and "Limited Inc. abc," tr. Samuel Weber, *Glyph* 2 (1977).

his or her intentions in the act of writing or speaking itself. And the "reading" of intentions poses problems analogous to those involved in the reading of texts.

It is significant that an intention is often formulated retrospectively, when the utterance or text has been subjected to interpretation with which the author does not agree. The first time around, one may feel no need to make one's intentions altogether explicit, or one may feel that this is impossible, perhaps because one is writing or saying something whose multiple meanings would be excessively reduced in the articulation of explicit intentions. Along with the "projection" of a goal that in part directs the writing process, an intention is a kind of proleptic reading or interpretation of a text. A retrospectively formulated intention is more manifestly a reading or interpretation, for it is rarely a transcription of what the author meant to say at the "original" time of writing. Insofar as there is a proprietary relation between the author and the text, especially in cases where the author's responsibility is at issue (for example, in cases at law), one may want to give special weight to statements of intention, at least to the extent that they are plausible interpretations of what actually goes on in a text. But even if one is content merely to extend the relevant analogy, one can argue that, to some significant extent, tradition expropriates the author, for the texts of the tradition have entered the public domain. Here the intentions of the author have the status of either aspects of the text (for example, when they are included in a preface) or interpretations of it which the commentator should certainly take into account but whose relation to the functioning of the text is open to question.

The idea that authorial intentions constitute the ultimate criterion for arriving at a valid interpretation of a text is motivated, I think, by excessively narrow moral, legal, and scientific presuppositions. Morally and even legally, one may believe that a person should bear full responsibility for utterances and have a quasi-contractual or fully contractual relation to an interlocutor. Scientifically, one may seek a criterion that makes the meaning of a text subject to procedures of confirmation that leave minimal room for disagreement over interpretation. At times responsibility may be great enough to meet moral or legal demands, although this eventuality would satisfy neither the theoretical nor the practical conditions for *full* freedom or intentionality. In any case, to believe that authorial intentions fully control the meaning or functioning of texts (for example, their serious or ironic quality) is to assume a predominantly normative position that is out of touch with important dimensions of language use and reader response. The scientific demand is closely related to the moral one. It might be acceptable if it were applicable. To insist upon its applicability is to sacrifice more dialogical approaches and to obscure the role of argument in matters of interpretation, including the interpretation of intentions themselves. It is, moreover, commonplace to observe that a sign of a "classic" is the fact that its interpretation does not lead to a definitive conclusion and that its history is very much the history of conflicting or divergent interpretations and uses of it. It is less commonplace to apply this insight to the process of argument that engages its interpreters. Insofar as an approach supplements the documentary with the dialogical, informed argument in it is to be seen not merely as an unavoidable necessity but as a valuable and stimulating activity bound up with the ways interpretation may be related to forms of renewal, including the renewal of beliefs to which one is deeply committed. The point here is to do everything in one's power not to avoid argument but to make argument as informed, vital, and undogmatically open to counterargument as possible.

These considerations bear upon the question of criteria for a "good" interpretation. The latter should of course resolve documentary matters that are amenable to ordinary procedures of verification, and it should seek mutual understanding on larger issues of interpretation. But, equally important, it does not settle once and for all the question of how to understand a work or a corpus. A "good" interpretation reactivates the process of inquiry, opening up new avenues of investigation, criticism, and self-reflection. This is not to say that one should make a fetish of the new or become a slave to current ideas about what is interesting. But it is to say that basic differences in interpretation (or mode of discourse) rarely turn on simple matters of fact—and that on certain levels these differences may have a value that is not entirely subordinated to the ideal of consensus in interpretation. For they may relate to processes of contestation that have a critical role at present and that one would want to retain in some form in any social context.

2. *The relation between the author's life and the text.* This approach is inspired by the belief that there may be relations between life and text that go beyond and even contradict the author's intentions. What is sought in a psychobiographical perspective is the motivation of the author, which may be only partly known to him or her or even unconscious. A difficulty analogous to that with the intentionalist view arises, however, when there is an assumption of full unity or identity between life and texts that allows both to be situated in parallel or homologous fashion in a cycle of development or a pattern of breakdown.[12] The temptation is then to see the text as a sign or symptom of the life process even when the resultant understanding of their relationship is left on the level of suggestion rather than elaborated into a full-blown causal or interpretative theory.

Here again, what is taken as a solution should be posed as a problem. There may of course be symptomatic aspects of texts. But life and text may also be both internally marked and related to each other by processes that place identity in question. A text or a life may question itself in more or less explicit ways, and each may question the other. Insofar as they are distinguishable, life and text may be characterized by patterns of development or by forms of repetition that are not simply coincident and that may even challenge one another. A problem common to a written text and a lived "text" may be worked or played out differently in each, and these differential relations pose important problems for interpretation. And we read significant written texts not only because they are

12. This assumption and the difficulties attendant upon it affect even so careful and well documented a study as Jerrold Seigel's *Marx's Fate: The Shape of a Life* (Princeton, 1978).

compensatory but also because they are supplementary: they add something to the ordinary life that as a matter of (perhaps unfortunate) fact might not exist without them.

In addition, for a writer who takes what he or she is doing seriously (an attitude not necessarily divorced from a view of art or even of writing in general as a form of serious play or of jesting in earnest), writing is a crucial way of life. At times the writer may be more willing to defend the writings than other dimensions of the life. One may find this attitude in certain ways objectionable or "alienated," but one has to take it into account. It may (as with Kierkegaard) be proffered not to establish the innocence of the writings or to promote a vision of art for art's sake but to articulate a situation of which the writer is himself critical. In other words, the writer too may want a world in which writing is less distinctive because the text of life is itself "written" in a better way.

The general problem for an attempt to relate life and texts is to arrive at an understanding of the "text" of a life and of the use of language in texts, and of the relation between these signifying practices, that is sufficiently nuanced to do justice to them. To believe that a relatively simple idea of identity or of breakdown does justice to a life may at times be plausible, although certain lives are rather complex. To believe that a relatively simple understanding of "real-life" problems provides the causal or interpretative key to the meaning of the texts or to the interaction between life and texts is altogether implausible. This belief almost invariably prefaces an excessively reductive interpretation of the texts and their relation to life. By contrast, the investigation of the relation between life and texts does more to complicate the problem of interpretation than it does to simplify it, for it supplements the difficulty of interpreting demanding texts with the difficulty of cogently relating them to existential processes. The text to be interpreted then becomes larger and probably more intricate, for it includes the written texts, in cases where writing itself may be a highly existential process, and other dimensions of the life that are not simply external to these texts. Simplification occurs only to the extent that it is plausible to read texts, or aspects of texts, as secondary elaborations or projective rationalizations. And here there is always the possibility that a psychobiography will tell us more about its author than about the author being studied.[13]

3. *The relation of society to texts.* At this point the intersecting nature of the categories I am using becomes evident. One cannot discuss the individual life without significant reference to society and vice versa. But I shall attempt to focus on problems that have been taken to be more specifically social or sociological in nature. (And I shall do so not from the perspective of a social history that inquires into the uses of texts for the empirical reconstitution of past society but from the distinctive perspective of an intellectual history that inquires into the relationship between social processes and the interpretation of texts.) These problems have often been seen in terms of the "before" and "after" of the text: its genesis and its impact.

I have already indicated that the problem often elided or not emphasized in a social history of ideas is that of the relation of social to textual processes—a relation that notions of "genesis" and "impact" may be inadequate to formulate. Foucault, aware of this problem, has elaborated a notion of discursive practice which signals the interaction between institutions and forms of discourse. But he has not altogether succeeded in relating the discursive practice to the significant text or, even more generally, in articulating the relationship between more or less formalized modes of discourse and written or lived "texts," for he often treats written texts and other phenomena in a similar manner by falling back on the notion

13. This problem may arise in a rather subtle form. The psychohistorian may make a dichotomous opposition between fully logical or rational arguments and illogical or irrational arguments in the text and assert that psychohistorical methods apply only to the interpretation of the latter. For a well-reasoned and careful exposition of this view, see Gerald Izenberg, "Psychohistory and Intellectual History," *History and Theory* 14 (1975), 139–155. The problem here is whether this extremely neat opposition applies to the text in question or whether it reflects the perspective of the analyst. In any case, it obviates inquiry into the interaction between the "logical" and the "illogical" in the functioning of the text itself.

that they are instances or tokens of the discursive practice—signs of the times. In certain respects, this understanding may be accurate. A text may exemplify discursive practices or modes of discourse in a relatively straightforward way. Marxist interpretation has often seen a similar relationship between ideology and text, and while Foucault's notion of discursive practice is more comprehensive than the notion of ideology as false consciousness, it relies on an understanding of relationship comparable to the more orthodox Marxist type.

But in both Foucault and in certain Marxists a different possibility at times arises. The text may then be seen not only to exemplify discursive practices or ideologies in a relatively straightforward way but also to engage in processes that, whether consciously or not, render them problematic, at times with critical implications. The question then becomes how precisely the discursive practice, deep structure, or ideology—even the prejudice—is situated in the text other than in terms of instantiation or simple reflection. The *locus classicus* of this kind of inquiry may still in certain respects be Lukács's investigation of the relationship between conservative ideology and what the text discloses about social processes in the works of Balzac.[14] But in Lukács the understanding of language use and textual process was often not subtle or searching enough to account for the interaction between text and society. The almost Platonic vehemence of his condemnation of modernist literature not only illustrates this point; it points to problems that are intimated in Lukács's texts themselves but in a manner that remains "unthought" or not rendered explicit.

This is where Derrida's work may hold our possibilities for the type of inquiry into the interaction between text and social process that Derrida himself rarely seems to undertake overtly. His elaborate critique of Foucault's reading of Descartes in *Histore de la folie* should not, I think, be seen as a simple rejection of Foucault's interpretation.[15] Rather it directs attention to the question of pre-

14. See Georg Lukács, *Studies in European Realism* (New York, 1964).

15. Michel Foucault, *Folie et déraison: Histoire de la folie à l'âge classique* (Paris, 1972; first pub. 1961); in an appendix Foucault responds to Derrida. For Derrida's essay, published in French in 1967, see *Writing and Difference* (Chicago,

cisely where and how the exclusion of madness takes place in Descartes's text and whether that text may be understood as a straightforward sign of the times. Derrida's argument in "*Cogito* et histoire de la folie" must be seen in the broader context of his understanding of the long and tangled tradition constituting the history of metaphysics. It must also be seen with reference both to the problem of relating a text to its times and to the way texts may place in radical question their own seemingly dominant desires and themes.

The manifest division between Derrida and Foucault takes place over the local interpretation of a passage in Descartes's first *Meditation*. Where Foucault locates the exclusion of madness that inaugurates or confirms its status in the classical age, Derrida sees a "pedagogical" and dialogical discursive process that instead includes madness in a movement of increasing hyperbole. Derrida in effect gives a new turn to the very classical argument that one cannot take the passage in question out of context but must relate it to the overall movement of the text. Given the uncertainty in the passage concerning whether Descartes is speaking in his own voice, it may be impossible to decide whether Derrida or Foucault gives the better account. There is something to be said for both—and that may be the thought-provoking feature of the passage in question.

A more forceful moment in Derrida's analysis comes when he discusses the point of hyperbolic doubt in Descartes, which seems to be open to the possibility of madness and to occur on a level that

---

1978), 31–63. In "The Problem of Textuality: Two Exemplary Positions," *Critical Inquiry* 4 (1978), 673–714, Edward Said argues that Derrida's "deconstructive" criticism remains within the text while Foucault's history of discursive practices takes one into "thick" historical reality where various "discourses of power" and related dominant institutions have ruled the production of texts. In a valid attempt to stress the political importance of Foucault's concerns, Said ignores Derrida's extension of "textuality" beyond the confines of the book, and he fails to see how Foucault's view at times tends to reduce the complex text to a token of a mode of discourse. Nor does Said pose the problem of how the complex text may both "reflect" or inscribe dominant modes of discourse and also challenge them, at times with significant critical effects. The view of modern history that emerges from this perspective veers toward a rather monochromatic story of repression in which the contestatory role of certain texts is not investigated. The consequences of this limited view mark Said's own *Orientalism* (New York, 1978).

undercuts the opposition between madness and reason. But this point of extreme hyperbole is almost immediately followed in Descartes by a gesture that seems definitively to exclude madness and to establish a firm foundation for reason. Thus for Derrida, Descartes also excludes madness, but in a manner that repeats in modified form both the traditional philosophical desire for a firm and fully unified foundation for reason and the hyperbole that, at least momentarily, seems to subvert or contest that desire. In fact, in Descartes the moment of hyperbolic doubt and radical contestation is more explicit than it is in many other philosophers as Derrida himself interprets them. The larger question raised in Derrida's analysis is that of relating long and intricate traditions, such as the history of metaphysics, the specific period or time (including some delimited structural or epistemological definition of it), and the specific text. The attempt to delineate the mode of interaction among them requires an interpretation of the text in all its subtlety, and it indicates the importance for historical understanding of a notion of repetition with variation over time. In this respect, the relation among long tradition, specific time, and text cannot be determined through a notion of either simple continuity or discontinuity. Nor can the text be seen as a simple instantiation or illustration of either the long tradition or the specific time. Rather the problem becomes that of the way long tradition, specific time, and text repeat one another with variations, and the matter for elucidation becomes the degree of importance of these variations and how to construe it. The text is seen as the "place" where long tradition and specific time intersect, and it effects variations on both. But the text is not immobilized or presented as an autonomous node; it is situated in a fully relational network.

This network is the context for one of the most difficult issues for interpretation: that of how the critical and the symptomatic interact in a text or a work of art. Only by exploring this issue in a sustained way can one avoid the one-sidedness of analyses that stress either the symptomatic and representative nature of art (as did even Lukács and Lucien Goldmann, for whom art was critical solely as an expression of larger forces) or the way "great" art is itself an exceptional critical force for constructive change (as those affiliated with the Frankfurt school tended to argue). Stated in somewhat different terms, the issue is the extent to which art serves the escapist function of imaginary compensation for the defects of empirical reality and the extent to which it serves the contestatory function of questioning the empirical in a manner that has broader implications for the leading of life. One might suggest that texts and art works are ambivalent with respect to this issue but that they differ in how they come to terms with the ambivalence. A criterion of "greatness" or at least of significance might well be the ability of certain texts or works of art to generate a heightened sense of the problematic nature of this ambivalence and yet to point beyond it to another level of ambivalence where the very opposition between escapism and criticism seems to become tenuous—indeed where oppositions in general founder and emerge in the passage between radical hyperbole and delimited structures. There is no ready formula for "decoding" the relations among the symptomatic, the critical, and what Derrida terms the "undecidable," but the attempt to interpret significant modern works forces one to confront the problem of what to make of these relations.

The question of "impact" is best seen in terms of complex series of readings and uses which texts undergo over time, including the process by which certain texts are canonized. Any text reaches us overlaid and even overburdened by interpretations to which we are consciously or unconsciously indebted. Canonization itself is a procedure not only of selection but of selective interpretation, often in the direction of domestication. We as interpreters are situated in a sedimented layering of readings that demand excavation. But the process of gaining perspective on our own interpretations does not exclude the attempt to arrive at an intepretation we are willing to defend. Indeed the activity of relating the existing series of interpretations, uses, and abuses of a text or a corpus to a reading that one tries to make as good as possible is essential to a critical historiography. Of course, this is not to say that the interpretation one offers is definitive and exhaustive. Not only is it open to revision through argument and reconsideration. It may actively address the issue of how the text itself resists the "closure" of definitive and exhaustive interpretation. And it should be agitated by the realization that we are inevitably blind to certain limitations of our own perspective. But we interpret nevertheless. And, unless we interpret, our reference to a text becomes purely nominal, and we trace the movement of an "I-know-not-what" across time. To proceed in this manner is to abandon all hope of attaining a critical understanding of what is involved in the "impact" of texts. Indeed one might well argue that what is needed at present at the intersection of intellectual and social history is precisely an approach that relates an informed interpretation of complex texts to the problem of how those texts have been adapted to—and in certain ways have allowed—important uses and abuses over time. The cases of Marx, Nietzsche, and Heidegger call for treatment of this kind.[16]

16. George Steiner's *Martin Heidegger* (New York, 1978) is one of the best short introductions to Heidegger's thought, and it raises the problem of the relation between that thought and Heidegger's life. But the way Steiner addresses the latter issue is too summary and extreme to be altogether acceptable. He asserts an "organic" relation between the "vocabulary" of *Being and Time* (especially its later sections) and Heidegger's addresses of 1933 as well as "instrumental connections" between the "language" and "vision" of Heidegger's treatise and Nazi ideology (121–123). The mixing of metaphors to designate the nature of the relationships at issue itself indicates that they demand a more careful and extensive investigation than Steiner allows. He provides some crucial steps in this investigation by stressing the dangers of the more mesmeric sides of Heidegger's thought and the combination in it at times of near total criticism of the present and vague apocalyptic hope for the future. These aspects of Heidegger's thought may well have helped to induce the belief that the Nazis were the bearers of the fundamental change in modern civilization that Heidegger desired. And Steiner is, I think, justified in insisting upon the question of why Heidegger after 1945 remained publicly silent about his brief affiliation with the Nazis. What is also significant is that Steiner, in spite of his strictures about Heidegger's relation to the Nazis, wants to argue that Heidegger's work remains a basic and valuable contribution to modern thought. But the elucidation of the relation of that thought (notably *Being and Time*) to Nazi ideology and to Heidegger's own brief participation in politics requires an interpretation that inquires into the question of how the "same" themes or "ideas" function differently (or even in opposed ways) in different texts and contexts and how they may be both used and abused, not only by others but by the author

46

One important area for the study of impact that has not been sufficiently investigated is that of the readings texts receive at trials. The trial serves as one instance of social reading that brings out conventions of interpretation in an important social institution. It is significant that in their basic assumptions about reading, the prosecution and the defense may share a great deal, and what they share may be quite distant from, or even placed on trial in, the work itself. (One thing a trial must repress is the way style, as Flaubert realized, may be a politically subversive or contestatory force, more unsettling than the revolutionary message packaged in conventional forms.) In the modern West, the most famous and momentous trials of writers have involved "literary" figures. This may be one sign of the more contestatory character of literature in comparison with other varieties of "high" culture in modern society, at least on levels where a more general public may sense that something disconcerting is happening—although the reasons given for trial often neutralize this sense by appealing to very conventional criteria of judgment, for example, "prurient interest." Writers of "theoretical" or philosophical works in the West are tried more informally through critical responses to their works. This has happened to Nietzsche, Heidegger, Derrida, and even Wittgenstein—philosophers who have perhaps gone farthest in challenging traditional understandings of philosophical discourse. In this sense, the history of critical response, including the book review, is an important chapter in the history of social impact, especially with reference to the constitution and development of disciplines. One can often

---

himself in certain circumstances. Steiner does not provide this extremely difficult kind of interpretation. His own categorical response not only creates unexamined divisions in his own account (for Steiner himself argues that certain discussions in *Being and Time* constitute a radical critique of totalitarianism). It also leads him to the extremely dubious and unsupported assertion that the later sections of *Being and Time* (the ones presumably closer to Nazi ideology) are less persuasive and more opaque than the earlier portions of the text. The specious but useful separation between "good" and "bad" parts of the text is, I think, too simple an answer to the admittedly intricate question that Steiner has the merit of raising.

47

learn more about the operative structure of a discipline from its book reviews and their distribution in different sorts of journals than one can from its formal institutional organization.

4. *The relation of culture to texts.* The circulation or noncirculation of texts among levels of culture is an intricate problem, and difficulties arise even at the stage of deciding how to identify "levels." The approach to intellectual history I have been defending is directed at what has been traditionally (and now is often derogatorily) called "high" or "elite" culture. The dissemination of the "great" texts of at least the modern period to a larger audience is frequently at best a desideratum. At times it is actively opposed by important writers and intellectuals, although one may wonder to what extent this reaction is a defense against rejection, for modern texts often make demands upon the reader that few readers—even those in the so-called educated class—are willing to accept. One crucial function of a more "recuperative" or domesticating kind of intellectual history has been to disseminate these texts to the "generally educated" class in a "digestible" or "assimilable" form that may have little in common with the texts themselves and may even function as an excuse not to read them. Here I would note a general difference between a documentary and a dialogical approach to history. Insofar as an approach is documentary, it may validly function as a processing of "primary source material" that enables the nonexpert reader not to go to the sources or the archives themselves. But the very point of a dialogical approach is to stimulate the reader to respond critically to the interpretation it offers through his or her own reading or rereading of the primary texts.

To the extent that a text is not a mere document, it supplements existing reality, often by pointing out the weaknesses of prevailing definitions of it. In a traditional context, texts may function to shore up norms and values that are threatened but still experienced as viable. For example, Chrétien de Troyes had the quests of his knights test and ultimately prove the validity of courtly values that were threatened in the larger society.[17] In a revolutionary context,

17. The example of Chrétien de Troyes is discussed by Wolfgang Iser in *The Act of Reading* (Baltimore, 1978), 77–78.

texts may help to break down the existing system and suggest avenues of change. But it is at times difficult to distinguish clearly between the traditional and the revolutionary context. And any text that pinpoints weaknesses in a system has an ambivalent function, for it may always be read against its own dominant tendency or authorial intention—a "conservative" text being used for "radical" purposes or vice versa. The fate of Marx in the hands of his liberal and conservative critics—or even certain of his putative followers— is illustrative in this respect.

Most modern writers of note have seen their period as revolutionary or at least as "transitional." Indeed they have often been "alienated" from what they perceive as the dominant society and culture. Even significant conservatives, such as Burke and Maistre, do not simply defend a status quo but often inveigh against it in defense of values they believe to be under full siege and rapidly disappearing. They may advocate a context in which the attachment to values, norms, and communal groups is prereflective or quasi-instinctive, but they are forced to become highly reflective intellectuals in spite of themselves. More often than not, the modern conservative is a divided self who may even harbor rather radical tendencies. This tension is quite evident in Dostoevsky and Balzac. And, for conservatives and radicals alike, the very notion of a popular culture to which they might relate arose largely as an ideal, a critical fiction, or a goal to be opposed to "modern" forces that jeopardized those at times vestigial forms of popular culture they judged to be desirable.

One might argue that the global society or culture is too large and undifferentiated a unit for the investigation of the most relevant community of discourse for intellectuals. The more delimited school, movement, network of associations, or reference group would seem to provide the more immediate complex of shared assumptions or pertinent considerations that operate, tacitly or explicitly, to shape the intellectual's sense of significant questions and modes of inquiry. Hence intellectual history should be a history of intellectuals, of the communities of discourse in which they function, and of the varying relations—ranging in often complicated ways from insulation to openness—they manifest toward the larger culture. Thinkers as diverse as T. S. Kuhn, Quentin Skinner, R. G. Collingwood, and Michel Foucault may be drawn upon in the attempt to elaborate and apply this view. This approach has much to commend it, but I want to point out at least two problems it sometimes generates.

First, it may be used to restrict historical inquiry to the historicist and documentary attempt to recreate the dialogue of others, prohibiting the extension of that dialogue to include the interpretations of the historian, perhaps on the grounds that epochs are primarily if not exclusively dissociated in their forms of understanding. (Those grounds give rise to damaging aporias that are too well known to be rehearsed here.) Even more often, the assumption is made that historical understanding itself is (or should be) purely "objective" and that the very notion of an informed dialogue with the past is absurd or at least nonhistorical. This position not only identifies the historical with the historicist and the documentary. It may also construe the notion of dialogue in a simplistic way (for example, in terms of drawing immediate lessons from the past or projecting our own particular or subjective concerns onto it). One may, however, argue that the reconstruction of the dialogues of the dead should be self-consciously combined with the interpretative attempt to enter into an exchange with them that is itself dialogical only insofar as it actively recognizes the difficulties of communication across time and the importance of understanding as fully as possible what the other is trying to say. To the extent that the past is investigated in terms of its most particularized aspects, dialogue with it becomes minimal. But the subsequent question is whether historical research should be directed primarily to aspects of this sort, which restrict the historian's use of language to predominantly informational and analytic functions. When it is applied to the works of major figures, an approach that attempts to be exclusively documentary is often deadly in its consequences. And when we historians who are trained to believe in the primacy of the documentary ideal do venture to put forth interpretations or critical judgments, the latter may well be of little interest, for they are not the products of a rich and varied discursive background. Here, of course, we face the traditional problem of how the educator is himself to be educated.

Second, the focus on communities of discourse must be cogently related to the problem of textual interpretation. It is not enough to establish influence or the existence of a shared "paradigm" through the enumeration of common presuppositions, questions, themes, or arguments. One must elucidate in a more detailed way how the borrowed or the common actually functions in the texts in question. To document common assumptions or lines of influence may suffice to debunk the myth of absolute originality. But this procedure easily gives rise to its own forms of self-deception or even mindless chronicling when debunking goes to the extreme of not recognizing why there is, for example, a major difference between a Fliess and a Freud. Influence studies are of minor interest unless they address the issue of how common ideas function differentially in different texts and corpuses, and even the attempt to dethrone a reigning "great" must face up to the problem of interpreting his works in their complexity. All too often the focus on the community of discourse leads the historian to limit research to minor figures or to highly restricted and unsituated aspects of the thought of a major figure (for example, Nietzsche's elitism, Marx's utopianism, or Freud's biologism). In addition, the delimited "communities" in which important modern intellectuals participate may themselves be made up more of the dead or absent than of the living or present. The most significant reference group may prominently include dead or distant (even future) "others" who become relevant largely through their works, which the "creative" intellectual helps bring to life in his or her own works through emulation, selective appropriation, parody, polemic, anticipation, and so forth. The contemporary person-to-person group may have a lesser significance for the actual production of "ideas" and in any case its role is always supplemented by relation to others through their texts or other artifacts. The dialogue with the text may even be experienced as more immediate and engrossing than most conversations. Indeed one of the re-creative implications of reading might well be to attempt to create social and cultural conditions in which the literal conversation and the general text of life are more like the processes stimulated by an encounter with a great text.

This last consideration provides a limited avenue of reentry into the question of the relation between "great" texts and general or popular culture. The processes that Mikhail Bakhtin discusses in terms of "carnivalization" help to identify at least one kind—or one vision—of popular culture activated or reactivated in the texts of many significant modern writers and often desired by them as the larger context to which their writings might relate. "Carnivalization," in Bakhtin's own normative, indeed visionary conception, is epitomized in carnival as a social institution but not confined to it. In its larger sense, "carnivalization" is an engaging process of interaction through which seeming opposites—body and spirit, work and play, positive and negative, high and low, seriousness and laughter—are related to each other in an ambivalent, contestatory interchange that is both literally and figuratively "re-creative." It is set within an encompassing rhythm of social life, and one might argue that its nature and functions depend upon that larger setting. While Bakhtin provides little description or analysis of actual carnivals, he does note broad variations in the role of carnival in society and of carnivalization in literature, and he stresses the importance of the carnivalesque as a vital dimension of life itself.

According to Bakhtin, a lively interchange among carnival as a social institution, popular culture, and high culture existed in Rabelais's Renaissance. While aspects of elite culture were closed to the common people (for example, works written in Latin), the elite participated in popular culture, and aspects of that culture affected high culture. Thus, with some underemphasis of their erudite and esoteric side, Bakhtin can interpret the works of Rabelais as drawing upon, and feeding into, a rich and vital popular culture. The modern period witnessed the decline of carnival, the separation of the elite from popular culture, and the detachment of processes of carnivalization in literature from significant public institutions. Indeed great literature is for Bakhtin the primary repository of the modern carnivalesque in its more restricted but still potent state. Social forms of carnivalization have tended to be appropriated for official political purposes, as in the parade and the pageant, or to withdraw to the private sphere, for example, in the domestic celebration of holidays. And the modern literary carnivalesque has itself often gravitated toward more reduced extremes, such as largely negative irony and hysterically shrill laughter. Bakhtin's analysis of the works of Dostoevsky, however, itself indicates the more recreative possibilities of carnivalization and "grotesque realism" in modern literature. [18]

The decline of carnival was directly related to religious reform and indirectly related to the multiple processes gathered together under the label of "modernization." The withdrawal of the elites from popular culture was a long-term process extending from 1500 to 1800, and what had been everyone's second culture was rediscovered as an exotic residue of the past. In the nineteenth century, the turn toward folklore and other forms of popular culture was often one aspect of various responses to the perceived "excesses" of the Enlightenment. In post-Enlightenment writing, there is often, moreover, an adversary relation to the dominant society in which "carnivalization" is underplayed or repressed. Here, for example, we have one basis for Nietzsche's critique of positivism as a eunuchlike flight from carnivalesque contestation—the Nietzschean version of the "betrayal of the intellectuals." We also have one way of viewing Flaubert's "postromantic" notion of art as an ironic and stylistically insurrectionary variant of the transformed carnivalesque. More generally, the notion of carnivalization provides one way of interpreting the contestatory styles with political overtones that have been so characteristic of modern writing. In-

18. See Mikhail Bakhtin, *Rabelais and His World* (first submitted as a dissertation in 1940), tr. Hélène Iswolsky (Cambridge, Mass., 1968), *Problems of Dostoevsky's Poetics* (1929), tr. R. W. Rotsel (Ann Arbor, 1973), and *The Dialogic Imagination*, tr. Caryl Emerson and Michael Holquist (Austin, 1981). For an application of certain of Bakhtin's views, see Natalie Z. Davis, *Society and Culture in Early Modern France* (Stanford, 1975).

deed, official resistance to carnival-type behavior may stem from political and cultural insecurity. And processes of carnivalization can themselves be related to social action in part inspired by a desire for a context of "lived experience" more open to revitalizing, contestatory forms. One need not look to the distant past for examples of these phenomena. Not only may aspects of the work of recent French figures (for example, Foucault, Deleuze, Sollers, Kristeva, and Derrida) be seen in terms of processes of carnivalization. But the events of 1968 in France have been interpreted in this way, often with the term "carnival" being used in a pejorative sense by opponents and at times with the vision of "carnivalization" becoming a pretext for romanticization in defenders of the *événements*. [19] The larger problem these considerations bring out is that of the way innovatory "elite" responses in the modern period may appeal to more or less transfigured versions of older "popular" culture in the

19. For a treatment of early modern culture (or cultures), with a discussion of the role of carnival, its decline over time, and the withdrawal of the elites from popular culture, see Peter Burke, *Popular Culture in Early Modern Europe* (New York, 1978). For a study of French culture emphasizing the problem of carnivalization, including its role in 1968, see Maurice Crubellier, *Histoire culturelle de la France* (Paris, 1974). A more detailed discussion of the history of the carnivalesque and its relation to various writers would require qualifications and discriminations that I have not provided. For an analysis of Flaubert and carnivalization, see Arthur Mitzman, "Roads, Vulgarity, Rebellion, and Pure Art: The Inner Space in Flaubert and French Culture," *Journal of Modern History* 51 (1979), 504–524. It must, however, be noted that the danger in Flaubert is that the leveling tendency he saw operating in modern culture affected his own approach in an uncritical way, leading him at times to a homogenized and nearly nihilistic condemnation of both modern society and humanity in general. In his most lapidary and famous formulations of the ideal of "pure art," Flaubert "sublimated" the carnivalesque into its opposite: an ascetic negation of reality and an attempt to transcend it into an inviolate sphere of beauty or absolute style. The more compelling and subtle dynamic in his stories is that whereby a vision of pure art is not simply exemplified but contested and even "carnivalized," notably through the treatment of analogous forms of the quest for the absolute and the empathetic-ironic modulations of narrative voice in the so-called "free indirect style." In general, art was for Flaubert the most important commitment in the world and the work of a clown. It is important to recognize that he affirmed both these conceptions with great intensity and that there is in his works a variable tension between a pathos of belief and critical forms such as irony, parody, and self-parody. On these issues, see my *"Madame Bovary" on Trial* (Ithaca, 1982).

radical critique of what is perceived as the dominant sociocultural context.

5. *The relation of a text to the corpus of a writer.* The notion of context provided by other texts is itself apparently textual in nature (although one must recall that "corpus" here may also mean "body"). And it raises the problem of the relationship between a text and the texts of other writers as well as other texts of the same writer. For what is at issue here is precisely the unity or identity of a corpus. Often the corpus is seen in one of three ways: continuity among texts ("linear development"); discontinuity among texts (change or even "epistemological break" between stages or periods); and dialectical synthesis (the later stage raises the earlier one to a higher level of insight). The corpus is thus unified in one way or another (developmental unity, two discrete unities, higher unity), and so seen, it is like a single text writ large, for the single text may be interpreted through the use of these categories. The question, however, is whether these categories are too simple for interpreting the functioning of both a complex text and the corpus of complex texts. The relation among aspects or elements of a text, and a fortiori among texts in a corpus, may involve uneven development and differing forms of repetition or displacement that put in question simple models of intelligibility. Indeed the "corpus" of a writer may be at least partially dismembered, sometimes in ways that are intended or explicitly explored by the writer himself. Carnivalization as described by Bakhtin involves dismemberment or creative undoing that may be related to processes of renewal. One strategy of dismemberment is the use of montage and quotation through which the text is laced or even strewn with parts of other texts—both written texts and elements of social discourse. In Flaubert, for example, the text is punctuated with parodic citations from other novels and from the clichés of daily life. In Mann and Joyce, the montage technique assumes panoramic proportions in its ability to piece or graft together various uses of discourse. In Sollers and Derrida, dismemberment (involving textual distribution of the "self") at times seems to attain Dionysian heights or depths. The larger question raised by

these strategies is that of the interaction between the quest for unity, which may continue to function in direct or parodic ways, and challenges to that quest operative or experimented with in the texts themselves. The texts, however, do not become hermetically closed upon themselves; they differ from and also defer to other texts both written and lived.

6. *The relation between modes of discourse and texts.* In the recent past, considerable attention has been paid to the role of more or less formalized modes of discourse, structures of interpretation, and conventions or rules. Many theorists have argued that writing and reading are informed by structures or conventions that should be a primary, if not an exclusive, center of critical interest.[20] Hayden White has attempted to arrive at a level of deep structure that undercuts the opposition between literature and history to reveal how modes of emplotment inform all coherent narratives and how tropes construct the linguistic field. He has also indicated that figurative uses of language connect the levels of description and explicit interpretation or explanation in prose narratives. This last point serves to raise again a question that has been insufficiently explored in structuralist accounts of discourse: the question of how various modes of discourse, rules, or conventions actually function in texts or extended uses of language. In this regard, the reading of "minor" texts is certainly important for the attempt to establish what the dominant rules or conventions of a genre were at a given time. But the relation of a "great" text to genres—both the ones it is placing in question and the ones it is helping to establish—is always problematic, and even a "minor" text may hold out some surprises here. Often, however, it is assumed that this relation is one of coverage on the part of structures and instantiation on the part of texts. This view (which may actually be held by theorists who in other respects criticize the subordination of the humanities to "positivism" with its

20. For one especially forceful elaboration of this view, see Jonathan Culler, *Structuralist Poetics* (Ithaca, 1975). For an equally forceful exploration of some of its limitations, see Culler, *Flaubert: The Uses of Uncertainty* (Ithaca, 1974).

"covering laws") leads to the belief that there are unproblematic realms of discourse, illustrated by texts that fall within them.

This view is misleading as it relates to the status of analytic distinctions or structural oppositions and to the question of how these distinctions or oppositions function in texts.[21] Analytic distinctions such as those drawn between history and literature, fact and fiction, concept and metaphor, the serious and the ironic, and so forth, do not define realms of discourse that unproblematically characterize or govern extended uses of language. Instead, what should be taken as a problem for inquiry is the nature of the relationships among various analytically defined distinctions in the actual functioning of language, including the use of language by theorists attempting to define and defend analytic distinctions or oppositions in their conceptual purity. To say this is neither to advocate the obliteration of all distinctions nor to offer a purely homogeneous understanding of a mysterious entity called the "text." It is rather to direct attention to problems that are obscured when one relies uncritically on the concept of "realms of discourse." For example, it is common to distinguish history from literature on the grounds that history is concerned with the realm of fact while literature moves in the realm of fiction. It is true that the historian may not invent his facts or references while the "literary" writer may, and in this respect the latter has a greater margin of freedom in exploring relationships. But, on other levels, historians make use of heuristic fictions, counterfactuals, and models to orient their research into facts, and the question I have tried to raise is whether historians are restricted to the reporting and analysis of facts in their exchange with the past. Conversely, literature borrows from a factual repertoire in multiple ways, and the transplantation of the documentary has a carry-over effect that invalidates attempts to see literature in terms of a pure suspension of reference to "reality" or transcendence of the empirical into the purely imaginary. Even

---

21. I try to develop this assertion with reference to the thought of Jürgen Habermas in "Habermas and the Grounding of Critical Theory," below.

when literature attempts to "bracket" empirical reality or to suspend more ordinary documentary functions, it engages in a self-referential work or praxis through which the text documents its own mode of production. The very prevalence of literature about literature or art about art raises the question of how to interpret self-referential activity with respect to a larger historical context. Thus there certainly are distinctions to be drawn, but the problem is the manner in which these distinctions function in texts and in our reading or interpretation of them.

In the last-mentioned respect, there are different possibilities, ranging from the dominance of a given analytic distinction or type to more open interplay and contestation among various uses of language. But dominance implies some form of subordination or exclusion, and how this relationship is established must be investigated. Any critique of pure identities, pure oppositions, and attendant hierarchies must pay close attention to the way these categories function, for they have indeed been of decisive importance in thought and in life. One has certainly witnessed a quest for pure fact, pure fiction, pure philosophy, pure poetry, pure prose, and so forth. For those committed to some variant of it, the quest is taken at face value and defended. It may also be institutionalized in disciplines that organize themselves around conventions and rules that restrict language to certain uses and prohibit or sanction the attempt to raise questions that problematize these restricted uses. One of the largest of these questions is whether the quest for purity and the direct projection of analytic categories onto "reality" are related to a "metaphysics of the proper" whereby one's own identity, propriety, or authenticity is established through the identification of a totally different "other," an outsider who may even become a pariah or scapegoat. In any case, the problem is how seeming purity (or unmarked identity and unity) is established and whether the quest for it in language use is contested by other aspects of the text or more general linguistic context in which this quest takes place. A text itself may of course seek purity by engaging in procedures of exclusion or domination that tend to neutralize or reduce its more dis-

58

concerting or contestatory movements. These procedures provide points of entry for interpretations or entire disciplines that "found" themselves upon the purity and autonomy of "realms of discourse" putatively emanating from certain master texts. But complex texts may well involve other movements that test the desire for unity in a variety of ways. Indeed certain texts that seem to rely exclusively on one function or analytic dimension of language—for example, analytic dissociation or simulated denotative usage and attendant metaphoric deprivation in Beckett—may involve parody and stimulate in the reader an awareness of other possible uses of language. In fact the question is whether any text that seems successful in the sustained reliance on one function or analytic aspect of language, for example, the accumulation of facts or of theoretical reflections, is engaged in intentional or unintentional parody or self-parody, or at least may always be so read.

These points indicate that analytic distinctions are useful for purposes of clarification and orientation as pursued on an ideal level in their pure or "laboratory" form but that they never function "as such" in actual discourse or in texts. When they do seem to be used purely as such, other processes are at work or at play. The critique of these processes is perforce prone to its own excesses (discursive delirium, political quietism, anomic disorientation, the quest for full liberation either of or from libidinal demands). At its best, however, this critique may raise the problem of a more viable interaction between forms of language and forms of life. The exploration of this problem in the great texts of the tradition constitutes an especially engaging adventure that at times involves a strangely disconcerting way of making us think seemingly alien thoughts that are in fact within us and that may well return in unmitigatedly destructive ways when they are simply repressed or excluded. This problem may not be seen or appreciated when texts are read in an excessively reductive way or delegated exclusively to discrete disciplines. No discipline has the imperial right to dominion over a Freud, Marx, Nietzsche, or Joyce. (The practical advantage of intellectual history in this respect is that it can, without excuse or subterfuge, explore the problem of reading various texts together and thus raise questions about their functioning as language that might not otherwise be apparent.) Indeed, as I have already intimated, a discipline may constitute itself in part through reductive readings of its important texts—readings that are contested by the "founding" texts themselves in significant ways.[22] These readings render the texts less multifaceted and perhaps less critical but more operational for organized research. Here the decisive role of certain disciples and practitioners lies not in the fine-tuning of a paradigm enunciated in "founding" texts but in the active reduction of those texts to their paradigmatic level.

The "great" texts should be part of the pertinent record for all historians. They are certainly part and parcel of a general historical culture. Something excessively reductive has already taken place when they are assigned to the subdiscipline of intellectual history, which may then function as a park or reserve for them. But at least within that subdiscipline, they should be read with an eye for the broader and occasionally uncanny processes they engage and that engage us. One such process is precisely the interaction between the desire for unity, identity, or purity, and the forces that contest it. The investigation of this process does not imply a simple rejection of conceptions of unity or order in a mindlessly antinomian celebration of chaos and dismemberment. What it calls for is a rethinking of the concept of unity and its analogues in more workable and critical terms. It also requires a sensitivity to the way these concepts are related to their "adversaries" in the texts we study and in our own attempts at theoretical self-understanding. One practical implication of these considerations is the possibility of reconstructing norms and conventions in forms that may be more durable precisely because they enable us to contend better with criticism and contestation. In this respect, a function of dialogue with the past is to

22. This view motivates my study of Durkheim in *Emile Durkheim: Sociologist and Philosopher* (Ithaca, 1972).

further the attempt to ascertain what deserves to be preserved, re-habilitated, or critically transformed in tradition.

I want to conclude by returning to the distinction I drew between intellectual history as a reconstruction of the past and intellectual history as a dialogue or conversation with the past—a distinction that should not be taken as a purely dichotomous opposition. The reconstruction of the past is an important endeavor, and reliable documentation is a crucial component of any approach that claims to be historical. But the dominance of a documentary conception distorts our understanding of both historiography and the historical process. Indeed I have tried to suggest that a *purely* documentary conception of historiography is itself a heuristic fiction, for description is never pure, in that a fact is relevant for an account only when it is selected with reference to a topic or a question posed to the past. The simplest fact—a dated event—relies on what is for some historians a belief and for others a convenient fiction: the decisive significance of the birth of Christ in establishing a chronology in terms of a "before" and "after." Yet a purely documentary conception may function as an unexamined assumption or it may give rise to a paradoxically self-conscious and sophisticated defense of a "naive" idea of the historian's craft—a defense that may border on anti-intellectualism. In any case, insofar as it achieves a position of dominance, a documentary conception is excessively restrictive, especially in the results it yields in the analysis of significant texts. And it obscures the problem of the interaction between description and other uses of language in an account. The idea of a purely descriptive, objective rendering of the past can allow for uses of language that escape it only in terms of the exiguous category of unavoidable bias or particularistic subjectivity. This category may apply to certain aspects of historiography. But the simple opposition between self-effacing objectivity and subjective bias fails to accommodate the range of language uses in any significant history.

The purely documentary view of historiography often coincides with a historicist definition of the historical that identifies the object of study as changing "particulars" in contrast with extratemporal or synchronic types or universals. This venerable view ignores the historical process of repetition with variation or change that functions to mitigate the analytic opposition between the particular or unique and the typical or universal. Yet it is this historical (and linguistic) process that is operative in the past and that raises the problem of the historicity of the historian in his or her attempt to come to terms with it. A documentary historiography that tries to exclude interpretation or to see it only in the guise of bias, subjectivity, or anachronism also has a bizarre consequence. It presents historical truth in an essentially nonhistorical way, for, by attempting to restrict historiography proper to the description and analysis of verifiable facts (ideally in the form of a definitive and exhaustive account), it strives for an unchanging representation of changing "particulars" that would itself transcend the historical process. As the work of Ranke amply documents, the narrowly historicist and the ahistorical are extremes that meet in the ideal of a purely documentary historiography. And the desire to transcend history reappears in a form that may be invisible precisely because it has become so familiar. Indeed, a belief that historiography is a purely documentary or descriptive reconstitution of the past may be prone to blind fictionalizing because it does not explicitly and critically raise the problem of the role of fictions (for example, in the form of models, analytic types, and heuristic fictions) in the attempt to represent reality. The result is often a tacit reliance upon the most conventional narrative structures to combine documented fact, *vie romancée*, and unsubstantiated judgments about the past or flimsy analogies between past and present.

With specific reference to intellectual history, I would argue for a more "performative" notion of reading and interpretation in which an attempt is made to "take on" the great texts and to attain a level of understanding and perhaps of language use that contends with them. This notion, which valorizes the virtuoso performance in reading, is easily abused when it becomes a license for reducing the text to little more than a trampoline for one's own creative leaps or political demands. Certainly, the act of interpretation has political dimensions. It is not an autonomous hermeneutic undertaking that moves on the level of pure meaning to establish a "fusion of horizons" assuring authoritative continuity with the past. In some relevant sense, interpretation is a form of political intervention that engages the historian in a critical process that relates past, present, and future through complex modes of interaction involving both continuities and discontinuities. But it is misleading to pose the problem of understanding in terms of either of two extremes: the purely documentary representation of the past and the "presentist" quest for liberation from the "burden" of history through unrestrained fictionalizing and mythologizing. In relation to both these extremes (which constitute parts of the same complex), it is necessary to emphasize the status of interpretation as an activity that cannot be reduced to mere subjectivity. A significant text involves, among other things, creative art, and its interpretation is, among other things, a performing art. But art is never entirely free, and the art of the historian is limited in specific ways. He must attend to the facts, especially when they test and contest his own convictions and desires (including the desire for a fully unified frame of reference). And even when he attempts to think further what is thought in a text, he cannot reduce the text to a pretext for his own inventions or immediate interests. The belief in pure interpretation is itself a bid for absolute transcendence that denies both the finite nature of understanding and the need to confront critically what Freud discussed in terms of "transference."

The genuine alternative to a purely documentary and contemplative conception of the past "for its own sake" is not its simple opposite: the futile attempt to escape the past or to identify it through projection with the present. Rather, texts should be seen to address us in more subtle and challenging ways, and they should be carried into the present—with implications for the future—in a dialogical fashion. Historiography would be an exercise in narcissistic infatuation if it amounted to a willful projection of present concerns upon the past. The notion of "creative misreading" (or active "rewriting") is itself misleading when it legitimates one-sided, subjectivist aggression that ignores the ways texts may actually challenge the interpreter and lead him to change his mind. Even if one accepts the metaphor that presents interpretation as the "voice" of the historical reader in the "dialogue" with the past, it must be actively recognized that the past has its own "voices" that must be respected, especially when they resist or qualify the interpretations we would like to place on them. A text is a network of resistances, and a dialogue is a two-way affair; a good reader is also an attentive and patient listener. Questions are necessary to focus interest in an investigation, but a fact may be pertinent to a frame of reference by contesting or even contradicting it. An interest in what does not fit a model and an openness to what one does not expect to hear from the past may even help to transform the very questions one poses to the past. Both the purely documentary and the "presentist" extremes are "monological" insofar as they deny these possibilities. Indeed the seeming anomaly should be seen as having a special value in historiography, for it constrains one to doubt overly reductive interpretations and excessively "economical" shortcuts from understanding to action.

The conception of the field that I have tried to defend complicates the task of the intellectual historian. But it also keeps intellectual history in touch with questions that are raised in "great" texts and that are forever old and new in a manner that cannot be reduced to some *philosophia perennis* or to a subjectivistic relativism. And it defines intellectual history more in terms of a process of inquiry than in terms of rules of method or of a body of information about the past. This is the most fruitful kind of "definition" possible for an approach that both addresses historical problems and understands itself as historical. The demand for documentation serves to keep responsive interpretations from becoming irresponsible. But to use this demand to attempt to escape our own dialogical relation to the past is to attempt to escape our own historicity. We need to understand more clearly what is involved in a relationship that is dialogical and historical without being either "historicist" or "presentist." The historian who reads texts either as mere documents or as formal entities (if not as Rorschach tests) does not read them historically precisely because he or she does not read them as texts. And, whatever else they may be, texts are events in the history of language. To understand these multivalent events as complex uses of language, one must learn to pose anew the question of "what really happens" in them and in the reader who actually reads them. One of the most important contexts for reading texts is clearly our own—a context that is misconstrued when it is seen in narrowly "presentist" terms. I have only alluded to ways in which this context involves the reader in an interaction among past, present, and future—an interaction having a bearing on both understanding and action. But it is precisely here that intellectual history opens out to other modes of interpretation and practice. This "opening" relates to the way the power of dialogue and of reflection is itself effective only when it comes with the "working through" of existential problems that are perforce also social and political problems.[23]

I shall here append a few observations that have a specific bearing upon this volume. My overall purpose is to arrive at some conception of where the subdiscipline of intellectual history finds itself at present and where it should be going. I want to emphasize that this essay is largely programmatic. It tries to raise questions about exist-

---

23. I will simply mention one limited way in which intellectual history should address this issue. The intellectual historian should, I think, recognize his or her audience as a tensely divided one made up of both experts and a generally educated public. The intellectual historian is required to come as close as possible to an "expert" knowledge of the problems being investigated. But a goal of intellectual history should be the expansion of the "class" of the generally educated and the generation of a better interchange between them and the "experts." This means helping to put the generally educated in a position to raise more informed and critical questions. It also means attempting to prevent expertise from becoming enclosed in its own dialect or jargon. In these senses, intellectual history faces complex problems of "translation," and its own concerns bring it into contact with larger social and cultural questions. One such question is how to resist the establishment of common culture on a relatively uncritical level and to further the creation of a more demanding common culture that, within limits, is genuinely open to contestation.

ing approaches and to sketch alternative ways of addressing issues. It does not itself show how to practice the approach it somewhat presumptuously defends on a relatively theoretical level. Only in footnotes do I attempt to indicate possible approaches to reading and interpretation that relate to the more general issues.

I nonetheless think that there is a need today for more programmatic and relatively theoretical statements in the field of intellectual history. This need is conjunctural, and my insistency in urging it is to some extent transitional. At issue is the process of recognition and even of naming with respect to various approaches to history. One important question facing us is that of the type of research that should be called intellectual history, indeed that of the type of research to be recognized as historical. We are, I think, in a situation analogous to that about which Confucians spoke in terms of the issue of a "rectification of names."

The idea that the mansion of history has many chambers or that we should not build walls between approaches bespeaks a false generosity insofar as there exists a hierarchy among various perspectives and even an unwillingness to recognize certain approaches as validly historical. The issues of recognition and naming relate to practical as well as cognitive matters, for example, job placement. Material interests are involved in processes of recognition and nonrecognition. These interests cannot be separated from questions of professional or disciplinary politics. When a position in intellectual history is to be filled and candidates with different perspectives apply for it, what approach to research will be considered relevant and which candidates will be accorded preferential treatment? I think that there is at present an excessive tendency to give priority to social or sociocultural approaches and to downgrade the importance of reading and interpreting complex texts. The recent shift from the more statistical methods of the earlier version of *Annales* historiography to a concern with problems of social and cultural "meaning" does not remedy the problem, for it often leads to a definition of intellectual history as retrospective symbolic or cultural anthropology. This definition frequently brings about what might be called an anthropological bulldozer effect, whereby the significance and the specificity of interpreting complex texts is plowed under in the attempt to reconstruct a common or collective "discursive culture." But certain cultures provide "mechanisms" for the preservation and reinterpretation of their exceptional products; intellectual history is one of these "mechanisms."

Let me immediately add that I recognize the importance of reconstituting institutional practice and social discourse. But I must also stress that the focus upon this problem often involves a very restricted interpretation of complex texts (when the latter are considered at all). Conversely, the focus on the understanding of complex texts may bring certain losses in the more general reconstitution of institutionalized or shared social discourses in various classes, groups, or occupations. The comprehensive problem is to understand how complex texts relate to their various contexts and vice versa—and this problem itself involves an appreciation of the losses and gains attendant upon a research strategy. Without more programmatic or even polemical statements, studies employing certain research strategies may easily be written off as beyond the pale of historiography or merely marginal to its main concerns. In an ideal world, each historian would be responsible for the treatment of all problems from the most comprehensive of all possible perspectives. In the real world, certain choices must be made. Only when these choices are self-conscious and thought out can genuine cooperation among historians with different emphases be undertaken in a noninvidious spirit. My concern is that the specific problems involved in the understanding of complex texts are becoming radically deemphasized in intellectual history and that the latter is being defined in ways that obscure or avoid these problems.

In the most general terms, where does the perspective on intellectual history that I have tried to elaborate lead? What implications does it have for the relation between past and present and between "theory and practice"? The field of humanistic studies today seems increasingly divided by two opposed tendencies. One tendency attempts, more or less self-consciously, to rehabilitate conventional approaches to description, interpretation, and explanation. It stresses the need to discover or perhaps to invent, on some decisive level, unity and order in the phenomena under investigation and, by implication, in one's own life and times. It may recognize chaos or disorder in phenomena, but its overriding goal is to uncover order in chaos, for example, through delimitation of topics, selection of problems, empirical and analytic procedures of investigation, and perhaps even synthesis of results by means of causal or interpretative models. In the reading of texts, it emphasizes the importance of determining central arguments, core meanings, dominant themes, prevalent codes, world views, and deep structures. In relating texts or other artifacts to contexts, it seeks some comprehensive, integrative paradigm: formally, by arguing that once texts "internalize" contexts, the latter are subjected to procedures "internal" to the text; causally, by arguing that the very problems or, indeed, the formal procedures operative in texts are themselves "caused" or generated by changes in the larger context; or structurally, by arguing that both texts and contexts attest to the agency of deeper forces homologous to them. A single account may variously employ all three of these paradigms of integration, or it may seek to include them in some higher "order of orders."

The other tendency tries to bring out the ways in which debates that agitate those taking the first approach actually rest on common assumptions, and it points to the limitations of those assumptions. What is assumed in conventional approaches is the priority, perhaps the dominance, of unity or its analogues: order, purity, closure, undivided origin, coherent structure, determinate meaning at least at the core, and so forth. Those working within the other, more "experimental" tendency (often identified, at times misleadingly, as "deconstructive") will thus stress the importance of what is marginal in text or life as seen from the conventional view—what is uncanny or disorienting in terms of its assumptions. But the danger in this other tendency is that it will remain fixated at the phase of simple reversal of dominant conventional assumptions and replace unity with disunity, order with chaos, center with absence of center, determinacy with uncontrolled plurality or dissemination of meaning, and so forth. In so doing, it may aggravate what its proponents would see as undesirable tendencies in the larger society, become symptomatic where it would like to be critical, and confuse ordinary equivocation and evasiveness—or even slipshod research—with the kind of transformative interaction between self and other (or language and world) it would like to reactivate.

Reversal may be necessary as a type of shock therapy that enables a critique to register, but its inadequacies are blatant, especially when it has become familiar and fails to shock. What is then needed is a general rethinking of problems, including a modulated understanding of the relation between tradition and its critique. Involved in this process of rethinking is the realization that both full unity and full disunity (or their analogues) are ideal limits more or less approximated in language and life. The general problem then becomes that of how precisely these limits have been related in texts and contexts of the past and how they should be related in the present and future. An informed dialogue with the past, which investigates significant texts and their relations to pertinent contexts, is part of an attempt to come to terms with this problem. It is premised upon the conviction that the intellectual historian is both intellectual and historian and that he or she, as intellectual, does not simply cease being a historian. Indeed, the relationship between the "critical" intellectual and the "scholarly" historian (or traditional *érudit*) is essential for the internalized dialogue that marks the intellectual historian. [24]

24. A recent book is highly relevant to the problems rehearsed in this essay. Timothy J. Reiss, in his immensely learned and stimulating *Discourse of Modernism* (Ithaca, 1982), traces the emergence and rise to dominance of what he calls an "analytico-referential class of discourse," one based upon the assumption of a logically coherent sign system having a relation of full adequation or correspondence to both reality and the "scientific" mind. (The "analytico-referential" might be taken as the extreme variant of what I have termed a documentary approach to problems.) Reiss distinguishes this discourse from a "patterning" or "conjunctive" discourse (analogous to Lévi-Strauss's *bricolage* or *pensée sauvage*) which he sees as dominant ("prevalent" might be a more accurate term) in the pre-modern period. Reiss's own method of investigation tends, as he notes, to be "analytico-referen-

tial," and his understanding of the hold of a given discursive mode over a period is often too rigid. Indeed there is a correspondence among his reliance upon a relatively unproblematic analytic category such as "class of discourse" (or "episteme" in the terminology of Foucault, who is his acknowledged guide), his documentary view of the way texts instantiate epistemes, his idea of the "dominance" of an episteme in a period, and his underemphasis of all basic, nontransitional contestation or difference in a period, text, or individual. Reiss's own tendencies in interpretation not only tend to be too narrowly "analytico-referential" in bias; they obscure the problem of how dominance may come to be established and questioned. Especially dubious is his rather homogeneous—almost fictional—notion of the way "patterning" was "dominant" in pre-Renaissance Europe. ("Dominant" is an especially unfortunate word to the extent that this discourse is genuinely tolerant of, or even generously open to, other discourses.) He rejects the claim that figures such as Aristotle and Aquinas elaborated significant aspects of an analytic and referential discourse because they lacked what is for him a criterion of the latter: a concept of the subjective will (or the willful, possessive subject) as center of knowledge and power. He does not confront Heidegger's argument that the modern subject is a specific displacement of—one involving both continuity and discontinuity with respect to—the metaphysical "ground" that had other articulations in earlier philosophers. He also omits mention of Lévi-Strauss's view that la pensée sauvage includes a "science of the concrete" that remains a basis as well as a goal of later science. And he does not come to terms with the understanding of historical process as both repetition and change—an understanding that would mitigate certain damaging aporias of his own text (such as the one generated by the historicist belief that "our" position within analytico-referential discourse renders impossible an understanding of a putatively alien "patterning" discourse—although it somehow permits the unproblematic assertion that there was a total break with that unknowable discourse). Reiss's own hyperbolic idea of the dominance of the analytico-referential after 1600 may have limited polemical value. But it presents Kepler as anomalous and converts modernity into the image of Bacon writ large—a "modernist" Bacon interpreted in terms of his own self-image as the agent of a total break with the past and the "instauration" of an entirely new discourse. It also threatens to be too domineering in its underemphasis of the significance of challenges to the analytico-referential that rely on relational and contestatory modes, including the carnivalesque, which Reiss treats rather dismissively. But, despite its own reductively "analytico-referential" bent, Reiss's book is quite valuable in its elucidation of the rise of the "analytico-referential" and in its discussion of certain texts of the early modern period, especially when Reiss does not insist on making those texts fit his model with no remainders or countercurrents. His thesis (as well as his blank apprehension of the modern period as the "nether end" of the analytico-referential) might be modified to permit the claim that analytico-referential discourse tended after 1600 to become relatively dominant—but in a way that calls for the close study (as well as the elaboration) of more relational perspectives complementing and contesting the relatively dominant discourse. Indeed the variable tensions between modes of discourse as they are worked and played out in significant texts are, I think, more widespread than Reiss allows, and they problematize assertions of the relative dominance of a discourse in specific cases, even

Request for Clerical Work

Staff Member ___Lasinski___

Course Chairman Approval _____

Date of Request ___1/16___

Date Needed ___1/19___

Course/Section # ___438/4___

Completed By ___[signature]___

Type	Xerox		
___ Letter(s)		5	Number needed
___ Manuscript		___	Number of pages
___ Critique		x	Clean copy attached
___ Syllabus		___	Type new master
___ Examination		___	Keep master on file
___ Class Handout	x	___	Return master to me
___ Other			

x	Double run
___	Single run
x	Collate & Staple

Other instructions: ___Copy pp 13-71 and make 5 copies___

Note: Complete this form, attach it to your work, and drop in "Work Request" Tray. **PLEASE TRY TO HAND IN ALL SHORT JOBS 24 HRS. IN ADVANCE OF THE DATE NEEDED: ALLOW A LONGER PERIOD FOR MORE EXTENSIVE PROJECTS.**

in the early modern period. Ignoring these tensions leads Reiss (like Foucault himself at times) to rely implicitly on a very old philosophy of history: a unified vision in the past, which has now become incomprehensible, was ruptured by a "dissociation of sensibility" attendant upon the rise of science and capitalism; transitional texts *circa* 1600 mark the break; at present all we have are faint glimmerings of another break that may apocalyptically instate a radically new discourse of the future. This venerable view has recurrently been heralded as representing a turning point in literary and intellectual history. Here we perhaps have the hallmark of the "discourse of modernism" in a sense unintended by Reiss to the extent that his own remarkable text—a text that is well worth careful reading—is indebted to its questionable but still alluring heritage.

[2]

A Poetics of Historiography:
Hayden White's *Tropics of Discourse*

> How can the fundamental polysemanticity of the word be reconciled
> with its unity? To pose this question is to formulate, in a rough and
> elementary way, the cardinal problem of semantics. It is a problem
> that can only be solved dialectically. . . . In the alternating lines of a
> dialogue, the same word may figure in two mutually clashing
> contexts. . . . Contexts do not stand side by side in a row, as if
> unaware of one another, but are in a state of constant tension, or
> incessant interaction and conflict. The change of a word's evaluative
> accent in different contexts is totally ignored by linguistics and has no
> reflection in its doctrine of the unity of meaning.
>
> V. N. Vološinov, *Marxism and the Philosophy of Language*

No one writing in this country at the present time has done more
to wake historians from their dogmatic slumber than has Hayden
White. One cannot overemphasize his importance for contemporary historiography in general and intellectual history in particular.
In the recent past, intellectual history has departed from the
rigorous if formalistic approach followed by Ernst Cassirer and
Arthur O. Lovejoy. The result has often been its reduction to superficial contextual reportage of little interest to those in related disciplines. One might, without undue hyperbole, say that White's writings have helped to reopen the possibility of thought in intellectual
history.

The collection of essays in *Tropics of Discourse* constitutes an invaluable supplement to White's masterwork of 1973, *Metahistory*, where he elaborated and applied the theory of tropes that serves as a leitmotif in the current volume.[1] The range of the essays is ambitiously broad: problems of historiography and the related disciplines of literary criticism and philosophy; the notions of the wild man and the noble savage in Western thought; Vico; Foucault; structuralism and poststructuralism. The tense unity of the book is provided by the recurrent concern with interpretation in history and with the need for historians to become apprised of more modern, experimental developments in literature, literary criticism, and philosophy. White's far-ranging hermeneutic interests transcend disciplinary boundaries and his critical observations apply beyond professional historiography, for they address more traditional methods in related areas, for example, in the writing of literary history. Indeed White often looks to literary criticism for interpretative methods that may illuminate problems in historiography. This gesture is altogether in keeping with his insistence upon the importance of the problem of language, of rhetoric, and of theoretical self-reflection in the writing of history. His purpose is to question the invidious distinction between those who write history and those who write about writing history—a distinction that functions to reinforce theoretical "know-nothingism" among historians. (This distinction is often combined with the concept of the "working" historian, who is opposed, I imagine, to the historian on welfare.)

Allowing for the necessary leaven of exaggeration in all committed polemic, one will find White's criticisms of powerful tendencies in the historical profession to be quite telling. The following pastiche of quotations gives some sense of the nature of his comments about the great commonplace book of conventional historiography:

> The "proper historian," it is usually contended, seeks to explain what happened in the past by providing a precise and accurate reconstruction of the events reported in the documents. [P. 52]
> History is perhaps the conservative discipline par excellence. Since

1. Hayden White, *Tropics of Discourse* (Baltimore, 1978); all page references in the text are to this edition. See also Hayden White, *Metahistory* (Baltimore, 1973).

the middle of the nineteenth century, most historians have affected a kind of willful methodological naivete. [P. 28]

What is usually called the "training" of the historian consists for the most part of study in a few languages, journeyman work in the archives, and the performance of a few set exercises to acquaint him with standard reference works and journals in his field. For the rest, a general experience of human affairs, reading in peripheral fields, self-discipline, and *Sitzfleisch* are all that are necessary.   [P. 40]

Since the second half of the nineteenth century, history has become increasingly the refuge of all those "sane" men who excel at finding the simple in the complex and the familiar in the strange.   [P. 30]

It may well be that the most difficult task which the current generation of historians will be called upon to perform is to expose the historically conditioned character of the historical discipline, to preside over the dissolution of history's claim to autonomy among the disciplines, and to aid in the assimilation of history to a higher kind of intellectual inquiry which, because it is founded on an awareness of the *similarities* between art and science, rather than on their differences, can be properly designated as neither.   [P. 29]

In more specific form, White's critique is addressed both to positivism and to the unself-conscious employment of traditional narrative in the writing of history. The more elaborate positivistic understanding of science, in terms of causal "covering laws," had little effect upon the practice of historians. But the attraction of a more loosely understood "scientific" model has been of paramount importance in contemporary historiography. The comprehension of history as art—art itself being equated with traditional narrative—is still very much alive, but it exists on sufferance in the shadow of the scientific ideal. White points out a number of highly significant similarities between scientific and narrative history as they are generally practiced. (1) Both are largely pre-twentieth century in inspiration. The paradigm of science is late nineteenth century, and that of art is the pre-Flaubertian novel. "When historians claim that history is a combination of science and art, they generally mean that it is a combination of *late-nineteenth century* social science and

74

mid-nineteenth century art. . . . Historians continue to act as if they believed that the major, not to say the sole, purpose of art is to tell a story" (p. 43). (2) Both share a precritical conception of "facts" as the indubitable, atomistic baseline of history—the ultimate "givens" of an account. (3) Both reduce interpretation to a marginal status, conceiving of it as a more-or-less plausible way of imaginatively filling in gaps in the historical record. For both, metahistory is much too speculative to live in the same neighborhood as "proper" history. (4) Both rely in relatively unreflective fashion on tropologically based sense-making structures—the one on schematic models and metonymic causal mechanisms and the other on the "emplotment" of events in a chronologically arranged story.

For White, the rigid opposition of history "proper" and metahistory obscures more than it illuminates. The distinctive criterion of metahistory for him is the attempt to make interpretative and explanatory strategies—which remain implicit in traditional historiography practiced as a craft—explicit, self-conscious, and subject to criticism. In this sense, his own approach is militantly metahistorical. Interpretation is not a necessary evil in the face of a historical record that is always too full (hence the need for selection) and too empty (hence the need for auxiliary hypotheses to stop gaps). Interpretation is at the heart of historiography, for it relates to the way in which language prefigures and informs the historical field. Historians should not attempt to escape the need for interpretation through an illusory "positivistic" purity or experience this need as an exile from objective truth. On the contrary, they should inquire into its nature, implications, and "positive" possibilities in the reconstruction of the past.

As White develops his own program for the understanding of history, however, certain difficulties arise. In putting forth the following sympathetic criticisms of White, I would stress that my intention is to bring out and even to force certain tensions that exist in his own writings, for I think that White's own relation to traditional historiography and, more generally, to traditional philosophical assumptions is at certain points not fully thought out.

White continues to write what he conceives of as a history of consciousness (rather than, let's say, a history of texts or of uses of language in various contexts). Language and discourse are seen predominantly as instruments or expressions of consciousness. "A discourse is itself a kind of model of the process of consciousness by which a given area of experience, originally apprehended as simply a field of phenomena demanding understanding, is assimilated by analogy to those areas of experience felt to be *already* understood as to their essential nature. . . . This process of understanding can only be tropological in nature, for what is involved in the rendering of the unfamiliar into the familiar is a troping that is generally figurative" (p. 5). This movement through the figurative toward the familiar is basic to White's own systematic effort in providing a theory of language in historiography. It is contested by the less predictable movement through which tropes move from the familiar to the unfamiliar—a process White recognizes and at times defends as necessary for renewal.

White's own systematic theory of language as an expression of consciousness is necessarily reductive of its object. It is much more indebted to Vico, Kant, and Hegel than it is to Nietzsche, Heidegger, and Derrida. (Indeed, the latter are interpreted at times quite negatively in the light of the former.) White's theory is also "constructivist" in that it affirms a "making" function of consciousness, identified with *poiesis*, in contrast to the "matching" function stressed by the mimetic epistemology common to positivism and traditional narrative. The title, *Tropics of Discourse*, itself refers to the prefigurative and projective function of tropes in constituting a field of discourse. In articulating this function, White's metahistory becomes a metalanguage for historiography. The problem is that, in the systematic understanding he attempts to provide of figurative language, White assumes the mastery of "logocentric" philosophy over rhetoric. In other words, he writes from a position itself constituted and secured after an important battle has seemingly been won and without inquiring into the *casus belli*. In the process, he provides what Derrida would see as another version of "White Mythology" and what Heidegger would see as a subjectivist and voluntaristic distortion of the poetic.

For White, as for Vico, there are four Master Tropes (which function theoretically as masters of troping): metaphor, metonymy, synecdoche, and irony. These tropes are presented as the origin or fundamental ground that structures discourse and gives rise to other discursive levels (emplotment, argument, and ideology). Modal patterns further coordinate the relationships among the primary tropes and the other typological levels of discourse. White's own thought is here close to a genetic structuralism. Although the tropes are originative and basic, they are nonetheless seen as informed by narrative and dialectical patterns in a directed process of "encodation." Metaphor, metonymy, and synecdoche are related to one another cyclically as beginning, middle, end and as identity, difference, higher identity. (Thus the traditional patterns, shown out through the front door, re-enter through the back.) Irony has a paradoxical position as both one trope among others and as a trope-killer that— coming at the end of an era—effects a generalized displacement of the "tropics of discourse." White more than recognizes the importance of irony for any critical self-consciousness. But the primary sense of irony in White (especially in *Metahistory*) is what one might call epigonal irony—negative, decadent, dissolving, and destructive. This is the serious and even pious understanding of irony in Vico (although Vico himself is not without internal contestations on this, as on other counts). Given this understanding, one's ultimate goal must be to transcend irony with its cold and deadly effects. White even sees Nietzsche as attempting to transcend an ironic apprehension of the world in order to arrive at a restored metaphoric contact with reality that seems dangerously close to blind faith or mythologizing. But this very partial and largely misleading interpretation of Nietzsche is itself "prefigured" by White's own placement of irony in a narratively and dialectically informed cycle of the tropes. This placement of irony renders impossible a relationship between it and figuration that is repetitive, carnivalesque, contestatory, and affirmative—the relationship Nietzsche sought in his *gaya scienza*. It also renders White incapable of seeing the way in which Derrida's strategy of deconstruction and double inscription of traditional assumptions may be understood in the light of a "gay science" not reducible to Vico's "new science."

In fact, the only serious lapse in the high level of argument in *Tropics of Discourse* is to be found in the last essay, "The Absurdist Moment in Contemporary Literary Theory." Here figures as diverse as Poulet, Barthes, Foucault, and Derrida are lumped together, labeled absurdist, and discussed in a way that is at best caricatural. They have merely symptomatic significance as the most recent manifestation of Western self-doubt and the final blow-up of the modern crisis. White's harshest comments are reserved for Derrida, who is presented as little more than an irresponsible "wild man." The interesting problem, I think, is how a writer of White's intelligence and perspicacity could possibly have arrived at these analyses and conclusions. There is, of course, a point at which everyone feels inclined to become Horatius at the bridge. The question is where one locates that point. I would suggest that one way to see White's reaction is as a turn toward secure "sanity" and conventional irony in the face of the "other," who actually articulates things that are "inside" White himself—but an "other" whose articulation is perhaps too disconcerting or at least too alien in formulation to be recognizable. At present one may indeed be wary of the way an institutionalized deconstructive discourse can become an ideology for the projective reprocessing of all texts rather than an approach to reading that is critically sensitive to its own assumptions and limitations. But one need not lose all power of discrimination to recognize both the value of much deconstructive criticism and Derrida's own importance. Derrida has raised the problem of the text and renewed the problem of rhetoric in a manner that both acknowledges the desire for systematicity, as well as the importance of the classical tradition, and furnishes the basis for a critical response to them. (It is significant that White himself observes of Vico's "new science": "The internal dynamics of the system represents a projection of the theory of the tropes and of the relationships between them that he took over entire from classical poetics" [p. 216].) Just as the romances of chivalry would have been more easily forgotten (or repressed) had it not been for Cervantes's battles—both mock and real—so the assumptions and hopes of the metaphysical tradition would have been more peacefully laid to rest (or covertly resurrected, *faute de mieux*) had it not been for Derrida's contestation of them in both their ancient and modern forms. But Derrida's enterprise requires genuine respect for tradition, which must be confronted in its most forceful expressions (or "inscriptions")—even reinvigorated and made more engaging through "reinscription"— for the contest to be possible. Derrida has made it less plausible to indulge in a falsely complacent oblivion of classical forms in philosophy and poetics. Indeed, through a fruitful paradox, the "founding fathers" of the tradition have taken on renewed interest because of Derrida's critical inquiry into their work and its legacy.

Another reading of Derrida might have provided White with the means to investigate more fully certain of his own internal tensions. For the things Derrida discusses *are* inside White. They relate to the problem of the relationship among history, discourse, and the text. It is curious that White's own constructivist tendencies, which construe the tropes as the informing forces of a creative consciousness, lead him at times to lend credence to the idea of an unprocessed historical record.[2] The record is presented as the inert object to be

2. This notion of the historical record is the analogue of the idea of life or reality that White often presents in stark, dichotomous opposition to the formally ordering aesthetic imagination. Indeed the view of consciousness as imposing formal order of a fictive sort upon a virtual chaos or void of contingent events is quite prevalent, and it derives in part from a restricted reading of Kant, Nietzsche, and Sartre. Given this view, narratives are on the side of the imagination, and the dialectical pattern structuring the cycle of tropes provides their higher-order articulation. (Narrative may even be interpreted in terms of a closed, progressive, and fully concordant dialectical pattern that denies or obscures the role of a more repetitive temporality in narrative itself.) Paradoxically, this universalistic or at least typical projection of an extreme, modern perspective (one is reminded of Antoine Roquentin's reflections on the relation between life and art in *Nausea*) is linked to a relativistic idea of historiography. In the face of existence (or the historical record) as unformed chaos, the historian is free to choose (or else is constrained by) the tropes and narrative structures by which he "emplots" the past. White has in-

animated by the shaping mind of the historian. This gesture, however, simply reverses the positivistic mythology of a mimetic consciousness and substitutes for it an idealistic mythology which converts the former meaningful plenum of the "record" into dead
matter or even a void, thereby giving rise to another avoidance of
the problem of interplay between structure and play in the text and
in one's relation to it. But, at other times, a second view emerges in
White's own approach to this problem. Then White astutely notices
the way in which the historical record is itself a text "always already"
processed in a manner that makes the historian begin as situated in
the context of more-or-less vital or exhausted traditions of discourse.
The very notion of an unprocessed historical record may in this
light be seen as a critical fiction. What we perceive as unprocessed is
actually a heuristic zero point in historiography. This zero point
itself is, however, not a pure, primary "given." It is derived through
a critical process that attempts to disengage "facts" from their implication in story, plot, and myth.

The latter understanding of the historical record contests any

---

creasingly seen the ground of this choice as moral or ideological. I think that this
entire way of posing problems oversimplifies the relations between chaos and
(moral or narrative) order in life, in art, in historiography, and in the interactions
among them. I would argue that life is informed by various, at times conflicting,
sometimes—perhaps, in the modern context, often—gap-ridden narrative structures; modern literature explores differing approaches to narrativity, including the
problem of repetitive temporality (frequently misinterpreted as "spatial form" or
synchronic structure); and historical accounts are suspect to the extent that they
furnish *fully* rounded or concordant narratives. To say this is obviously not to assert
that lives are typically led in conformity with the stereotype of the "traditional"
novel; but it is to suggest that we attempt to live and to conceive our "lived"
narratives forward as well as in retrospect, and this attempt cannot be reduced
simply to "false consciousness." Historiography seeks to provide versions of those
narratives with a claim to truth; intellectual history seeks to relate those narratives to
processes (including narrative processes) occurring in texts and other artifacts. The
problem is of course the status of the claim to truth and its relation to other claims
bearing upon our exchange with the past, including our own attempt to live and to
promote the social role of certain narratives rather than others. Insofar as it is a
fruitful metaphor, the notion of a "general text" relating life and writing tries to
further our understanding of this problem.

rigid categorical opposition between fact and fiction or between "matching" and "making" ("mirroring" and "lamping") functions in the writing of history. In addition, it points to a notion of discourse as other than the projection of consciousness, and it raises the problem of the actual uses of language in the text—or rhetoric in a sense not reducible to the four Master Tropes but certainly involving the question of figurative language. This different understanding of discourse is formulated by White himself:

> [Discourse] is both interpretive and preinterpretive; it is as much *about* the nature of interpretation itself as it is *about* the subject matter which is the manifest occasion of its own elaboration. . . . Precisely because it is aporetic, or ironic, with respect to its own adequacy, discourse cannot be governed by logic alone. Because it is always slipping the grasp of logic, constantly asking if logic is adequate to capture the essence of its subject matter, discourse tends toward metadiscursive reflexiveness.   [P. 4]

White tends to resist an understanding of the text as the scene, in writing and in life, where discourse in this sense takes place. Indeed, he identifies the text with the book and accuses Derrida of fetishizing or mystifying the text. Yet what he writes of Foucault's conception of the text could be applied to his own often dominant understanding of it: "The names of individuals that do appear are merely shorthand devices for designating the texts; and the texts are in turn less important than the macroscopic configurations of formalized consciousness that they represent" (p. 238). What one at times misses in White is an analysis of the way in which the formalized schemata and patterns he elicits actually function in texts. In *Metahistory*, there was a Procrustean tendency to see texts as embodiments of patterned variables or modal sets of tropes, emplotments, arguments, and ideologies. Yet, in the present work, he himself says something which would indicate that the tense interplay among elements in the language of the text should be a focal point of historical and critical investigation:

Now, in my view, any historian who simply described a set of facts in, let us say, metonymic terms and then went on to emplot its processes in the mode of tragedy and proceeded to explain those processes mechanistically, and finally drew explicit ideological implications from it—as most vulgar Marxists and materialistic determinists do—would not only be very uninteresting but could legitimately be labelled a *doctrinaire* thinker who had "bent the facts" to fit a preconceived theory. The peculiar dialectic of historical discourse—and of other forms of discursive prose as well, perhaps even the novel—comes from the effort of the author to mediate between alternative modes of emplotment and explanation, which means, finally, *mediating between alternative modes of language use* or *tropological* strategies for originally describing a given field of phenomena and constituting it as a possible object of representation. . . . This aim of mediation, in turn, drives him [White is discussing Tocqueville here] toward the ironic recognition that any given linguistic protocol will obscure as much as it reveals about the reality it seeks to capture in an order of words. This *aporia* or sense of contradiction residing at the heart of language itself is present in *all* of the classic historians. It is this linguistic self-consciousness which distinguishes them from their mundane counterparts and followers, who think that language can serve as a perfectly transparent medium of representation and who think that if one can only find the right language for describing events, the meaning of the events will *display itself* to consciousness. [P. 130]

The question raised in this passage is precisely that of the text. I think that White is right in believing that formalized schemata are necessary for interpretation. The problem is how one is to understand them and their relation to actual discourse and texts.[3] In this respect, one has a great deal to learn from Nietzsche, Heidegger, and Derrida. The linkage of irony and *aporia* invariably evokes the

3. In a recent essay, White approaches this problem in terms of "code-switching." See his "Method and Ideology in Intellectual History: The Case of Henry Adams" in Dominick LaCapra and Steven L. Kaplan, eds., *Modern European Intellectual History: Reappraisals and New Perspectives* (Ithaca, 1982), pp. 280–310. The question is whether this important modification of a structuralist problematic accounts fully for the relation between codes and texts.

threat of infinite regress in discourse. But this linkage is itself related to a one-sided, negative understanding of irony, which is of course a threat. The more affirmatively contestatory understanding of irony might be related to the possibility of endless egress and renewal, which is implied in Nietzsche's notions of *Heiterkeit* and gay science. Indeed, one sign of the intellectual vigor of White's own work is that it stimulates this kind of contestation. *Tropics of Discourse* is a book that engages one on every page. It should be of immense interest to literary critics, historians, and philosophers.

[3]

Reading Exemplars:
Wittgenstein's Vienna and Wittgenstein's *Tractatus*

Exemplary 1. Serving as a pattern; deserving imitation. 2. Serving
as a warning; monitory. . . . 3. Serving as a type, instance, or
illustration.
>> *Webster's New Collegiate Dictionary*

"I don't know what you mean by 'glory,'" Alice said. Humpty
Dumpty smiled contemptuously. "Of course you don't—till I tell
you. I meant 'there's a nice knock-down argument for you!'"
  "But 'glory' doesn't mean 'a nice knock-down argument,'" Alice
objected.
  "When *I* use a word," Humpty Dumpty said, in a rather scornful
tone, "it means just what I choose it to mean—neither more nor
less."
  "The question is," said Alice, "whether you can make words mean
so many different things."
  "The question is," said Humpty Dumpty, "which is to be master—
that's all."
>> Lewis Carroll, *Through the Looking-Glass*

The problems arising through a misinterpretation of our forms of
language have the character of *depth*. They are deep disquietudes;
their roots are as deep in us as the forms of our language and their
significance is as great as the importance of our language.
  —Let us ask ourselves: why do we feel a grammatical joke to be
deep? (And that is what the depth of philosophy is.)
>> Wittgenstein, *Philosophical Investigations*, I, no. 111.

Reading Exemplars

Wittgenstein's Vienna is a book that has by now been assimilated into the standard repertory of the intellectual historian. It has even been presented as a path-breaking contribution to "contextualist" studies—one marking a significant departure from an ahistorical, formalist interpretation of texts and ideas.[1] Indeed, it is a rarity within the context of a certain approach to intellectual history, for it not only provides much "historical" information concerning the life and times of Wittgenstein. It also puts forth a striking argument about a text often seen as the exemplary statement of logical positivism: Wittgenstein's Tractatus Logico-Philosophicus. It might be plausible to construe Wittgenstein's Vienna itself as an exemplary expression of an important and influential approach to intellectual history—an exemplar that invites a reconsideration of what is to count as a historical approach to the interpretation of texts. One valuable aspect of the book is that it manifests in a direct and militant form assumptions that operate elsewhere in a more latent and complacent manner. For, in one way or another, "contextualism" is often identified with historical understanding itself in a gesture that opposes it to an "internal" or formalist account of ideas

1. Allan Janik and Stephen Toulmin, Wittgenstein's Vienna (New York, 1973. All references in the text are to this edition). This work has been hailed (along with Steven Marcus's Engels, Manchester, and the Working Class) in the following way: "Neither can be called an unqualified success in its own terms, yet each can boast substantial achievement in the way in which it uses biographical and sociological materials to elucidate a philosophic text, thus registering a novel stance in contemporary critical studies. Not, indeed, an absolutely new approach: rather a conscious and sustained protest against the Platonism which has more or less dominated literary and philosophical criticism since the ascendency of I. A. Richards, T. S. Eliot, Cleanth Brooks, and the New Criticism, of Hutchins, Adler, and Leo Strauss at Chicago, and of the influential school of British Analytic Philosophy. For the prevailing dogma of the established church—the autonomy and auto-intelligibility of the rigidly sealed off and isolated text—finds here in these two books its empirical refutation" (Albert William Levi, "De Interpretatione: Cognition and Context in the History of Ideas" in Critical Inquiry 3 [1976], 153). Levi sets contextualism off against internalist formalism and argues that cognition derives its meaning from context. He believes that Wittgenstein's Vienna supports his views by lending "great plausibility to the primacy of an essentially 'ethical' interpretation of the Tractatus" on the basis of contextual considerations (p. 157).

and their relationships. The obvious question is whether the presentation of these seemingly opposed methods as comprehensive alternatives fosters a truncated conception of the relation between texts and contexts and functions to obscure certain assumptions they both may share, notably an essentialist theory of meaning.

Although it involves neglecting certain features of this eminently readable and ambitious book, my procedure will be to concentrate upon the more general problems raised by *Wittgenstein's Vienna* as an exemplar of a contextualist approach to interpreting the meaning of an important text. One of the most pointed ways of investigating these problems is, I think, to inquire into the dissonance between *Wittgenstein's Vienna* and Wittgenstein's *Tractatus* (a dissonance that in certain respects becomes more pronounced in the context of Wittgenstein's later thought). Both these "exemplary" texts tend paradoxically to place in question that which they attempt to establish as valid. But the paradoxes of the *Tractatus* are more fruitful, and they often pass unnoticed in Janik and Toulmin's commentary. This hermeneutic declension between the "primary" text and the commentary is significant. In terms of it, one may raise the issues of whether Janik and Toulmin's operating assumptions about the nature of interpretation blind them to important aspects of the *Tractatus* and whether a different approach to reading is necessary for the interpretation of certain texts.

The explicit intention of Janik and Toulmin is to relate the *Tractatus* (first published in 1921) to a precise context: fin-de-siècle Vienna. This context was characterized by a widespread cultural concern with the crisis of language and the problem of ethics. Their argument is that the ignorance of this context has led to significant distortion in the way the *Tractatus* has been read. For them, the interpretation of the *Tractatus* as a foundation for logical positivism was altogether misguided. Even the interpretations of later analytic philosophers lead one astray. English and American commentators such as G. E. M. Anscombe and Max Black have read the *Tractatus* primarily as a treatise in logic, and they have seen Bertrand Russell and Gottlob Frege as furnishing the most salient and important points of departure for Wittgenstein's thought. More generally, the increased specialization, division of labor, and professionalization of the disciplines since the time of Wittgenstein have induced a tendency to read the *Tractatus* in terms of technical philosophical interests that distort its meaning. By marked contrast, the placement of the *Tractatus* back in its Viennese context reveals that it is to be read also—indeed essentially—as ethical.

In Janik and Toulmin's account, the idea that the *Tractatus* is essentially "ethical" rather than "logical" in meaning depends upon an extremely reductive interpretation of the text which, not surprisingly, coincides with an extremely reductive interpretation of the context. This dual reduction serves the interest of a fully unified interpretation. The reduction of the text is apparent: the text becomes a vehicle for ideas, discursive arguments, and essential positions. The function of the context is to reveal the true meaning of these elements—an ethical meaning in the light of which the function of these elements in the text need not be interrogated. The dominant method for interpreting the text may appropriately be that of synoptic content analysis periodically illustrated by quotation. Whatever it is that makes a text a text—its language, style, structure, movement, power, asperities, and silences—simply becomes grist for the interpretative mill. In their own reductive approach to the text, Janik and Toulmin share something with commentators, such as Anscombe and Black, whom they criticize—something perhaps more compelling than putative disagreement about whether the *Tractatus* is essentially a "logical" or an "ethical" text.[2] In Janik and

2. Anscombe asserts: "in his Introduction [*sic*] Wittgenstein suggests that'he may be understood only by people who have had the same thoughts as he; certainly he can only be understood by people who have been perplexed by the same problems. His own writing is extraordinarily compressed, and it is necessary to ponder each word in order to understand his sentences. When one does this, they often turn out to be quite straightforward, and by no means so oracular or aphoristic as they have been taken to be. But few authors make such demands on the close attention and active cooperation of their readers. In my account, I have not followed the arrangement of the *Tractatus* at all. That, I think, is something to do when one reads the book for enjoyment after one has come to understand its main ideas. I have chosen what seem to me to be the most important themes and

Toulmin, the context serves ultimately to saturate the text with meaning. The paradoxes and silences of the text are not questioned precisely because they are filled in or smoothed over by generous helpings of context, and the paradoxes of the context itself are transcended through a methodology that ties everything together. A "cross-disciplinary" study of the Viennese context makes its "features . . . become wholly intelligible and lose their paradox" (p. 16). For Janik and Toulmin, there is apparently no level on which interpretation explores paradox without transcending it. "Paradox" is reduced to "puzzle" open to full (one is tempted to say "positivistic") solution through contextual analysis. (It is curious that Janik and Toulmin themselves quote Kierkegaard on paradox in a sense they see as close to Wittgenstein's own: "to explain the paradox would then mean to understand more and more profoundly what a paradox is, and that the paradox is a paradox" [p. 160].) As they candidly state concerning their treatment of the *Tractatus:* "the evidence that Wittgenstein's aim in the *Tractatus* was as much ethical as logical cannot, accordingly, be looked for within the text of the book itself. What we must here point to, accordingly, is the circumstantial evidence which allows us to support that claim" (p. 191). There is, I think, "evidence" in the text of the *Tractatus* that it is as much ethical as logical, but that "evidence" resists a reductive understanding of the text and, by implication, of the context.

---

problems of the book" (*An Introduction to Wittgenstein's "Tractatus"* [Philadelphia, 1959], 19). Anscombe's cavalier dichotomy between "ideas" and "arrangement" with the attendant oppositions it evokes (logic and rhetoric, literal and literary, understanding and enjoyment, etc.) gives one pause. Max Black also recommends a method that avoids reading the text as a text: "a serious reader must labor strenuously to reconstruct Wittgenstein's thoughts from cryptic and elliptical suggestions, getting what help he can from a succession of images that dazzle as much as they illuminate. The difficulties can be overcome by patient collocation of the scattered passages where Wittgenstein re-examines a topic from a new perspective" (*A Companion to Wittgenstein's "Tractatus"* [Ithaca, 1964], 1). The philosophical stakes must indeed be high when a commentator of unquestioned ability sees the text simply as an aid to the serious interpreter who labors strenuously to reconstruct thoughts by overcoming (or repressing) difficulties. One may note that it is precisely this method that Arthur C. Danto uses to reconstruct Nietzsche's texts in terms of a systematic philosophy in *Nietzsche as Philosopher* (New York, 1965).

The introduction appeals to two Wittgensteinian expressions to characterize the ensuing account—one borrowed from the *Tractatus* and the other from the later Wittgenstein. Man, text, society, and culture constitute a fourfold complex in which each element serves "as a mirror in which to reflect all the others" (p. 14). Janik and Toulmin are to "assemble reminders" of the way in which this great mirroring process takes place. In this way, they hope to show that the immediate Viennese context represents "the most significant fact" about the phenomena they discuss—"that they *were* all going on in this same place at this same time" (p. 18). The categories that orient the heavily ideological "description" of fin-de-siècle Vienna are those of decadence and divorce between reality and appearance. Hapsburg Austria was a house divided against itself in almost every conceivable way, and its citizens were the true people of paradox. The Viennese context is appropriately seen in the light of Robert Musil's presentation of Kakania. There is apparently no problem in relating reality and appearance for Janik and Toulmin themselves. They simply take the "representations" of figures such as Musil and Karl Kraus and identify them with Viennese "reality." At least two questions are begged here. How adequate were these "representations" as a portrayal of Viennese "reality"? How adequate is it to read Musil's novel as a document representing reality? More generally: What is the relationship among descriptive "representation," fiction, and reality? One might observe that this is a question not altogether alien to Wittgenstein's concerns in the *Tractatus*.

If fin-de-siècle Vienna is the locus of full intelligibility for reading Wittgenstein's *Tractatus*, Karl Kraus is the *genius loci*. His influence somehow pervades the context and informs all serious thought in it. What is relatively clear is that Kraus becomes the interpretative center of Janik and Toulmin's own text. It is primarily in the light shed by Kraus that Wittgenstein stands forth as an "integral and authentically Viennese genius" (p. 22). Wittgenstein apparently intended what Kraus wrote—an identity established through a comparison of what Wittgenstein did not say with what Kraus said:

"Wittgenstein's critique of language, as expressed in the *Tractatus*, is in fact—as he himself claimed—only *half* a critique. The half that he did not write ('this second part, that is the important one') comprises the corpus of Karl Kraus's writings" (p. 196). In relating Kraus to other figures—for example, in treating Wittgenstein as a "Krausian" or as "one of Kraus's 'integral men'" (p. 207)—Janik and Toulmin simply conflate the problem of "intertextuality" with that of empirical influence. The evidence that Wittgenstein was influenced by Kraus is minimal. The problems of an "intertextual" reading comparing the two are hardly broached in the extremely general and superficial discussion in *Wittgenstein's Vienna*. Janik and Toulmin do, however, make one point that would indicate a very important difference between Kraus and Wittgenstein. "In the case of Kraus, his highly idiomatic, punning, colloquial, and consequently untranslatable German has prevented him from becoming widely known" (p. 36). Wittgenstein, on the contrary, is not rooted in the Viennese context in terms of his style and allusions or, more generally, his use of language. Here one has a marked contrast between Kraus and Wittgenstein that raises problems not only for a putative relationship between them but more generally for an interpretation of Wittgenstein of the sort Janik and Toulman attempt. On a sentence by sentence basis, Wittgenstein reads like pattern practice in German. But, on other levels of discourse, Wittgenstein is very "strange," even in translation. The more general point is that the presentation of Kraus as the unifying center of Viennese high culture is dubious. And the dubiousness of taking Kraus as microcosm is compounded by the treatment of the larger Viennese macrocosm, for the notion of "context" is employed by Janik and Toulmin in an uncritical way. It simply refers to anything going on in fin-de-siècle Vienna somehow related to the theme of decadence and presumably present to the young Wittgenstein—the generational "here and now" into which Wittgenstein grew up. ("And—in the absence of more direct evidence—we can hope to answer the question, What philosophical problems did Wittgenstein originally have in mind?, only if we are prepared to look first at the situation into which he grew up" [p. 29].) In a circular fashion, the notion of context as a synchronic whole, situated in time and place, further serves to bring about a coincidence between the author's intentions and the meaning of the text. Janik and Toulmin believe that their interpretation is closest to Wittgenstein's intentions in writing the *Tractatus*. The "holistic" (or hall-of-mirrors) assumption underlying their account prevents them from raising as explicit problems the relation between intention and text and the question of what is to be included in the Viennese context, what is to be excluded, and why. It also relieves them of the need to inquire into the relationships in history of the synchronic and the diachronic, the continuous and the discontinuous, the particular and the general. The paradoxical result is that their argument harbors unjustified exclusions, unexplicated inclusions, and indiscriminate movements—all in the interest of a seemingly unified interpretation.

One exclusion is especially noteworthy. In contrast to an almost chapter-long discussion of Fritz Mauthner, the handling of Freud is so brief as to be inconsequential. The extensive analysis of Mauthner is hard to justify, for its results are inconclusive. Janik and Toulmin term their discussion of the relations between Mauthner and Wittgenstein "frankly conjectural" (p. 10). It is perhaps more fitting to see it as an extreme instance of interpretative overkill (even Humpty-Dumpty hermeneutics) in the overriding attempt to make contextual sense of an elliptical comment in the *Tractatus*: "4.0031 All philosophy is a 'critique of language' (though not in Mauthner's sense)." The upshot of the extremely general and somewhat confused analysis seems to be that Wittgenstein was explicitly opposed to Mauthner's views in the *Tractatus*—although in retrospect he described the work as an elaborate metaphor in terms reminiscent of Mauthner—but came close to Mauthner's ideas in the *Philosophical Investigations*. I shall return to the one precise aspect of their argument in their attempt to determine the univocal meaning of *Bild* in the *Tractatus* by contrasting it with "metaphor" in Mauthner and associating it with "model" in Heinrich Hertz. The point here is that in any historical recreation of the Viennese context the attention paid to Mauthner in contrast to Freud is excessive. Freud is discussed almost exclusively in terms of Kraus's critique of vulgar psychoanalysis. The approach of Janik and Toulmin is especially noteworthy in that Freud is one of the very few writers concerning whom we do have at least reports of Wittgenstein's views (those of Rush Rhees).

A second and perhaps related point refers to considerations that at present necessarily involve conjecture and the appeal to circumstantial evidence. It is difficult to know whether one should, in this respect, allude to another possible exclusion in the account of Janik and Toulmin. The problem here touches upon the moot issue of Wittgenstein's homosexuality—an issue which Janik and Toulmin do not mention. This issue in all its interpretative dimensions does not itself fall into the realm of gossip, but the "evidence" bearing upon it is at present often of a gossipy nature. In a work published the same year as *Wittgenstein's Vienna*, W. W. Bartley assembled hearsay evidence, specifically with reference to the "Austrian decade" (1919–1929) in Wittgenstein's life, which separated his two prolonged periods in Cambridge.[3] One might observe that Bartley's "evidence" is, in its own way, as circumstantial as that provided by Janik and Toulmin, but in Bartley's case it is addressed to a question where the "text" no longer exists and the likelihood of further documentation may be remote. Bartley's discussion verges on the feuilletonistic, and it even lapses into dubious innuendo concerning Wittgenstein's later Cambridge years. (In the former respect, it bears another puzzling resemblance to Janik and Toulmin's account.) But it does at least serve to raise a question that other studies of Wittgenstein simply omit—an omission that is questionable if only because "underground" rumors do circulate and should be displaced through more critically responsible procedures of research and interpretation. Especially with reference to the so-called "Austrian decade," Janik and Toulmin's account itself involves curiously contradictory movements that render it suspect. They refer to a

3. W. W. Bartley, *Wittgenstein* (Philadelphia, 1973).

personal crisis of Wittgenstein's in these terms: "he writes repeatedly in tones of self-disgust about his own 'lack of decency' [*Unanständigkeit*]; and he hints at emotional pressures which it was equally difficult for him to suppress or to sublimate." Again, they turn precipitately to the Viennese context as an explanatory deus ex machina: "Still, to grope after the ultimate source of Wittgenstein's deepest intellectual attitudes in his personal temperament and makeup would, very likely, betray us into unprofitable and irrelevant speculations. . . . Instead, we shall do better to recall the social and cultural parallels that we came across in earlier chapters. . . ." (pp. 236–37). (These comments might themselves invite psychoanalytic interpretation inquiring into the relationship between reverence and repression or suppression. It may further be noted that no interpretative problems are posed to Janik and Toulmin by the recognition that, precisely in this instance, their contextual account would not conform to Wittgenstein's own intentions: "however much we may see a connection in retrospect between the collapse of the Hapsburg Empire and Wittgenstein's own personal crisis of the early 1920's, he himself would probably have seen no connection between these two things" [p. 243].) One might well be sensitive to the difficulty of even formulating cogently the problem of the relative significance of Wittgenstein's homosexuality (assuming Bartley is right) for a reading of his texts. But any investigation into the relationship between life and texts would at least have to confront this problem.4

4. For a recent rehearsal of the problem of the relationship between Wittgenstein's putative homosexuality and his thought, see the following exchange: Albert W. Levi, "The Biographical Sources of Wittgenstein's Ethics," *Telos* 38 (1978–1979), 63–76; Thomas Rudenbush and William M. Berg, "On Wittgenstein and Ethics: A Reply to Levi," *Telos* 40 (1979), 150–160; Steven S. Schwarzschild, "Wittgenstein as Alienated Jew," *Telos* 40 (1979), 160–165; Albert W. Levi, *Wittgenstein Once More: A Response to Critics*," *Telos* 40 (1979), 165–173; Ulrich Steinvorth, "The Ideological Sources of Wittgenstein's Ethics: Reply to Levi," *Telos* 41 (1979), 167–172; Allan Janik, "Philosophical Sources of Wittgenstein's Ethics," *Telos* 44 (1980), 131–144. This debate is conducted on an admirably high level and is well worth careful reading, but it tends to take the form of a rather categorical opposition of positions that share more basic contextualist assumptions.

A general function of Janik and Toulmin's understanding of "context" is to foreclose prematurely the problem of relating textual processes to contexts—a problem that encompasses their own text. Despite their castigation of the distorting effects of the division of academic labor in the interpretation of the *Tractatus*, they do not see as dubious one significant instance of it in their text. The chapters on the context are written by Janik and those on the *Tractatus* primarily by Toulmin. Another sign of the avoidance of any significant interaction between text and context in their account is the very structure of *Wittgenstein's Vienna*. The problem of interpreting the *Tractatus* is mentioned in the introduction only to be deferred to concluding chapters: "having stated the key question about Wittgenstein which it will be our central purpose to answer, we must now set it to one side. For the first step toward answering it must (if we are right) be to engage in a complex, cross-disciplinary study—namely, to set the political and social, cultural and philo-

---

Levi argues in unqualified fashion that Wittgenstein's homosexuality is the true key to his view that no propositions are possible in ethics and to his guilt-ridden anguish. Levi's critics argue that Wittgenstein's homosexuality is at worst irrelevant (or philosophically uninteresting!) and at best inadequate to account for views that can better be explained through other contextual considerations, notably ideas or attitudes that Wittgenstein shared with others at the time or that constituted variants of more traditional perspectives. The prior problem of how precisely contextual factors both interact with one another and relate to a complex text is not posed. A fortiori, it is not explored in the specific case of Wittgenstein. Nor is the issue of the relation between the content of Wittgenstein's arguments in the *Tractatus* and his rhetoric or style of writing. Janik, moreover, conjoins the point that for Wittgenstein there could be no absolute foundational theory in ethics (or logic) with the point that Wittgenstein accepted a total opposition between practice and theory such that the goal of moral life was pure practice devoid of theoretical self-reflection. The latter point constitutes a domestication of the perplexities and silences of the *Tractatus*, but it may in one sense be a plausible inference from its assertions, especially in the light of its relation to other pertinent texts, including those of Wittgenstein. Yet this point is not a necessary consequence of the critique of foundationalism, and it would seem to rest on the dubious assumption that if an absolute theoretical foundation is impossible, then theory is utterly worthless and has no link whatsoever to practice. It also is based upon an idea of pure moral (or "spiritual") practice (and self-presence) that begs the question of the relation between the use of language in moral practice and its use in moral theory.

sophical preoccupations of Austria alongside one another and see them as framed and reflected in one another" (p. 29). By the time the *Tractatus* is treated, it is itself "framed" all too well. It becomes the "epitome" or straightforward, quintessential expression of its fin-de-siècle Viennese context.

When the reader reaches the postscript, he is witness to an incredible narrative double-take, a now-you-see-it-now-you-don't maneuver that is quite bewildering. Until the postscript the text played variations on the "only-in-Vienna" motif. ("In order to have had the same thoughts as the author of the *Tractatus Logico-Philosophicus*, one would have to have lived in the milieu of *fin-de-siècle* Vienna" [p. 200].) In the postscript, one leaps without transition or mediation from the particular to the general. To justify a sketchy analogy between Wittgenstein's Vienna and contemporary America, we are told: "Austria was only an extreme case of a more general phenomenon; its characteristic distortions and artificialities, as we have studied them here, are reproduced in miniature wherever similar conditions and relationships exist" (p. 264). Thus the book oscillates from historicist particularism to abstract generality in the way it draws analogies and makes comparisons. What is left out or silenced is the entire problem of history, which obligates one to give an account of continuity and discontinuity, of similarity and difference, of repetition and change as a requirement of an informed dialogue between past and present. Here one perhaps has an important context for the reading of *Wittgenstein's Vienna* itself— the counter-cultural movement of the 1960s with its enthusiasms, hopes, and illusions. *Wittgenstein's Vienna* tries to effect a kind of "greening" of Wittgenstein, and the terms in which it "brings it all together" recall the type of rhetoric one finds in "descriptions" of context by Marcuse, Laing, and Charles Reich.

The context, in the sense desired by Janik and Toulmin, does not exist. The search for it is a quest for a will-o'-the-wisp generated by a questionable theory of meaning. The context itself is a text of sorts; it calls not for stereotypical, ideological "descriptions" but for interpretation and informed criticism. It cannot become the occasion for a reductive reading of texts. By contrast, the context itself raises a problem analogous to that of "intertextuality." For the problem in understanding context—and a fortiori the relation of context to text—is a matter of inquiry into the interacting relationships among a set of more or less pertinent contexts. Only this comparative process itself creates a "context" for a judgment that attempts to specify the relative importance of any given context. The view of fin-de-siècle Vienna itself as the "cradle" of modernity serves as a suggestive stimulus to research insofar as it remains on an allusive level. Promoted to the status of an interpretative framework for understanding the relation between texts and contexts, it becomes problematic in the extreme and may function as a pretext for avoiding or foreclosing an investigation into significant issues in historical interpretation. [5]

5. Recently Carl Schorske has published in book form the essays that were instrumental for the work of Janik and Toulmin. See *Fin-de-Siècle Vienna: Politics and Culture* (New York, 1980). Schorske provides an impressive panorama of high culture that is unified by the focus upon a given city, the response of figures to a common set of problems (notably political and cultural crisis), and a combination of "synchronic" interpretation of the role of cultural artifacts in their contemporary context and "diachronic" inquiry into their place in the history of genres. Thus a coordination of topical delimitations and methodological procedures is intended as a remedy for the problem of fragmentation that has beleaguered and intrigued intellectuals for at least the past two centuries and not only in Vienna. For reasons that are not altogether clear, Schorske does not discuss Wittgenstein. (Is he atypical or insufficiently Viennese?) Schorske's treatment of Freud's *Interpretation of Dreams* is his most sustained case of textual analysis, and it shares certain of the difficulties of Janik and Toulmin's handling of the *Tractatus*. What distinguishes Schorske's approach is the insistent stress on politics and the reliance on modes of interpretation that depend a great deal on a certain understanding of psychoanalysis itself. He centers his analysis on what Freud presumably shared with other exponents of Viennese high culture: a growing tendency to turn away from political problems toward private, aesthetic, and psychological concerns. Schorske's emphasis upon the circumscribed theme of Freud's "escape" from politics (in the conventional sense) has limited validity in the context of his study. But it also threatens to present Freud as yet one more frustrated liberal and, in the process, to construe history in terms that eliminate or obscure signs of alternatives to the state of affairs Schorske explicitly deplores. A different view of Freud would raise difficulties for Schorske's central theme, but it would have the merit of highlighting the way Freud generalized the problem of politics by seeing the psyche and family relations in terms of relations of power and authority. It might also further a conception of politics more closely bound up with problems of daily life.

Janik and Toulmin often rely on an equivocal notion of a "Viennese, German-language" context in opposition to an English one. But the relationship between the Viennese and the more generally Continental is itself a problem slurred over in their account. Kierkegaard and Schopenhauer are not specifically Viennese figures, and Janik and Toulmin's analysis of them, while unobjectionable on a general level, is not specific enough to get at either their "intertextual" relation to Wittgenstein or the distinctive features of the way they were read in Vienna. In addition, the reference to a larger Continental context brings up further questions unexplored by Janik and Toulmin. Nietzsche was perhaps the first modern thinker to provide a radical critique of both the metaphysical tradition and the modern context as "decadent." Husserl put forth an analysis of the modern "crisis" and developed an approach to philosophy revealing highly significant similarities and differences in comparison with the early Wittgenstein of the *Tractatus*.[6] The later Wittgenstein seems to move in a direction comparable to that of Heidegger (as Gadamer, among others, has pointed out).[7] In the novel more or less contemporary with Wittgenstein's *Tractatus*, Thomas Mann (among others) was exploring the problem of decadence, for example, in *Death in Venice* and *The Magic Mountain*. Why do not these figures form part of a context as relevant as Vienna for the reading of Wittgenstein? Indeed, at times the analysis of Janik and Toulmin is so broad that it seems to relate to the entire "modern" context—as their own discussion of contemporary America (and Russia!) seems to indicate in a relatively uncritical way.

6. This question is broached by Sande Cohen, "Structuralism and the Writing of Intellectual History," *History and Theory* 17 (1978), 175–207.

7. Hans-Georg Gadamer, "The Phenomenological Movement" in *Essays in Philosophical Hermeneutics* (Berkeley and Los Angeles, 1976), 130–181. Newton Garver, in his preface to *Speech and Phenomena and Other Essays on Husserl's Theory of Signs*, by Jacques Derrida (Evanston, 1973), makes a number of suggestive points. He observes that the relation between the early and the later Wittgenstein may be compared to that between Husserl and Derrida. In this respect, one important issue is that of the relationship between "logic" (based on concepts of identity and noncontradiction) and textual problems that exceed, contest, and situate it.

The discussion of England is little more than caricatural. "One of the gravest misfortunes that can affect a writer of great intellectual seriousness and strong ethical passions is to have his ideas 'naturalized' by the English. . . . The preconceptions with which his English hearers approached [Wittgenstein] debarred them almost entirely from understanding the point of what he was saying" (pp. 19, 22). Here a number of things must be noticed. First, England is not restricted to the Cambridge (or even Oxbridge) academic society that Janik and Toulmin focus upon, and even those involved in that society had second thoughts or critical tendencies not investigated by Janik and Toulmin (e.g., John Maynard Keynes and Virginia Woolf). If decadence and reactions to it form the theme, where does one place Oscar Wilde and D. H. Lawrence? Second, the positivistic interpretation of the *Tractatus* was in certain ways distorting, but the precise nature of the distortions and the extent to which the *Tractatus* invited misreading are themselves historical and interpretative issues of great interest. Janik and Toulmin provide no close analysis of the uses and abuses of Wittgenstein in the English context. Their assertions are so extreme and superficially rhetorical that they fail to convince even the sympathetic reader. There is, however, an entire history to be written here, one that would include the story of how even Wittgenstein's gestures and turns of speech were often transmitted to his disciples and admirers. Third, living in the milieu of fin-de-siècle Vienna was no assurance of immunity against misinterpretation, for, as Janik and Toulmin themselves observe—without being concerned in the least about its relevance for their contextual argument—one of the most extreme positivistic interpretations was the work of the Vienna circle.

A final contextual consideration may at least be mentioned. A crucial question is that of the relation of the *Tractatus* to the entire tradition of Western metaphysics—a tradition for which the divorce between reality and appearance and even the concern about decadence are stories forever old and new. This question arises peripherally in Janik and Toulmin's account through discussions of Kant, Schopenhauer, and Kierkegaard, but, given their assumptions, it is never so much as formulated as a problem. A relatively informed discussion of the relation of a thinker to the tradition of Western metaphysics would be an impossibly tall order were it not for the critical foundation laid in the works of Heidegger and Derrida. As Ms. Anscombe herself remarks (but fails to explore): "the investigations prompted by [Wittgenstein's] questions are more akin to ancient, than to more modern, philosophy."[8] There is, for example, a sense in which Plato may be more pertinent than Karl Kraus for a reading of the *Tractatus*. (This is not to say that Plato is irrelevant for an understanding of Kraus's quest for "integrity.") One highly important issue is that of the relationship between traditional "mimetic" or representational theories of symbolism and the argument of the *Tractatus*. To provide an acceptable account of this relationship, one would at the very least have to attempt an intertextual reading of the *Tractatus* in relation to the *Cratylus*, the *Theaetetus*, and the *Sophist*.

In practice, it would of course be humanly impossible to treat adequately all these contexts—although the awareness of the "intercontextual" horizon of any contextual reading serves both as the (recurrently displaced) ideal limit for research and as a check against unsubstantiated claims for the primordiality of any given context. My point in bringing up this issue is not to fault Janik and Toulmin for not being exhaustive. On the contrary, it is to question the concept of exhaustiveness, including the form it takes in Janik and Toulmin: that of contextual saturation of the meaning of a text. The most that can be argued for fin-de-siècle Vienna is that it is one pertinent context among others for the understanding of the *Tractatus*. Its relative importance is contestable, and the attempt to constitute it as *primus inter pares* remains a matter of relatively loose judgment. One plausible way to test its significance is to examine critically the extent to which it informs a reading of the text.

How, then, does the Viennese context inform a reading of the

8. Anscombe, *Introduction to Wittgenstein's "Tractatus,"* 13. She quotes the *Theaetetus*, which was one Platonic dialogue to which Wittgenstein recurrently referred. In addition, one may note that Wittgenstein's critique of the account of naming in Saint Augustine, which comes at the beginning of the *Philosophical Investigations*, of course applied to his own view of naming in the *Tractatus*.

Tractatus for Janik and Toulmin? As I have already mentioned, their essential point is that Wittgenstein's essential point in the *Tractatus* is ethical. In essence, this point is culled not from the text but from the context, especially from Wittgenstein's intentions as expressed in his correspondence with Paul Engelmann and Ludwig Ficker. It shows that the last five pages of the text are not mere *obiter dicta* but the very essence and identity of the text, and it meaningfully fills in the silences of those pages. As Paul Engelmann wrote:

> A whole generation of disciples was able to take Wittgenstein as a positivist, because he has something of enormous importance in common with the positivists: he draws the line between what we can speak about and what we must be silent about just as they do. The difference is only that they have nothing to be silent about. Positivism holds—and this is its essence—that what we can speak about is all that matters in life. *Whereas Wittgenstein passionately believes that all that really matters in human life is precisely what, in his view, we must be silent about.* [P. 220]

And, as Wittgenstein himself wrote to Ludwig Ficker:

> The book's point is an ethical one. I once meant to include in the preface a sentence which is not in fact there now, but which I will write out for you here, because it will perhaps be a key to the work for you. What I meant to write, then, was this: My work consists of two parts: the one presented here plus all that I have not written. And *it is precisely this second part that is the important one.* My book draws limits to the sphere of the ethical from the inside as it were, and I am convinced that this is the ONLY rigorous way of drawing those limits.
>
> In short, I believe that where many others today are just *gassing*, I have managed in my book to put everything firmly into place by being silent about it. And for that reason, unless I am very much mistaken, the book will say a great deal that you yourself want to say. Only perhaps you won't see that it is said in the book. For now I would recommend you to read the *preface* and the *conclusion* because they contain the most direct expression of the point of the book. [P. 192]

Thus Wittgenstein stood in the tradition of Kraus in making a "creative separation" between fact and value, and he tried to preserve silently what was of value. Value could only be shown (*gezeigt*) and not said (*gesagt*). In the realm of fact and the sayable, descriptive propositions represented reality. Representation took place through a *Bild*. The standard translation of *Bild* is "picture." For Janik and Toulmin, this is a misleading translation. Appealing to the context, they argue that Wittgenstein's use of *Bild* should be contrasted with Mauthner's use of metaphor. The *Bild* was not "merely metaphoric" (*sic*). Its use by Wittgenstein should be associated, perhaps identified, with Hertz's use of mathematical models. They stress the active, constructivist sense in which we make *Bilder* of reality in propositions for Wittgenstein. In addition, they assert that Hertz used *Darstellung* in contrast to *Vorstellung* in relation to his models and that Wittgenstein rarely uses *vorstellen* in the *Tractatus*. They associate *Vorstellung* with the senses and with "ideas" as used in the English empirical tradition. By contrast, they link *Darstellung* with model-building and argue that this is what goes on in propositions for Wittgenstein. They accurately point out that Wittgenstein, unlike the positivists, never tied his elementary propositions and facts to observation and verification procedures. In the light of Wittgenstein's critique of language, what could be said in science was purely descriptive and relatively unimportant; everything of genuine value was unsayable.

The picture presented by Janik and Toulmin is an extremely tempting one. If it were altogether accurate, the *Tractatus* would be a much simpler and less enigmatic text to interpret than it is. Nor should one fail to appreciate the many insightful aperçus marking their account and having an unexplored and often blind-sided relation to their principal argument. It would perhaps be beside the point to say that Janik and Toulmin are, in their own way, like positivists in attempting to fill in Wittgenstein's silences. The difference is that positivists at least tried to specify the nature of scientific propositions and became agitated over the problematic status of verification, while Janik and Toulmin remain oblivious to the para-

dox inherent in their attempt to identify the ethical both with Wittgenstein's silence and with what was said in the Viennese context.
In any event, it would, at the present time, be superfluous to argue
that an author is not invariably his own best interpreter. It is more to
the point, I think, to observe that Wittgenstein's comment to
Ficker, in which the Kierkegaardian echoes are almost deafening,
cannot be read either in a simply literal way or as an open invitation
to a contextual *Erfüllung* of the meaning of the text. One may,
however, notice what Wittgenstein says about the preface and the
conclusion and inquire into the relationship between what is "directly expressed" there and the rest of the text. What is the relation
between saying and silence, the direct and the indirect, in the
Tractatus, and does it authorize one to say that the text is essentially
ethical—or essentially anything else for that matter?

In addressing this question, I shall in the main confine myself to
assembling certain reminders from the text. On the level of explicit
or direct statement, the world presented by the *Tractatus* seems to
be at least a threefold one. First, one has the realm of representation
of reality in propositions. This is the realm of the sayable, facts, and
science. Determinate meaning in it requires simple names for simple objects. Names refer to (*bedeuten*) objects and stand as proxies
for (*vertreten*) them in propositions. Names cannot be analyzed or
defined. They are used in propositions that describe and correspond
to facts. Complex facts (*Tatsachen*) may be analyzed into simple
facts or states of affairs (*Sachverhalte*) that are expressed in elementary propositions. Meaningful propositions may be either true or
false. They are *Bilder* in that they represent (*abbilden*) reality. On
this level, one seems to have the most extreme form possible of a
descriptive or literal theory of meaning guided by an analytic logic
of identity and difference.

Second, one has logic. Logic is not a metalanguage in that it does
not represent reality, including the reality of language. In this sense,
it is meaningless (*sinnlos* but not *unsinnig*). Logic is a question of
formal necessity in tautologies and contradictions. It is closely akin
to mathematics but does not include numbers. It is expressible in

symbolic notation. It seems to correspond to the purely formal aspect of reality. The content of reality, by contrast, is contingent and represented in propositions. Formal properties of the world are in a sense sayable—in logic.

Third, one has the unsayable or mystical. To say something about the unsayable is to speak nonsense (*Unsinn*). Metaphysics is not false but nonsensical. The unsayable includes ethics and aesthetics (which are one) as well as the metaphysical subject (which is both the center and the limit of one's world). It also includes the form of representation (*Abbildung*) or logical form in virtue of which a *Bild* or proposition may be said to represent reality. A proposition may represent reality but it cannot represent the "something identical" it shares with reality—the essence—that is seen by Wittgenstein as necessary for representation. Logic expresses pure form, but what a representation has in common with reality—what is in a sense necessary for logic to connect with the real world—is not sayable. It is noteworthy that Wittgenstein discusses the form of representation early in the text and does not bring it up again in the last five pages. But it seems closely related to his discussion there.

Everything in the radically transcendental realm of the mystical or the unsayable is identical—but not in a purely logical sense. The metaphysical self as center and limit of the world would seem to "be" ethical, aesthetic, and the form of representation in virtue of which representations correspond to reality. The "I" shrinks to an extensionless point, and solipsism becomes identical with pure realism. The unsayable, moreover, may be shown or mirrored forth. How precisely remains a mystery that Wittgenstein makes no attempt to dispel. It is significant that Wittgenstein does not take a step that might be expected here. One might argue that what can be shown can be seen—at least with the "inner eye" or ideal faculty. The form of representation seems close to the Platonic *eidos*. But Wittgenstein (in contrast with Husserl) does not talk of a vision or intuition of essences. One might also observe that he does not talk (as Russell did) of a direct acquaintance with reality. His concept of reality remains vacuous and is discussed only in terms of formal requirements for determinate meaning. Nor does he provide any examples of elementary, irreducibly simple states of affairs (*Sachverhalte*) or elementary propositions.

The foregoing synopsis of the *Tractatus* would not seem to be too great a misrepresentation of its more direct and discursive argument, although I have shot a few gaps and made connections Wittgenstein does not explicitly make. I have presented it to facilitate a comparison of it with what I think are greater distortions in Janik and Toulmin's argument and with other aspects of the *Tractatus* itself. Ethics has an important place in the argument but cannot plausibly be termed the essential point of the text. A notion related to essence is discussed by Wittgenstein—that of identity. But it is related to the form of representation shared by representation and reality. Although Janik and Toulmin refer to Wittgenstein's later self-criticism concerning a belief in a direct *Verbindung* or connection between language and reality, they do not treat adequately the relation of the *Verbindung* to identity and the form of representation. The reason may be that this relation is important for an essentialist theory of meaning and interpretation that is operative in their own text. This theory is affirmed in the more "direct" argument of the *Tractatus* but it is radically contested on other levels of the text—"directly" in the preface and conclusion and indirectly in multiple ways throughout the text.

In its explicit argument, the *Tractatus* seems to (re)present representation as unproblematic. Yet the theory of seemingly literal description and fully determinate meaning is conveyed in a use of language that is not altogether fixed or certain. The English "represent" (or the noun "representation") covers a number of German terms and masks a play of terminological substitutions (e.g., in the use of *vorstellen*, *darstellen*, and *abbilden*) that is damaging for the explicit theory of meaning in the *Tractatus*. In addition, the term *bedeuten* is used both for the direct reference of names to objects—"3.203 The name refers to the object"—and for the way in which philosophy indirectly refers to the unsayable—"4.115 It will refer to the unsayable in that it clearly represents [or presents: *darstellt*] the sayable." The relationship among representation, presentation, and phenomena such as picturing and modeling is not crystal clear. The actual usage of *bedeuten* itself refers one not to essential meaning that provides a fully determinate "fix" on reality but to an intricate network of interacting terms, meanings, and objects mutually implicated in one another in both direct and indirect ways. It shows that *deuten* (interpretation) can never be totally bracketed off from *bedeuten* (reference)—or from *Sinn* (meaning).

In his explicit argument, Wittgenstein distinguishes sharply between the symbol bearing a resemblance to its object and the perceptible sign having an arbitrary relation to what it signifies. The ambiguity of ordinary language is that in it often "the same word signifies in two different ways—and therefore belongs to two different symbols—or that two words, which signify in different ways, are apparently applied in the same way in the proposition" (3.323). The logical problem is to arrive at signs univocally corresponding to symbols—"a symbolism, that is to say, which obeys the rules of *logical* grammar—of logical syntax" (3.325). The "real name" would be "that which all symbols, which signify an object, have in common" (3.3411). This understanding of the essential relation of logic to language gives an implicit legislative or normative role to logic as an instrument of clarification in spite of the paradoxical assertions that logic says nothing or is purely tautologous and that "all propositions of ordinary language are, just as they are, completely in order logically" (5.5563). It also justifies a conception of pure logic that need not concern itself with problems of actual usage. In addition, the fundamental conditions of possibility for fully determinate meaning—simple objects, undefinable names, elementary or "atomic" facts, and elementary descriptive propositions—are in fact neither shown nor said by Wittgenstein; they are simply posited as requirements. No explicit question is raised concerning this nonmanifest, ideal, and virtual status of the seemingly axiomatic grounds of representation.

In accordance with the views developed by the later Wittgenstein, one might argue that in actual usage (including that of Wittgenstein in the *Tractatus*) language and world arise together, and names are implicated in their interplay. This interplay is neither purely arbitrary (and fully indeterminate, subjectivist, or relativist) nor purely necessary (and fully determinate, natural, or absolute): it both stimulates and contests the desire for fully unified meaning and logical mastery over discourse, for it constitutes a relational network in which one is always already situated and which forms the context for the problem of representation. Within this context, logically precise factual propositions do not institute the ruling paradigm for the legitimate use of language—the positivistic paradigm through which "a proposition must pin reality down to two alternatives: yes or no," agreement or disagreement in the relation of language and world (4.023). Indeed, in terms of this context, one may ask whether names can have a logically primitive, purely designative relationship to simple objects other than through an appeal to univocal definitions that involve a questionable attempt to fixate and to dominate the object of thought. In actual discourse, language cannot be reduced to a nomenclature (paradoxically supplemented by logic); and, in it, names name in a complex way. The very title of the *Tractatus*, which was substituted, presumably at the suggestion of G. E. Moore, for Wittgenstein's earlier and more straightforward *Der Satz*, was itself a name enmeshed in a traditional network of allusions that included an indirect reference to Spinoza's *Tractatus*. Not only was the traditional network revised and reworked by Wittgenstein's *Tractatus*, with the assumptions of a *mathesis universalis* becoming, if anything, more problematic. But the name *Tractatus* itself was something of a misnomer, given the text's dubious relation to the traditional treatise in continuous and methodical prose form. (The numerical system of the highly aphoristic *Tractatus* might even be read as a parody of the use of numerals in the "geometrically" arranged arguments of Spinoza.) Here, as elsewhere, the *Tractatus* both helped to institute positivism and to place it in radical jeopardy.

The notion of *Bild* is at the center of the problem of representation. What is significant is that Wittgenstein uses such a notoriously ambiguous word in such a strategic place in his argument—a word which evokes the problematic position of the imagination in between the senses and sense. Indeed *Bild* would seem to be undecided among all the crucial oppositions essential for identity and fully determinate meaning. It can be neither identified with metaphor nor simply opposed to it. When Wittgenstein asserts that a proposition is a *Bild*, he enunciates a literally meant metaphor that implicitly questions a rigid categorial opposition between the literal and the metaphoric. He also raises doubts about *both* the conversion of the distinction between "iconic" symbol and "arbitrary" sign into a pure opposition *and* the attempt to conflate it into a pure identity. If one translates *Bild* as "likeness," then Wittgenstein's own proposition about the proposition says (and conceals) that the proposition is (like) a likeness. Thus he approximates the proposition to a metaphor of metaphor and indirectly indicates the need for an understanding of the relation between language and world that situates a representational theory of symbolism (or, conversely, that is situated by a generalization of "representation"—a gesture which, departing critically from the classical subordination of representation to presence, itself broaches the problem of a generalized referential network). If one translates *Bild* as "image," the unexplored implication is that image and language arise together, bringing with them the possibility of metaphor as a displacement of being. The status of language and image as supplements to the represented would indicate their necessary function for the constitution of the represented which, in turn, could no longer be seen as a pure presence. More explicitly, Wittgenstein states: "4.015 The possibility of all imagery [*Gleichnisse*], of all our pictorial modes [*Bildhaftigheit*] of expression, rests on the logic of representation." Yet the *Bild* obviously pertains to sense, for it circumscribes meaning itself.

The translation of *Bild* as "picture" seems superficially to decide crucial issues in interpretation. But Janik and Toulmin's opposition of *Bild* to metaphor and association of it with model-building abuses the power of translation even more, and in a more misleading way, for it makes it appear as if certain problems in interpretation did not even exist. Nor does it really decide issues. Rather it begs questions. What is the relationship between metaphor and model or between model and mathematics? That these relationships are not altogether self-evident should be abundantly clear to anyone who has examined even a small portion of the vast literature on these topics. In the context of the *Tractatus* itself, there is also a problem with the idea of mathematical model. Mathematics is related to logic rather than to propositional representation, and numbers are excluded from logic. How mathematics even applies to "reality" remains problematic in the *Tractatus*. (It may be pertinent to recall that for Kant all mathematical judgments, including those of arithmetic, are synthetic a priori—a status seemingly outlawed by the radical opposition between formal necessity and contingent reality in the argument of the *Tractatus*.)

The dichotomy traced by Janik and Toulmin between *Vorstellung* (on the side of the senses and metaphor) and *Darstellung* (on the side of models) hardly scratches the surface of the history of the problematic relations between these two terms in German thought. In any case, it does not apply to the *Tractatus*. *Vorstellen* is employed in relation to the *Bild* (e.g., 2.11). *Darstellen* is used in a variety of ways: in relation to the sayable (4.115), propositions and reality (4.12), the impossibility of "representing" the logical form shared by propositions and reality (4.12), and the way in which the conditions of correspondence or representation are canceled out in tautologies (4.462). Most important, the *Tractatus* does not entirely succeed in whisking away the problem of the relation among the senses, propositions, signs, and sense. It explicitly links propositions to the senses through signs (3.1, 3.32) and to sense through "representation" (*darstellen* in 2.221). The *Bild* would seem to straddle the senses and sense, and Wittgenstein's discussions of the *Bild* are at times quite figurative: "2.1515 These co-ordinations [of the elements of the *Bild* and things] are as it were feelers of its elements with which the *Bild* touches reality."

These considerations point to what may at least initially be formulated as a more or less systematic tension or internal contestation between the explicit, direct argument of the *Tractatus* and its own use of language or style. (On further reflection, one would want to question the neat distinction between the "direct" and the "indirect" levels of discourse in the *Tractatus*, not simply to obliterate it but to indicate how each level is already implicated in the other.) The stark and seemingly uncompromising opposition between the sayable and silence is itself contested by the more subtle interplay between what is said and silence in the text. One may notice that I have not as yet referred to the "critique of language" in the *Tractatus*. Verbal language plays a relatively minor role in the explicit argument of the *Tractatus*. It is only one form of representation, and an especially misleading one at that. The first extended discussion of language comes in a very subordinate place, if one remembers the numerical system of the *Tractatus* (4.001 and 4.002). The explicit theory of language is understandably quite traditional: language is a mere expression or "clothing" for thought and it disguises the true form of thought.[9] In this respect, Wittgenstein's gesture is highly equivocal, and it relies upon an extremely paradoxical "line" of argument.

9. One important difference between the *Tractatus* and the *Investigations* is that, in the later Wittgenstein, one always "begins" as already situated in language when one explores its relation to "reality" (or to anything else). (In contrast to the explicit overture of the *Tractatus* with its oracular pronouncement that "the world is everything that is the case," the *Investigations* itself begins in a historically situated way with a quotation from Saint Augustine.) In addition, while the process of making *Bilder* is in some sense seen as active, the *Tractatus* presents no account of the mutual implication of language and action in *Lebensformen*. In the later Wittgenstein, a metalanguage is, in any strict sense, still impossible, but what might be called its conditions of impossibility differ from those posited in the *Tractatus*, for it is no longer a question of the tautologous nature of logic but of the conceptually relevant fact that one is always historically situated in language. Nor is language reduced to the status of mere expression or clothing for thought. In the later Wittgenstein, language may still "veil" meaning and logic, but the "imprecise" interplay of concealment and disclosure in actual language is no longer the seemingly disparaged object of a comparison with a "strict" calculus of meaning or logical form. As Janik and Toulmin observe, there is a sense in which "language games" occur in ethics, aesthetics, and religion. One might also mention the relevance of Carlyle's *Sartor Resartus* for the problems rehearsed in the *Tractatus*.

Wittgenstein refuses to privilege verbal language and stresses the importance of "hieroglyphic writing, which pictures the facts it describes" (4.016). But this appeal to hieroglyphics functions not merely to problematize the role of verbal language but to relegate it further to a markedly subordinate position among forms of representation. The "pictographic" nature of hieroglyphic writing enables one to understand "the essence of the proposition" as a picture. And hieroglyphic writing is itself transcended when Wittgenstein makes the hyperbolic assertion that things themselves could be arranged into a "proposition." The order of things could then simply (and silently?) be "read" or beheld, and the gap between the representation and what it represents—a gap indicated by the proxy nature of signs—could be closed. The ideal of an essential identity between representation and reality would then be realized only through a collapse or extreme reduction of representation itself. "3.1431 The essential nature of the propositional sign becomes very clear when we think of it as made up of spatial objects (such as tables, chairs, books) instead of written signs. The mutual spatial position of these things then expresses the sense of the proposition." The book is, needless to say, a strange supplement to the series of spatial objects, for the book, once it is opened, raises the very problems that have ostensibly been eliminated by the extreme reduction of the sign to the thing itself. The apparent "intention" of the argument is, however, to provide not so much a "critique" of language as grounds for de-emphasizing the significance of language in the matter of representation. In this light, it is indeed curious that the *Tractatus* has been taken as a beginning of the "linguistic turn" in modern philosophy: one of its most forceful movements involves a resolute turn away from language.

By contrast, what is radical in the *Tractatus* is its own use of language, and even its numbering system takes on a paradoxical coloration. The only footnote in the book tells us: "the decimal numbers assigned to the individual propositions indicate the logical importance of the propositions, the stress laid on them in my exposition. The propositions n.1, n.2, n.3, etc., are comments on proposition no. n; the propositions n.m1, n.m2, etc., are comments on proposition no. n.m; and so on." This explanation seems plausible, for at times there does seem to be something like a logical progression connecting propositions. At other times, this is not the case. (For example, why is 1.13 situated where it is, and, on another level, why, as Russell queried, is *Tatsache* introduced before the logically more elementary *Sachverhalt?*) More shockingly, the text itself tells us that "there are no numbers in logic. There are no pre-eminent numbers" (5.453). In indicating the stress or weight of propositions, numbers in the *Tractatus* would seem to function in a largely figurative way.

The very discontinuous, aphoristic structure and gnomic quality of the "propositions" of the *Tractatus* are features of the text that cannot be eliminated as insignificant by a straightforward reconstruction of its discursive argument. For these are textual features that forcefully contest the explicit discursive argument of the *Tractatus* itself. The medium seems to be at loggerheads with the message. A univocal, indeed dogmatic, theory of meaning is conveyed in an extremely open form—one that seems almost "pre-Socratic" in nature. It is rare that a discursive unit of the *Tractatus* is more than a sentence long. Wittgenstein was never able to catch his discursive breath or to compose a "proper" book (a fact he continues to worry in the preface to the *Philosophical Investigations*). Yet, even when Wittgenstein in his later work developed more "open" theories of meaning and shifted his attention from the proposition and logic to actual discourse and "language games," he in one sense used a less open form, for his conceptually picaresque investigations moved to the paragraph level of articulation.

The paradoxical structure implicit in the entire text becomes more explicit in the preface and, especially, the concluding sections. In any longer study of the *Tractatus*, the preface would have to be quoted in full and discussed in detail, for it seems intensely earnest in intent, yet it reads like an incredible joke—a serious joke coterminous with philosophy itself. The justly famous concluding passages are especially pertinent to the problem of the way in which the text presents itself:

> 6.54 My propositions are elucidatory in this way: he who understands me finally recognizes them as nonsensical, when he has climbed out through them, on them, over them. (He must so to speak throw away the ladder, after he has climbed up on it.) He must transcend these propositions; then he sees the world rightly.
>
> 7. Whereof one cannot speak, thereof one must be silent.

If something is expressed "directly" in this conclusion, its meaning is not clear and distinct. One may offer two rather different interpretations of it. On the one hand, the conclusion seems to appeal to the traditional ladder metaphor as a way of indicating a final turn toward silence: the *Tractatus* would culminate in mute mysticism. This conclusion would seem to resonate with a statement in the preface—a statement which the use of language in the book renders radically problematic: "[The book's] whole meaning could be summed up somewhat as follows: What can be said at all can be said clearly, and whereof one cannot speak, thereof one must be silent." On the other hand, the conclusion seems to intimate that the use of language in the *Tractatus* was not simple nonsense but, at least in part, a deconstructive strategy simultaneously using the terms and operations of traditional philosophy and critically sounding them out, thereby indicating the need for a radically different way of posing problems.[10] This interpretation would appeal to the use of language in the *Tractatus* in order to contest the neat opposition in the preface that seemed to ban the interplay between limits and transgression in language: "The limit [to the expression of thought] can, therefore, only be drawn in language

10. Sylviane Agacinski informs her extremely "active" interpretation of the *Tractatus* with a sustained effort to disclose the deconstructive impetus of Wittgenstein's thought. See "Découpages du *Tractatus*" in *Mimesis désarticulations*, ed. S. Agacinski, J. Derrida, and S. Kofman (Paris, 1975), 19–53.

and what lies on the other side will be simply nonsense." In some sense (but how could one articulate it?), the "nonsensical" propositions of the *Tractatus* did "think" the other side of this limit in a complex and significant way.

In what may still be termed, for sake of convenience, the explicit or "direct" argument of the *Tractatus*, however, certain traditional metaphysical assumptions were affirmed, notably the idea of an essential identity between representation and reality and the reduction of language to a mere expression or clothing for thought. It is noteworthy that the *Notebooks* and Wittgenstein's letters to Russell do not always seem to take for granted what was dogmatically expressed in the *Tractatus*:

> If sign and signified *were not* identical in respect of their total logical content then there would have to be something still more fundamental than logic. . . . Identity is the very Devil and *immensely important*; very much more so than I thought. It hangs—like anything else—directly together with the most significant questions. . . ."[11]

One fruitful way of seeing the later Wittgenstein is, I think, in terms of a more explicit exploration of the paradoxes of the *Tractatus*. In the process, he did not simply reject the picture presented in the *Tractatus* (one is not in an area where simple rejections are pertinent) but reinscribed it in a critical way, often pointing out where its views were misleading. It is significant that the problem of identity and essence was a particular object of critical scrutiny.

11. Ludwig Wittgenstein, *Notebooks 1914–1916*, ed. and tr. G E. M. Anscombe (New York, 1969), 43, 122. It is remarkable that Janik and Toulmin, who are so intent on eliciting Wittgenstein's intentions, make only two relatively marginal references to his *Notebooks*. Even if one rejects the identification of the *mens auctoris* with the true meaning of the text, the *Notebooks* should nonetheless be considered in any intertextual reading of the *Tractatus* addressed to the problem of context. In them, Wittgenstein's sense of indebtedness to Frege and Russell and his relation to Russell as a significant interlocutor are beyond question. It may further be observed that Lewis Carroll, whom Janik and Toulmin do not mention, is an important reference point for Wittgenstein in the English context. See George Pitcher, "Wittgenstein, Nonsense, and Lewis Carroll," *Massachusetts Review* 6 (1965), 591–611.

When Wittgenstein argues that the same concept is not applied in the light of a shared essence and when he chooses the game as an example of the concept, elucidating the concept of game through an appeal to the metaphor of family resemblances, he is doing explicitly what was implicitly at work in the *Tractatus*. But in his later thought, his endeavor is directly related to a critique of the notion of essential meaning and to an investigation into the interaction between structure and play in the use of language. His inquiry then begins with language seen as a labyrinth or as an ancient city which philosophical demands for law and order (purity, precision, univocity, full meaning, etc.) may regulate but never entirely master. Indeed, the later Wittgenstein often reads like a *Vindiciae Contra Tyrannos* in a world where logic threatens to assume the dominant role of tyrant. Wittgenstein's later views do not imply that there is no basis for stable meaning, knowledge, and communication. Nor do they imply a simple rejection or denial of the function of logic in language. But they do raise radical doubts about a notion of essence or identity as an incontestable ground or *archon* of meaning. And they direct interpretation toward a careful and detailed investigation of the interplay, in actual usage, of order and openness, convention and transgression, logic and rhetoric, the literal and the literary, and so forth. As Wittgenstein himself put it in the *Philosophical Investigations*:

> The more closely we examine actual language, the sharper becomes the conflict between it and our requirement. (For the crystalline purity of logic was, of course, not a *result of investigation*: it was a requirement.) The conflict becomes intolerable; the requirement is now in danger of becoming empty.—We have got on to slippery ice where there is no friction and so in a certain sense the conditions are ideal, but also, just because of that, we are unable to walk. We want to walk; so we need *friction*. Back to the rough ground. [I, no. 107]

This "rough ground" designates the place where philosophy, literary criticism, and intellectual history meet. The problem of the relationship between text and context is situated on it. But "contextualism" in the sense practiced by Janik and Toulmin is itself a powerful orthodoxy in the humanities that arrives by another route at the same result as "Platonism": an idealized notion of full, essential meaning.[12] And what may seem liberating in contrast with a narrowly literary or "history-of-ideas" point of view may be overly restraining from a more critical perspective on historical problems, for contextualism may readily serve to underwrite the newer tendency that tries to establish social history as the only true way to address problems in historiography. Here one has a final paradox of Janik and Toulmin's text, for—despite their good intentions—their critique of professionalism and the academic division of labor diverts attention from the manner in which their own operating assumptions function to reinforce dogmatism in interpretation. Here the "true" question may, in Humpty-Dumpty fashion, be largely political—a question of what is recognized as a "historical" or an "unhistorical" method of inquiry, with all of the professional implications a recognition of this sort entails. Given the limitations of discourse addressing the politics of disciplines, what lapidary conclusions may be drawn for a revision of processes of recognition

12. At the risk of confusing a bad pun with a grammatical joke of deep philosophical significance, one may observe that there is more in Plato than meets the *eidos*. (On the role of "supplementarity" in Plato, see Jacques Derrida, "La pharmacie de Platon" in *La dissémination* [Paris, 1972], 69–199.) In criticizing the notion of essential or fully determinate meaning, however, the later Wittgenstein still insisted that answers must somewhere come to an end. His rationale seemed to be in part pragmatic, but it may be precipitate to see his later thought as leading to an unproblematic defense of ordinary language and convention. Nothing seems less ordinary than ordinary language after Wittgenstein has finished with it. His own later works, moreover, made use of a "dialogical" form in which questions often remained open after they had been explored and elucidated. As K. T. Fann notes: "according to Anthony Kenny, the *Investigations* contains 784 questions, only 110 of these are answered and 70 of the answers are *meant* to be wrong." Fann also notes: "It has been reported that once Wittgenstein flew at one of his students for suggesting that he was a 'systematic philosopher'" (*Wittgenstein's Conception of Philosophy* [Berkeley and Los Angeles, 1969] 109, 101). It is nonetheless true that a major difference between Wittgenstein, on the one hand, and Nietzsche, Heidegger, and Derrida, on the other, is that the latter make a sustained attempt to relate their thought to an explicit critique of traditional metaphysical systems and of assumptions in "ordinary language" that are related to them.

concerning the nature of a historical approach to the interpretation of texts?

Insofar as the approach taken in the present essay is convincing, it would indicate that the extremes of fully determinate and fully indeterminate meaning are ideal limits approximated in varying degrees by actual uses of language or "texts." In this sense, the text is not to be identified with the self-enclosed, unique aesthetic object, which is as much an idealization as is the eternal form or the fully unified structure. The text is rather the scene of an interplay between different forces—forces of unification and dissemination—whose relation must be taken as a matter of inquiry. Philosophers as seemingly diverse as Nietzsche, Heidegger, Derrida, and Wittgenstein have inquired into the problem of textuality. If one were to draw an implication for intellectual history from their tensely related inquiries, it would be that the specific problem for interpretation is that of how structures, paradigms, or patterns of meaning actually inform or fail to inform a text and its readings. A further implication would be that the argument in defense of an essential, dominant, or even primary meaning for a text (and, a fortiori, for a tradition) would be unjust to the extent that it did not include, and evaluate the importance of, elements that constituted counterevidence, or even the basis of a "counter-story," vis-à-vis the essentialist claim or its weaker analogues. A crucial issue would be that of the manner and extent to which any text generally recognized as a classic renders that claim problematic. (The question would then be whether and how classics both help to institute something—a system, a pattern, a genre—and challenge it.)[13] In addition, the context itself

13. These comments raise the entire problem of the relationship between textuality and structures, and they point to an entire field of historical research. Figures like Wittgenstein, Marx, and Freud may be seen as "initiators of discursive practices" (in the phrase of Foucault) or as founders of "paradigms" (in the term popularized by T. S. Kuhn). But it has become increasingly evident that these figures do not simply initiate or found a discursive practice or a paradigm. The alternative view, however, should not be to present their work in terms of the opposite extreme of "historical" particularity and the purely individual intellectual biography. In an intricate and often internally divided way, the texts and other

would have to be seen as a text of sorts. Its "reading" and interpretation pose problems as difficult as those posed by the most intricate written text. The systematic defect of much traditional historiography has been the attempt to employ the simplest documentary texts—or documentary texts subjected to a simplistic interpretation—as the basis for an understanding of the past or the "context" to which complex texts are made to conform. A fruitful reversal of perspectives would propose the complex text itself as at times a better model for the reconstruction of the "larger context." The relationship between text and context would then become a question of "intertextual" reading, which cannot be addressed on the basis of reductionist oversimplifications that convert the context into a fully unified or dominant structure saturating the text with a certain meaning. Meaning is indeed context-bound, but context is not itself bound in any simple or unproblematic way.

---

related activities (e.g., clinical, professional, and social practice) of these figures both put forth seemingly comprehensive structures and, more or less explicitly, indicate ways in which they are problematic. "Orthodox" followers do not merely apply or refine a discursive practice or a paradigm. At times in collaboration with the "founding father," they are instrumental in reducing the "master's" texts to their paradigmatic or structural level. On this level, the texts may function unproblematically to found a discipline or a practice by providing a core of identity for followers and a means of clear differentiation from competing schools, parties, movements, etc. To some extent, the relation between the early Wittgenstein and positivists (or the later Wittgenstein and analytic philosophers) may be understood in the light of this decisive process of reduction. More generally, the historical function of much intellectual history (whether of a narrative, analytic, or contextual kind) has been to facilitate the process of reducing complex texts to a relatively simple level of intelligibility. This process cannot be entirely circumvented, but it can be limited and contested through certain approaches to reading.

[4]

Who Rules Metaphor?
Paul Ricoeur's Theory of Discourse

Truth is not a minted coin that can be given and pocketed ready-made.

> Hegel, Preface to *The Phenomenology of Mind*

What, then, is truth? A mobile army of metaphors, metonyms, and anthropomorphisms—in short, a sum of human relations, which have been enhanced, transposed, and embellished poetically and rhetorically, and which after long use seem firm, canonical, and obligatory to a people: truths are illusions about which one has forgotten that this is what they are; metaphors which are worn out and without sensuous power; coins which have lost their pictures and now matter only as metal, no longer as coins.

> Nietzsche, "On Truth and Falsity in Their Extramoral Sense."

Paul Ricoeur is an important presence on the contemporary critical scene. His rigorous thought and lucid prose style have made him an especially influential exponent of phenomenology and hermeneutics, one whose works play a noteworthy role in the human sciences. The odds are that an anthropologist, sociologist, or historian who has read little or no Husserl or Heidegger will have read Ricoeur. With the publication of *Freud and Philosophy*, a broad-gauged study of Freud and the problem of understanding in the sciences of man, Ricoeur clearly emerged as one of the foremost philosophically oriented theorists in the humanities and social sciences.[1] The publication of *The Rule of Metaphor* marks a synthetic moment in his career, for in it he gathers together his thoughts on language and employs them to combat what he sees as dangerous tendencies in the field of discourse.[2] This magisterial book, which I think will receive recognition as a minor classic, deserves careful study.

Ricoeur's specific goal is an attempt to provide a crucial chapter in a modern treatise on rhetoric. Metaphor forms the guiding thread in the richly woven fabric of Ricoeur's theoretical discussion, but the broader ambition of the book might be seen as a reformulation of Aristotle's conception of the relationships among three modes of discourse: poetry (the realm of metaphor), philosophy (the conceptual realm of theoretical reflection on being), and hermeneutics or interpretation—the latter displacing the Aristotelian notion of history. Indeed Aristotle, completed and complemented by Husserl, is Ricoeur's *maître à penser*. Ricoeur pays little attention to Plato and seems to agree with Aristotle's criticism of his predecessor's idea of participation as overly metaphoric for philosophical speculation proper.

Ricoeur's study might also be seen as a limited response to the call for "reunion in philosophy" sounded a generation ago by Morton White, for Ricoeur discusses extensively both rhetorical studies in France (notably by structuralists) and theories of metaphor in the Anglo-American world of philosophy and literary criticism (Max Black, Monroe Beardsley, Nelson Goodman, and others). Thus one valuable function of the work is to serve as a critical handbook of influential theories of metaphor in France, England, and America. As Ricoeur himself observes, he tends to de-emphasize or even omit German contributions from the romantics through Nietzsche to more contemporary theorists. He does, however, conclude his

1. Paul Ricoeur, *Freud and Philosophy*, tr. D. Savage (New Haven, 1970).
2. Paul Ricoeur, *The Rule of Metaphor*, tr. Robert Czerny, with Kathleen McLaughlin and John Costello, S. J. (Toronto, 1977; all page references in the text are to this edition).

work with a moderately critical appreciation of Heidegger, which he links to a more militantly critical reaction to Jacques Derrida.

The translated title of the book exemplifies both the problems it treats and the problems that confront it. The French title was *La métaphore vive*—"Live Metaphor"—a title with a rather different connotation or metaphoric ring than the seemingly staid and strait-laced English title. The English title, however, is itself ambivalent at first blush. It could mean the (somewhat unruly) "rule" of metaphor in language or the rule over metaphor by language or some particular, privileged mode of discourse or language use. The translators decide the ambiguity in favor of the latter interpretation. Given the dominant line of argument and the actual use of language in the book, they are probably right. There are very few "live metaphors" in *The Rule of Metaphor*—a crucial feature of Ricoeur's own discursive practice. The translators quote "Aristotle's assertion, often quoted by Ricoeur, that 'the greatest thing by far is to be a master of metaphor.'" And they add: "Besides rule as mastery of metaphor, the reader will encounter the language rules that impinge on metaphor, and the domains of discourse in which metaphor holds sway" (p. vii). These latter "domains" are poetic and literary. Ricoeur's central thesis might be summarized by saying that metaphor is all right in its place, but it must be kept securely in its place. The task of philosophy as the privileged "realm" of discourse *par excellence* is to be the "vigilant watchman" (Ricoeur's own biblical metaphor) that makes limited use of mastered metaphor in a way that keeps it in its "literary" or "poetic" place and prevents its movement from impinging in an unsettling or seductive way upon speculative discourse proper. This argument emerges most forcefully in the Eighth Study, which concludes the principal text and includes the stringent reprimands addressed to the imp of the perverse mingling of the domains in the works of Heidegger and, especially, Derrida. This is the argument to which I shall devote most attention here, for it constitutes one of the strongest reaffirmations of a basically traditional understanding of philosophy, literature, and interpretation in the face of what would seem to be its most disorienting and uncanny challenge. It transports one to the scene of what might be called the contemporary conflict over interpretations of interpretation. This is the scene involving what Heidegger refers to quite simply as "thought"—a scene impinging upon historical interpretation itself.

Ricoeur begins *The Rule of Metaphor* with a discussion of Aristotle's definition of metaphor and ends it with a train of thought defending Aristotle's conception of philosophy as theoretical speculation that grounds thought by seeking purity, autonomy, and unity (*pros hen, ad unum*) in addressing the ontological question What is being? Ricoeur devotes a long discussion to Aristotle's seeming answer to the question of unity in the apparently diverse meanings of being—the analogy of being—and to the elaboration of the analogy of being in scholastic philosophy. Ricoeur seems to concede that the Aristotelian quest for unity encountered aporias that made it a *beau désastre*, but he insists that the quest itself was essentially right in establishing the nature of philosophy and that it marked philosophical discourse in a unique way. His own argumentation would seem to imply a belief that the more successful alternative to the analogy of being is to be found in Husserlian phenomenology with its reliance on transcendental reduction in the establishment of unified eidetic essences. One might conjecture that Aristotelian analogy was not far enough removed from Platonic participation (or Freudian transference, for that matter) to establish a unified, pure, and autonomous realm of speculative discourse. Ricoeur fails to discuss Derrida's analysis of Husserl in *La voix et le phénomène*,[3] which attempted to indicate that Husserlian phenomenology encountered analogous difficulties. The only text of Derrida that Ricoeur treats—indeed one of the very few texts in Ricoeur's book as a whole receiving detailed treatment that departs significantly from a synopsis or summary of themes—is Derrida's "White Mythology."[4] He does not even discuss the Heideggerian text which would seem to be the closest analogue to Derrida's

3. Jacques Derrida, *La voix et le phénomène* (Paris, 1967). *Speech and Phenomena*, tr. David B. Allison (Evanston, 1973).
4. Jacques Derrida, "La mythologie blanche," in *Marges de la philosophie* (Paris, 1972).

"White Mythology": "The Origin of the Work of Art."[5] It is significant that in a recent essay, which includes a partial response to Ricoeur's critique, Derrida does refer to "The Origin of the Work of Art" as marking a significant twist in Heidegger's reflection on Being.[6] Derrida's essay also marks a significant twist in his own extremely intricate relationship to Heidegger, for in it he does not argue, as he formerly tended to do, that Heidegger's thought represents perhaps the strongest defense of the quest for unified presence in the reflection on Being. He reveals how Heidegger, while never simply abandoning that quest, also places it in radical question in an explicit and "thematized" way, especially in his later works.

For Ricoeur, Aristotle's famous definition established the frame of reference for later thought on metaphor in the Western tradition: "Metaphor (*metaphora*) consists in giving (or transfering to: *epiphora*) the thing a name that belongs to something else; the tranference being either from genus to species, or from species to genus, or from species to species, or on grounds of analogy." Aristotle's definition also indicated the difficulty in the attempted conceptual mastery of metaphor, for it repeated the metaphoric process (transfer) in the definition itself. Metaphor in Aristotle was not a specific figure of speech distinguished from others, for example, metonomy and synecdoche. It referred to the general problem of figurative uses of language. And it stressed the work of resemblance in the metaphoric articulation of similarities among logically and literally distant or different things. What is especially significant for Ricoeur is that in Aristotle metaphor (in a properly subordinate place) was linked to philosophy, and it was situated at the crossroads of rhetoric (teleologically defined in terms of persuasion) and poetics (teleologically defined in terms of the *mimesis* of human action in tragic art). Rhetoric itself was controlled by philosophy, but it was broad enough to include argumentation, composition, and style. Over time, rhetoric became restricted to a taxonomy or classification of

5. Martin Heidegger, "The Origin of the Work of Art," Albert Hofstadter, in *Poetry, Language, Thought* (New York, 1975).
6. Jacques Derrida, "The Retrait of Metaphor," in *Enclitic* 2 (1978), 5–33.

figures of speech, as rhetoricians became concerned with elaborate and shifting differentiations between metaphor and other figures. The rhetoric that was pruned from curricula in the nineteenth century was but a wilted image of its former self. Yet the seeds of decline could in one sense be found in Aristotle's conception itself, for he focused the theory of metaphor on the word (especially the name) and the substitution of words.

Ricoeur would like to reinvigorate rhetoric under the auspices of philosophy. He distinguishes among semiotics (the level of the word), semantics (the level of the sentence), and hermeneutics (the level of discourse, text, and interpretation). He argues that much modern theory has followed the less fruitful strain in Aristotle by centering a conception of metaphor on word substitution. Without rejecting the importance of the word as the carrier of the effect of metaphorical meaning, he argues for an insertion of the word and the name in a larger context allowing for the importance of predication in metaphoric usage. On the level of the word, metaphoric transfer is a case of deviant denomination in contrast with literal or standard usage. On the level of the sentence, it is a case of impertinent predication. Here Ricoeur quotes Nelson Goodman's serio-comic "definition" of metaphor: "Metaphor is an affair between a predicate with a past and an object that yields while protesting." In this sense, what is a "category mistake" in literal or logical terms may constitute metaphoric vision in the revision of a mode of discourse or a way of seeing problems. Ricoeur does not add the obvious: the necessarily "transgressive" revision may be seen as a mistaken or even "nonsensical" venture by those whose unfamiliarity with, or resistance to, its demands or strategies fosters the "natural" tendency to defend established approaches. What is less obvious is the status of criteria of critical evaluation and judgment in cases of this sort.

Ricoeur argues most insistently for the need to account for both sense and reference in metaphoric usage. Philosophers and literary critics have too readily restricted reference to scientific usage and seen metaphor, poetry, and literature solely in terms of sense, expression, and self-reflexivity. At least on the levels of semiotics and semantics, Ricoeur combines his insistence on reference with a tension and interaction theory of metaphor. Word substitution itself becomes intelligible only within the context of semiotic and semantic tension and interaction: between the literal and the metaphoric in the work of resemblance; between identity and difference in the metaphoric copula; between discovery and creation in metaphoric invention; and between belief and critical distance in metaphoric predication. The metaphoric "is" signifies both "is like" and "is not." The "is like" is not marked grammatically in metaphoric predication; it becomes marked only in simile, which may be seen as extended metaphor. The "is not" signals the intervention of the literal. Metaphor implies a kind of conditional belief: "Can one create metaphors without believing them and without believing that, in a certain way, 'that is'?" (p. 254). Metaphoric vehemence is related to belief and to the sense of finding one's metaphors, not simply making them. But simple belief would amount to myth and the elimination of tension in the metaphoric copula.

> The paradox consists in the fact that there is no other way to do justice to the notion of metaphorical truth than to include the critical incision of the (literal) "is not" within the ontological vehemence of the (metaphorical) "is." In doing so, the thesis merely draws the most extreme consequence of the theory of tension. . . . It is this tensional constitution of the verb *to be* that receives its grammatical mark in the "to be like" of metaphor elaborated into simile, at the same time as the tension between *same* and *other* is marked in the relational copula. [Pp. 255–56]

One might think that these comments would lead to an understanding of language as a generalized referential network that raises the question of the possibilities and limits of sense-making. But, as he approaches the level of interpretation, discourse, and text, Ricoeur draws back from the "most extreme consequence of the theory of tension." Indeed his argument undergoes a curious reversal, for tension, interaction, and interpretation itself assume a definitely subordinate or *merely* supplementary position with reference to "realms" of discourse. The tense interaction among modes of discourse, which Ricoeur himself ultimately sees as the creative dynamic in thought, is given at best only minimal room in which to operate. Ricoeur adamantly resists what may be called, with some oversimplification, the primacy of interaction and tension on the discursive level. This resistance is evident in the specific gloss he places on the notion of "split reference" in poetic and literary texts and in his attempt to establish the unity, autonomy, and purity of philosophical discourse proper. In the process, he covertly repeats on his third level of language that which he criticizes on the first two levels: the primacy of nominalization and the marked secondariness of relational interaction. In this unannounced reversal, one has what might not altogether facetiously be called Ricoeur's essential tension about the problem of tension. I would not want to eliminate this tension, for it is an essential tension attesting to importance of problems which are not easily resolved, but I would like to ask whether it can be better articulated through an inquiry into the relationship between the desire for unity, autonomy, and purity and forces that contest or resist it. This is, I think, an inquiry that becomes more explicit in the works of Heidegger and Derrida in ways that Ricoeur refuses to recognize. This nonrecognition renders Ricoeur less able to address an important question: does the desire for unity (*pros hen, ad unum*), with the postulation of ontological and epistemological realms that seems to satisfy it, become prey to unthematized inconsistency, damaging repetition, and specious argumentation when it fails to pose as an explicit problem its relation to what contests it? Does the desire to be fully in control of certain essential problems make one less able to attain the measure of critical control that is possible in discourse?

The passage from semiotics and semantics to hermeneutics poses special problems for Ricoeur, and these problems become especially knotty with reference to the literary or poetic text, for the literary text does not seem to have a reference in the usual sense. For

Ricoeur, the sense of the text is its structure, and its reference in the most comprehensive sense is its world. The literary text does refer to a world and, to elicit its peculiar features, Ricoeur appeals to Roman Jakobson's notion of "split reference."

In discussing Jakobson's theory of split reference, Ricoeur notes certain telling qualifications, but his own gloss fails to explore and even represses them. For Jakobson, the poetic function of language is not identical with the poem as a literary genre or with the specific text. The poetic function is defined in two related ways: the dominance of message and verbal structure over other aspects of the communicative act and the overlay or projection of the axis of selection or resemblance on the axis of combination or contiguity through rhythm, meter, rhyme, and so forth. Jakobson notes that "the supremacy of poetic function over referential function does not obliterate the reference but makes it ambiguous" (quoted by Ricoeur, p. 224). To illustrate this split reference, Jakobson quotes the usual exordium of Majorca storytellers: "It was and was not." Jakobson also argues that the poetic genres are distinguished not by the poetic function per se but by the way the poetic is mixed with nonpoetic functions of language. Thus third-person epic poetry entails a great deal of reference; first-person lyric poetry is intimately linked with the emotive function; and second-person poetry is imbued with the conative function.

Ricoeur's gloss is quite reductive of the ambiguity of split reference in the relation of the poetic to the nonpoetic, both in specific texts and in the definition of genres. "The literary work through the structure proper to it displays a world only under the condition that the reference of descriptive discourse is suspended. Or to put it another way, discourse in the literary work sets out its denotation as a second-level denotation by means of the suspension of the first-level denotation of discourse" (p. 221). What this second-level denotation might be is never clear, but what is clear is that the appeal to the Husserlian *epochè*, or bracketing of empirical reality, saves the reference of the literary work only by etherealizing it. One seems to have a "two-worlds" theory of reference. In the process, the entire range of referential possibilities in the literary work is collapsed into one limiting possibility. And the implications for the understanding of the literary work are conservative and contemplative. What is lost is the "heuristic power" of fiction that Ricoeur himself notes, for the redescription of reality which he presents as the achievement of literature amounts to little more than a purely aesthetic way of seeing things differently with no implications for understanding or action in the ordinary world.

In contrast to Ricoeur's interpretation of split reference, one might make the following limited observations. There is a sense in which literature invokes a suspension or virtualization of ordinary reference, and the risks of the reader may not seem as "immediate" as they sometimes are in everyday life. Yet the reader does confront at least mediate risks through the implications of what is written and his or her own implication in the text. These risks are more forceful to the extent that the text has a critical relation to everyday life, including the everyday uses of language. In this respect, one has an entire range of possibilities in the relation of the literary work to ordinary reality and ordinary usage. There may be elements of denotative reference in the more ordinary sense, most significantly on the level of a reading of the times. Even particular references, for example, to a historical figure or event, involve a carry-over effect that makes their use in fiction something other than a pure suspension or virtualization of denotation or factual assertion. Here one may speak of a quasi-documentary dimension of the literary work which is interwoven in a variety of ways with its other dimensions. In significant modern literature, there are often markedly critical elements in the way the work reads the times and its various "discourses." (Lukács, in however restricted a fashion, makes this point a theme of his readings of Balzac and others, indicating the importance of a tension between the explicit ideology of the writer and what his works may be argued to disclose about the times.) There may also be simulated denotative reference in the literary work, giving rise to the criterion of verisimilitude or lifelikeness in the interpretation of the work. More subtly, there may be simulated denotative usage, at times in an experimental form that questions Ricoeur's understanding of literature as the "realm" of metaphoric usage. Some of the strongest "literary" effects of Flaubert, Beckett, or Kafka depend upon simulated literal or denotative usage (often in parodic form) and the more or less systematic avoidance of metaphor. This is not to say that in their works the interaction with the metaphoric is entirely suspended, for—aside from the role of parody—part of the effect of their works is to stimulate in the reader a desire for metaphor and a tendency to read entire texts as extended metaphors or allegories—a tendency both invited and undercut by the texts themselves. A final example from the novel is particularly apposite, for it concerns a writer who on one level sought the more idealistic and contemplative virtualization of ordinary reality that Ricoeur's theory of split reference evokes. In Virginia Woolf's *To the Lighthouse*, violent events and abrupt changes that might disrupt the quest for "higher reality" and unity (which is definitely not restricted to philosophy) are explicitly placed in brackets. (One may note that "bracket" may be traced etymologically to the Latin *bracae* and the French *braguette*—breeches and codpiece. Ricoeur observes that etymology is significant not in a purely literal sense but in the reanimation of dead metaphor, and the function of the bracket, including the phenomenological *epochè*, might well be seen as a means of covering or repressing aspects of empirical reality that disorient purely speculative philosophical discourse.) The altogether explicit use of the bracket in Virginia Woolf directs attention to its more implicit function (as well as to nonidealistic movements in Woolf's own texts), and it sets up a fascinating interplay between what is revealed and what is concealed in certain uses of language.

What one misses in Ricoeur's interpretation of split reference in the literary text and poetic discourse is precisely the tension between the metaphoric and the literal that he himself stresses on semiotic and semantic levels. Indeed Ricoeur inquires very little into the tense interaction of modes of discourse with one another or with pertinent institutional contexts and not at all into their actual function in specific texts. Instead the mode of discourse is promoted into a largely detached "realm" of discourse. And analytic types and analytic distinctions, which have heuristic value when they are seen as methodological guides and employed to stimulate research or foster processes of clarification, are given epistemological and even ontological status in defining discontinuous "realms" of discourse. Thus Ricoeur simply assumes that a mode of discourse (e.g., the literary or the philosophical) does and should define at least the dominant structure and world of the text. This assumption is, of course, facilitated by his summary way of dealing with texts and by the fact that his understanding of discourse eliminates rather than poses the problem of the text. The text seems like little more than a token or instance of a type or mode of discourse. What is not posed as a problem for inquiry is precisely the way in which more or less formalized modes of discourse actually function in texts or extended uses of language. As a consequence, Ricoeur is in no position to investigate how dominant structures and worlds relate to more submerged aspects of the text and whether there is always some measure of tension, with dominance seeming entirely pacific or neutral only through a reliance on the dead metaphors that Ricoeur criticizes. A fortiori, he cannot raise the question of whether this dominance is always desirable or whether other forms of relationship, involving relative stress or perhaps mutuality and creative strife among more equally matched modes of discourse, both exist in certain texts and have their justification. The Menippean satire and the more general processes that Mikhail Bakhtin refers to as "carnivalization" underscore the pertinence of this question, for they explore the tense interaction of genres in a way that may be impertinent enough to test the limits of a conception of genre.

These considerations become especially pressing in Ricoeur's understanding of philosophy and its relation to interpretation. And it is here that the covert, unthematized internal contestation and even inconsistency of Ricoeur's argument become most pronounced, for in his own dominant line of argument, Ricoeur would like to present philosophy as autonomous, discontinuous in relation to the poetic or literary, and allowing only for securely marginal and mastered interaction with metaphor. For Ricoeur, the question of the philosophy that is implied in his investigation "requires a global decision concerning the collective unity of modes of discourse, such as poetic discourse, scientific discourse, religious discourse, speculative discourse, and so on" (p. 257). Hence it is "important to recognize in principle the *discontinuity* that assures the autonomy of speculative discourse" (p. 258).

> The possibility of speculative discourse lies in the semantic dynamism of metaphorical expression and yet . . . speculative discourse can respond to the semantic potentialities of metaphor only by providing it with the resources of a domain of articulation that properly belongs to speculative discourse by reason of its very constitution. [P. 259]
>
> That speculative discourse finds something like the sketch of a conceptual determination in the dynamism [of metaphor] does not bar it from beginning in itself and from finding the principle of its articulation within itself. By itself, it draws on the resources of a conceptual field, which it offers to the unfolding of a meaning sketched metaphorically. The *necessity* of this discourse is not the extension of its possibility, inscribed in the dynamism of the metaphorical. Its necessity proceeds instead from the very structures of the mind, which it is the task of transcendental philosophy to articulate. One can pass from one discourse to the other only by an *epochè*. [P. 300]
>
> The signifying aim of the concept works free of interpretations, schematizations, and imaginative illustrations only if a horizon of constitution is given in advance, the horizon of speculative logos. . . . Because it is a system, the conceptual order is able to free itself from the play of double meaning and hence from the semantic dynamism characteristic of the metaphorical order. [P. 302]
>
> [The question of being] is entirely outside of all language games. For this reason, when the philosopher is confronted by the paradox that "being is said in several ways" and when, in order to rescue the diverse meanings of being from dispersal, he establishes between them a relation of reference to a first term that is neither the univocity of a genus nor the mere chance equivocalness of a simple word, the plurivocity that is thus brought to philosophical discourse

is of a different order than the multiplicity of meaning produced by metaphorical utterance. . . . What is important is that a connection be identified among the multiple meanings of being, one which, though not proceeding from the division of genus into species, nevertheless constitutes an order. This order is an order of categories. . . . The regulated polysemy of being orders the apparently disordered polysemy of the predicative function as such. . . . Philosophical discourse sets itself up as the vigilant watchman overseeing the ordered extensions of meaning; against this background, the unfettered extensions of meaning in poetic discourse spring free. [Pp. 260–261]

This set of quotations gives some sense of the forcefully "logocentric" field that Ricoeur would like to establish for speculative philosophy. In terms of it, the dream of traditional philosophy, resurrected and rearticulated by Husserl, is not dead. It is indeed vigorous enough to combat successfully the doubting waywardness of Heidegger and Derrida. And the defense of tradition makes strange bedfellows, for Ricoeur would like to enlist Anglo-American analytic philosophy in support of his claims. His theoretical energy is not in the least dissipated by the fact that his claims tend to remain on the level of flat assertion and that his own text is marked by metaphor and by secular analogues of religious notions. He is willing to give up the virgin birth of speculative philosophy. It is somehow generated by metaphor and the productive imagination. But through some process of transfiguration or conversion it achieves full or at least masterful functional autonomy of its origins. On its own proper level, speculative philosophy attains immaculate conception. The concept is not at all marked by the play of double meaning characterizing the metaphorical copula. Ricoeur insists that the mutually implicated similarity and difference of metaphor are different from the "same" established by conceptual meaning, and without argument he equates the same with the identical and frees identity from the play of difference. The concept gives a pure grasp of the identity and essence of its object. Speculative philosophy, as the discourse of pure concepts, is paradoxically a metalanguage fully in control of its linguistic repertory and a liberated movement of pure thought which seems to transcend the play of language games and empirical involvements. It is the necessary language or nonlanguage of pure reflection, and Ricoeur notes its strange proximity to "religious non-discourse." In it, language becomes the vehicle of an essential message that may be ineffable or border on silence (a message that, from a different perspective, might be seen as the vivid imaginary form or waking conceptual dream of speculative philosophy). And, through it, polysemy seems to become accidental, for it is fully mastered and detached from the risk of dissemination. This extremely "strict" understanding of philosophical language accompanies an excessively libertarian or permissive notion of poetic or literary language which does not seem to allow for the interaction of discipline and play in literature.

Ricoeur argues that live metaphor is essential for philosophical creativity, but it is not clear how live metaphor inseminates a conceptually pure philosophy. If metaphor is reduced to a fully instrumental level, how can it be alive? The problem Ricoeur faces is whether philosophy may appear autonomous only to the extent that it breaks the spirit of language and deals in domesticated or even dead metaphors. His confrontation with this problem does not lead him to question the idea of a discontinuous realm of speculation or to ask whether Derrida's critique is compatible with a more modulated notion of the relative specificity of philosophy. Instead it provokes Ricoeur's most insistent affirmation of a proper realm of philosophy. And it is related to two extremely dubious arguments: the argument that Derrida derives philosophy exclusively from dead metaphor, and the argument that Heidegger's critique of a certain understanding of metaphor does not pertain to Ricoeur's own thought, since Ricoeur does not adhere to the "obsolete semantic notion" that applies the distinction between proper and figurative to individual words (p. 282). In contrast to Ricoeur, one might argue that Derrida in "White Mythology" critically poses the problem of the interacting losses and gains in the relationship between metaphor and concept and that Ricoeur does articulate and defend the understanding of metaphor criticized by Heidegger, not on the semantic level but on the level of realms of discourse where a "metaphysics of the proper" is very much at work in Ricoeur's text. Indeed Ricoeur's pivotal discussion of the relationship between dead metaphor and speculative philosophy epitomizes the difficulties of his argument, and it reveals why he turns to overly reductive interpretations of those he sees as his adversaries.

Ricoeur refers to a passage in Hegel's *Aesthetics* that is also discussed in Derrida's "White Mythology." He provides this synopsis:

Derrida bases his work here [in "White Mythology"] on a particularly eloquent text in Hegel's *Aesthetics*. It begins by stating that philosophical concepts are initially sensible meanings transposed (*übertragen*) to the spiritual order; and it adds that the establishment of a properly (*eigentlich*) abstract meaning is bound up with the effacement of what is metaphorical in the initial meaning, which, once proper, has become improper. Now Hegel employs the term *Aufhebung* to describe this "raising" of sensible "worn away" meaning into the spiritual meaning, which has become the proper expression. Where Hegel sees an innovation of meaning, Derrida sees only the wearing away of metaphor and drift towards idealization resulting from the dissimulation of this metaphorical origin. [P. 286]

Ricoeur counters what he believes to be Derrida's interpretation with this gloss on Hegel's text:

This text describes two operations that intersect at one point—dead metaphor—but remain distinct. The first operation, which is purely metaphorical, takes a proper [*eigentlich*] meaning and transports it [*übertragen*] into the spiritual order. Out of this expression—nonproper [*uneigentlich*] because transposed—the other operation makes a proper abstract meaning. It is the second operation that constitutes the "suppression-preservation" which Hegel calls *Aufhebung*. But the two operations, transfer and suppression, are distinct. The second alone creates a proper sense out of an improper sense coming from the sensible order. The phenomenon of wearing away [*Abnutzung*] is only a prior condition allowing the second operation to be constituted on the ground of the first. [P. 272]

What is curious in Ricoeur's gloss (and in the "divide and rule" strategy on which it relies) is that he "defends" Hegel against Derrida at the price of reducing Hegelian dialectics to something it was supposedly to "overcome": a rather narrowly analytic way of understanding problems. Not only does one have what Derrida terms "a movement of idealization" in the Hegelian text. One presumably has a pure and simple categorial affirmation of the ideal. How this involves a process of conservation as well as of suppression and elevation in dialectical "interiorization" (*Erinnerung*) becomes more of a mystery than it was in Hegel—or rather, Hegel's argument is "straightened out" in the direction of a pure phenomenology by simply eliminating the "conservation" (residue or resonance?) of the sensible in the ideal. Given his interpretation, Ricoeur does not notice a number of problematic elements in Hegel's text—problematic both for the movement of dialectical idealization and for Ricoeur's reductive hermeneutic. (For the sake of convenience, I shall continue to refer to the textual segment or fragment which Ricoeur discusses out of context as Hegel's "text," thereby repeating the synecdochic movement of Ricoeur's argument and leaving in abeyance its problematic implications.)

The status of the "original" metaphor that "begins" the process of thought is radically ambivalent. It seems from any ordinary perspective to be neither metaphoric (for it cannot be contrasted with a prior proper, conceptual, or literal meaning) nor simply proper, conceptual, or literal (for this would confuse the distinction between metaphor and its "opposites"). In an unexamined (repressed?) manner, it seems to place all of language in a "metaphoric" position and to shift the grounds of argument to the recurrent and rather unsettling interplay between various tendencies in the use of language—an interplay that itself raises the question of "originary mimesis" or undecidable interinvolvement of "Being" and "language games." As Derrida remarks in "White Mythology": "The primitive meaning, the original figure which is always sensible and material . . . is not exactly a metaphor. It is a sort of transparent figure, equivalent to a proper meaning. It becomes metaphoric when philosophical discourse puts it into circulation."[7] (This is, of course, precisely the frame of reference that *is* questioned or "solicited" in "White Mythology"—an interrogation to which Derrida returns in "The Retrait of Metaphor.")

Hegel, moreover, refers to the role of usage (*Gewohnheit*) in transforming an improper sensible meaning into a proper spiritual meaning in a manner that at least implies an approximation of the proper to cliché rather than to innovation. Here he seems very close to Nietzsche in a famous passage from "On Truth and Falsity in their Extramoral Sense" (which Derrida quotes and alludes to in "La mythologie blanche," p. 258). In addition, Hegel describes the role of *usure* (*Abnutzung*) in terms of a wearing away or "fall" from "live" or effective metaphors into "proper" expressions. (He does so in arguing that this process is easy to establish in "living" in contrast to "dead" languages and that in the latter only an appeal to etymology—presumably as opposed to usage—can determine whether a seemingly picturesque word has lost its first sensible signification as well as the memory of it.) Thus, in at least one aspect of his extremely complex text, Hegel does seem to support the thesis that Ricoeur falsely ascribes to Derrida.

Not only does Derrida not simply base his "work" in "White Mythology" on Hegel's text. He does not even inquire into its internally contestatory movements (as he does, by contrast, in "Hors livre," "Le puits et la pyramide," and *Glas*). He somewhat atypically contents himself with noting that the "system" identifying the movement of metaphorization with the movement of idealization is nowhere more explicit than in Hegel. And he observes that it is precisely this system that inspires Heidegger's mistrust of the concept of metaphor.[8] In "White Mythology," Hegel's "text" is employed in a relatively restricted way as a significant "example" of a philosophical "problematic," as are—with certain variations—the "texts" of other "figures," including Nietzsche. Derrida's intricate

7. Derrida, "La mythologie blanche," 251. My translation.
8. Ibid., 269.

discussion does not simply conform to this "problematic" or to its opposed options: metaphorization as a linear process of either loss of sensible meaning or gain of spiritual meaning. Derrida is quite explicit on this point:

> It goes without saying that the question of metaphor, as we are repeating it here, far from belonging to this problematic and sharing its presuppositions, should on the contrary delimit them. It is not, however, a question of consolidating in symmetrical fashion the position which Polyphilos [one might almost substitute "Ricoeur," for the character from Anatole France's *Jardin d'Epicure*, whom Derrida discusses toward the beginning of "White Mythology," is also engaged in a "false dialogue"] chooses as his target; it is rather to deconstruct the metaphysical and rhetorical schemes that are at work in his critique, not in order to reject or to discard them, but to reinscribe them in a different way, and above all to begin to identify the historico-problematic terrain on which it has been possible to ask systematically of philosophy the metaphorical credentials of its concepts.[9]

In order to conduct his "critique" in the way he does, Ricoeur must remain blind to the deconstructive impetus of Derrida's essay. And to establish a seemingly pure realm of speculative philosophy, he must also be oblivious to the aporetic relation between concept and metaphor upon which Derrida insists[10]—as well as to the problems and possibilities it poses for the "rethinking" of philosophy.

Ricoeur sees Heidegger's philosophy as an "intermingled and inescapable attempt and temptation. It is an attempt from which we must draw inspiration whenever it manifestly contributes to clarifying speculative thought in accordance with the semantic aim that animated Aristotle's investigation into the multiple meanings of Being; and it is a temptation we must shun when the difference between speculative and poetic threatens once again to disappear" (p. 309). He presents Derrida as radicalizing even further Heideg-

9. Ibid., 256. My translation.
10. Ibid., 272–73.

ger's more dubiously radical tendencies in the direction of "un-bounded deconstruction," the simple collapse of the difference between the poetic and the speculative, the absolute loss of control in the use of language, and eventual submergence in a nihilistic abyss. Ricoeur thus makes short shrift of a number of complex problems: the attempt to discriminate between various or divergent ("good" and "bad"?) tendencies in Heidegger's thought; the relation of Derrida to Heidegger; and the attempt to discern the general cast as well as the implications of Derrida's discourse. It seems evident that these questions must arise in one form or another. The obvious difficulty is that, in addressing them, one is prone—especially within the limits of a review-essay—to fall prey to the same recuperative strategies one might criticize in Ricoeur. Since Ricoeur's general characterizations are both highly questionable and potentially quite influential, it seems important to resist them frontally. I shall, then, attempt briefly to counter them with different characterizations, even at the risk of synoptic reduction and the prolongation of a false dialogue. Here the problem may be not whether one can totally avoid "recuperation"—one cannot—but whether one can offer recuperative interpretations that at least indicate how certain strategic considerations must remain active.

Both Ricoeur and Derrida (in "The Retrait of Metaphor") comment upon a famous statement of Heidegger: "The metaphorical exists only within the [bounds of the] metaphysical." The statement implies neither a blanket indictment of "metaphor" (as Ricoeur himself recognizes) nor simply a criticism of "a manner of casting metaphors as particular philosophical statements" (p. 282)—the latter being Ricoeur's Aristotelian interpretation of the statement. Nor does Heidegger's saying pose the alternative of either conflating philosophy and metaphor or asserting their discontinuity, as Ricoeur thinks. Rather it raises the issue of the interaction between philosophy and metaphor in less reductive and/or dichotomous terms, and it casts doubt upon the alternative as Ricoeur conceives it. One might suggest that the problem "exemplified" in Heidegger's saying is that of how to combine a radical critique of an

137

intrametaphysical "concept" of metaphor, a process of thought that might appear to be highly "metaphorical," and a powerful desire for "presence" having a problematic relation to metaphysics itself. Can the "metaphoric" spring free as other than merely metaphoric and as other than an inducement to leap into an "abyss"?

In his own intricate commentary (which I shall adapt in a scandalously general way), Derrida inquires into Heidegger's notion of the "withdrawal of Being." This notion, which is neither properly literal nor properly metaphoric, has the liminal or threshold status of a "metaphor of metaphor"—a term precariously positioned in the gap between distinctions and functioning so as to inscribe their condition of possibility. The "withdrawal of Being" occurs with the appearance of language and of forms of representation in general. It points to the status of language as a displacement or alterative "doubling" of Being, and it places all language in a "tropical" position with reference to Being. In this sense, nothing in language happens without metaphor. But the withdrawal and concealment of Being with the appearance of language are at the same time the revelation or disclosure of Being in its different determinate forms whose highest-order names are recorded in the history of metaphysics. Thus language on the most "fundamental" or "essential" level conceals while it discloses and vice versa. It is both the "cause" of the withdrawal of Being and the house of Being. And, as Being withdraws—Being is that which has "always already" withdrawn—the attempt to speak it is redressed or redrawn time and again. Metaphysics itself exists within the bounds of the metaphoric, for it cannot fully master its guiding tropes. Yet its basic concepts would suppress or sublate the grounding processes of interaction in which they are engaged. This tense and recurrent interplay between a desire for firm conceptual mastery and a letting-be of language that holds out the hope of "presence" while marking and re-marking its elusiveness is itself a nonlinear story that cannot be altogether confined within the bounds of philosophy.

These considerations of a Heideggerian cast jeopardize Ricoeur's view of reference, and they signal a somewhat different interpretation of metalanguage from Ricoeur's. Ricoeur refers to a non-linguistic referent as if this notion were immediately self-evident. One might object that once there is a referent, language is involved and there is no purely nonlinguistic referent. But this is not to say that the referent then becomes purely linguistic. Rather one has a relational network in which the appearance of language comes with the postulation of a referent that language itself cannot fully possess. Metalanguages are implicated in that relational network even as they attempt to work free of it. Metalanguages are signs of the withdrawal of Being and have, with reference to so-called "first-order" or "natural" languages, a position analogous to that of metaphors of metaphor. In Ricoeur's words, they mark "the reflective capacity [of language] to place itself at a distance and to consider itself, as such and in its entirety, as related to the totality of what is" (p. 304). But this capacity does not simply render speculative discourse possible; it also renders it impossible as a fully successful or definitive achievement in the mastery of language and its relation to Being.

One especially curious and, I think, internally inconsistent argument is important for Ricoeur's over-all position. He accuses both Heidegger and Derrida of having too homogeneous and self-serving a view of "the" metaphysical tradition.

> This inclosure of the previous history of Western thought within the unity of "the" metaphysical seems to me to express a sort of vengefulness—which this thinking [Heidegger's], nevertheless, calls us to renounce—along with a will to power that seems inseparable from it. The unity of "the" metaphysical is an after-the-fact construction of Heideggerian thought, intended to vindicate his own labor of thinking and to justify the renunciation of any kind of thinking that is not a genuine overcoming of metaphysics. [P. 311]

Ricoeur also intimates that it is precisely in this respect that Heidegger is traditional, for all creative philosophers of the past have criticized tradition in similar terms and called energetically, even hyperbolically, for a new beginning in philosophy. Ricoeur's assertions are not altogether wrong, but they do obscure a number of issues. Heidegger and Derrida, in different but related ways, attempt to work out an understanding of the historical process that cannot be decided in terms of simple continuity and discontinuity, similarity and difference. Indeed the beginning point for an attempt to understand the relationship between Heidegger and traditional philosophy or between Derrida and Heidegger would seem to be the process of repetition with variation (or alteration) that they bring to bear in the understanding of historical processes more generally. This process would not amount to an abstract, homogeneous *Geschichtlichkeit*; it would have to be specified in terms of precise modes of recurrence and change including, for example, the role of an active "reinscription" of the process, and a rather sustained "dialogue" with Heidegger, in Derrida's texts. Derrida effects a "translation" of Heidegger, at times with remarkable changes in style and emphasis. What is not marked in Derrida is the more incantatory, even mesmeric—some might say ritualistically "poetic"—side of Heidegger. And the quest for unified "presence" is more insistently scrutinized in a critical way or "thematized" as a problem.

The inconsistency in Ricoeur is that in his own dominant line of argument, he not only lends credence to a notion of "the" metaphysical tradition but does everything in his power to reaffirm it. In Derrida, and in certain ways in Heidegger, the full "closure" of metaphysics emerges as a metaphysical representation of metaphysics. What they oppose to this self-image is a "representation" or reenactment of metaphysics that questions its own *mise-en-scène* by eliciting or soliciting its internally contestatory tendencies, certain of which seem to be dominant (precisely the quest and self-image relating to full "closure") and others of which are submerged and represented (if at all) as *merely* supplementary, marginal, or borderline. The originality of Heidegger and Derrida—which they would be the last to see as absolute—is to stress the marginal in traditional philosophy, rethink the border or threshold, and enter it into a more open "contest" with the dominant or principal. Rather than follow the dominant tradition by stressing the differences *be-*

tween philosophy and poetry, they insistently explore the submerged differences *within* philosophy and poetry that bring the two into an often repressed "internal" exchange or "dialogue" with one another. Heidegger does at times—for example, in his reading of Nietzsche—almost willfully ignore, in the texts of others, the self-questioning exploration of liminality and the "playful" yet deadly serious displacement of "presence" which would seem closest to the forceful "solicitation" of presence itself that becomes most evident in his later texts. (In one sense, Ricoeur's "reading" of Heidegger approximates that of Derrida in "Structure, Sign and Play" or in *Positions*—a "reading" whose emphasis shifts in "The Retrait of Metaphor," perhaps because of Ricoeur's "critique.") Throughout his own texts, Derrida stresses traditional philosophy's own aporetic impasses that are not of a purely "negative" character—the incandescent yet evanescent moments of irrecuperable loss, hyperbolic disorientation, and "undecidability" that both bring the philosophical "machine" to a grinding halt and motivate it to get under way again. And in Derrida perhaps even more than in Heidegger, what is meant by a "genuine overcoming of metaphysics" becomes extremely problematic. But one thing that is blindingly clear is that it cannot be equated with a simple rejection or denial of traditional philosophy and that it involves a critical "reinscription" of the tradition in an attempt to displace its dominant assumptions. The active implication in Derrida is a loss of absolute control over language and an understanding of language as punctuated by losses that are both "pure" (in the sense of not being altogether subject to *Aufhebung*) and "impure" (in the sense of not being autonomized in a negative theology or in a theory of a purely liberated, self-referential system of signifiers).

This rather intricate notion of loss cannot, I think, be identified with an absolute loss of control over language in any carte blanche way. At least one controlling "mechanism" is the recurrent, critical, and self-critical attempt to think through one's relation to traditional philosophy. And, in Derrida's texts themselves, the quest for a lost origin or an absolute ground, with its essential tensions, is "repeated" in a way that in one sense makes it more unforgettable than it hitherto was—an aporetic necessity of the deconstructive variant of "active forgetfulness." (This quest, it should be noted, is not restricted to the books of philosophers, although these may well put forth arguments in their most careful and intricate forms. Those who criticize Derrida for not moving beyond the "realm" of philosophy often forget that, for him, philosophy, despite its desire for closure, is not a realm and that traditional philosophical assumptions may be most uncritically active in those who believe that in turning to social "reality" or even to the "social text," they have transcended those assumptions.) Only on a foundational level is Derrida "acritical" in that he unsettles the basic decisions that lead to pure opposites. But the questioning of pure oppositions does not imply the simple obliteration of all distinctions. In these respects, certain observations in "White Mythology" are apposite.

> This operation of Nietzsche's [the generalization of metaphoricity through the *misc en abyme* of a determinate metaphor] is only possible by risking a continuity between metaphor and concept, as between man and animal, knowledge and instinct. To avoid ending up with an empiricist reduction of knolwedge and a fantastic ideology of truth, we should no doubt have to substitute for the classical opposition (maintained or eliminated) between metaphor and concept, another articulation. This articulation, without bringing in the whole metaphysics of the classical opposition, would also have to account for the specific gaps which epistemology cannot ignore between what it calls metaphorical and scientific effects. Undoubtedly the need for this new articulation is already announced in Nietzsche's discourse. It would provoke a displacement and an entire reinscription of the meaning [*valeurs*] of science and of truth, which is to say, of some other terms as well.[11]

What would seem to be indicated here is the need to make the recognition of aporia eventuate not in an infinite regress—which would, however, always be a possible risk—but in a renewal of

11. Ibid., 313–314.

modes of using language. This would militate against a formalist reduction of "deconstruction" or an understanding of it in terms of an involuted and increasingly conceit-laden process of unveiling aporias in any and every text ever written. The "interminable" problem of textuality would remain; but it would acquire a new insistence by being extended to areas that in the past have often seemed immune to it.

It would be self-deceptive to equate a turn toward the "social text" with turning the page of Derrida or with relegating Plato and Hegel to the "scrap heap" of history. Yet the relation between written texts (in the ordinary sense) and various "lived" texts is an issue of obvious importance, as is the investigation of the role of textuality in social life. In this respect—with the notable exception of educational reform in France—Derrida's publications have thus far been limited to noting what seem, from any "ordinary" perspective, to be general implications. Even in the extremely important area of feminist criticism inspired by Derrida, the political implications of micrological and allegorical readings of texts often remain very allusive. The problem is to draw out those implications—implications attendant upon Derrida's own problematization of any rigid boundary between the political and the seemingly apolitical—and to "apply" them without either forgetting or mechanically remembering what one has learned from Derrida. The result might be the creation of a stronger bond between "deconstruction" and critical theory as well as the ability to transfer more directly to social criticism those often unrecognized carnivalesque tendencies that exist in so lively and subtle a form in Derrida.

Ricoeur is himself concerned with the excessive encroachment of the poetic upon the philosophic in Heidegger and with what he takes to be the dubious radicalization of this process in Derrida. I have tried to raise doubts about Ricoeur's own reading of Derrida. What has become apparent is the urgency of an attempt to decipher the relation of the nature, use, and abuse of Heidegger's thought to political and social issues—including its use and abuse in Heidegger's own hands. Ricoeur does not raise this problem or the others to which I have alluded toward the end of this essay. What I have attempted to argue more generally is that Ricoeur does not inquire into the ways in which Heidegger and Derrida investigate and enact the interaction among tensely related forces on the "levels" of interpretation, text, and discourse. A fortiori, he is unable to ask how their texts broach certain problems. Yet Ricoeur's discussion of semiotics and semantics does bear upon those problems and—*mirabile dictu!*—it is in an appendix that he informs us of his intention to pursue further an inquiry into text and discourse. A question that must, I think, arise in the latter respect is whether the rules, norms, and processes of reflection upon which Ricoeur would like to rely are too weak, exhausted, or dubious to have the binding function he seeks—and whether the more disorienting and at times disoriented "alternatives" he fears (and too readily projects onto those he sees as his adversaries) are in fact the historical complements of his centers of reliance. The related question is how to work and to play out a nexus between more credible and creditable norms on all levels (including language use) and more compelling but limited forms of "transgression"—a "project" that requires a revised "reading" of tradition. In Heidegger and Derrida, an extensive and radical critique of the larger context that includes both Ricoeur's neotraditionalist loyalties and their seeming opposites may harbor necessary complicities with both. But just as it is misleading to see in either Heidegger or Derrida a simple denial of tradition or a fatuous denigration of metaphysical desire, so it is equally misleading to see in them a merely symptomatic aggravation of that which they help to situate and to criticize. By contrast, their intricately related overtures may hold out the possibility of at least posing certain questions in a manner that provides a self-critical perspective on questionable complicities and a chance of coming to terms with them in more effective ways.

[5]

Habermas and the
Grounding of Critical Theory

In this realm one cannot prove anything, but one can point out a
great deal.
                        Heidegger, Preface to *Identity and Difference*

Representations and descriptions are never independent of standards.
And the choice of these standards is based on attitudes that require
critical consideration by means of arguments, because they cannot be
either logically deduced or empirically demonstrated. Fundamental
methodological decisions, for example such basic distinctions as those
between categorial and noncategorial being, between analytic and
synthetic statements, or between descriptive and emotive meaning,
have the singular character of being neither arbitrary nor compelling.
They prove appropriate or inappropriate. For their criterion is the
metalogical necessity of interests that we can neither prescribe nor
represent, but with which we must instead *come to terms*.
                        Habermas, Appendix to *Knowledge and Human Interests*

THE PROBLEM

Jürgen Habermas is perhaps the most important recent exponent
of a critical theory of society and culture in the tradition of the
Frankfurt school. He provides what has often been seen as the
theoretically "strongest" attempt to inquire into the relations of
critical theory to epistemology and philosophical anthropology.
This essay is written from a position sympathetic to Habermas's

critique of positivism and to his more general attempt to establish a bond between knowledge and critical theory. And its purpose is not to offer a general survey of Habermas's impressive achievements. To the extent that any such venture is not premature given Habermas's continued productivity, it has already been undertaken by other commentators.[1] The limited purpose of this essay is rather to inquire critically into the most problematic elements of Habermas's attempt to ground critical theory in a philosophical anthropology having certain epistemological correlates. A central problem in this respect is the nature and status of cognitive interests and their relation to an ideal speech situation.

The existence of a tension in Habermas's thought has been noticed by his more acute commentators.

> There is . . . a deep unresolved conflict in Habermas between the transcendental pole of his thinking which emphasizes the a priori categorical distinctions, and more pragmatic tendencies that emphasize the continuity and overlapping similarities and differences in all forms of rational inquiry. Habermas has been extremely perceptive and forceful in exposing various forms of reductionism, whether they take a physicalist or historicist form. But the alternative he proposes is suspect. It is a fiction—and not a useful methodological one—to suggest that there are categorically different types of inquiry and knowledge. But it is not a fiction—rather, it is the locus of the most

1. For general accounts of Habermas's thought which include some pertinent criticisms, the reader is referred to Richard J. Bernstein, *The Restructuring of Social and Political Theory* (New York, 1976); Martin Jay, "Recent Developments in Critical Theory," in *Berkeley Journal of Sociology* 18 (1973–1974), 27–44; Dick Howard, "A Politics in Search of the Political," in *Theory and Society* 1 (1974), 271–306; and the series of articles appearing in *Philosophy of the Social Sciences* 3 (1973). Rather than summarize or develop the more or less cogent criticisms of Habermas, which may be found elsewhere, I have tried to elaborate their conditions of possibility, especially with reference to the thought of recent French figures (notably Jacques Derrida) who are not accounted for either in critical appraisals of Habermas or in the works of Habermas himself. For a somewhat comparable attempt, appearing after the original publication of the present essay, see Charles C. Lemert, *Sociology and the Twilight of Man* (Carbondale, 1979), 194–225. See also Thomas McCarthy, *The Critical Theory of Jürgen Habermas* (Cambridge, Mass., 1978).

important controversies about the nature and limits of human knowledge as it pertains to social and political inquiry—to see how the battle of competing technical, practical and emancipatory cognitive interests continues to rage.[2]

This quotation points to the important problem of the logical status of analytic distinctions in their relation to social and political inquiry. With reference to this problem, the conflict in Habermas can be seen, I think, in terms of a tendency to think simultaneously in two directions without being able to articulate theoretical notions which account for this tendency. On the one hand, Habermas thinks in terms of categorical distinctions that are not rendered problematic on the level of theory. Indeed, categorial or analytic distinctions are promoted to positions of dominance as conceptual dichotomies that are given quasi-transcendental grounding and justification. The concepts involved come to define separate and distinct areas of life or disciplinary activity whose relations can be seen only in one-directional ways. (For example, a technical interest defines empirical-analytic sciences, and a communicative or "practical" interest defines hermeneutic or interpretative sciences.) The result is that Habermas is in no position to recognize and confront aspects of life or thought that are either obscured by, or in secret complicity with, the dominant tendencies he singles out for attention. And his own thought threatens to be influenced if not reappropriated by the very tendencies he deplores in society and its dominant ideology. Thus Habermas will explicitly criticize the growing dominance in modern society of technological ideology and related structures of power or surveillance. But, in attempting to account for this tendency, he will employ a frame of reference which on one level accepts a notion of technology "as such" in dichotomous opposition to a sphere of practice, of symbolic interaction, and of institutional structure. The only relationship he can theoretically articulate between technology and its opposite number is either one of an ab-

2. Bernstein, *Restructuring of Social and Political Theory*, 223.

sence of institutional control with the dominance of technology or one of control of technology from above by institutions. This formulation of the problem functions to obscure the role of institutions and values in modern life and makes Habermas's own framework indebted to a "logic" of domination that he explicitly criticizes. More generally, the very form of rationalism which Habermas attempts to ground in an unproblematic way itself relies upon modes of analysis and dialectics geared to mastery and control of the object under investigation. What Habermas often refuses to entertain is the possibility that rationalism need not be abandoned if it is rendered problematic in certain explicit ways, and that his own thought, in failing to make this "problematizing" process explicit, itself makes rationalism problematic in unexamined and, therefore, even more defenseless ways.

On the other hand, there are countertendencies in Habermas which place in question and contest all of the tendencies specified in the preceding paragraph. These countertendencies concern what is left out or repressed in the above-mentioned theoretical framework. Often these countertendencies are implicit, and the internal contestation in a text by Habermas is largely inadvertent. These "blind spots" in the thought of Habermas do not invalidate his insights into modern problems, but they do raise often unexplored questions about their theoretical basis. In certain of Habermas's more recent works, however, his self-questioning becomes more explicit. But Habermas never seems fully able to work out notions that account theoretically for his forms of self-contestation as well as for "overlapping similarities and differences in all forms of rational inquiry." His immanent self-critique thus seems to be relatively unsituated in terms of theory.

This essay attempts to explore the internal contestation in certain texts of Habermas. One might begin by repeating what has often been noticed: German thought and French thought at times reveal a deplorable insularity. Habermas became relatively well known in France in the wake of the events of 1968. Yet there has not appeared in France a more or less systematic attempt to come to terms with Habermas's version of critical theory in the light of recent currents in French thought. Habermas himself, given his desire to integrate elements of traditional philosophy, analytic philosophy, Marxism, psychoanalysis, systems theory, and the like, has often been accused of eclecticism. But Habermas has not extended his overwhelmingly ambitious interests to include recent French thought. Perhaps the most direct comparison on the level of philosophical assumptions and forms of internal self-contestation could be made (strange as it may at first seem) with Jean-Paul Sartre. I shall in the course of this essay forgo an extended comparison of this sort. Instead I shall appeal to recent French thinkers—especially to Jacques Derrida—who may provide some critical perspective on the "problematics" of both Habermas and Sartre. I shall explicitly and implicitly "confront" Habermas with selected elements of Derrida's thought in the hope that approaches to the text developed in their most forceful form by Derrida can help to account for theoretically unsituated tensions in Habermas.

DERRIDA

Even a slight acquaintance with Derrida's texts immediately reveals why this "confrontation," especially insofar as it attempts to avoid the bind of an *obscurium per obscurius*, requires a "translation" of Derrida's thought that involves significant distortion. Derrida defies translation (in all senses of the term) partly because in his texts the problem of style cannot be detached from the movement of thought itself. In one of the best discussions of his work, he has been fittingly termed *"un philosophe 'unheimlich'"*—an uncanny philosopher;[3] the juxtaposition of French and German is itself significant.

3. Sarah Kofman, *"Un philosophe* 'unheimlich'" in *Ecarts*, ed. Lucette Finas (Paris, 1973), 109–204. For a stimulating introduction in English to the writings of Derrida see Gayatri Chakravorty Spivak's preface to her translation of *Of Grammatology* (Baltimore, 1976), ix–lxxxvii. For an excellent discussion of the relations between Habermas and Hans-Georg Gadamer, see Martin Jay, "Should Intellectual History Take a Linguistic Turn? Reflections on the Habermas-Gadamer Debate," in Dominick LaCapra and Steven L. Kaplan, eds., *Modern European Intellectual History: Reappraisals and New Perspectives* (Ithaca, 1982), 86–110. In France Jean-François Lyotard has recently put forth certain criticisms of Habermas. See his *La condition post-moderne* (Paris, 1979).

It is entirely problematic to attempt to apply his "ideas." (One may at best speak of emulating, at the risk of parodying, his textual strategies.) The result in this essay at times will be a crude Esperanto developed to facilitate a reading of Habermas in terms which provide some insight into his theoretical tensions. The loss in relation to an understanding of Derrida may be compensated for by a gain in creating a preliminary "dialogical" context with which to inquire into Habermas's elaboration of the grounds of critical theory. It is of course a dialogical context which is the goal of Habermas's own endeavors and the leitmotif of his conception of immanent critique. It may not be entirely fatuous to suggest that the countertendencies in Habermas, which become more explicit in the course of his self-criticism, move in the direction of the primary tendencies of Derrida. In Derrida, the theoretically unaccounted-for "remainders" or anomalies in Habermas's dominant framework become an object of sustained inquiry.

In one sense, it would be appropriate to defer a discussion of Derrida to the section of this essay in which I discuss *Knowledge and Human Interests*. Derrida could then be discussed in the more general context of thinkers whom Habermas omits from his study of the decline of critical epistemology and the rise to dominance of positivism in modern thought. These omitted thinkers furnish a critique of positivism which mitigates Habermas's thesis concerning the dominance of positivism and which places in question his own attempt to ground critical theory. (In this context, one would have to stress the importance of a figure about whom Habermas is extremely wary and with whom Derrida is in continual critical dialogue: Heidegger.) Derrida's thought begins with an elaborate "deconstructive" reading of the philosophical tradition—what Habermas would term "immanent critique." In Derrida, however, the fundamental concepts of the tradition are subjected to a more radical and sustained critique than that to be found in Habermas, and they include the very categorial opposites upon which Habermas would ground critical theory. Derrida's critique is not half-hearted. But it does include the realization that the present "epoch" may be defined in terms of an undecidable tension between an attachment to nearly exhausted traditional forms and an attempt to overcome the tradition of Western metaphysics. Moreover, any "overcoming" or displacement cannot take the reassuring form of a secure dialectical synthesis. The dialectical model with its progressivist impetus is too simple to account for the uncanniness of any movement beyond the forms of thought (including analysis) that are essential for dialectics itself. This movement is open and dangerous in a sense which dialectical sublation can only conceal. But traditional notions, if they are not overcome in a dialectical fashion, are not simply dispensed with either. They are resituated or reinscribed in a different way, for they are interpreted (as they were in Nietzsche) as recurrent functions of a differing "play" which repeats them in continually displaced forms. An extreme and somewhat mechanical schematization of the strategy of the fine art of "deconstruction" might present it in the following terms: a continual reference to the texts of the tradition with their terms, analytic oppositions, and dialectical sublations; a "double inscription" of that tradition which simultaneously uses its terms (the only ones we have) and critically sounds them out, thereby placing them *sous rature* (under erasure); an investigation of how the problematic language of the tradition contains submerged elements that place in question its own dominant motifs and desires; an initial "moment" of reversal of hierarchical oppositions which violently gives priority to the "oppressed" member of the hierarchy; displacement of the repeated terms of the tradition in which the "revolutionary" member of the opposition is denied sovereignty in its turn and disclosed as "always already" inside its opposite; the attempt to make room for new possibilities not governed by the oppositions of the "old regime" yet actively forgetting (therefore, in a certain sense, remembering) them; a constructive affirmation of the disseminating play of "supplementarity" which gives rise to an active interpretation of the text and of the world.

To crystallize the notions evoked in the preceding paragraph and to make them applicable to the problem discussed in this essay, I shall single out Derrida's conception of supplementarity. To privilege this "concept" (and even to call it a concept) is to distort Derrida's thought, for supplementarity cannot be conceptually defined, and its function is to question the status of any central or dominant concept by revealing what it leaves out or "represses." (Hence in Derrida's writings, one finds an intentional proliferation of terms that serve as substitutions for "supplementarity" and prevent it from attaining the status of a "master" concept or a key that opens all locks.) To oversimplify, one might say that supplementarity reveals why analytic distinctions necessarily overlap in "reality" and why it is misleading to take them as dichotomous categories. Analytic or polar opposites always leave a problematic difference or remainder for which they do not fully account. In more positive terms, supplementarity refers to the undecidable interplay of excess and lack between the same and the other. One (e.g., one of a pair of opposites) is the same as the other but as differed or deferred. (The French term *différer* brings out this dual meaning. To mark it, Derrida coins the term différance, in which the anomalous "a" is apparent only in writing and not in speech.) The supplement is added to its "other" or "opposite" in a way that both exceeds it and simultaneously indicates a lack that needs to be supplemented. This entire notion of relationships departs from a "logic" of identity and difference which analysis formulates and dialectics attempts to "overcome" through sublation.

Reason (*ratio*) itself might be seen as an attempt to ration and limit the play of supplementarity. Analysis provides clear and distinct ideas which define boundaries and confine ambiguity or overlap to marginal, borderline cases. Insofar as analysis defines polar opposites, it constructs ideal types or heuristic fictions. When these polar opposites or dichotomies are erected into transcendental conditions of knowledge and projected onto the world as defining separate disciplinary or life activities, one has the operation of a logic of surveillance and control if not domination. Supplementarity does not obliterate distinctions, and it cannot be identified with confusion. But it does situate dichotomies as functions of a "logic" of identity and difference which serves to control the object. Dialectics, in a sense, compensates for the excesses of analysis. (If analysis may be seen on the analogue of a ritual of purification, dialectics recalls an agonistic or even a sacrificial ritual process.) Dialectics takes analytically defined opposites and relates them in processes of becoming. As negative dialectics, it tracks forms of alienation and attempts to explode them. In so-called "identity-theory," dialectical sublation may seek a reconciliation of opposites in a totality or harmonious whole which amounts to an end-game fiction. It thereby tries to make supplements entirely complementary by eliminating all problematic residues and remainders. By contrast, the notion of an open or unfinished dialectic converges in certain ways with a "logic" of supplementarity. It attempts to think through dichotomies and double binds and to prefigure a more creative interplay among aspects of the world. But it recognizes that structures of domination may always be regenerated, and thus insists upon the role of recurrent critique. To account for the very openness of a dialectical structure, a notion of supplementarity is necessary.

The foregoing preliminary discussion of the thought of Derrida (whose explicit formulations I have partially gone beyond in the preceding paragraph) will, I hope, take more concrete form in its use in a reading of Habermas. One of Derrida's reiterated points is that a seemingly subordinate supplement to a text—an introduction, appendix, postscript, footnote, or such—may bring in considerations that are left implicit or repressed in the "principal" body of the work. In discussing Habermas, I shall be primarily concerned with three such textual supplements: "Technology and Science as 'Ideology'" of 1968; the appendix to *Knowledge and Human Interests* of 1968 (first given as Habermas's inaugural address at Frankfurt in June 1965); and the introduction to *Theory and Practice* added to the other texts comprising this volume in 1971.4 These texts dis-

---

4. All references will be to the following editions: "Technology and Science as 'Ideology,'" in *Toward a Rational Society*, tr. Jeremy J. Shapiro (Boston, 1970); *Knowledge and Human Interests*, tr. Jeremy J. Shapiro (Boston, 1971); *Theory and Practice*, tr. John Viertel (Boston, 1973). A fourth "supplementary" text might be

close interesting similarities and differences. Both the appendix to *Knowledge and Human Interests* and the introduction to *Theory and Practice* explicitly have the status of supplements. And the difficulties inherent in the principal texts, as in other of Habermas's writings, come to a head in the supplements. "Technology and Science as 'Ideology'" may be seen as a supplement only in a more metaphoric sense: in certain ways it reads like a companion piece to a larger study in comparative social history and theory. It offers *en raccourci* a theory of historical change and of modern society. All three texts begin their arguments in a similarly oblique or indirect fashion as a critique of a critique. And, in different but related ways, all three texts broach the problem of supplementarity, which they fail to thematize as a primary problem of the text. "Technology and Science as 'Ideology'" is the "blindest" of the three texts in this regard, for it requires the notion of supplementarity in a manner which at one point seems to undercut its argument. Perhaps the introduction to *Theory and Practice* is most self-conscious about its own status, for it is at times most explicit about the problematic aspects of the ideas it explores. Also, certain of its formulations point in the direction of a "logic" of supplementarity to situate the problem of cognitive interests in relation to an ideal speech situation.

"TECHNOLOGY AND SCIENCE AS 'IDEOLOGY'"

Let us begin with "Technology and Science as 'Ideology'" in an attempt to trace the play of blindness and insight in these three

---

added to the three texts upon which I am focusing: "A Postscript to *Knowledge and Human Interests*," in *Philosophy of the Social Sciences* 3 (1973), 157–185. For reasons of economy, I shall forgo an analysis of this text, which in most relevant respects may be inferred from the present essay. For three brief pieces on Heidegger that Habermas wrote in the 1950s, see the latter's *Philosophisch-politische Profile* (Frankfurt am Main, 1971), 67–92. Habermas is especially trenchant concerning Heidegger's political views and the way his philosophy was in complicity with them. For an extremely restricted and harshly negative appraisal of "poststructuralism," see Habermas's recent "Modernity versus Postmodernity," *New German Critique* 22 (1981), 3–14.

somewhat peculiar texts of Habermas. "Technology and Science as 'Ideology'" begins circuitously as a critique of Marcuse's critique of Weber. Marcuse argued that Weber's concept of formal rationality concealed an unacknowledged political function. For Marcuse, technology is always a historical-social project; and the very form of technical reason masks a substantive political and historical project of domination. If this is so, Habermas argues, social emancipation requires a complementary revolutionary transformation of science and technology themselves. He further observes that in several passages Marcuse "is tempted to pursue this idea of a New Science in connection with the promise, familiar in Jewish and Protestant mysticism, of the 'resurrection of fallen nature.'" This theme, for Habermas, is present in Marx's *Paris Manuscripts*, central in Bloch's philosophy, and even noticeable "in reflected forms" in the "more secret hopes" of Walter Benjamin, Max Horkheimer, and Theodor W. Adorno.[5]

Habermas objects that modern science can be interpreted as a historically unique project only if at least one alternative project is thinkable. And an alternative New Science would have to include the definition of a New Technology. "This is a sobering consideration because technology, if based at all on a project, can only be traced to a 'project' of the human species *as a whole*, and not to one that could be historically surpassed."[6]

By contrast, Habermas argues, like Arnold Gehlen, that there is an immanent connection between the technology known to us and the structure of purposive-rational action in human beings that constitutes the structure of work. As long as "the structure of human nature" does not change, we cannot conceive of a qualitatively different technology. To justify the idea that modern technology is the logical culmination of the structure of purposive-rational activity or "work" in human beings, Habermas offers what amounts to a just-so story. "In any case technological development lends itself to being interpreted as though the human species had taken the

5. Habermas, "Technology and Science as 'Ideology,'" 85–86.
6. Ibid., 87.

elementary components of the behavioral system of purposive-rational action, which is primarily rooted in the human organism, and projected them one after another onto the plane of technical instruments, thereby unburdening itself of the corresponding functions."[7] This "as if" reconstruction of the history of technology amalgamates two features of the technical cognitive interest which Habermas will try to come to terms with in other texts: the natural history of the human species and a quasi-transcendental status.

On the level of possible social and cultural change, Habermas asserts that "Marcuse has in mind an alternative *attitude* to nature, but it does not admit the idea of a New Technology."[8] This different attitude would involve treating nature not as the object of technical control but as the opposing partner in a possible interaction. In other words, it would require a movement from the framework of technical rationality or work (the "technical cognitive interest") to that of symbolic interaction (the "practical cognitive interest").

The introductory argument of Habermas is circular insofar as it depends for its cogency upon the validity of Habermas's own framework. In this essay, Habermas promotes an analytic distinction between technology and its sociohistorical context into a dichotomy which serves to introduce his own dichotomous typology of work and interaction. The typology is in turn a methodological correlate of a philosophical anthropology relying upon a notion of quasi-transcendental human interests. The typology of work and interaction depends for its truth-value upon the distinction between a technical and a practical cognitive interest. The emancipatory cognitive interest and the ideal speech situation are at most the implicit horizon of "Technology and Science as "Ideology.'" In the diagram that codifies the typology of work and interaction, the last box on the side of symbolic interaction and the institutional framework relates to the emancipatory interest and the "extension of communication free of domination." Habermas notes that he neglects to

7. Ibid.
8. Ibid., 87–88.

discuss the emancipatory interest in this essay but that "it refers to the very problem for whose solution [he is] introducing the distinction between work and interaction."[9]

The difficulty in Habermas's essay comes when he promotes a possibly fruitful analytic distinction between work and interaction into a typology of dichotomous polar opposites which are directly applied in an analysis of history and society. The absence of a theoretically thematized "interaction" between work and interaction that recognizes the way they overlap and supplement one another blinds Habermas to certain relationships and even leads him paradoxically to undercut his own argument. For it is manifest that Habermas explicitly intends to attack the separation between work and interaction in modern society. Yet he fails to provide a "deconstructive" critique of the categories of work and interaction and the logic of domination in which they function. Instead, he implicitly replicates the separation between them in his own categorial opposition and can conceive of their relationship not in terms of a

---

9. Ibid., 92–93. In the preceding argument, Habermas seems to accuse Marcuse of identity-theory both in the latter's analysis of existing phenomena (modern technology is a political project) and in his utopian hope for the future (a radically new science and technology totally reconciling man and nature are possible). Despite his partial leanings toward this crucial element of the Hegelian legacy, Marcuse also takes a somewhat different approach, for example in *Eros and Civilization*. Here Marcuse does not obliterate distinctions, but he does insist upon the overlapping interplay of analytic opposites which could be made more creative in a transformed society. The significant issue is not attitude in the psychological sense but institutional change that might bring about significantly and even qualitatively different relations among science, technology, and their "life-world." In philosophical terms, the emphasis is upon the possible relation of technology to a receptive openness to nature in contrast to the domination "from above" of nature by man in technology. Habermas mentions Sartre with reference to the notion of technology as a world-historical project. But, given Marcuse's own intellectual biography, a more pertinent reference would be to Heidegger. More generally, earlier critical theorists placed great emphasis upon the disastrous effects of man's attempt to dominate nature, at times even going to the extreme of making this a focal point in critical reaction to Marx. The role of critical theory was to "remember" the possibility of a more reciprocal relation to nature, and a primary goal of social action was to attempt to provide its institutional bases. This side of critical theory threatens to be radically de-emphasized in Habermas's approach.

more creative interaction but only in terms of hierarchy or domination of the one by the other.

A first major problem with the typological dichotomy between work and interaction appears when values related to symbolic interaction are surreptitiously introduced into the category of work. In Habermas's words, "purposive-rational action realizes goals under given conditions. But while instrumental action organizes means that are appropriate or inappropriate according to criteria of effective control of reality, strategic action depends only on the correct evaluation of possible alternative choices, which results from calculation supplemented by values and maxims."[10]

The key phrase is "calculation supplemented by values and maxims." Into the category of work or purposive-rationality (the technical cognitive interest) is imported the supplement of values and maxims. This "supplement" is not accounted for theoretically by Habermas. Not only does it show the limitations of his typological dichotomy, it also conceals very important problems about the nature of critical theory. Technical rationality or work does imply goals, values, and maxims which from a purely technical viewpoint are accepted as simple data or "givens." The question is whether, from the viewpoint of critical theory, they should ever be accepted merely as "givens." Their very acceptance as unproblematic data and their categorial legitimation in a concept of technology "as such" may itself be indicative of an impairment of a critical approach to problems.[11]

---

10. Habermas, "Technology and Science as 'Ideology,'" 92.

11. This tendency also appears in Habermas's uncritical acceptance of systems theory in its own terms as an adequate approach for the investigation of certain problems. For example, in *Legitimation Crisis* (Boston, 1975), Habermas writes: "From the life-world perspective, we thematize the normative structures (values and institutions) of a society. We analyze events and states from the point of view of their dependency on functions of social integration (in Parsons' vocabulary, integration and pattern maintenance), while the non-normative components of the system serve as limiting conditions. From the system perspective, we thematize a society's steering mechanisms and the extension of the scope of contingency. We analyze events from the point of view of their dependency on functions of system integration (in Parsons' vocabulary, adaptation and goal-attainment), while the

Habermas applies his typology of work and interaction in a general theory of history which includes an attempt to designate the specificity of modern society. For Habermas, all history is at some significant level the story of the breakdown of a limiting institutional framework with its legitimated forms of symbolic interaction by a breakthrough of purposive-rational activity or work in the technical sense. Traditional societies limit change by controlling "work" from above through institutional checks and symbolic forms. The specificity of modern society as well as the criterion of modernization is the unlimited expansion of purposive-rational or technical subsystems. These subsystems undermine the legitimating efficacy of shared cultural norms and convert them into random, merely subjective or private values.

Habermas sees important changes in the modern period itself. His interpretation of these changes leads him to take his distance from Marx. Habermas rehearses the familiar idea that the nineteenth century was the period of classical liberalism. The economy was separated from the state. The state was reduced to night-watchman functions. And there was a legitimation of social action on the economic level through an ideology of just exchange in the market. (This model probably applies in a relatively adequate way only to England during a brief period of time in the nineteenth century.)

Habermas argues that in the late nineteenth and twentieth centuries there have been important changes related to the formation of technical rationality as an ideology that excludes appeal to the practical and critical interests of man. In "Technology and Science as 'Ideology,'" Habermas focuses on three changes: (1) the state intervenes in the domestic economy, but it does so with the technical, negative intention of eliminating dysfunctions; (2) there is a growing interdependence of science and technology which has turned them

---

goal values serve as data" (pp. 4–5). The elided question is, of course, whether the critical theorist is justified in accepting the language and framework of an approach in this manner and whether, for him, "goal values" can ever be taken simply as "data."

into the leading productive forces generating surplus value in modern society; (3) there emerges a distinctive kind of ideology—technology-as-ideology. (In a later work, *Legitimation Crisis*, Habermas continues this analysis and argues that contradictions within the economic order have been displaced to the political and cultural orders and that crises of legitimation center around the spheres of politics and administration.)

For Habermas, the modern conjuncture has given birth to a technocratic ideology which passes itself off as the end of ideology. For him, technology-as-ideology is specific. It does end ideology in the older sense, but it represents a more mystifying, one-dimensional ideology in its own right. Older ideology, in Marx's sense for example, was a form of distorted communication in which values, needs, and utopian hopes relating to an image of the good life, were systematically twisted to justify or legitimate dominant interests in society. In relation to older ideologies, one strategy of critique was to extricate the values from the ideology and to show how social reality failed to live up to them. In technology-as-ideology, according to Habermas, there is no longer an appeal to values or norms at all. An aseptically anti-utopian technocratic consciousness brackets out values and norms as unscientific and subjective. Technology-as-ideology addresses itself only to questions of adaptation or the elimination of dysfunctions within the established system. And it poses as the one right way to approach problems in public life. Habermas recognizes that technocratic consciousness and all that it implies are far from prevailing in a total way in modern life. But the dominance of technology-as-ideology poses for him what one might perhaps term a real, clear, and present danger.

Habermas's analysis of modernization, however forceful and cogent it may at times be, nonetheless replicates the difficulties of his typology of work and interaction. His dichotomous typology when applied to historical situations or developments prevents him from distinguishing on a theoretical level among different kinds of institutions and forms of symbolic interaction which may divide the same society or, within limits, characterize different societies. One key question not fully elucidated is whether "modernization" involved the development of different kinds of institutions and forms of symbolic interaction from those prevalent in so-called traditional societies. Habermas's own typology allows for only one conception of institutions and symbolic interaction—a basically "traditional" one where institutions limit purposive-rational activity. Habermas will make mention of institutions that further the unlimited expansion of technology and the economy. ("Capitalism is the first mode of production in world history to institutionalize self-sustaining economic growth.")[12] However, he has no place in his typology to account for institutions that do not limit and may even further limitless expansion, for limitless expansion is categorically on the side of work and the technical cognitive interest. Moreover, Habermas is in no position theoretically to explicate the often concealed relations between technology as ideology and older forms of ideology. Yet what appears as technology-as-ideology is often an implicit, unexamined adaptation to the limitless ends built into modern institutions and ways of life. The concept of drift brings this out, for drift implies movement in the direction of established aims or established aimlessness. And in the values of profit-maximization, growth, achievement, and national security, one has important elements of ideology in the older sense. In fact, one might argue that an important question for critical theory is whether, as shared ends and values become less open to critical scrutiny, the adherence to them becomes more docile and blind if not fanatical. The point is not that these observations are new or that Habermas would disagree with them but that his frame of reference renders him unable to elucidate them in relation to this own concerns in this essay.

Habermas asserts that his typology of work and interaction reveals

---

12. Habermas, "Technology and Science as 'Ideology,'" 96. It is also important to note that traditional societies (if this catch-phrase still has meaning) do not simply limit technical rationality "from above." This view may be an illusion generated by typologies such as that of Habermas. Traditional societies provide different ways of relating to the interplay of excess and limits within institutions and symbolic forms. Institutions, like sacrifice, ritual sacrilege, and role inversion, function to limit historical change by playing with and playing out excess.

what is common to the older typologies of polar opposites in classical sociology (*Gemeinschaft/Gesellschaft*, mechanical/organic solidarity, traditional/bureaucratic authority, and so forth). It also attempts to show how these typologies referred to the transition from traditional to modern society. But there are significant ways in which Habermas's typology and the analysis of history based upon it fail to do full justice to the insights of earlier social thinkers such as Marx, Durkheim, and Weber. I would suggest that on the most general level of a theory of history, earlier social thinkers were concerned about the breakthrough of various kinds of excess in history. Newer developments supplemented traditional forms in ways that exceeded their limits and proved them lacking. Durkheim, for example, was initially interested in the "supplementary" role of demography and, if anything, always de-emphasized the importance of technology. Weber stressed the impact of breakthroughs on the ideological level itself. Marx inquired into the breakdown of established relations of production with the breakthrough of newer forces of production. (I shall defer a discussion of why Marx's distinction between forces and relations of production may be more fruitful than Habermas's typology of work and interaction in that Marx's distinction allows for overlap—relations may become forces of production—and is an aspect of a more critical frame of reference.)

On the question of the specificity of modern society, thinkers like Marx, Durkheim, and Weber—whatever their highly significant differences in other respects—were more pointed than Habermas concerning the theoretical and practical importance of what seemed distinctive in modern institutions and symbolic forms. They all had some theoretical awareness of the way modern institutions furthered endless expansion by subordinating purposive-rational means to limitless ends. In the economy, profit-maximization built limitlessness into a commodity system. More generally, classical sociologists, in contradistinction to Habermas, tended to focus theory on the specificity of modern institutions and symbolic forms. These institutions, which furthered technical rationality on the level of means, built limitlessness on the level of ends into the modern institutional and symbolic framework in ways that made the established order into an established disorder. The privatization of ends and the constitution of values as subjective were aspects of a broader development which the notions of privacy and subjectivity sometimes functioned to conceal, for private ends and subjective values (for example, which commodity to buy) in the most institutionally strategic instances fell within the general range prescribed by institutions or shared values—but in ways which obstructed solidarity and aggravated limitless expansion. These crucial points for critical theory threaten to be submerged by Habermas's use of his typology.

Basing oneself on the work of classical sociologists, one might hazard the generalization that all history is in some sense the story of often violently and uncontrolledly disruptive supplementarity in the breakdown of limiting institutions and symbolic forms by the breakthrough of varieties of excess which those institutions or forms cannot adequately "house." Modern society seems specific in that—in secret complicity with privatization and the furtherance of technical rationality—it institutionalizes limitlessness and thereby builds "history" into its open-ended structures and forms. What Habermas's typology threatens to blind one to is the specific nature of modern institutions and the social relations within them.

KNOWLEDGE AND HUMAN INTERESTS

Habermas's often familiar criticisms of Marx in "Technology and Science as 'Ideology,'" which stress the pertinence for social theory of socioeconomic changes since Marx's time, are frequently convincing. But, in spite of Habermas's belief, their cogency does not, I think, derive from the typology of work and interaction as Habermas formulates it. To gain further perspective both on this typology and on Habermas's response to Marx, I shall turn to *Knowledge and Human Interests*. In this book, Habermas attempts simultaneously to trace and to provide a critical perspective upon the emergence and eventual dominance of positivism and the decline of a critical epistemology since the time of Kant. The interpretative strategy of Habermas is to argue that however much a given thinker approached critical theory in Habermas's sense in a more or less important dimension of that thinker's work, the thinker nonetheless became ensnared in a positivistic self-misunderstanding. In certain cases, for example, those of Marx and Freud, Habermas's argument is in good part cogent. In other cases the result is highly dubious, as with Nietzsche, whom Habermas analyzes according to a method of selective quotation in which the text, much less the position of the quotation in the text, is often not cited—and on this basis one could use Nietzsche to prove anything. But the systematic defect of the work is the omission of certain thinkers, such as Heidegger, and of dimensions of the thought of thinkers Habermas does discuss that would evidence a critique of positivism in terms that place in question Habermas's own conception of critical theory. Habermas in this work tries to center his analysis upon a self-reflecting epistemological subject and to ground critical theory in a philosophical anthropology based upon quasi-transcendental cognitive interests and an ideal speech situation involving a consensus theory of truth. Dimensions of the thought of others that radically place in question these attempts and that might provide a notion of supplementarity with which to situate Habermas's own self-contestations are not investigated. Recent French thinkers like Lacan and Derrida have elaborated a notion of the text that highlights the similarities between figures like Freud and Nietzsche. They have argued that both Freud and Nietzsche decenter the subject and situate it in a broader and problematic field of concern. The subject or ego is besieged and allured by drives, desires, and phantasms. Also, the texts of Freud himself are seen as heterogeneous objects of a "Freud on Freud" strategy, which explores the way in which the writings of the master were the scene of Freudian conflicts, repressions, significant silences, uncanny detours, and the like. The unconscious in Freud is not viewed as a text present beneath the text of consciousness, ready to be reappropriated by an in-depth interpretation. It is what is radically other, different, left over, and supplementary vis-à-vis the text of consciousness; it leaves traces and deferred effects that can never be fixated in an original source open to the ego in quest of identity. The unconscious is a paradoxical name for the way one differs from oneself. In what is perhaps the best analysis in his book, Habermas also stresses the problem of textuality in Freud, but the text he sees is very different from that revealed in the French Freud. The text in Habermas is the object of hermeneutic interpretation rather than the symptomatic scene where desire, meaning, and dream have their strangely disconcerting rendezvous. And Freud is presented as a theorist of systematic distortion which the psychoanalytic process disentangles and raises to the level of public communication in the interest of enlightenment and ego-identity. Repression is seen by Habermas in a one-sided linguistic manner in terms of excommunicated interpretations, and the unconscious is interpreted as a text beneath the text of consciousness decoded through analysis and made public through intersubjective communication. The result is a de-eroticized Freud of ego-psychology in whom one does not see the irritating and fascinating role of the body and desire or the uncanny threat of radical alterity. The insight of Freud into the human being as the scandalous and even incestuous site of intercourse between nature and culture—a being who is always other to himself—is elided in the purifying reflection of Habermas. [13]

13. The comments in this paragraph rely primarily on the works of Derrida. An extended comparison of Derrida and Jacques Lacan is beyond the scope of this essay. For some pertinent texts on Freud, see *French Freud, Structural Studies in Psychoanalysis*, ed. Jeffrey Mehlman, *Yale French Studies* 48 (1973). This includes a translation of Derrida's "Freud and the Scene of Writing" and Lacan's "Seminar on 'The Purloined Letter.'" See also Jacques Lacan, *Écrits* (Paris, 1966). It is interesting to note the textual position of Habermas's discussion of Nietzsche in *Knowledge and Human Interest*. It is situated as an oddly dangling supplement to the section on Freud, which ends the principal body of the text and comes immediately before the appendix. This somewhat "castrated" position is symptomatic of Habermas's treatment of Nietzsche, in which Habermas often seems at a loss to know what to do with Nietzsche. His analysis, in which Nietzsche emerges as a paradoxical "virtuoso of reflection that denies itself," tends to obscure the nature of Nietzsche's critique of both positivism and the metaphysical tradition—a critique that recent French thinkers have emphasized. For a critical discussion of Habermas's use of Freud, see Russell Keat, *The Politics of Social Theory* (Chicago, 1981).

For Habermas, psychoanalysis and Marxism provide complementary contributions toward a paradigm for a critical theory of society. Marx is viewed as a thinker who had the basis of a critical theory in Habermas's sense. But Marx increasingly became caught up in a "positivistic self-misunderstanding," which led him to conceive of his own thought in the guise of a purely empirical-analytic science of the laws of motion of society. Habermas is, I think, correct in finding in Marx a positivistic current of thought which becomes more pronounced in Engels and the theorists of the Second International. His assertion that one can discover in Marx the rudiments of a critical theory in Habermas's sense also has limited validity. What Habermas fails to confront is the existence of another dimension in Marx through which Marx provides a basis in supplementarity for his understanding of dialectics and critique.

MARX

To illustrate this point in a necessarily schematic manner, I will refer to three widely separated "moments" in the thought of Marx—an analysis in the *Paris Manuscripts*, the beginning of *The German Ideology*, and the discussion of commodity fetishism in *Capital*. In the *Manuscripts*, Marx's application of a Feuerbachian transformative criticism to Hegel seems to generate an argument in which the Hegelian lexicon is changed but the grammar remains the same. Man or the proletariat becomes the surrogate for Hegel's Absolute Spirit, and the mysterious powers of *Geist* working its way through history toward a utopian reconciliation with itself become displaced onto man. But there is a current in the *Paris Manuscripts* themselves which contests this version of anthropogenesis tied to a certain conception of species-being or essence in a philosophical anthropology. The human being is seen as both "an active natural being" and "a *suffering*, conditioned, and limited creature." Indeed, bodily forces and drives are among the forces of production which man does not simply generate. Human essence itself is described in terms of existence as free, self-conscious activity. But the analysis is not centered on a meaning-generative human subjectivity. Essence from which one is alienated is not seen as a presence but rather as what is missing when one is controlled by alien "others" beyond one's control. Essence in this sense is not a present in the past (a golden age) or a present in the future (a utopia of total reconciliation of opposites) but a virtual object projected by the play of "supplementary" forces in the human being. [14]

In the *Theses*, Feuerbach, who was employed in the critique of Hegel in the *Manuscripts*, is himself criticized. And in *The German Ideology*, what was marginal in the *Manuscripts* becomes explicit as a *force majeure*. We are told that there was a mystification in the questions asked by the German ideologists and not simply in the answers given. Here the grammar or structure of Hegel's thought is being placed in question. Marx asserts that his premises in contrast to those of the German ideologists are real, concrete individuals. The force of this gesture must be recognized. In any logical sense, an individual cannot be a premise of an argument. Marx's move is to disrupt logocentrism and any attempt to center thought on a logical or epistemological starting point, origin, or end. The way in which his argument develops is highly significant. Twice Marx resorts to repetition in explicating the historical process, not in terms of temporal stages but in terms of interacting aspects. First the production of means to satisfy needs is called the first historical act, and then a second "moment," the production of new needs, is called the first historical act. Similarly, the third moment in the role of social relations, especially in the family, is repeated in the fourth

14. For the analysis of the human being in the *Paris Manuscripts* or the *Economic and Philosophic Manuscripts*, see especially the passage on p. 325 of *Writings of the Young Marx on Philosophy and Society*, ed. and tr. Loyd D. Easton and Kurt H. Guddat (Garden City, N.Y., 1967). The interpretation of Marx in terms of a theory of anthropogenesis is developed by Shlomo Avineri, *The Social and Political Thought of Karl Marx* (Cambridge, England, 1968). It is criticized in *For Marx* (New York, 1970) by Louis Althusser, who—whatever may be the distortions in his extreme insistence upon the discontinuity or "epistemological break" in Marx's thought—does bring out the radical nature of Marx's critique of Hegel.

moment. Here the idea that Marx stresses work and reduces interaction to the level of work in a technical sense is misleading. Rather, Marx stresses that the production of life, both of one's own in labor and of fresh life in procreation, appears as a "double relationship": a natural and a social relationship. He adds that a certain mode of production is always combined with a certain mode of cooperation which is itself a productive force.

In *The German Ideology*, Marx offers a succinct account of labor as life activity or praxis in relating man and nature in history. Concrete individuals are "always already" situated in history, and any beginning "moment" of the historical process has always already begun and been repeated. There is no simple origin or center of history. Thus the human being or the subject is not the center of the analysis. As Marx was to put it in *The Eighteenth Brumaire of Louis Bonaparte*, men make history but not in conditions chosen by themselves. Nor are these conditions presented exclusively either in terms of contingent facticity or counter-finality. These conditions are always sedimented with meaning and nonmeaning. As Marx notes as early as in the *Economic and Philosophic Manuscripts*, labor in some sense always objectifies the human being but it does not necessarily alienate him. Perhaps one might say that objectification is compatible with a supplementary or an open dialectical relationship between the same or the self and the other. Alienation intervenes at the point of a fatal split or dissociation which subordinates the one to the control from above or the domination of the other. In *The German Ideology*, it is interesting that language appears in the text before the discussion of ideology as distortion. Language is said to appear first in the form of sounds or agitated layers of air. The ideological use of language is an aspect of alienation. And alienated language as something other than the expression of existing practice is attendant upon the split between material and intellectual labor. At this point, pure theory arises as theology, philosophy, ethics, and so on. This split is, of course, also related to the appearance of classes and class conflict. At times in *The German Ideology*, one is close to a utopia of distortion-free language and communication as well as to a vision of the total transcendence of the division of labor. But the entire "logic" of the argument with its repetitions and its insistence upon the interaction of all its aspects moves in the direction of a notion of supplementarity which is always threatened and is at times frustrated by alienation and a "logic" instituting domination.

In *Capital* the discussion of commodity fetishism does seem to appear as a return of the repressed notion of alienation which retrospectively situates the preceding analysis not as a purely positivistic account of the laws of motion of the modern economy but as a characterization of alienated relations in a commodity system. The treatment of commodity fetishism presents a delineation of the form of alienation in a commodity system. Labor split in two in a commodity system is on one level reduced to instrumental, purposively rational work in the production of commodities. On another level, meaning stripped from labor as life praxis is mystified and idealized in symbolic forms, as, for example, in the commodity as fetish. The danger in Habermas's dichotomy between work and interaction is the formalization and codification of the constituents of what Marx discussed as alienated labor. Marx in his notion of labor as life praxis does not reduce symbolic interaction to work in a technical sense. Rather, he sees symbolic interaction and work as supplementary aspects of life praxis which relate man and nature. It is Habermas's dichotomous typology of work and interaction which threatens to present alienated labor in a theoretically unsituated way.[15]

15. See the partially convergent analyses of Göran Therborn, "Frankfort Marxism: A Critique" in *New Left Review* 63 (1970), 65–96, and "Habermas: A New Eclectic" in *New Left Review* 67 (1971), 69–83. For the more general problems evoked in my discussion of Marx, see Jacques Rancière, *Lire le "Capital"* (Paris, 1973), chap. 3, and Jean-Joseph Goux, *Economie et symbolique* (Paris, 1973). For the relevant sections of *The German Ideology* (New York, 1947), see 1–43. The pertinent section of *Capital* is "The Fetishism of Commodities and the Secret Thereof," vol. 1, pt. 1, chap. 1, sec. 4. It must be emphasized that my largely suggestive indications of "supplementarity" in Marx are in no sense intended as inclusive and exhaustive accounts of his thought even on the level of drastic schematization. Nor do they deny the presence of "humanistic" and "positivistic" elements in Marx, which, moreover, cannot be neatly distributed in terms of

APPENDIX TO *KNOWLEDGE AND HUMAN INTERESTS*

The appendix to *Knowledge and Human Interests* places the typology of work and interaction in the context of three primary cognitive interests that provide the epistemological framework for Habermas's conception of critical theory. The technical cognitive interest guides work in the empirical-analytic sciences, which are geared to the control of objectified processes. The practical cognitive interest provides a fundamentally different framework for the historical-hermeneutic sciences, which are not constituted in the interest of technical control. In these sciences, the access to facts is provided by the understanding of meaning, not causal explanation. The verification of lawlike hypotheses has its counterpart in the interpretation of texts. And the "practical" in this specific sense is related to processes of communication or symbolic interaction within a normative order. The emancipatory cognitive interest embodied in critical social science encompasses both the technical and the practical, but it also goes beyond them. Critical social science attempts "to determine when theoretical statements grasp invariant regularities of social action as such and when they express ideologically frozen relations of dependence that can in principle be transformed." Critical social science effects this determination by invoking a methodological framework that guides inquiry into "the validity of the meaning of critical propositions" through the concept of self-reflection. "The latter releases the subject from dependence on hypostatized powers." Thus self-reflection is determined by an emancipatory cognitive interest that recognizes "the connection of its knowledge with the human interest in autonomy and responsibility (*Mündigkeit*)."[16] Indeed, this connection is implicit in language,

Marx's early and later texts. (For a forceful analysis of positivistic elements in *The German Ideology*, written from a perspective close to that of Habermas, see Albrecht Wellmer, *Critical Theory of Society* [New York, 1971], chap. 2.) The more general problem in the interpretation of Marx might initially be seen in terms of the precise relations in his texts among humanism, positivism, dialectics, supplementarity, and critical theory in Habermas's sense.

16. Habermas, *Knowledge and Human Interests*, 308–315.

which has as its *telos* an ideal speech situation implying a consensus theory of truth. Habermas's ideal speech situation might be seen as an analogue of Kant's kingdom of ends, of Hegel's vision of a mutual recognition of self and other, and of Peirce's notion of an ideal community of inquirers.

> The human interest in autonomy and responsibility is not mere fancy, for it can be apprehended a priori. What raises us out of nature is the only thing whose nature we can know: *language*. Through its structure autonomy and responsibility are posited for us. Our first sentence expresses unequivocally the intention of universal and unconstrained consensus. Taken together, autonomy and responsibility constitute the only Idea that we possess a priori in the sense of the philosophical tradition. Perhaps that is why the language of German Idealism, according to which "reason" contains both will and consciousness as its elements, is not quite obsolete. Reason also means the will to reason. In self-reflection knowledge for the sake of knowledge attains congruence with the interest in autonomy and responsibility. The emancipatory cognitive interest aims at the pursuit of reflection as such. [17]

Yet in the appendix as well as in the principal text at times, the status of cognitive interests, their relation to one another, and their relation to the ideal speech situation, which appears as the epitome of the emancipatory interest, are problematic. And Habermas is divided between a dominant self-understanding in terms of clear and distinct cognitive interests with an a priori or "quasi-transcendental" status and a submerged intimation of interacting, supplementary relationships which place his own categorial determinations in question. It is undecided whether he is continuing the tradition of German Idealism or displacing it.

The appendix itself takes the indirect form of a critique of Husserl's critique of positivism—Husserl, who himself tried to respond to modern crisis by renovating and purifying the philosophical tradi-

17. Ibid., 314.

tion which reached its culmination in German Idealism. Habermas contrasts Husserl's concept of traditional theory with Horkheimer's idea of critical theory, but he does not explicate the relations between Horkheimer and himself. In certain ways, he seems closer to Husserl. He apparently agrees with Husserl's centering of philosophy on the intentional consciousness and the meaning-generating subject, although he socializes the subject in an intersubjective community and does not identify it with the transcendental ego. Further, he extends Husserl's idea of the relation of science to a life-world in an assertion of the partial continuity of positivism and traditional philosophy. Positivistic science shares for Habermas two fundamental assumptions with traditional philosophy. It affirms "a theoretical attitude that frees those who take it from dogmatic association with the natural interests of life and their irritating influence." And it retains the "intention of describing the universe theoretically, just as it is." Habermas agrees with Husserl's critique of the "objectivist illusion" in the second assumption shared by positivism and traditional philosophy, which is "the basic ontological assumption of a structure of the world independent of the knower." But he criticizes Husserl for following positivism in detaching pure theory from practice and for paradoxically believing that theory without the bond between knowledge and interest might be relevant for life. It is important to note that Habermas is not rejecting Husserl's notion of theory as a purifying reflection that brackets the world of empirical reality. This point will become manifest in the introduction to *Theory and Practice*. He is in effect criticizing Husserl for failing to recognize that pure theory itself conceals a practical interest—precisely, an interest in purification. In Greece, pure theory hid within itself the interest in domesticating the gods and demons and in purifying the subject from the "irritating influence" of the "drives and affects that enmesh man in the empirical interests of his inconstant and contingent activity." Pure theory was in a sense a ritual of purification which held out to the votary-theorist the promise of a soul not only in harmony with the cosmos but in a state of "ecstatic purification" from empirical contingency and the harassment of the body. [18]

One might object to Habermas that the philosophical tradition itself harbors a submerged tendency that places in question the dominant tendencies that he specifies. This submerged tendency—which again points to a "logic" of supplementarity—is not absent from the texts of Plato with their connection of philosophy, wonder, and divine frenzy and their "undecidable" concepts. [19] The gods, demons, and erotic forces of the body were not altogether silenced or conjured away in Greek philosophy. And the submerged tendencies of the philosophical tradition are the very ones raised to prominence in the texts of figures—notably Nietzsche and Heidegger—whom Habermas either tends to ignore or interprets in a way which silences these tendencies. But the interesting textual point is that the notion of cognitive interest in Habermas seems to gesture undecidably in two different directions: the direction of pure traditional theory, which attempts to transcend the irritating and contingent empirical realm, and the direction of critical theory, which is engaged or committed in that very empirical realm through self-reflection, the critique of ideological mystification, and the process of secular enlightenment.

The undecidable status that applies to the notion of cognitive

18. One may observe that Habermas at times seems to draw an analytic or categorial opposition between science and metascience in relation to positivism. But Habermas is not altogether consistent on this point. He does not simply argue that empirical-analytic science per se is all right and that only dominant forms of modern metascience fall prey to the illusory ideology of positivistic self-understanding. He also argues that science—whatever may be the ideology of the scientist—is intrinsically open to technological application in the control of the object under investigation. In this latter sense, science itself in some sense has an inherent relation to "positivism." (On these points, contrast, for example, pp. 308–309 and pp. 315–316 of *Knowledge and Human Interests.*) The problem in relating "science" and "metascience" is similar to that in relating other categorial oppositions in Habermas's thought, and it is included in the more general problem of relating a "language" to a "metalanguage."

19. On the problem of "undecidables" in Plato, see Jacques Derrida, "La pharmacie de Platon," in *La dissémination* (Paris, 1972), 69–199.

interest in general is repeated on the level of the specified trinity of cognitive interests. The emancipatory interest seems at times to be beyond the technical and the practical and at other times it seems to refer to the interacting, supplementary relation between them. And the cognitive interests are explicated through a terminology and a network of distinctions whose pertinence they seem to render dubious. They refer undecidably to a natural history of the human species, and they are a priori or quasi-transcendental. They distinguish the contingent or the empirical from the a priori or the transcendental, and they overlap these categorical distinctions. They seem both to renovate the dominant philosophical tradition and to contest or displace that tradition, for they seem to place in radical question the truth-value of the very categories they require to define themselves. Habermas himself is on the very threshold of thinking through the "logic" of supplementarity in a passage such as the following, which presents "cognitive interest" as a scandalously contaminated, "incestuous" term transgressing the limits of ordinary distinctions: "'Cognitive interest' is therefore a peculiar category, which conforms as little to the distinction between empirical and transcendental or factual and symbolic determinations as to that between motivation and cognition. For knowledge is neither a mere instrument of an organism's adaptation to a changing environment nor the act of a pure rational being removed from the context of life in contemplation."[20]

INTRODUCTION TO *THEORY AND PRACTICE*

The way in which the notion of cognitive interest approaches the question of what Nietzsche would term "dangerous knowledge" is never fully brought to light by Habermas. But certain of his internal contestations are repeated in an interesting way and to a certain extent clarified in the introduction to *Theory and Practice*. This introduction takes the form of a critique of Habermas's critics as

20. Habermas, *Knowledge and Human Interests*, 197. See also p. 312.

well as a self-criticism. Habermas notes certain changes in his thought in a somewhat deceptive manner, for in this introduction he is not so much changing his mind as making explicit what was at times implicit in his earlier works.

> The formula "quasi-transcendental" is a product of an embarrassment which points to more problems than it solves. On the one hand, I have relinquished the position of transcendental logic in the strict sense in my attempt to clarify the systematic relations between the logic of scientific investigation and the logic of the contexts in which the corresponding sciences are constituted and applied. I do not assume the synthetic achievements of an intelligible ego nor in general a productive subjectivity. But I do presuppose, as does Peirce, the real interrelationship of communicating (and cooperating) investigators, where each of these subsystems is part of the surrounding social systems, which in turn are the result of the sociocultural evolution of the human race.[21]

The introduction is subtitled "Some Difficulties in the Attempt to Link Theory and Practice." Habermas intends to elucidate these difficulties by clarifying the status of cognitive interests as well as the extent to which a psychoanalytic model is valid as a paradigm for a critical theory of society. I shall not follow him in all the detailed elaborations and applications of these distinctions,[22] but shall conclude with a discussion of the relation of these distinctions to the problem of tension in Habermas's attempt to ground critical theory. Somewhat embarrassingly, the distinctions which are intended on an analytic level as means of resolving tensions in Habermas's thought take the form of two overlapping sets of distinctions whose relations are not altogether clarified: the distinction among discourse, enlightenment, and tactics or strategy, and the distinction

---

21. Habermas, *Theory and Practice*, 14.

22. A good description of these applications, as well as an extensive account of the often conflicting criticisms to which Habermas tries to respond, may be found in Fred R. Dallmayr, "Critical Theory Criticized: Habermas's *Knowledge and Human Interests* and Its Aftermath," in *Philosophy of the Social Sciences* 2 (1972), 211–229.

between reconstruction and reflection. Again, these distinctions are not entirely new in Habermas. To a certain extent, they may be seen as a way of making explicit what was already at work in his texts. And at times they seem to displace rather than to overcome the tensions and the equivocations of his earlier texts. The crucial problem which is repeated is that of the extent to which the distinctions should be seen as categorial dichotomies and the extent to which they should be taken as supplements.

Discourse recalls the notion of pure theory that provides an "ecstatic purification" from empirical contingency and the constraints of action in the real world. Here discourse is presented as an ideal means of testing the factually raised claims to validity based upon a naive consensus in ordinary experience and action. Indeed, Habermas explicitly relates discourse to Husserl's *epochè* or phenomenological reduction, which, through a purifying reflection, brackets the thesis concerning the empirical reality of objects of consciousness and enables an "intuition" of essences or eidetic forms.

> Discourse . . . requires the virtualization of constraints on action. This is intended to render inoperative all motives except solely that of a cooperative readiness to arrive at understanding, and further requires that questions of validity be separated from those of genesis. Discourse thereby renders possible the virtualization of claims to validity; this consists in our announcing with respect to the objects of communicative action (things and events, persons and utterances) a reservation concerning their existence and conceiving of facts as well as of norms from the viewpoint of *possible* existence. To speak as Husserl does, in discourse we bracket the general thesis.[23]

This purifying thought-experiment is necessary as a ground for hypotheses and counterfactuals. Habermas stresses the importance of the institutionalization of contexts for discourse free from the immediate pressure of empirical reality. And he relates such institutionalization to the birth of philosophy in Greece. Discourse in this

23. Habermas, *Theory and Practice*, 18–19.

sense has a special relationship to the emancipatory interest, which is beyond the two "lower" interests, and it is essential for a consensus theory of truth based upon an ideal speech situation.

> Solely the structure of this peculiarly unreal form of communication guarantees the possibility of attaining a consensus discursively, which can gain recognition as rational. Because truth (in the most broadly conceived traditional sense of rationality) is distinguished from mere certainty by its claim to be absolute, discourse is the condition of the unconditioned. With the aid of a consensus theory of truth, which would have to justify, in the face of competing theories of truth, why a criterion of truth independent of discourse cannot be meaningfully postulated, the structure of discourse would have to be clarified with respect to the unavoidable reciprocal anticipation and presupposition of an ideal situation of discourse (*Sprechsituation*).[24]

Discourse in this sense moves in the direction of traditional pure theory, and its relation to action in the real world can only be indirect. Habermas asserts that in his earlier notion of reflection, he did not sufficiently distinguish between reconstruction and reflection in the sense of critical recollection. But certainly this distinction was implicit in the opposition between "theoretical statements [which] grasp invariant regularities of social action as such" and statements expressing "ideologically frozen relations of dependence that can in principle be transformed" through critical reflection and social action. Reconstruction originates within discourse and is, in a sense, the discourse of discourse: it provides the conditions of possibility of discourse. Rational reconstructions deal with anonymous rule-systems, such as those in logic and linguistics, which "do not encompass subjectivity" and have "no practical consequences." "By learning logic or linguistics I acquire theoretical knowledge, but in general I do not thereby change my previous practice of reasoning or speaking."[25] By contrast, critical reflection which works through

24. Ibid., 19.
25. Ibid., 23.

distorted forms of communication, such as social ideology or psychological rationalization, leads to insight relevant for change in life, for what was previously unconscious or hidden is made conscious in a manner rich in practical consequences. It is in this latter sense that psychoanalysis retains qualified validity as a model for critical theory.

Habermas reacts strongly against the tendency to reduce or collapse the levels of discourse and reconstruction, or even the level of critical reflection in processes of enlightenment, to the level of strategy and tactics in the conduct of political struggle. He sees the danger of a domination of political organization and tactics over theory in Lenin and Lukács. And he argues convincingly that there can be no direct derivation of political action from theory. For "no theory and no enlightenment can relieve us of the risks of taking a partisan position and of the unintended consequences involved in this."[26] Habermas is, as always, forceful in criticizing reductionism and in arguing for a relative autonomy of levels of thought and action. This leads him to see the limits of attempts at dialectical reconciliation or synthesis. He notes as "Adorno's central insight" the role of negative dialectics in tracking and exploding structures of domination by critically "reconstruct[ing] that which has been repressed from the historical traces of repressed dialogues." But he asserts that in negative dialectics, "our problem is merely deferred. For the structure of distorted communication is not ultimate; it has its basis in the logic of undistorted language communication."[27] And he rejects the idea of a dialectical sublation of the distinctions and differences his own analysis has taken pains to elaborate.[28]

The problem, however, is whether, in rejecting reductionism and dialectical synthesis, Habermas goes to the extreme of analytical dissociation which is itself constitutive of a logic of domination. Habermas does not directly see how his own analytic distinctions,

26. Ibid., 36.
27. Ibid., 16–17.
28. Ibid., 20–21.

which are useful within limits, may be rendered problematic, especially when they are taken as categorical definitions of realms of thought or action. The notion of "a special, a pure knowledge; in logic, mathematics, epistemology, and linguistics" which as the object of discursive reconstruction "remains untouched by the technical as well as the practical interest"[29] is not above suspicion. For, as Habermas himself recognized in *Knowledge and Human Interests*, an interest is concealed in this notion. And this notion depends for its cogency upon an extreme logic of identity and difference based upon a law of noncontradiction. It is this formal logic which a "logic" of supplementarity places in question by relating it to a repression or oblivion of originary ambiguity and overlap. When Habermas asserts that the areas of "pure knowledge" he specifies form the "core of the philosophic disciplines," he may be correct with reference to analytic philosophy but not with reference to figures such as Nietzsche, Heidegger, and Derrida.

On one level, the ideal speech situation and a consensus theory of truth, which are intimately connected to the notions of discourse and rational reconstruction, constitute an extreme utopian vision of communication free of distortion. But this dimension of Habermas's thought is not free of internal contestation. In one sense, the ideal speech situation is a paradoxical dialogical context insofar as communicants in it would, without the play of enabling as well as disabling distortions, have little to say to one another beyond the rules of logic and linguistics. What Habermas fails to emphasize is that a dialogical context requires "distortion" to permit communication short of the limiting ideal (or fiction) of perfect mutual understanding. The critical question is the nature of the distortion, for one can distinguish between playfully creative ambiguity (including humor, irony, and parody) and destructive equivocation—although in any real context the two will interfere with one another. The strategic issue for social and textual praxis is to prevent the latter from dominating or repressing the former. In this respect, the focus

29. Ibid., 24.

upon an ideal speech situation in the elaboration of a critical theory of society may function as a diversion from the attempt to conceive of and implement concrete projects in real situations. Habermas indicates that "in advanced capitalism changing the structure of the general system of education [*Bildungssystem*] might possibly be more important for the organization of enlightenment than the ineffectual training of cadres or the building of impotent parties."[30] Also his general political position is one of "radical reformism," which brings to mind the "revolutionary reformism" of André Gorz, the French associate and friend of Sartre. But Habermas is much less incisive in discussing the specific nature of the political organization of enlightenment than he is on more formal levels of theory. And, more clearly, his emphasis upon discourse, reconstruction, and an ideal speech situation in the theory of language and society does divert him from an inquiry into literary and poetic language, which for certain thinkers (including the recent Sartre in the impressive "Plea for Intellectuals") is a crucial concern of critical thought. It is curious that Habermas will invoke Wittgenstein in defense of the idea that an ideal speech situation and a consensus theory of truth constitute the *telos* of language.[31] And it is noteworthy that in explicating the relations among discourse, enlightenment, and political strategy or tactics, the implicit model in Habermas (as in Peirce) is closer to that of research design in the sciences than to that of textual interpretation.[32] If anything, Wittgenstein resisted the notion of an ideal language or the attempt to model the understanding of ordinary language on rules of discourse drawn from the natural sciences and, at least in his later thought, insisted that "ambiguity" in ordinary language was not always a defect but a requirement of certain uses of language. In this respect, there is an element of continuity between ordinary and literary language, which raises doubts about Habermas's use of ordinary language as a basis for a projective ideal speech situation. To oversimplify, one

30. Ibid., 31–32.
31. Ibid., 17.
32. Ibid., 32ff.

might say that literary language often bares or highlights concealed ambiguities of ordinary language, critically explores their disabling features, and renders more precise their enabling qualities. From the perspective of ordinary and literary language, the ideal speech situation might in one sense appear to be a technocratic fantasy.

Habermas's conception of the ideal speech situation is, however, far from clear. There are aspects of his thought about it which question the pertinence of conceptions of it in terms of a substantive dialogical context or a projected "present" reality. While it is a center for Habermas's theory of language, it is not a concrete, fixed center or a projected end-game fiction on the model of traditional utopias or Hegel's Absolute Knowledge. In a highly significant sense, it is a formal or functional center which is continually displaced, for Habermas will stress the importance of an open *process* of inquiry having certain formal conditions of possibility and certain institutional underpinnings. He does not refer to substantive conclusions or contents of thought and experience. And, in the introduction to *Theory and Practice,* the ideal speech situation (somewhat like Marx's notion of essence in the *Paris Manuscripts*) is explicitly presented in terms of virtuality, unreality, and ideality. One may perhaps raise a question that Habermas does not explicitly raise: whether the ideal speech situation is a formal fiction or functional center for an intersubjective theory of language generated by the play of supplementarity (e.g., between the technical and practical interests in human beings) which is required insofar as thought retains its orientation in terms of the dominant philosophical tradition and its conception of truth. The ultimate appeal in defending a notion like the ideal speech situation may be to piety, for—to misappropriate a quote from Habermas—a lodestar of this sort may at least function "to provide immunity against the more dangerous bewitchments of misguided reflection."[33] One point of this essay

---

33. Habermas, *Knowledge and Human Interests,* 315. Here a comparison with Vico in his conclusion to *The New Science* (Ithaca, 1948) might not be out of place: "To sum up, from all that we have set forth in this work, it is to be finally concluded that this Science carries inseparably with it the study of piety, and that if one be not pious he cannot really be wise" (p. 383).

has been to suggest, with reference to the more risky and disorienting but not, I think, altogether misguided thought of recent French figures, that if there is a need for forms of purifying reflection—and certainly for limits—there is also a need to reflect critically about their relation to problems such as that of supplementarity.

A CONCLUDING ASIDE

The more parochial problem indirectly addressed in this essay has been that of the nature and direction of intellectual history. The shortcomings of certain well-established tendencies have become increasingly evident. Internalist formalism ignores context in the history of ideas. Externalist or contextual reportage ignores the "logic" of ideas and often results in a relatively mindless form of intellectual history relying on conventional paradigms to tack between ideas and events in a seemingly unified narrative. And psychobiographical models, if they do not lead to reductionism, hover between the internal and external approaches and attempt to provide criteria of selection to decide upon the appropriateness of one or the other method. In any event, they share the problems of unself-questioning "dialectical" syntheses in general. One might suggest that, by contrast, newer currents attempt to displace these options as inclusive and exhaustive definitions of the field. But, with greater or lesser degrees of self-understanding, newer currents in intellectual history are divided between approaches to the problem of textuality and intertextuality, on the one hand, and the project of constituting the field as a branch of critical theory, on the other. Derrida is a powerful hidden persuader in favor of the former tendency, as Habermas is a more manifest proponent of the latter option. I think that these two tendencies can supplement one another in interesting and creative ways. But two obstacles to further insight have been the relative ignorance or mutual avoidance of these two tendencies vis-à-vis one another and the largely unexplored "problematics" of Habermas's grounding of critical theory. This essay has attempted to address simultaneously both of these issues by applying approaches to the text developed by Derrida to the question of Habermas's grounding of critical theory. To the extent that the attempt made here has been successful, it has cleared the ground a little for a more extensive "dialogue" between two critical tendencies with important implications for intellectual history and, more generally, for the philosophy and methodology of the "human sciences." Here a crucial issue is how to articulate ways in which a decisive critique of political, social, and economic institutions may be related to a "critique" of foundational philosophy whose critical decisions divide the world into dichotomous opposites. [34]

34. This essay, of course, focuses on Habermas's works up until 1975. It does not seem to me, however, that works published after this date have addressed the issues raised here. In his recent publications, such as *Communication and the Evolution of Society*, tr. Thomas McCarthy (Boston, 1979), Habermas elaborately details the program for a reconstruction of the conditions of communication ("universal pragmatics") and specifies his theory of the evolution of the human species. In addition, he still makes the commendable effort to integrate a semiotic conception of society with a critical theory that adapts historical materialism to an analysis of contemporary social conditions. He continues, however, to downplay or to ignore "supplementary" and carnivalesque dimensions of language use as they bear upon his model of an ideal speech situation or context for mutual understanding. And the implications of his thought for political action or social reconstruction remain extremely abstract. Indeed his growing emphasis upon the "rational reconstruction" of the conditions of communication and the formation of "ego identity" takes Habermas in a markedly formalistic direction wherein the proliferation of categories and distinctions approaches neoscholastic extremes. But to put forth these observations is in no sense to deny the difficulty and importance of the problems Habermas poses—especially the problem of rationally grounding a normative concept of legitimacy.

[6]

Sartre and the Question of Biography

If I relegate an impossible Salvation to the prop room, what remains?
A whole man, composed of all men and as good as all of them and
no better than any.

Sartre, *Les mots*

It is no fanatic that speaks here.

Nietzsche, *Ecce Homo*

Few writers of note have lives as fascinating or worthy of extended
commentary as are their writings. Sartre is among the exceptional
few. At times he seemed to live the gripping, heroic narrative whose
possibility his writings denied. Indeed his ideal-typical and quasi-
mythological status on the contemporary scene is due in part to the
fusion in his popular image of Sartre the writer and Sartre the man.
My own attempt to disentangle and to interpret the strands that
make up this image will be oriented in a certain direction. In the
conventional approach to biography, one tries to develop a narrative
of the "ordinary" life of a figure in which his or her writings (or
other published verbal performances) serve as supporting evidence
of a documentary sort. By contrast, what I would like to investigate
is the relation between Sartre's "ordinary" life and his writings in
some larger and more problematic context of bio-graphy or textuality. This orientation implies that the writings (or, more gener-

ally, the published verbal performances) will not be used to fill in gaps in our knowledge of Sartre's "ordinary" life. Nor will a conception of the life, itself derived from other documents or, in a more circular fashion, from his own writings, be used as a key to interpret those writings. Rather the very context of interpretation will be one formed by a notion of the interaction between the life and the writings, and the problem for investigation will be the nature of that interaction. Since a full-scale treatment of this problem, to the extent that it is feasible at all, escapes the limits of an essay, I shall restrict myself to raising a number of questions that any extensive treatment would have to take into account. I shall, moreover, choose as a leitmotif the conception of freedom in Sartre's life and writings, especially with respect to the issue of marginality and commitment. And, in keeping with Sartre's own later emphases, I shall focus upon political and social considerations.

The notion of biography as designating the space in which there is an interaction between lived and written texts (or "ordinary" life and writings) implies that written texts are themselves important events in a life, especially in the life of someone who wrote so much and with such great existential investment. *Les mots* (*The Words*), in subtly communicating this message, may perhaps be compared to Nietzsche's *Ecce Homo*, for both texts render dubious a simple identification as well as a simple dichotomy between the discursive events that are written texts and "real-life" events that are always related to discourse. And the two texts further intimate that in comparing lived with written events, we are not merely comparing raw data with discursive or narrative representation—although this assumption may in one sense be a necessary heuristic fiction; we are also comparing signifying practices which pose the problem of mutual translatability and transformation. Sartre broaches this problem in a self-critical, earnest jest when he tells us that he committed "the mad blunder, in a grim century, of taking life for an epic."[1]

1. Jean-Paul Sartre, *Les mots* (Paris, 1964), 96. Unless otherwise indicated, all translations in this essay are my own.

But the more general form the problem takes is that of relating theory and practice—or the role of the marginal intellectual possessed of (or by) critical distance and the role of the committed political "man of action" (or, in the later Sartre, the "friend of the people"). And the open question is the extent to which a text may be equated with pure, abstract theory and the extent to which it is itself a use of language that is never simply a means to a political end but itself already part of that end.

In *Question de méthode*, or *Search for a Method*, Sartre himself stresses the complex, nonreductive nature of the relationship between life and "works."[2] But in Sartre this emphasis is bound up with the notion of a totalizing intentionality as essential to dialectical practice and to the "progressive-regressive" method that tracks it, for one of Sartre's crucial postulates is that life is informed by a totalizing intentionality that is experienced and comprehended without being conceptually known—what he in his earlier thought referred to as the prereflective, original choice to be in-itself-for-itself and what in his later thought is transmuted into the more expansive notion of *le vécu* (lived experience). In addition, in Sartre's own existential biographies, a second factor often deflects inquiry along paths I do not wish to follow. This is the tendency to center interpretation on the life (as ordinarily understood) and to read the writings as symptomatic indexes of the life process—a tendency that at times brings Sartre's interpretations alongside more conventional approaches to biography, including that of orthodox Freudians.

My own guiding assumption is somewhat different from the one often uppermost in the Sartrean hermeneutic; it is that there is, in both written and lived texts, a contestatory interaction between unifying and counteracting forces. The forces that counteract unification cannot, moreover, be reduced to counterfinalities or unintended consequences of a dominant, totalizing, intentional praxis, for the challenge they pose resists this form of containment or

2. See Jean-Paul Sartre, *Search for a Method*, tr. Hazel E. Barnes (New York, 1963), 142.

"recuperation." Indeed they both offset the unifying process and help to set it off. This interaction between unifying (or, at the limit, totalizing) forces and offsetting, decentering or disseminating ones is often active in the very relation between Sartre's writings and his "ordinary" life as well as in each of them insofar as they may be considered separately. In his writings, this interaction, while always powerful, leads an uneven existence, and it is often subordinated to the notion of totalization, which is the explicit center of Sartre's theoretical attention. The interaction emerges most challengingly in certain of his "literary" works (notably *La nausée* and *Les mots*) and in the way in which "literary" currents confront "philosophical" theses in a treatise such as *L'être et le néant* (*Being and Nothingness*). It also surfaces in some of his interviews. It is, I think, more thoroughly contained but not entirely suppressed in *La critique de la raison dialectique* (*The Critique of Dialectical Reason*)— for good or ill, depending upon one's understanding of philosophy—and it has a moot function in his existential biographies, especially *L'idiot de la famille* (*The Family Idiot*).

One must note that I am referring to an interaction between unifying and decentering forces and not to the submergence of life and thought in sheer flux. This interaction permits a highly significant role for the intentional praxis of the human agent. But it contests a totalizing "dialectical" comprehension of the object of Sartre's study as well as of Sartre's own written and lived texts. Thus it places in radical question the pattern that has guided various emulatory interpretations of Sartre, both sympathetic and hostile, notably those that position his life and writings in an oriented or directed movement from an early apolitical, aesthetic individualism through crises or conversion experiences (such as World War II) to an existential Marxism and, after 1968, to a *gauchiste*, or New Left, politics of liberation. This pattern accounts for only one stratum of Sartre's written and lived texts, and it represses or suppresses some of their most significant movements.

Allow me to add a final consideration of a prefatory nature. On the conception of "interaction" I am suggesting, one's very understanding of history shifts from Sartre's dominant idea of a totalizing,

globally progressive process of human liberation subverted by counterfinalities to a view that allows for a notion of repetition with
variation. In this manner, the historical process itself may be understood in terms of an agonistic interaction between unifying and
decentering forces that recur with more or less significant changes
in them and their relationship over time. History in its movement
thus comes to resemble the process occurring in the use of language
itself, and what happens in written and lived texts becomes emblematic of historical processes at large. I vary a theme in observing
that this notion of history does not eliminate the significance of
human beings as subjects and agents, but it does situate it in a rather
different way from Sartre. For it renders problematic an attempt to
ground history totally on the praxis of free, conscious subjects or
agents as the ultimate source of meaning and value in the world. It
detects arrogance and a variant of species-imperialism even in the
generous and militant humanism that Sartre defends, for it leads
one to argue that the activity of the human being be countered by
receptivity in relation to natural and cultural processes—receptivity
that cannot be reduced to passivity or escape from action. Nor can
repetition be seen exclusively as counterfinality and regression, although it certainly includes this possibility, which, as Sartre insists,
has been all too evident in recorded history. Repetition also includes more regenerative modes that keep action located in traditions and institutional contexts that may be transgressed and transformed—at times radically—without being totally transcended.
And it helps to situate the very notion of a "realm of freedom" as a
problematic utopia that contests existing reality to open up risky
historical possibilities.

I begin with these all-too-general considerations to give some
sense of the approach I shall take to Sartre—an approach that will
be modified as I discuss his written and lived texts in more specific
terms.[3] And I have intimated that the model of agonistic interaction

3. I try to develop certain perspectives employed in this essay in A *Preface to
Sartre* (Ithaca, 1978) and *"Madame Bovary" on Trial* (Ithaca, 1982). See also my
"Interpreting Sartre," *Telos* 44 (1980), 145–150.

I have briefly sketched is related to Sartre's own explicit theoretical emphases not as their abstract negation but as the more submerged but at times powerful dimension that internally questions what often seem to be Sartre's dominant views. Its submerged status, especially in Sartre's theoretical texts, means that its implications are often not drawn out by Sartre and made explicitly to confront his more dominant ideas and ideological interests. To perform this task is perhaps the function of the devil's advocate in Sartre's case—but an *advocatus diaboli* that is his inner double, for the repetitions and variations in the interaction between his dominant theoretical emphasis upon totalization and the forces that decenter it help to account for the nonlinear and other than totalizable movement of his texts over time. It provides a "pattern" of internal contestation—even of carnivalization—with which to appreciate at least two aspects of Sartre's texts: those moments when he himself seems to thematize the problem of interaction without relying initially upon pure dichotomies (freedom/counterfinality, consciousness/thing, for-itself/in-itself, praxis/practico-inert, and so forth) and the placement of all positive value on one side of the dichotomy and everything negative on the other; and those textual movements when a more open and reciprocal interplay between unifying and decentering forces intervenes despite Sartre's reliance upon contradictory opposites and their sublation in a totalizing process that gives rise to newer contradictions in its turn.[4]

The general considerations I have put forth can be supported only through a close investigation of Sartre's written and lived texts, which is, unfortunately, impossible here. I can at most propose a schema or sketch and illustrate it in limited ways. I would add that my designation of a certain side of Sartre as dominant and another

4. I find the former especially prominent in the notion of transphenomenality in *L'être et le néant*, the treatment of language in "Plaidoyer pour les intellectuels," and various dimensions of certain interviews. I find the latter most notably in the challenge posed by Sartre's "literary" texts or textual currents to his dominant theoretical and philosophical emphases. Except for the notion of transphenomenality, these are discussed later in this essay. For a discussion of transphenomenality, see LaCapra, *A Preface to Sartre*, 123–126.

as submerged is itself based upon a general estimation of tendencies in his texts that courts the status of premature totalization and that is tentative and open to debate. A more probing inquiry into his "ordinary life" than I am able to undertake might, for example, reveal that the type of interaction that often seems submerged in some of his most important written texts is much more prevalent in his "lived" relations with others. This would seem to be indicated in the countless testimonials to Sartre's remarkable sense of humor and an ability to spend himself generously despite difficulties posed to his chosen projects, his personal preferences, or even his health. But part of the fascination exerted by Sartre's life stems from the fact that it is not a simple story, and the interest and relevance of his written texts may be enhanced by an attentiveness to the modes of self-contestation and agonistic (but not simply antagonistic) reciprocity they enact. For, although the willingness to thematize or render explicit the problem of internal contestation may, within limits, increase the measure of responsible control in discourse, the way Sartre's writings question themselves is not merely a matter of formal contradiction or lack of theoretical insight. It is part of their creative challenge and vitality. And their inner dissension at times takes place on a level where it is specious to conceive of one side winning and the other losing; the "contest" may be the essential thing.

Before I turn to a discussion of certain of Sartre's texts that will at least suggest how the investigation I am proposing might proceed, I would like to indicate briefly how it applies to what is, on Sartre's own account, the key notion of his lifework—that of freedom or liberty. As Sartre put it in an interview of 1970, "the idea that I have never stopped developing is that, in the last analysis, a person is always responsible for what one has made of him."[5]

What I have termed the agonistic interaction between unifying and decentering forces may, I think, be detected in Sartre's conception of freedom itself, for Sartre's notion of freedom is a tensely

5. Jean-Paul Sartre, *Situations IX* (Paris, 1972), 101.

divided one that goes in two directions—directions, however, that are not simple opposites or alternatives but mutually implicated forces of contention. One direction often tends to be dominant, especially in the theoretical texts. It provides the semblance of full unity for consciousness or praxis, and it culminates in either total marginality or total commitment. Freedom in this first, rather puritanical sense is seen in hyperbolic terms: within its own sphere of action, it is totally unconditioned and internally pure, and it is the transcendental origin of meaning and value in the world. It is identical with nihilation of the given as the source of determinate processes of negation. It is also radically contingent, for man does not choose to be free in this exorbitant sense; he is paradoxically condemned or predestined to freedom. And he is cast in the larger existential drama of being a being who is both predestined and ultimately responsible for his use of a totalizing, secular freedom. Vis-à-vis this sense of freedom, not only is God dead but nature and woman are often perceived as vessels of receptivity that threaten to entomb man's creative autonomy.

In an interview of 1975, Simone de Beauvoir observed with surprise that Sartre, despite his concern for the oppressed, never addressed the crucial issue of woman's liberation and that there is a certain "machismo" (*machisme*) in his approach.[6] At the same time, she acknowledged that she had experienced her relation with Sartre not as oppressive but, on the contrary, as one of reciprocity and equality. De Beauvoir's memoirs do reveal a number of tensions in the relationship, for example, in the way Sartre's generosity in dispensing his ideas threatened to overwhelm others and in her sense of panic when so-called contingent relationships with others (especially Sartre's liaison with "M" in the mid-1940s) threatened to become a little too "necessary."

In this interview, Sartre goes so far as to assert that woman's liberation is so important in a revolutionary movement as to take priority over the class struggle in modern societies. And, in his very

6. Jean-Paul Sartre, *Situations* X (Paris, 1976), 116–132.

first response, he attributes his neglect of "the question of women" to the fact that in his childhood he was surrounded by women and, given this "natural milieu," he "always thought that there was in him a sort of woman."[7] De Beauvoir observes that this does not fully account for his neglect of the oppression of women once he became an adult and insists that one may find traces of "machismo" and even of "phallocratism" in his works. Sartre feels that she may be exaggerating a little but he seems to concede the point.

One might add that Sartre has very little to say about "the question of ecology." Indeed the predominant relationship between man and nature in his writings is an irremissively adversary one—a feature manifest in the binary opposition between the for-itself and the in-itself (or, with the upsurge of the "other," between consciousness and the body) in *L'être et le néant* as well as in that between praxis and the practico-inert in *La critique de la raison dialectique*. What I would like to note here is the nature of the representation of woman in Sartre's philosophy as it relates to his more puristic and total idea of freedom. Woman has an appeal for the projecting for-itself because she is, in the words of *L'être et le néant*, condemned to be "in the form of a hole"[8]—an absence which the assertive freedom of man must try to plug at his peril, for woman also, in her motherly "moist and gastric intimacy," threatens to encompass freedom in intrauterine security. To be like woman understood in these terms is for Sartre an extreme danger, and threaded through his works is anxiety at being attacked from behind and put in a feminine position. This is so explicit as to seem ironic in his *prière d'insérer* for the first edition of *La nausée* (Nausea): "Then began his true adventure—an insinuating and sweetly horrible metamorphosis of all his sensations. It is Nausea. It grabs you from behind and then one floats in a lukewarm pool."[9] In *La nausée*, the sexual identity of Antoine Roquentin is very much in doubt: it is not existential he-

7. Ibid., 116.
8. Jean-Paul Sartre, *L'être et le néant* (Paris, 1943), 706.
9. Quoted in Michel Contat and Michel Rybalka, *Les écrits de Sartre* (Paris, 1970), 61.

roes who keep diaries; little girls do. The insistency with which an extreme sense of freedom is urged, especially in the early works, may itself be intimately related to ambivalence and anxiety over the relation of man and woman in man himself. One must await *Saint Genet* for the link between writing and homosexuality to be explicitly presented as one possible avenue of liberation in a situation that is specific but that nonetheless poses a threat to the *honnête homme*.

In the early Sartre, pure freedom takes the form of a prepersonal consciousness or for-itself that in *L'être et le néant* becomes personalized in a rather questionable way, thereby laying the groundwork for the idea of the lonely or uncommitted existential individual. Freedom as nihilation of the given also approximates an escapist or even pathogenic idea of the imagination that negates and transcends reality either to achieve narcissistic closure or to return to reality by "assuming" the situation through a gratuitous, activist leap into the "real" world. The fully marginal (or "ironic") individual conceived in terms of this freedom would seem to personify the limiting case of alienation in both its psychological and social senses, and this is the way he is at times portrayed by Sartre, for example, in Antoine Roquentin of *La nausée*.

Philosophically, however, this freedom is attendant upon the phenomenological *epochè* or eidetic reduction as presented by Husserl—a procedure that puts empirical reality in brackets or out of play. (There is a bizarre sense in which Antoine Roquentin in his schizoid relation to the world may be said to live the *epochè*.) Even in the early Sartre, however, phenomenological reduction was not employed solely as a technique of philosophical analysis. Nor was it a way of transforming the life of the theorist alone. The only project Sartre ever affirms in his own voice is the turn from the imaginary, "poetic" quest for redemption *from* the world to the interventionist attempt at redemption *of* the everyday world. This project begins to emerge at least as early as *L'être et le néant*, and it becomes fully explicit in the late 1940s. What precisely the activist leap is to bring about in terms of concrete social and political transformation is not specified by the early Sartre, and the more eschatological trend in his later thought also leaves the future in its most significant bearing on man a total blank. And, especially in the early Sartre, the proximity of extreme alienation and the hope of revolutionary transformation in the idea of living the *epochè* suggests the presence of extreme paradox. The notions of noncomplicitous reflection and radical conversion, which are explicitly left vacuous in *L'être et le néant,* and which in one sense seem to be identical with the idea of authenticity, would seem to imply the transfiguration of the world itself into a realm of pure and total freedom—an emancipatory realm in the full sense of the word. As Sartre states in the conclusion to *L'être et le néant:* "Ontology and existential psychoanalysis . . . must reveal to the moral agent that he is *the being by whom values exist.* It is then that his freedom will become conscious of itself and will reveal itself in anguish as the unique source of value and the nothingness by which the *world* exists." But the final words of *L'être et le néant* refer the explication of freedom and its relation to the situation to "a pure and not a complicitous reflection," which is properly ethical—an explication that is promised in a "future work" that remained among Sartre's uncompleted projects.[10]

One might be tempted to restrict this more exorbitant, willful notion of freedom to Sartre's early works. This would in important ways be a mistake, for, while the range of freedom's application is drastically narrowed in the later works, as its historical situation is understood in more concrete political and social terms, the nature of freedom is nonetheless at times still comprehended as pure, total, and originating—even when it takes the form of the translucent or translucid praxis of the organic individual. And nothing could be more dubious than the idea that the later Sartre becomes "nonjudgmental" because he realizes that individual praxis is determined or decisively shaped by social circumstance. Individual praxis and responsibility remain crucial for Sartre even when they are not given

10. Sartre, *L'être et le néant,* 722.

an exorbitant status. The early Sartre combined predestination and ultimate choice; the later Sartre combines social conditioning and significant—at times ultimate—responsibility in his understanding of his subjects as well as empathy and strenuous argument in his approach to interpreting them. Indeed, in *L'idiot de la famille*, the intended empathy of Sartre for Flaubert is sorely tested by the actual language used to account for his subject, for in it there is at times embedded vitriolic castigation and condemnation. (Intentions do not make words innocent.) In addition, in Sartre's later thought, the very idea of a neo-Marxist "realm of freedom," which signals a definitive break with history as we have known it, relies, as I have intimated, on a pure and uncompromising notion of freedom. Its heroic mission is secular redemption through a total transformation of the real world, and it may be used to justify a redemptive or therapeutic experience of violence. Yet one must be blind to the concrete object of this visionary freedom, for what it will be like to live it fully is beyond the analogical powers of our fallen, alienated state to conceive. Dedication to freedom in this sense may foster a belief in the need for total or at least overriding commitment to the group that seems to be the historical vehicle for transcending alienation. But given the very understanding of freedom, it is radically unclear whether its realization—not its betrayal—would amount to the realization of alienation. The realm of pure freedom might, in a sublime and extremely disconcerting paradox, be identical with a condition of alienation in the form of a total dissociation from anything hitherto known as reality for the collectivity as a whole.

Sartre's idea of pure freedom may be further elucidated by reference to a notion that is so intimately bound up with it as to be virtually indistinguishable from it. This is the notion of transparency. The freedom of the prepersonal consciousness or, later, of the individual is for Sartre initially fully transparent to itself, and this transparency is identical with its emptiness and spontaneity. The fall into bad faith is coterminous with the loss of self-transparency through self-deception, and the alteration of the self through objectification in history marked by scarcity is coeval with the reign of alienation. The full ontological transparency of the conscious for-itself—or the translucent practical individual—obviates the need for any notion of the unconscious, and it presents all alterity in a negative light. The self may become opaque to itself, but this is because of the alienation of originally free praxis which dispossesses the self by converting the internal and transparent into the external and opaque. And the prevalence of alienated social relations is coincident with the opaqueness of others and the role of secrets in social life. Here one has another crucial link between the early and the later Sartre, for the initial given and the ultimate goal of both is full transparency of the self to itself and to the other. In his "Self-Portrait at Seventy," Sartre insisted that the primary cause of the vitiation of social life lies in the fact that "each conserves in his relations with the other something hidden, secret. . . . I think that transparency ought always to be substituted for secrecy, and I can well imagine the day when two men will no longer keep secrets from one another, because they will have none to keep, because subjective life, as well as objective life, will be totally offered, given."[11] Although Sartre elsewhere—for example, in *Question de méthode*—states that one cannot conceive of the realm of freedom, he here intimates that one can imagine it in the form of a reign of total transparency. When the notion of communication is introduced, one gets the picture of an ideal communicative situation wherein language itself is the transparent medium of intentional, totalizing, communicating selves. Sartre's visionary utopia is one of full equality in fully transparent relations within and between selves. One's evaluation of this utopia as a concrete goal of historical action, which one actually attempts to realize, depends in part upon one's judgment about whether the attempt to live the vision will necessarily fail and, in failing, give way to the transparency of total power and control. On one reading, this is the message of *La critique de la raison dialectique*. But the larger if obvious issue is whether the vision of total transparency in equality still amounts to

11. Sartre, *Situations* X, 141–142.

total blindness, for we have had no experience of it, while we have had all too many experiences of its conversion into a pretext for the exercise of oppressive power. And the less obvious issue is whether the goal itself is highly dubious in that a society of total transparency or existential nudity without focus or relief would in any case be as unlivably hellish as an opaquely closed society, even assuming conditions of total equality.

Transparent freedom as the alpha and omega of the Sartrean hermeneutic has multiple avatars in the course of his career, and I shall single out a few at this point—certain of which I shall return to later in my discussion. All of these share what might be called an extreme marginalization, minimalization, or reduction to a zero point, for transparency in its various modifications has no content and is identical with nothingness.

Rhetorically, the transparent is the metaphoric at the point of exhaustion. The for-itself or consciousness in the early Sartre is self-identical and fully present to itself, while praxis that overcomes alienation, in the later Sartre, returns one on a higher level to a fully transparent "relation" with others as well as with oneself. But one can say nothing significant about this "relation" or the realm of freedom in which it is to be realized. They remain totally open (or *disponible*) and internally unencumbered by defining characteristics or meaningful qualities. Transparency in this sense is an empty formal metaphor in a world substantively defined by metonomy as difference, radical contingency, and alienation. As such, it is the repository of necessarily blind hope.

Philosophically, the transparent provides a limiting notion of essence as emptiness. In Sartre this essence covertly precedes existence, but its mode of precedence cannot be characterized, and it is immediately repressed or even foreclosed to give rise to its inverted mirror image: the idea that existence as radical—indeed necessary—contingency precedes essence. As the motor of dialectical praxis, transparency entails a process of totalization without a substantive end to orient it.

Psychologically, the transparent intimates a form of narcissism that is both primary in its unconditioned or absolute originality and secondary in its necessary fall into difference, alterity, and contingency in the world. But both variants of narcissism provide little motherly comfort for the self. Indeed the place of the mother with whom one identifies is taken by an absolutely hollow phallus or assertive and projecting emptiness. Its role is to transform history in some presently indefinable way. The problem of the relationship between Sartre's approach and narcissism becomes explicit in *Les mots* and *L'idiot de la famille*, and in them a specifically biographical orientation is combined with a more positive estimation of the importance of the loving mother in childhood. But the problem is active in other texts as well—often in ways that conflict with the emphasis in these two texts.

Socially and politically, one might relate Sartre's sense of freedom to a desire totally to transcend a context in which existing institutions seem either empty and exhausted or overly rigid and oppressive—what for Sartre is represented by the hierarchical bureaucratic institution and the social condition of serialization and atomization. In the terms employed and sounded out in *La nausée*, one might say that freedom appears to be pure, and consciousness, empty, to the extent that life is—for good or ill—not informed by narrative structures that give lived experience a significance which clothes contingency. Yet one might also suggest that Sartre is so affected by the modern condition at its most extreme that he is unable to come to terms with institutions in any comprehensive way. As both Sartre and Simone de Beauvoir intimated, there was a sense in which Sartre always refused to grow up and assume ordinary adult responsibilities; he approached problems from a perspective deeply sympathetic to the *enfant terrible*. As Sartre himself put the point in more muted terms in an interview of 1969: "While recognizing the necessity of an organization, I admit not to be able to resolve the problems that are posed to any stabilized structure."[12] One of the more questionable consequences of this inability

12. Sartre, *Situations IX*, 283.

is the absence of a sustained, multidimensional inquiry into the relation of freedom and institutions—including the possibility of transformed institutions, for the institution, in its collective patterns, norms, and sanctions, is a crucial instance of the *internal* constraints upon the freedom of the social individual, which are epitomized in the problems of obligation and duty. On his own admission, these are problems that Sartre has not seriously addressed in his writings—a fact that is literally astounding in one who has taken ethics and politics to be central theoretical and practical concerns.[13] For, politically, institutions are ways and means of converting power into authority or even of creating power through authority where it might not otherwise exist. How this legitimating authority and the power it confers relate to domination and exploitation is a question that has also received relatively scant attention in Sartre's works. "Hegemony" is, for example, not a key category in *La critique de la raison dialectique*.

In his life, of course, Sartre has had to confront existing institutions like everyone else, for even the preferred work place of his early life, the café, is a noteworthy institution in French life. Indeed it is precisely the type of institution that introduces into modern existence a modest element of the playful face-to-face encounter— the meeting with friends or chance acquaintances, the masklike possibility of looking without talking or being noticed, indeed the upsurge of the nonserious and the carnivalesque. The café has also been a locus of "serious" business, including political activity. And one might hypothesize that one of the problems with modern institutions in general is the lack of a more sustained and invigorating interplay between the serious or workaday and the carnivalesque. (This, I think, is a lesson of 1968 that is not anticipated in *La critique de la raison dialectique*.) In both Sartre's writings and life, there is a restricted institutional vision that brings with it a tendency

---

13. See Benny Lévy, "Today's Hope: Conversations with Sartre," tr. Douglas Collins and David James Fisher, *Telos* 44 (1980), 162. (The original French version was published in three parts in *Le nouvel observateur* in March 1980.)

to see institutions as constitutive of the workaday at its most oppressive and tedious; liberation often seems to amount to the escape from all institutions—even alternative institutions. In his ordinary life, Sartre—despite his avowed preference for the noninstitutionalized—has certainly accepted certain institutional responsibilities and obligations that stem from his unchosen implication in institutions. For example, after the death of his stepfather, Sartre lived with his mother from 1942 to 1962, and he quite openly stated: "This was a great sacrifice. Until then I had always lived in a hotel, worked in a café, ate in a restaurant, and that was very important for me, the fact of not possessing anything. It was a mode of personal salvation."[14]

One must, however, also recall that the sublime sense of freedom that approximates total marginalization is, in one form or another, a paradoxical mainstay of the Western tradition, hallowed in its theological and philosophical doctrines, and enshrined in popular mythology. This freedom to which the modern alienated intellectual is heir is palpably implicated in a secularized and somewhat desperate—but exhilarating—displacement of Christian eschatological beliefs which Sartre himself has recently seen as crucial components of the Western tradition.[15] It is also a post-postromantic phenomenon which in its desire for higher immediacy returns to a central aspect of the complex movement known as romanticism. And the enthusiasm generated by the promise of total emancipation from tradition—indeed from mediation in general—does not seem abated by the fact that this promise is itself a recurrent motif of our tradition. This freedom is also part of a Promethean sense of action with a special fascination for intense, demanding, and forceful personalities. The question, however, is whether it too may be transformed with the transformation of the larger context into something with a significantly different shape.

14. Quoted in the special May 1980 issue of *Libération* devoted to Sartre, supplement to no. 1932, p. 22.

15. See Lévy, "Today's Hope," 157. See also *L'idiot de la famille* (Paris, 1971), vol. 2, p. 2124.

Here one may turn to a second and often more submerged sense of freedom in Sartre that is understandably less captivating than the first. It is more measured both in its conception of the given or the traditional and in its hope for a transformed future. But it might also be said to involve a more radical if more earthbound understanding of freedom, for freedom in this second sense is experienced and apprehended as "always already" situated and at stake in the world. The meaning and value of the situation are not simply inscribed in things but neither are they the pure derivatives of an originating consciousness or intentional praxis. Rather the situation (or the world) and freedom (or praxis) are on a fundamental level interinvolved in a radically ambivalent relationship, and they are thus bound together in a way to be distinguished from the state of affairs on other levels where the structure of decision or choice may be more clear-cut. As Sartre himself put it in *L'être et le néant*: "The situation, the common product of the contingency of the in-itself and freedom, is an ambiguous phenomenon in which it is impossible for the for-itself to discern the contribution of freedom and the brute existent."[16] This formulation both uses the total oppositions pertinent to the first sense of freedom and places them in radical doubt, for it shows how they relate to a situation which they do not fully master—here, the very situation of being in the world. The human being, on this fundamental level, is a tense compromise formation or liminal phenomenon: a being at the intersection of founding oppositions such as that between the in-itself and the for-itself. And resistances to freedom are not simply "out there" in matter or unintended consequences; they are also internal to the human being, for example, in the insistence of the body and in the action of institutional norms constitutive of the social individual.

Freedom in this second sense does not require an activist leap that defines *ab ovo* the meaning and value of the situation. However far back it goes in its reflection on itself, if finds itself already engaged in situations that are in part defined by more or less vital or

16. Sartre, *L'être et le néant*, 568.

exhausted traditions and institutions. Its ultimate origins are lost or continually displaced. And its task is to take up a situation whose creation it cannot claim fully as its own and to do something with it. Situated freedom would seem to imply an initial interinvolvement of marginality and commitment which gives rise to the more specific problem of the relation between critical distance and engagement in particular social and political circumstances. It would also indicate a different postulation of the connection between tradition and critique—one wherein a promise of transformation might be radical without being total in that traditions and norms bearing some significant relation to the past would always be regenerated. In this light, the radical conversion mentioned in *L'être et le néant* would refer to the turn away from the metaphysical project to be a *causa sui* or a synthetic totality—as well as a totally free being—and it would entail a new beginning in history that would have to be rewon time and again in recreated situations. It would also require a sustained critical analysis of the institutions one wanted to change and some idea of the directions in which one wanted to go.

There is in Sartre, as I have intimated, relatively little explicit theoretical development of this second sense of freedom or of its interaction with the first sense. In the major theoretical works, such as *L'être et le néant* and (even more so) *La critique de la raison dialectique*, the traditional desire to provide an ultimate grounding for a given perspective tends to be dominant. But even these texts are not entirely homogeneous, and other texts—notably the "literary" ones—raise problems for traditional "foundational" philosophy. And at times—for example, in some of Sartre's latest statements—there is a manifest recognition of the need to make certain assumptions explicit while rethinking problems in a significantly different way. This is one prominent feature of the book *On a raison de se révolter* (One is right to revolt)—actually the revised transcript of conversations in the early 1970s between Sartre, Philippe Gavi, and Pierre Victor (later named Benny Lévy). Thought in this text is intently—perhaps too intently—situated as it works in and out of particular problems, and the style of argument is insistently dialogical—not simply in the sense of being a literal dialogue but in the sense of enacting a questioning and self-questioning process whereby a speaker (or author) is able to argue with his own positions. In addition, there emerges some idea of a "punctual" politics in which the "decentering" potential of situated freedom is related to more unifying tendencies in political action that would attempt to coordinate initiatives without bureaucratically straitjacketing them. More generally, Sartre's interviews—notably his last interview with Benny Lévy—are especially important in these regards. Sartre's interviews are significant verbal performances which he made into a veritable subgenre—a subgenre whose obviously threshold or liminal position itself undercuts any rigid opposition between life and writing. Sartre's interviews provide self-commentaries or retrospective statements of intention that may be compared with the texts they are supposed to illuminate. But at times they go beyond this restricted function to make substantial contributions to his thought in their own right. And they are crucial examples of the way "mediation" was for Sartre (in contrast to many contemporary theorists) more than a purely theoretical concept, for in them Sartre himself mediates—and perforce partially "recuperates"—the import of his written and lived texts for a larger audience. In the process, there is a periodic loss in theoretical sophistication, but there is a gain in directness and accessibility. And there is also an insistency that provides numerous openings for a more situated sense of freedom to deploy itself.

With these schematic, preliminary remarks in mind, I shall now turn to a brief discussion of how the interaction between unifying and decentering tendencies as well as Sartre's related notion of freedom may be seen to work themselves through certain of his written and lived texts. I shall perforce be highly selective, and my account will have significant gaps.

There is by now a standard version of the relation between the novel *La nausée* and Sartre's life. It is reinforced by certain of Sartre's self-commentaries, including a cross-reference in *Les mots*.

And it fits nicely into a relatively linear, dialectical conception of Sartre's overall development. I quote from a recent book which provides a good statement of this view:

> Because meaning and value fell outside the limits of observation, Sartre concluded, they must be presumed to be absent altogether. Both the human and the physical world, he argued, were "contingent"; they obeyed no inner logic, stemmed from no higher design. His novel portrayed the narrator, Roquentin, as progressively overcome by the sheer materiality and senseless profusion of nature. At length, he begins to perceive even his own hand as inert matter. Human beings, he realizes, exist with no more justification for their presence than a stone or a tree. "Everything is gratuitous, this garden, this city, and myself. When one realizes this, it turns one's stomach and everything begins to waver. . . . That is nausea." Only a few bars of jazz heard in a café seem to escape from the "sin of existence," and inspire Roquentin with the faint hope that he, too, might create a redeeming work of art, "beautiful and hard as steel."
>
> Though Roquentin strips the daily world of its surface in an effort to discover a bedrock of reality and "salvation," the inhabitants of his adopted city, Bouville, make no such attempt to examine the raison d'être of their lives and habits. Sartre's description of Sunday in Bouville seen through the eyes of Roquentin reduces the town's inhabitants to marionettes, prisoners of their own "ready-made solutions," mechanical and purposeless. Roquentin's one claim to superiority is that he perceives the hollowness of these lives, including his own, while they do not. This insight provides a clue to Sartre's own placid situation in 1938. His negative verdict on the values of the interwar period was itself a justification for his privileged position. As he later admitted [in Les mots], "I succeeded at age thirty in . . . writing in Nausea—very sincerely, believe me—of the unjustified and brackish existence of members of my own class and in putting mine beyond discussion. I was Roquentin, I showed in his character, without complaisance, the pattern of my life. At the same time, I was myself, the elect, the annalist of hell."[17]

17. James Wilkinson, *The Intellectual Resistance in Europe* (Cambridge, Mass., 1981), 32–33. Although I am proposing an interpretation of *La nausée* that differs from the one formulated by Wilkinson, I would note that his book is a remarkable and extremely insightful synthesis of a vast range of highly significant material.

This interpretation of *La nausée* as an existential *Bildungsroman* is, on one level, unobjectionable. Indeed it resembles Sartre's own *prière d'insérer* for the novel. And the understanding of the relation of the novel to Sartre's life has Sartre's own retrospective authorization. Yet one might argue that Sartre himself is refusing (or is unable) to see certain things which suggest a very different relation between the novel and his "ordinary" life. For there are important ways in which Antoine Roquentin—as well as the Sartre who enunciated certain philosophical theses—are themselves being called into question in the novel. And, insofar as this is the case, the very writing of the novel may be seen as an act which, apparently unconsciously, helped Sartre to work out of positions he adhered to in "ordinary" life or, in other. respects, in his more philosophical pronouncements.

La nausée is a highly paradoxical first-person narrative (or "I-novel") in which the "I" is deconstructed in multiple ways to generate the problem of the interaction between unifying and decentering forces in the self. The narrator Roquentin is an isolated intellectual who seeks salvation through art, and he is placed on trial in *La nausée* as a text. Indeed "Antoine Roquentin" is converted from a proper name into an abstract or common noun signifying a disembodied consciousness or free-floating "I." And there are numerous indications that his form of uncommitted freedom is as open to doubt as the thing-like bad faith of the bourgeoisie he detests. Antoine is a coupon clipper, parasitic on the class that revolts him, and he lives in a hotel for traveling salesmen just this side of the tracks in the bourgeois section of town. He can interpret the world with disdain but do nothing to change it. His ability to see through the bad faith of others seems less a mark of superiority than a complement to his blindness to his own form of bad faith in attempting to save himself by indulging a noncomplicitous freedom and an entirely detached marginality.

The ending of the novel constitutes perhaps the most blatant way in which Antoine's position is placed in radical jeopardy, for Antoine does not really change in formulating his final project: he still is in quest of a freedom not involved or implicated in the world.

Antoine intends to write a book, a novel that is to redeem him at least retrospectively, just as the song "Some of These Days" presumably salvaged the existence of its negress singer and Jewish writer. Through art, the alienated bourgeois intellectual will transcend the banal, plotless contingency of life and enter the charmed circle shared by other outcasts of bourgeois society. Yet the novelistic technique of *La nausée* as a text is to set up an expectation of meaning which the text itself frustrates—a technique that might be called that of the aborted apocalypse or eschatological double-take. The nonlinear dimension of the plot is itself traceable in terms of these recurrent expectations of redemptive meaning or "adventure," which are frustrated with at times funny effects. By the end of the novel, this device almost attains the proportions of a novelistic repetition compulsion: it has been "bared" so many times that it is textually threadbare. And the ending itself must be affected and rendered at least somewhat ironic by it. Antoine may take his ultimate project seriously, although there are hints of irony in him (for example, his reflection just before the appearance of the novelistic project about his Aunt Bigeois, who is fatuous enough to think that people can console themselves by listening to music). Sartre as biographical author in the ordinary sense may have shared Antoine's project and felt complacent in the role of apolitical individualist seeking salvation through art—although one may suspect this depiction to be an oversimplification in part induced by the demand for a fully intelligible life history marked by a decisive turning point, conversion experience, or identity crisis. But *La nausée* as a text and, in some problematic sense, the Sartre who wrote it do not simply share this project. They situate it critically and provide the material for its deconstruction. Note also that anecdotal and seemingly aleatory facts support this interpretation as does the more literal ending of the novel, which tells us anticlimactically that tomorrow it will rain in Bouville. The song "Some of These Days" is not authentic jazz or Negro spiritual, and it was not recorded by a negress or written by a Jew. It is an artificial and highly imitative song made not by a Bessie Smith but by Sophie Tucker—

the last of the white red-hot mamas—and written by the black, Shelton Brooks, who went on to compose other commercial favorites. That Sartre as biographical author may not have known these facts attests to the difficulty of disentangling the "authentic" from the ersatz as well as to the unexpected textual power of the seemingly aleatory.

Allow me to summarize my argument. For Sartre as commentator on *La nausée*—and perhaps for Sartre as intentional author at the time *La nausée* was written—as well as for other commentators who follow these "Sartres," Antoine is Sartre's mouthpiece, and his views constitute the essential meaning or message of the text. My argument is that these views are placed in radical question in the text, and, insofar as Sartre was like Antoine, *La nausée* also contests his "biographical" existence in the ordinary sense. The larger scene of bio-graphy is one wherein this contestation takes place.

I would further note that the encounter of Antoine with the chestnut tree, often interpreted as the peak experience of contingency and explicitly so designated in one of the more lapidary philosophical interludes in the text, does not entirely conform to this interpretation in terms of its fuller textual treatment. Nausea itself is not simply equatable with the feeling of contingent existence stripped bare of the illusion of immanent or essential meaning, for there are processes and aspects of the text that give nausea a different and even a more affirmative meaning that prevents its identification with contingency in total opposition to necessity, fiction, or essentiality. In the very language of the text, for example, it is precisely when existence is revealed as radically contingent—and words presumably fall away to allow thinking "directly on, with things"—that a series of substitutive metaphors arise to name the ineffable. "Snake or claw or root or vulture's talon, what difference does it make."[18] The difference these metaphors for the root of the tree make is that they cast doubt upon the notion of total contingency itself, as well as upon the pure opposition between it and essential

18. Jean-Paul Sartre, *La nausée* (Paris, 1938), 181–182.

meaning, insofar as they are categorial attempts to get at the root of the problem of understanding, for they intimate that man, consciousness, and freedom are (in part) semiotic phenomena variably situated between the extremes of necessity and contingency, emptiness and fulness of content, transparency and opacity, and so forth.

Toward the end of the passage on the chestnut tree, one has a supreme paradox. Antoine sees a smile coming to him from the park. Given the thesis concerning the radical contingency of existence and the rejection of the putative illusion of immanent meaning, this smile is a logical and existential impossibility. Yet it happens, and it repeats an earlier experience. The fact that it happens is significant, for it signals the infiltration of meaning into things, and it indicates either the necessity of "illusion" or the dubiousness of ascribing the origin of meaning to an originating for-itself or free praxis alone. Some small residue of meaning is always there in the world already, however far back or deep down one goes in trying to get to its root. This "fact" poses a riddle that is more troubling than the vision of radical contingency for a philosophy that limits itself to analytic opposites and dialectical totalization. It points to the radical ambivalence between self and other (or between meaning and world) on a very basic level, and in this text it does so in terms of a smile from cultured nature—a smile from a park. In the text this smile is further related to the scene of writing, itself an attempt to come to terms with this radical ambivalence: "That little sense annoyed me: I *could not* understand it, even if I could have stayed leaning against the gate for a hundred and seven years; I had learned all I could know about existence. I left, I went back to the hotel and I wrote."[19]

19. Ibid., 190. One may note that a highly explicit dimension of the critique of totalization in *La nausée* is the radical questioning of the quest for full knowledge of another in conventional biography. Antoine Roquentin's project to write the life of the Marquis de Rollebon collapses as he witnesses the refractoriness of his subject to totally coherent representation in terms of either unity or contradiction. His experience is similar to that of Bouvard and Pécuchet in their ill-fated biography of the Duke of Angoulême. It might also be seen within limits as a premonitory critique of Sartre's own application of a totalizing method in his biographies.

This positioning of what Antoine could not understand even if he took a hundred years more than the Autodidacte took to read half the library of Bouville is a textual feature which makes *La nausée* one of the most forceful surfacings of the more submerged tendencies in Sartre—tendencies that Sartre often represses or suppresses, as in his own retrospective interpretations of *La nausée* itself. For the conception of *La nausée* as merely symptomatic of Sartre's own early life as a mystified intellectual and believer in salvation through art—a conception that fits neatly into his *Bildungsreise* toward commitment—obscures *both* some of the most significant features of the written text *and* some of its most potent challenges to the putative lived text.

A second group of texts I would like to discuss briefly treat precisely the problem of committed literature. In Sartre's prewar *L'imaginaire* (translated as *The Psychology of the Imagination*) all literature and art seemed to fall within the realm of an escapist imagination that is divorced from involvement in the real world. This text did not treat art in terms of salvation, but it seemed to imply that if art were a path toward salvation, it would have to be salvation from the world and not redemption of the world. The artist's pen was in this context a sacramental means of purification from implication in reality. The Second World War presumably led Sartre to discover history and the problem of commitment.[20]

20. It may be observed that Sartre gives conflicting signals on the significance of the war experience for the writing of *L'être et le néant*. In an interview of 1970, he asserts: "I wrote *L'être et le néant*, do not forget, after the defeat of France. But catastrophes do not bring any lessons unless they are the culmination of a praxis and one may say: 'My action has failed.' The disaster which befell our country taught us nothing." (*Situations IX*, 102) This idea that the war, at the time of its occurrence, had little immediate impact on his work and that he would assimilate its lessons only after the event is further substantiated by a comment in *Search for a Method*, where Sartre is criticizing an immediately contextual explanation offered by Lukács: "One needs a great deal of time to write a theoretical work. My book *Being and Nothingness*, to which he directly refers, was the result of study begun in 1930. . . . By the winter of 1939–40 I had already worked out my method and my principal conclusions" (p. 39). By contrast, in an interview in 1976 with Leo Fretz, Sartre asserts: "Do not forget that I wrote *Being and Nothingness* during the occupation. We were occupied here. I did some work in the resistance like every-

"Qu'est-ce que la littérature?", (What Is Literature?), first published in *Les temps modernes* in the immediate postwar context, was almost a position paper of committed literature, and it modified Sartre's own earlier theory of art. Prose was subtracted from the view of art as negation and transcendence of reality to be placed within the realm of commitment, communication, and reference to the real world. Poetry, on the other hand, became the repository of Sartre's earlier idea of art, but in "Qu'est-ce que la littérature?" salvation through art assumed an explicitly dubious status.

The first section of "Qu'est-ce que la littérature?" treats prose and poetry as ideal types or eidetic essences, and it posits a decisive analytic opposition between them. The specific terms of the analysis recall the ideas of the French Symbolists and the Russian Formalists. Put briefly, prose is the realm of language use that is referential and instrumental, while poetic usage is self-referential to the point of hermetic self-enclosure and the subversion of communication. Two important footnotes to part 1 extend the argument and also partially displace it. Footnote 4 identifies modern poetry as Sartre's particular point of reference in the somewhat deceptively general theory of part 1, and it presents this poetry in terms of the game of loser wins [*qui perd gagne*). Modern poetry stops the series of human projects and, through defeat in the real world, returns man to himself in his purity. Poetic language rises up out of the ruins of prose, and it testifies to the defeat every victory harbors. "The communication of prose having failed, the very meaning of the word

---

one else, and *Being and Nothingness* was also a book against the Germans. It has an anti-German aspect and there is most certainly some violence in it and more generally some antipathy, which undoubtedly can be explained in this way." ("An Interview with Jean-Paul Sartre," in Hugh J. Silverman and Frederick A. Elliston, *Jean-Paul Sartre: Contemporary Approaches to His Philosophy* [Pittsburgh, 1980], 238.) One might hypothesize that the war had little direct impact on the writing of *L'être et le néant* but that it had an important role in its reading at the time of its publication. It also continues to influence certain interpretations of the book, including at times Sartre's own self-commentaries. A more comprehensive interpretation, however, would have to investigate the extent to which the book and the war were both related to a larger sociocultural complex in similar and different ways.

becomes the pure incommunicable. . . . The absolute valorization of defeat . . . seems to me the original attitude of contemporary poetry. . . . Poetry is a case of loser winning. And the authentic poet chooses to lose, even to the point of dying, in order to win." The poet contests things but in the service of the defeat of the human enterprise, while the prose writer contests the world to further radical change, ultimately in the form of social revolution. "The contestation of prose is carried on in the name of a greater success; and that of poetry, in the name of the hidden defeat which every victory harbors [*recèle*]."[21] Sartre's modern poet is a voice in the wilderness who has lost faith in the visionary possibility of communicating or communing with the universe. He can only bear witness to failure. For with him the apostrophic succession has been broken, and the promise of renewal is reserved at best for the revolutionary society of the future.

Footnote 5 flatly states that "it goes without saying that in all poetry a certain form of prose, that is, of success, is present; and reciprocally the driest prose always contains a bit of poetry, that is, a certain form of defeat; no prose writer, even the most lucid, *entirely* understands what he wants to say; he says too much or not enough; each sentence is a wager, a risk assumed; the more one gropes, the more the word singularizes itself; as Valéry has shown, no one can understand a word to its very bottom." Yet in the principal text of "Qu'est-ce que la littérature?" these points did not go without saying. The fact that they were not made was related to the dichotomy between prose and poetry, which was discussed as if it did indeed govern actual usage in a nonproblematic way. At the end of footnote 5, Sartre returns to the dichotomy in a manner that raises the question of the relation between matters of degree and judgments of kind, and his final sentence leaves certain difficulties unresolved.

However, it need not be concluded that we can pass from poetry to prose by a continuous series of intermediate forms. If the prose writer tries to fondle his words too much, the *eidos* of "prose" is broken and

21. "Qu'est-ce que la littérature?" in *Situations II* (Paris, 1948), 85–87.

we fall into nonsense [*galimatias*]. If the poet narrates [*raconte*], explains, or teaches, poetry becomes *prosaic*. It is a matter of complex structures, impure but well delimited.[22]

The begged question is of course whether the structures are well delimited only on an ideal analytic or eidetic level but impure in actual usage. And the question of the degree to which that impurity is legitimate is the moot issue par excellence. What these footnotes, in contrast to the principal text, nonetheless bring about is an *internal* controversy of prose and poetry with one another in the same empirical text or use of language.

I would add that the principal text of part 1 of "Qu'est-ce que la littérature?" accords with my description of the probably dominant tendency in Sartre's thought, which combines analysis with a totalizing dialectic in a unifying mode of discourse. (In "Qu'est-ce que la littérature?" as a whole, dialectical motifs tend to predominate in parts 2 and 3.) What emerges, appropriately enough, in footnotes is the more submerged interaction between this dominant tendency and decentering contestants. (It also emerges, by the way, in the actual writing of part 1, for in contrast to the explicit theses put forth about the nature of prose, the language of the text is itself heavily allusive and suggestive—thus more on the side of the "poetic.") Yet in certain relatively "minor" writings, what is thematically or "thetically" confined to footnote status in "Qu'est-ce que la littérature?" is liberated to enter the principal text itself. *Orphée noir*, published about the same time as "Qu'est-ce que la littérature?", shows how the argument of part 1 was being challenged in significant respects in other writings of the same period, for it argues that in certain oppressive contexts, poetry may be the voice of social revolution.[23] Other texts of the 1950s might also be discussed to complicate further the picture of Sartre's development. But I would like to turn now to a few texts of the 1960s that are sufficiently heterogeneous among themselves.

22. Ibid., 87–88.
23. Jean-Paul Sartre, *Situations III* (Paris, 1949), 229–286.

In "Qu'est-ce que la littérature?" Sartre stated unequivocally that the politics of Stalinist communism were incompatible with the honest exercise of the literary métier. In the 1950s, the end of the Resistance euphoria, the failure of a third force in politics between the Communists and the Socialists, and the role of the cold war in dividing East and West led Sartre to take up a position as a more or less uncomfortable but at times extremely accommodating fellow traveler of the highly Stalinist Communist party in France. Sartre himself commented that in the play of 1951, *Le diable et le bon Dieu (The Devil and the Good Lord)*, he had Goetz bring off what he himself could not achieve: the resolution of the conflict between the intellectual and the man of action.[24] The extent to which Goetz does so in a convincing way is open to question. What is less questionable is that in Sartre's life the bond between theory and ordinary forms of political practice proved to be elusive. It was from a position of marked marginality that Sartre commented on events, provided rationales for the behavior of the Communists, or longed for the appearance of a group that might elicit full commitment. Writing and speaking were themselves signifying practices, but they apparently were not effective as constituents of the movement for radical social change that Sartre desired.

In 1956 the Soviet invasion of Hungary caused an estrangement between Sartre and the Communists, but Sartre still believed that the Communist party was crucial to any viable leftist movement in France, and he therefore tried to maintain some sort of dialogue with it. His *Critique de la raison dialectique* of 1960 tried to define the foundations of Marxism in terms that did not identify it with the ideology of the Communist party. But Sartre was not yet ready to argue for a sharp break with the party. In the late 1950s and early 1960s, Sartre was of course highly active in opposition to France's war in Algeria. And in the late 1960s, there would be Vietnam and then 1968 which led Sartre to believe in the viability of a left to the left of a Communist party that he now saw as a conservative force in

24. See Contat and Rybalka, *Les écrits*, 234.

French politics. In the mid-1960s, with a relative lull on the political scene, Sartre turned to more ideological controversy in attempting to stake out his position vis-à-vis structuralism. Structuralists had brought the problem of language to the foreground in ways that bore upon the prose/poetry opposition. But if one looks at Sartre's texts of the mid-1960s that are related to his debate with structuralism, no straightforward pattern of response appears. Rather the scene is one of heated internal contestation and multiple modifications of emphasis and nuance in Sartre's understanding of problems.

Two texts are relatively unmitigated condemnations of structuralism as a formalistic, neopositivistic ideology that avoids history and eliminates the role of man as practical agent. This indictment is, I think, at times warranted given the tendencies of certain forms of structuralism. Yet Michel Contat and Michel Rybalka, in their largely sympathetic *Les écrits de Sartre*, describe the nature of Sartre's performance in these texts in rather critical terms. Of his intervention in the December 1964 debate at the Mutualité, which also assembled Simone de Beauvoir, Yves Berger, Jean-Pierre Faye, Jean Ricardou, and Jorge Semprun, they write: "This was especially a confrontation between the proponents of '*telquelisme*' (J.-P. Faye and especially Jean Ricardou) and those of committed literature (Sartre, S. de Beauvoir, J. Semprun). . . . In his intervention—which, with its repetitions and its excessive abstraction, is no doubt not one of his best—Sartre defended himself against attacks upon him by placing the accent on the reader and not on language and redefining the relations of the reader to the work."[25] Of Sartre's interview with Bernard Pingaud, "Jean-Paul Sartre répond," which appeared in the October 1966 issue of *L'arc*, they write: "Rather than a considered response to criticisms of his philosophy formulated by researchers, thinkers, or writers affiliated in diverse ways with structuralism, this was a veritable counter-attack. Sartre expounds, in a manner at times abrupt and peremptory, his funda-

25. Ibid., 411–412.

mental objections to the latent philosophy he detects in the works of Foucault, structuralist linguists, Lévi-Strauss, Lacan, Althusser and the writers of the *Tel Quel* group. These works, in the eyes of Sartre, have in common the same *refusal of history* and participate in a *neopositivism* against which, in the name of Marxism, he rises up."[26]

Sartre's reaction to ideas often associated with structuralism is, however, rather different in the more congenial and less directly threatening contexts of his interview with Pierre Verstraeten—whom he considered, in the words of Contat and Rybalka, as "one of his rare 'disciples' who assimilated his thought in a creative manner"—and in the lectures delivered in the mid-1960s in Japan and published as "Plaidoyer pour les intellectuels" ("A Plea for Intellectuals").[27] Indeed the differences in Sartre's views attest to the importance of discursive contexts in shaping the formulation of ideas. "Plaidoyer pour les intellectuels" and the Verstraeten interview contain, I think, some of Sartre's most subtle comments about language in terms that expand the views he enunciated in the footnotes to part 1 of *"Qu'est-ce que la littérature?"*

In *"Plaidoyer pour les intellectuels,"* Sartre discusses the relations among the "technician of practical knowledge," the writer, and the intellectual with respect to the problem of commitment, and he devotes his third lecture more particularly to the question of art and language. Sartre presents the relation between the role of "technician of practical knowledge" (such as lawyer or physicist) and that of committed intellectual as relatively contingent in comparison with the more necessary but nonetheless historical and problematic con-

---

26. Ibid., 434.
27. For the comment of Contat and Rybalka on Pierre Verstraeten, see *Les écrits*, 420. The interview with Verstraeten first appeared in the July–December 1965 issue of the *Revue d'Esthétique*. It is republished in *Situations IX*, 40–82. The date for the delivery of "Plaidoyer pour les intellectuels" in Japan is given as September–October 1965 in Sartre's *Situations VIII* (Paris, 1972), 373–455 and as September–October 1966 in the chronology published in the special May 1980 issue of *Libération*. The later date, established by Michel Contat and Michel Rybalka, is probably the correct one. The translation by John Mathews appears in Sartre's *Between Existentialism and Marxism* (New York, 1974), 227–285.

nection between the intellectual and the writer. In discussing writing, he addresses his observations to the situation of "the contemporary writer, the *poet* who has declared himself to be a *prose writer* and lives in the post-World War II world."[28] This understanding of the problem focuses on the internal relations between poetry and prose that were confined to a footnote status in "Qu'est-ce que la littérature?" The analytic opposition between poetry and prose is itself replaced by a more flexible distinction among ordinary, literary, and technical uses of language. Ordinary language is seen as the matrix of the other uses, and the literary and the technical become polar opposites vis-à-vis the crucial issue of ambiguity. In "Qu'est-ce que la littérature?" all prose was discussed in terms now seen as technical. A technical language attempts to master ambiguity in order to communicate a maximum of information and a minimum of misinformation. It is conventionalized and specialized, and its code is as far as possible protected from the distorting influence of history. Literary usage by contrast is an exploration of ordinary language in which the writer "prefers to utilize a 'current' word and to charge it with a new meaning which is superadded to the old: in general, one might say that the writer has vowed to utilize the *whole* of ordinary language and nothing but it, with all the misinformative characteristics that limit its range."[29]

The literary writer is thus thoroughly situated in ordinary language, its problems, and its possibilities, and he supplements its standard usages in ways that may increase the plurality or multivocity of meanings. To emphasize the manner in which the writer does this, Sartre refers to a distinction drawn by Roland Barthes that Jean Ricardou had directed against Sartre himself in the Mutualité debate.

> Roland Barthes distinguished between *écrivants* and *écrivains* [translated in the English edition of "A Plea for Intellectuals" as "literal writers" and "literary writers"]. The literal writer uses lan-

28. Sartre, *Situations VIII*, 432.
29. Ibid., 435.

216

guage to transmit information. The literary writer is the custodian of ordinary language, but he goes beyond it and his material is language as nonsignifying or as misinformation. He is an artisan who produces a certain verbal object by working on the material of words; he takes the significations as means and the nonsignifying as end.[30]

For Sartre, the writer nonetheless communicates obliquely and beyond language his lived experience of the world. The "nothing" that literature says is an indirect communication of the silent non-knowledge or comprehension of the *vécu*. The heightened ambiguity of literary uses of language itself testifies to the position of man in the world as a being who comprehends what he does not fully or conceptually know. Sartre thus brilliantly relates to his own later perspective a train of thought that might seem to challenge it in a fashion that is less manageable than he intimates. In any event, in "Plaidoyer pour les intellectuels" he does not address the question of philosophical uses of language with respect to the distinctions he draws. Is the philosopher the transcendent technician in full control of language, or are his uses affected by the difficulties and overtures of ordinary or even literary language?

Here the interview with Pierre Verstraeten significantly supplements the argument of "Plaidoyer pour les intellectuels." Sartre often affirms a strictly classical conception of the rigid separation of genres such as literature and philosophy—although his later biographical ventures, in their quest for the "true novel," impertinently test the limits of generic classification. The point of the strictly classical conception, however, would seem to be to give philosophy a regal position as master of language—a master so seemingly secure in its rule that it need not even articulate the use of language as a problem in the pursuit of truth. It is in this spirit that Sartre begins the interview with Verstraeten. His very first responses present language as totally external to the self, thus confirming the absolute priority of a pure practical consciousness potentially open to full communication with the other. And he ini-

30. Ibid., 436–437.

tially sees philosophy as the rigorously technical realm of univocal usage wherein each sentence means only one thing and not something else. This idea of philosophy as the realm of pure conceptual communication par excellence, in sharp separation from the multivocity of literary usage, is justified by Sartre on *moral* grounds that one is tempted to call Platonic:

> If I allow myself [*me laisse aller*—note the connotation of "abandon"] to write a sentence which is literary in a philosophical work, I always have somewhat the impression that I am going to mystify my reader a little: there is an abuse of confidence. I once [in *L'être et le néant*] wrote this sentence—one remembers it because it had a literary aspect: "Man is a useless passion": abuse of confidence. I should have said that with strictly philosophical words. I believe that in *La critique de la raison dialectique* I have not committed any abuses of confidence.[31]

Sartre here assumes that it makes nonproblematic sense to speak of saying the same thing in other words—words which extract the rigorous kernel of meaning and leave aside the abusive husk of literary usage. He further assumes that there are such things as strictly philosophical words rather than more or less philosophical uses which literary and ordinary uses affect to some extent and which the philosopher may regulate or control within limits but not absolutely master. He also takes for granted the conventional assumption that maximal univocity makes for better philosophy than does usage in which unifying controls are contested or even at times carnivalized by other more ambivalent or multivocal tendencies. Sartre's assumptions seem to obviate the real problem: that of the extent to (and manner in) which various uses of language, which may be clearly opposed on a categorial or eidetic plane, do in fact and/or ought to interact in actual usage, including philosophical uses of language. Sartre never thematizes this problem in a way that would enable extensive theoretical reflection about it, and his domi-

31. Sartre, *Situations IX*, 56.

nant conception of philosophy requires that it not become an explicit problem. But, as the interview with Verstraeten progresses, Sartre begins to acknowledge and, to a certain degree, to explore the internal relations between the "philosophical" and the "literary."

Early in the interview, Sartre asserts that life brings an overcoming of the opposition between *écrivant* and *écrivain* and that "one cannot be a literary writer without being a literal writer or a literal writer without being a literary writer."[32] Indeed he finds in all usage the self-reflexive or "narcissistic" stasis that is for him especially pronounced in modern poetry. "I do not accept at all the idea that absolute communication does not presuppose moments of narcissistic solitude. There is a movement of expansion and contraction, dilation and retraction"[33]--what I have termed the interaction between unifying and decentering forces. And, in a movement of thought that takes him from Hegelian views to a critical estimation of Heidegger, Sartre goes so far as to admit the role of ambiguity in philosophical discourse itself:

> Philosophy ought to destroy itself all the time and be reborn all the time. Philosophy is reflection insofar as reflection is always the dead moment of praxis since, when it is produced, praxis finds itself already constituted. In other words, philosophy comes after, while nonetheless being constantly prospective, but it must forbid itself to have anything at its disposition other than notions; which is to say words. [Sartre elsewhere contrasts the notion with the concept in that the notion accounts for the *vécu* and time.] However, even thus, what serves philosophy is that words are not entirely defined, that is there is nonetheless in the ambiguity of the philosophical word something which one can use to go further. One can use it to mystify, and this is often what Heidegger does, but one can also use it to prospect, which he also does.[34]

I would simply interject here that *Les mots* (published in 1964), which Sartre classifies among his "literary" texts, also has philo-

32. Ibid., 46.
33. Ibid., 61.
34. Ibid., 69–70.

sophical import in its ability to counterpose unifying and disseminating tendencies in recounting the story of a life. Indeed it is
distinctive among Sartre's biographical efforts in its sustained, explicit use of parody and self-parody. In it Sartre establishes a joking
relationship with Freud that has rather serious implications, and
Freud comes to have on a theoretical level a position analogous to
Sartre's grandfather on an existential one. Sartre observes that the
death of his own father bestowed on him an incomplete Oedipal
experience, and he agrees with the opinion of an eminent psycho-
analyst that he has no superego. He also indicates that he looked
upon himself as a child of the miracle who was self-conceived. Yet
it is obvious that Sartre's grandfather had an ambivalent status as
buffoon and hidden God and that he substituted himself as authority figure at a number of crucial points in the young Sartre's life—
notably in the inverted castration, when his first haircut turned him
from a slightly feminine angel into an ugly little boy, and in his
"original choice" to be a writer. It was the grandfather's indifference
that lured Sartre into literature, and he still wondered later in life
whether he poured so many books onto the market in a mad desire
to please the old man. In fact the absence of a conventional authority in the person of a father helped generate in Sartre an overly severe
and totalizing superego that masochistically burned norms into his
skin and created the feeling that he was always on the line or under
the scrutiny of an Other.

Here certain speculative considerations are at least provocative.
What I referred to earlier as the notion of pure and total freedom
might—at least in condensed terms—be seen as freedom without a
father, which brings total responsibility for the self, while the more
situated understanding of freedom involves limited liability and the
problem of confronting the resistances posed by a father or a father-
substitute. The fatherless state might also be related to a primary or
pre-Oedipal narcissism providing full identity with the loving mother and the experience of all alterity as alienating. In *Les mots*, this
initial state precedes the genesis of a sense of seemingly total freedom, and it is presented as one that is lived in plenitude but re-

counted in the mode of parody. Sartre himself explicitly relates his sense of freedom to the death of his father, which placed his mother in chains but liberated him, and he gives special prominence to this point by situating it as a single-sentence paragraph. But the harmonious golden age of mother love and freedom may have been an idealized projection that gave way to the more ambivalent utopia of total freedom through events experienced as a "fall" in Sartre's early life. As Philippe Lejeune has remarked, two events related to a profound sense of loss or even betrayal are not given a salient position in *Les mots*; they are treated in an offhand or displaced manner.[35] One might, I think, suggest in lapidary terms what is inscribed in the text in subtle and fragile filigrain. The remarriage of Sartre's mother and the discovery of his own ugliness (notably at the time of his "castrating" haircut)—both of which events came when he was about eleven, that is, at the onset of puberty—combined to cut off the young Sartre from the putative earlier state of seemingly free and loving plenitude and to contribute to his anxiety-ridden sense of pure and total freedom. The loss of the mother and the recognition of the self as other than the one whom the mother formerly loved may indeed have been the traumatizing events that gave an uncanny and unsettling meaning to the death of the father as an anxiety-ridden liberation. At this point one seems to have had a dissociation of an anxious freedom from the love of the mother, with the latter now experienced as threatening. It is noteworthy that in later life the fatherless son never assumes the position of father; in his relations with others—even others much younger than himself—he recreates the ideal egalitarian peer group of his own desired youth. He also fictionalizes being—and becomes—a brother to a lover-sister who assumes the position attributed in *Les mots* to the mother. The role of the father—except for the idealized Hoederer in *Les mains sales* (Dirty hands), generally an absence or a "heavy"

---

35. Philippe Lejeune, *Le pacte autobiographique* (Paris, 1975), 221ff. Lejeune, however, attributes the success of *Les mots* to its integration of narrative and dialectical "totalization." He does not treat as a problem the relation of the latter to repetition and parody.

in Sartre—indicates the need to face up to alterity, including the problem of the relationship between authority and reciprocity as well as that of the secondary narcissistic identification with oppressive authority.

I would attribute the success of *Les mots* to its ability to work and play through this potentially leaden network of problems by setting up a delicate and, in part, contestatory interaction among narrative, dialectical "totalization," and repetition/displacement. And it is within the use of parody itself, which is far from purely negative, that a reinvigorating mode of contestation takes place, for one function of parody is the critique of ideology and rationalization as Sartre combines Marx and Freud in the serious business of critically excavating the illusions that nurtured him. Here Sartre almost fashions another avatar of the idea of pure freedom in that the goal of full enlightenment seems to give the adult Sartre the position of self-genitor who authoritatively fathers the text that includes little Poulou as homunculus. (One of the fascinations of autobiography is that it gives one the chance to become one's own father.) But a second function of parody is woven into the first, and through it Sartre actively carnivalizes himself and his beliefs in a recreatively dismembering and noninvidious spirit of self-contestation.

In an interview of 1970, Sartre proclaimed that "the conception of the *vécu* is what marks my evolution since *L'être et le néant.*"[36] The notion of lived experience is indeed crucial to Sartre's later thought, and its elaboration does introduce distinctive features into it in comparison with his earlier ideas. For example, in Sartre's early thought, "bad faith" was Sartre's substitute for the Freudian unconscious, while in his later thought the more expansive notion of *le vécu* (in its dialectic with the conceived) enables Sartre, on his own account, to accept facts stressed by Freud, such as repression and resistance, without appealing to the concept of the unconscious. But the difference from his earlier views is not, I think, as

36. Sartre, *Situations IX,* 112.

great as Sartre would lead one to believe. In *L'être et le néant*, the notion of prereflective consciousness, of which bad faith was a primary modification, covered a range of problems similar to those covered by *le vécu*. And there is an important element of continuity in Sartre's cogent reasons for suspecting the concept of the unconscious—its oscillation in Freud between teleological myth and mechanistic cause—as well as in his more questionable resistance to recognizing explicitly modes of internal alterity, such as processes of displacement, that place in radical question the role of a totalizing intentionality in "lived experience." Indeed his two major philosophical treatises, *L'être et le néant* and *La critique de la raison dialectique*, are related to one another by numerous instances of displacement (or repetition with variation); for example, both are variants of the quest for fundamental grounding and both employ key oppositions, such as for-itself/in-itself and praxis/practico-inert, in the organization of the argument.[37] In any case, the model of "totalizing" dialectical progress that leads from the putatively individualistic existential phenomenology of *L'être et le néant* to the collectivistic existential Marxism of *La critique de la raison dialectique* has only limited plausibility. This model excludes too many pertinent features of the two works to be altogether acceptable.

I have already noted that *L'être et le néant* does not simply begin in an individualistic way but with a notion of a prepersonal consciousness as does Sartre's earlier works, such as *La transcendance de l'égo* (The Transcendence of the ego). And the introduction of the person or the individual (in the ordinary sense) is problematic in the extreme, for it depends upon an unsubstantiated asymmetry between language and thought in the putative relations of I/me and we/us. "I," "me," and "us" presumably have ontological status, while "we" is termed a purely psychological experience. By significant contrast, *La critique de la raison dialectique* does accord vital historical reality to the "we" of the group-in-fusion, but it is equally significant that the group is nonetheless seen as part of a *constituted*

---

37. For a defense of this assertion, see LaCapra, *A Preface to Sartre*, chap. 4.

dialectic which is derivative in relation to a *constitutive* dialectic stemming from the intentional praxis of the organic individual. Strange as it may seem, *La critique* does "begin" with the individual as the ultimate origin of the historical dialectic.

The argument of *La critique* is in general a conceptualistic, foundational analysis of the historical structures of alienation and a restricted sketch of the negative dialectical relations between those structures and the people inhabiting them. It is extremely useful in providing a set of concepts and of possible processes in the analysis of alienated relations. But it is misleading in that it seems to present itself as a general theory of history as we have known or can conceive it, for it is insistently—and, once this is acknowledged, usefully—one-dimensional in its conception of problems. It is more unified in conception than *L'être et le néant*, but this very characteristic is related to the fact that it contains less powerful and sustained instances of self-contestation. With respect to the interaction between lived and written texts, it is difficult to determine whether the relatively atypical manner in which Sartre composed the book attests to an inspired breakthrough or to a repetition of old patterns in his thought, which *La critique* in certain ways may even deploy in extremely mechanical ways, for Sartre wrote *La critique* with a heightened sense of urgency and under extreme tension, and he kept himself going with large doses of amphetamines. In the words of Simone de Beauvoir:

> Sartre managed by writing furiously his *Critique de la raison dialectique*. He did not work as he usually did, with pauses, erasings, tearing up pages, beginning them again. For hours at a stretch, he sped from page to page without rereading them, as if waylaid [*happé*] by ideas that his pen, even at full tilt, could not keep up with. To keep up this pace, I could hear him crunching corydrame capsules, of which he swallowed a tube a day. By the end of the afternoon, his gestures would become uncertain, and often he would get his words all mixed up. . . . To think against oneself is fine, but in the long run it takes its toll. By breaking bones in his head he had damaged his nerves.[38]

38. Simone de Beauvoir, *La force des choses* (Paris, 1963), 407, 474.

It is noteworthy that *La critique,* in spite of its attempt to renew Marxism, is not based on a notion of the social individual, which would both obviate efforts to derive society from individual praxis and require a situated "beginning" that allowed for the role of institutions, including language, in the understanding of history or the relations between nature and culture. *La critique* (as distinguished from *Question de méthode* or *Search for a Method*) begins with individuals confronting nature or matter, and it has a purely negative comprehension of institutions, which appear only late in the text under the guise of what occurs with the "fall" from the spontaneous group-in-fusion into renewed forms of alienation. Hence the praxis of the individual is not perceived as internally "altered" from the very "beginning" of anything recognizable as human praxis—and in ways that need not be purely negative—by institutional and linguistic processes not freely and fully possessed by the individual. One is tempted to suggest that *La critique* begins with an imaginary initial state of pre-Oedipal, aggressive narcissism which is projected upon adult individuals in a deceptively unmediated way. In any case, it remains within a tradition in which there is no genuine tolerance for difference, for in that "dialectical" tradition otherness (or alterity) is seen as negative (or "fallen") in itself and positive (or redeemable) only as a means to a higher unity. And given the nature of Sartre's rendition of that tradition in *La critique,* it is difficult if not impossible to tell whether any projected *Aufhebung* of alienation involves the overcoming of all alterity.

Indeed the relation between alterity and alienation is an especially important and knotty problem in *La critique.* In beginning with the free and unconditioned praxis of individuals who are presumably possessed of totalizing intentionality and "translucency" or "translucidity," *La critique* would seem to take up where part 3 of *L'être et le néant* left off, and individuals as practical organisms have crucial defining characteristics of the for-itself. They are initially presented and understood by Sartre in total abstraction from the problem of institutions. Their alterity is not an internal feature which itself would be related to their role as social and signifying individuals in institutional contexts whose norms and practices generated inner constraints and "repression." Alterity follows freedom as a primary or primitive form of alienation brought about by the confrontation of projects with nature or matter interpreted in terms analogous to the probably dominant understanding of the in-itself in *L'être et le néant*. With objectification, matter "steals" freedom and gives rise to the practico-inert; free praxis returns to the initially translucid individual as alien or Other. Alterity is seen in exclusively negative terms, for there is no sense in which it may be a necessary condition for reciprocal relations of a more affirmative and fraternal sort as well as for aggression and alienation. And nature is itself experienced as alien *ab initio*; it is matter worked over by individuals. Indeed Sartre, like Hegel, sees it and, in a derivative way, archaic societies (*Naturvölker* in the older German designation) as constitutive of the realm of mere repetition in stark contrast to historical society. Sartre's approach does have the virtue of allowing for "alienation" in noncapitalistic societies, but the understanding of alienation returns to the uncompromising dualisms of his dominant tendency that are basic to his understanding of totalization.

What is less clear, however, is the precise relation of alterity or primary alienation to scarcity and "antagonistic reciprocity" among individuals themselves. Scarcity for Sartre is consubstantial with human history as we have known or can imagine it, and it is intimately connected with violence in human affairs. It is apparent that scarcity is bound up with all historical forms of alienation and that the transcendence of alienation in history requires overcoming scarcity. Sartre, moreover, insists upon a world-wide perspective that reveals the factual importance of scarcity in a context where three-quarters of the globe's population are undernourished. But the link between scarcity and alterity is itself not merely factual, especially in the way it is mediated by the relation of individuals to matter which, through praxis, becomes an initial form of the practico-inert. And there is an important sense in which Sartre's treatment of scarcity hypostatizes it.

Scarcity is the mode in which the "univocal relation of environing materiality to individuals manifests itself *in our History* under a particular and contingent form since the entire human adventure— at least until now—has been a rabid struggle against scarcity." Scarcity is contingent but in a sense close to the radical meaning of contingency employed in the early Sartre: it is a paradoxical contingent necessity. Indeed scarcity would seem to have the position of a historical a priori or condition of existential possibility—a status which here seems close to that of a structuralist analogue of ontology, for scarcity is a universal feature of our history that varies only in degree with specific circumstances. Not only is its reign coeval with history as we have known it. It shapes the very limits of our real historical understanding and concrete imagination, and, given our history, we can conceive of alternatives to it only in totally abstract, logical ways. To try to think beyond it would be like trying to think beyond our own existential horizon. It is part and parcel of our historicity. Thus, despite its contingency, "it is a fundamental human relation. . . . Any man today must recognize in this fundamental contingency the necessity which (across thousands of years and very directly, even today) forces him [*lui impose*] to be exactly what he is."[39]

Scarcity and alterity (or primary alienation) would thus seem to have a contingent but fundamental relationship throughout history as we have known it—or, more precisely, as we have lived and comprehended as well as can possibly imagine it. Sartre also states that primary alienation "expresses itself through other forms of alienation but it is independent of them and is on the contrary their foundation." This statement would seem to apply not to the bond between primary alienation and scarcity, which has a very special status, but to *institutional* forms, which for Sartre are derivative in relation to alterity *and* scarcity. Sartre explicitly criticizes Marx and

39. Jean-Paul Sartre, *La critique de la raison dialectique* (Paris, 1960), 201. For an attempt to argue that Sartre's conception of scarcity is historical rather than ontological, see Mark Poster, *Sartre's Marxism* (London, 1979). Poster's argument tends to lose its point, however, once one realizes that "historical" applies to all history as we have known or can imagine it.

Engels for not seeing scarcity as a ground of institutions: they interpreted scarcity not as the condition of possibility for history but as always already implicated in an institutional-historical context, for in their thought "the mode of production . . . , through institutions that it conditions, produces the social scarcity of its product." Thus for Sartre scarcity is *not* a phenomenon dependent upon the role of institutions and language, which limit and regulate as well as stimulate desire as a function of the nature of norms. Scarcity is not seen as specifying the excess of demand over need and differentiating culture from nature in and through the alteration of "being," attendant upon signifying practices. Indeed the very appeal of the group-in-fusion is what Sartre sees as its full transcendence of alterity and institutions, and this vision of unmediated democratic participation leads him to posit a total dichotomy between free praxis and alienation: "It is not that I am myself in the Other; it is that *in praxis* there is no Other, there are *myselves*. The free development of a praxis in effect can only be total or totally alienated."[40] And Sartre not only equates reciprocity with identity; he indicates a sense in which his notion of alienation, which reciprocity transcends, approximates that of Hegel:

> Alienation in the Marxist sense of the term begins with exploitation. Are we returning to Hegel who makes of alienation a constant characteristic of objectification of whatever sort? Yes and no. One must in fact consider that the original relation of praxis as totalization to materiality as passivity obligates man to objectify himself in a milieu which is not his and to present inorganic totality as his own objective reality. It is the relation of interiority and exteriority that originally constitutes praxis as a relation of the organism to its material environment; and it is not doubtful that man—from the time he no longer designates himself as simple reproduction of life—discovers himself as *Other* in the world of objectivity; totalized matter, as the inert objectification which perpetuates itself by inertia, is in effect *a non-man* and even, if one wishes, *a counter-man*. Each of us spends his life in engraving on things his maleficent image which fascinates

40. Sartre, *La Critique*, 202, 219. 420.

and leads him astray if he wishes to understand himself through it, while he is nothing other than the totalizing movement that culminates in *this* objectification.[41]

The only possibility for radical transformation in this context would seem to be a blind leap into an unknowable future. It is noteworthy that in the principal text of *La critique* there is no indication of a way out of the vicious circles Sartre traces. Even the evanescent but nearly perfect moment of the group-in-fusion—in which the Other is comprehended as the same and individual freedoms spontaneously meet in an identity without hierarchy or even organization—is inserted into larger cycles of alienated history. One might argue either that these motifs are in tune with the bleak pessimism of the book or that a durable apocalyptic and eschatological solution forms the silent center implied by its argument. In the latter case, the utopia of freedom would be one of fully transparent "relations," and the overcoming of scarcity would coincide with the overcoming of alterity: in an act of ultimate recognition, the self would be at one with other individuals if not with nature, and the group-in-fusion would somehow give birth to an ongoing society without the mediation of institutions.

It is significant that in *L'idiot de la famille*, which is in many ways a better sequel to *Question de méthode* than is *La critique*, Sartre does trace the manner in which the individual is "altered" within the family from his earliest participation in "lived experience." And Sartre attempts to show how Flaubert freely assumed the fate that his position in the family fashioned for him. Yet *L'idiot*, like *La critique*, continues to present alterity in general as negative, for its own textual practice grounds the possibility of transcending alienation on the viability of a totalizing comprehension of the life of another in which reciprocity takes the form of empathetic identification. The utopian hope of *L'idiot*, to the extent that it exists, relies on the basic nexus of transparency, identity, and totalizing com-

41. Ibid., 285.

prehension, and it is this nexus that presumably justifies the often confusingly labile—and even uncritical—blending of fact and fiction in Sartre's quest for the "true novel."

Concerning the interaction between Sartre's own life and writing during the composition of *L'idiot*, I would simply like to mention an issue which I cannot go into more thoroughly. After 1968, Sartre—despite certain reservations—affiliates himself politically with *gauchisme*, and he devotes considerable time and energy to writing *L'idiot*. Benny Lévy himself asked Sartre why his political commitments did not lead him to abandon his work on Flaubert and to write a popular novel instead, and Sartre felt defensive about the Flaubert study and tended to see it as the product of a residual "classical intellectual" in him—a product that might nonetheless, in some unforeseeable way, be of service in a future revolutionary society. Ronald Aronson in a recent study has seen *L'idiot* in particular as an expression of Sartre's own culminating flight into the imaginary—and the later Sartre in general as combining the active-less mind of his youth with the mindless activism of *gauchiste* politics.[42] What I would suggest is that although one may take issue in numerous ways with *L'idiot de la famille*, the difficulties in its argument do not stem from its putative apoliticism.[43] The book is a highly political statement, most ostensibly in its elaborate critique of formalism and art for art's sake. But what is remarkable is the initial contrast between the mode of political engagement evidenced in its intricate arguments and the more direct and "spontaneous" versions of commitment that brought Sartre into the streets. One might argue that at least on certain levels there is a powerful form of cross-checking involved in the contrast between the Flaubert project and *gauchiste* politics. The objects of criticism and the ultimate ends may be similar, but the means of attaining them are significantly different.

I shall conclude with a brief discussion of Sartre's last text—in

42. Ronald Aronson, *Jean-Paul Sartre—Philosophy in the World* (London, 1980).

43. For a development of this argument, see LaCapra, *"Madame Bovary" on Trial.*

fact a text that cannot be unambiguously ascribed to him as author. I have already referred to it in conjunction with another polyvalent text, *"On a raison de se révolter."* I am of course referring to Sartre's interview with Benny Lévy just before Sartre's death. This interview shares with *On a raison de se révolter* an intense dialogical quality that not only makes the ascription of ideas to individual authors problematic but also reveals how each subject is engaged in a process of self-questioning. In addition, both texts are very far from "foundational" thinking and, indeed, so situated as to seem at times circumstantial in nature. But their style and format do not exclude more rigorous thought that, while not pretending to provide ultimate principles, does enable inquiry into assumptions and presuppositions.

One prominent feature of Sartre's final interview is the way Lévy probes Sartre's assumptions at times almost to the point of badgering the old philosopher. The results are at times surprising. Raymond Aron has argued that Sartre in this interview was very much out of character—that he seemed other than his usual "delirious" self.[44] I would suggest that the interview brings out what I have been discussing as the more submerged side of Sartre and that it indicates that Sartre may have been ready to build upon it in a more extensive theoretical way than he had been earlier.

In his final interview, Sartre emphasizes the situated dimension of freedom and the need for an understanding of the traditional context of thought and action. In a sense, he returns to the questions raised at the end of *L'être et le néant* and explores alternative routes in answering them: "The moral modality implies that we cease, at least at that level, to place being as our goal; we no longer want to be God; we no longer want to be *causa sui*; we seek something else."[45]

Here Sartre does not see the political as a simple substitute for the

44. See "Le débat entre Raymond Aron, André Glucksmann, Benny Lévy, et Bertrand Poirot-Delpech" in the special May 1980 issue of *Libération* devoted to Sartre, pp. 48–9. Translated as "Sartre's Errors: A Discussion by Raymond Aron, André Glucksman [sic] Benny Lévy, et al., *Telos* 44 (1980), 204–208.

45. Lévy, "Today's Hope," 157.

moral but rather attempts to work out an ethicopolitical perspective. The consequences are that violence is not seen as redemptive and that fraternity is not a mere derivative of terror. In fact Sartre defines morality in terms of the problem of obligation (although he is not altogether happy with this word), and he admits that he failed to study this "sort of internal constraint which is a dimension of consciousness" in his philosophical works.[46] He also intimates that there is a need for some idea of internal alterity in understanding reciprocity: "I think that everything that takes place in a consciousness at a certain moment is necessarily bound, even conceived, by the presence or even the absence, at that moment, of the existence of the other."[47] And the very meaning of political action seems oriented not toward a leap into an unknowable future but toward punctual interventions of limited but possibly significant effect: "I believed that evolution through action would be a series of failures from which something positive, already contained in the failure and ignored by those who had wished to succeed, would result unexpectedly. This positive result would be these partial, local successes, difficult to recognize by those who had worked for them but which, from failure to failure, would accomplish some progress. It is thus that I have understood history."[48]

This account is dubious as a retrospective reconstruction of Sartre's "true" meaning in a work such as *La critique de la raison dialectique,* but it is noteworthy as an articulation of his views in the context of his final interview itself. It is complemented by a specification of the type of humanism Sartre defends—"the experience of what is best in us, an effort to go beyond ourselves within the circle of men—men who can be prefigured from our better acts."[49] Humanism thus seems to broach a transhumanism and not to be confined within invidious distinctions that confer an unconditioned, hierarchical privilege on the human species. Indeed

46. Ibid., 162.
47. Ibid., 163.
48. Ibid., 161.
49. Ibid., 162.

throughout this interview Sartre seems to approach a newer under-standing of the relationship between marginality and commit-ment—one wherein the intellectual would neither be initially re-moved from the world in a transcendent fashion nor uncritically ready to invest himself fully in a group or movement that offered the promise of solidarity and revolution.

One should not place undue emphasis upon this final interview or see it as a death-bed conversion to views one would like to promote oneself. But this interview does reveal Sartre at his dialogi-cal best, and it shows him in old age still ready to question himself in potentially unsettling ways. My own contention has been that it is precisely in the contestatory interaction between tensely related tendencies in Sartre—notably including the interaction between his written and lived texts—that one discovers problems most deserving of further exploration. For even in Sartre's at times exorbitant ap-prehension of freedom, one finds a paradoxical expression of meta-physical desire, which may be necessary in order to appreciate and to situate a more limited and conditioned understanding of freedom itself. The result may be a critical awareness of how the desire for full freedom, in conjunction with the demand for totalizing com-prehension and transparent immediacy of self to other, may bring egalitarian ideals in shocking proximity to the forms of oppressive power they intentionally try to escape.

[7]

Marxism in the Textual Maelstrom: Fredric Jameson's *The Political Unconscious*

The plurality of the *meanings* of History can be discovered and posited for itself only upon the ground of a future totalization—in terms of the future totalization and in contradiction with it. It is our theoretical and practical duty to bring this totalization closer every day.

Sartre, *Search for a Method*

The prefix "un" is the token of repression.

Freud, "The 'Uncanny'"

Fredric Jameson's *The Political Unconscious* is a major critical work that should be read by everyone interested in the relationship between history and theory.[1] It is an overwhelmingly ambitious attempt to "rewrite" Marxism in the light of challenges posed to it by contemporary theoretical perspectives ranging from psychoanalysis and myth criticism to poststructuralism, and it includes an extensive commentary on the problematic history of Marxist theory itself (Lukács, Sartre, the Frankfurt school, Benjamin, and especially Althusser, among others). It continues the project of Jameson's two earlier general Marxist studies, *Marxism and Form* (1971)

1. Fredric Jameson, *The Political Unconscious: Narrative as a Socially Symbolic Act* (Ithaca, 1981); all page references are to this edition.

234

and *The Prison-House of Language* (1972), providing a sustained instance of the dialectical hermeneutic called for by the former and extending the reckoning with structuralism begun in the latter. Indeed *The Political Unconscious* might be seen as a *summa marxologica* for our time—at least on the level of self-reflexive theory. In fact the neoscholastic metaphor applies to the book in more than one sense, not the least of which being its attempt to achieve the status of a dialectical synthesis (or, more properly, an *Aufhebung*) of the various perspectives it treats—rather than that of their eclectic combination or even their supplement in a *logomachia* or polemical contest.

Whether the book achieves its goal (*tout comprendre, c'est tout relever*) is a moot issue, but any criticism addressed to it must recognize its genuine intellectual effort, its sustained level of sophisticated intelligence, its impressive range, its honeycomb of stimulating insights and asides, and the value of the herculean task it undertakes. One must also recognize that Jameson is competing with figures such as Sartre (his mentor in more than one sense), and that his position in this country is a difficult one. It is perhaps epitomized by his position as Yale's token "literary" Marxist, running the gauntlet between the Scylla of traditional scholarship and the Charybdis of deconstruction—in its more formalistic and apolitical variant. (How he negotiates his way between the rock and the whirling place is one element of adventure in his book.) One must, in addition, acknowledge that the best basis for pertinent criticism relies on a crucial question enunciated by Jameson himself: to what extent is a work symptomatic or critically transformative (for Jameson: utopian) in relation to the contextual conditions in which all thought is enmeshed at the present time?

In discussing a work of the ambitiousness and scope of *The Political Unconscious*, one must either believe that one can deliver a condensed dialectical *summa* of what is—or aspires to be—an extended dialectical *summa* (and here I falter in theory and practice) or one must be selective and try to give reasons for one's choices. In taking the more soberly metonymic path, I shall focus on what I

235

take to be Jameson's major theoretical project for the rearticulation
of Marxism and of critical historical research in general. For it is
here, I think, that the book carries its greatest interdisciplinary significance, its maximal import for historians, and its greatest challenge to existing approaches. It is also here that the book encounters
its most formidable internal difficulties, for Jameson's venture is in
many ways an epitome of the promise and the problems of avant-
garde Marxist theory, especially in the context of the contemporary
American academy. Until I reach the concluding point of indicating how I think this is the case, I shall try to elucidate the difficult
and at times turgid "style" in which Jameson makes his argument—
a "style" in which the "work of the concept" is often mind-break-
ing—and, simultaneously, to examine critically certain of its turns
and procedures.

THE PROJECT

The book begins with an introductory chapter of nearly a hundred pages—"On Interpretation" is its appropriately Aristotelian
heading—which is almost a freestanding theoretical treatise in its
own right. It is followed by chapters on "Magical Narratives" and
on the novels of Balzac, George Gissing, and Joseph Conrad. The
guiding concept of a "political unconscious" is in Jameson's usage
as richly connotative and associative as in any "master" term or title
that is defined—insofar as it is at all—only by its multiple uses. In
its uncanny lability, it resembles the "unconscious" in Freud. Indeed Jameson's own use of "political unconscious" may be seen as
an initial point of internal contestation in his argument, for it sits
somewhat askew with respect to his dominant theme of dialectical
totalization: it is not entirely part of the story whose integral unfold-
ing it announces. At one point Jameson even refers to it as a "historical *pensée sauvage*" (p. 167). Its clearest meaning designates that
which has been repressed in contemporary thought, notably academic thought with its tendentious empiricism, formalism, and
disciplinary divisions: to wit, the social and collective substratum of

all culture, including literature and, more particularly, the Marxist vision of the historical process as the scene of class struggle culminating in utopian emancipation. Jameson hopes to contribute to the rebirth of a genuinely political discourse in the study of culture and history. Indeed one is tempted to say that for Jameson, Marxism is paradoxically the upstart and the sole, legitimate heir to the tradition of civic humanism. For it is Marxism that provides the political master code for the allegorical reading and "rewriting" of all cultural history, and it simultaneously reveals the coded truth of earlier allegorical modes. Only Marxism can decode the past in its utter "otherness" *and* in its bearing on the needs of the present. "These matters can recover their original urgency for us only if they are retold within the unity of a simple great collective story; only if, in however disguised a symbolic form, they are seen as sharing a single fundamental theme—for Marxism, the collective struggle to wrest a realm of Freedom from a realm of Necessity" (p. 19).

Jameson's method in pursuing his genuinely grand design is a combination of metacommentary and metahistory—a method that at times brings him paradoxically close to critics who, from a Marxist perspective, would appear formalistic. His focus is "the interpretive categories or codes through which we read and receive the text in question" (p. 9) and his objective, "the historical and dialectical reevaluation of conflicting interpretive methods" (p. 208). All reading or interpretation is allegorical, and codes—notably narrative codes—are the keys to the kingdom of allegory.

Jameson's approach to history is not the institutionalized empiricism familiar to most historians; he is out for big game, and one does not hunt elephants with a slingshot. His understanding of the past is informed by certain explicit narrative and dialectical motifs that attest to the proximity between the philosophy of history and practical historiography. Jameson is tactlessly forthright in baring his code: "This book will argue the priority of the political interpretation of literary texts. It conceives of the political perspective not as some supplementary method . . . but rather as the absolute horizon of all reading and interpretation" (p. 17). Given the nature

237

of poststructuralist critiques, it does not take much acuity to decode Jameson's assertive use of notions of "absolute horizon" and of centrality as a polemical gesture. Yet the declared centrality of his political perspective gives way to an elliptical formation whose two centers of concern do not entirely coincide: narrative and dialectics. The "movement of language and writing across time" is for Jameson "essentially narrative" (p. 13). And Jameson's own "specific critical and interpretive task" is "to restructure the problematics of ideology, of the unconscious and of desire, of representation, of history, and of cultural production, around the all-informing process of *narrative*, which I take to be (here using the shorthand of philosophical idealism) the central function or *instance* of the human mind" (p. 13). Given this centripetal conception of the nature of narrative, "it is in detecting the traces of that uninterrupted narrative, in restoring to the surface of texts the repressed and buried reality of this fundamental history [class struggle directed at wresting "a realm of Freedom from a realm of Necessity"], that the doctrine of a political unconscious finds its function and its necessity" (p. 20).

IDEOLOGY, SCIENCE, AND TEXT

What is, however, implicit in Jameson's own account is the idea that narrative is the central "instance" of the human mind only in an *ideological* sense—that is, in the sense of the ideological as specified by Althusser as centered on the subject or by Sartre as relating to lived experience (*le vécu*) in contrast to scientific, conceptual knowledge. Narrative is the story that is necessary ideologically not only for the "people" but for all human beings. It is both indirectly related to knowledge and inescapably subject to distortion; it also harbors utopian hope. "Any doctrine of figurality must necessarily be ambiguous: a symbolic expression of truth is also, at the same time, a distorted expression, and a theory of figural expression is also a theory of mystification or false consciousness" (p. 70). Narrative might almost be called a noble lie if we had some continuous but higher perspective from which to judge it. For Jameson, we do not. Indeed one of his more forceful themes is that Marxism has been "undialectically" one-sided in attempting to demystify ideologies without seeing their necessity and their well-nigh gravitational force of attraction. For even the most heinous ideology— fascism, for example—can take people in only because it seems to render subjectively comprehensible otherwise distant or opaque collective processes and to do so in ways that deliver utopian hope. The lesson for Marxism, which Jameson articulates in his concluding chapter, "The Dialectic of Ideology and Utopia," is that a negative hermeneutic demystifying ideology must be complemented by a positive hermeneutic sensitive to the necessity of ideology and its often concealed element of utopian promise. Indeed one of the more disorienting dynamics in this book is the partial shift in Marxism from a critique of ideology and utopia to an apology for ideology and utopia in a manner reminiscent of Durkheim at his most *exalté*.

The conception of Marxism as science is not, however, abandoned. It is situated on the level of dialectics which seeks conceptual knowledge of objective, collective processes that exert "action" only at a distance upon subjective, "ideological" phenomena and in ways that cannot be direct objects of experience. (One directly experiences the commodity as a fetish that crystallizes desire and dream; one does not directly experience the process of "commodification" and capitalization as it is analyzed in *Capital*.) Jameson never attempts to bring into focus the problems generated by the fact that Marxism has two foci for presumably "totalizing" accounts of history—one "ideologically" narrative and the other "scientifically" dialectical. But that there is a diacritical gap between these two processes is crucial to his account and to some of the partially unexplored questions it raises.

Indeed how precisely the gap is spanned but never closed by critical thought that demystifies ideology and engages practice is never really addressed by Jameson. Instead Jameson's own dominant emphasis tends to override the dual-focus problem within Marxism on a purely interpretative plane, for he insists that a centrally totalizing hermeneutic subsumes other modes of interpretation. "The limits of the latter can always be overcome, and their more positive findings retained, by a radical historicizing of their mental operations, such that not only the content of their analyses, but the very method itself, along with the analyst, then comes to be reckoned into the 'text' or phenomenon to be explained" (p. 47). The assertiveness of the desire for *Aufhebung* seems to obviate inquiry into the limits to it suggested by the supplementary relation between narrative and dialectics—or into the discursive status of critical thought that is not entirely accommodated by the binary opposition between narrative and science as Jameson "understands" them. Here one has a problem that will appear in other guises in our (meta)commentary on Jameson's project—a problem that both delimits the project and, in certain respects, may be said to motivate it.

Yet it must be confessed that this problem—call it "textual"—is precisely the sort of thing Jameson would like to resist, for one of the primary components of his "rewriting" of Marxism is a sinuous confrontation with structuralism and poststructuralism that seeks to integrate their "positive findings" and evacuate what are for him their debilitating excesses. Jameson is wary of—even hostile to— generalized "decentering" that culminates, he fears, in the glorification of extreme heterogeneity (indeed the "schizophrenic text"), the "pantextualist" inflation of language itself into a new paradoxical center, and the "rewriting" of all past history in postmodern terms. (The obvious question which the use of labels obscures is that of the extent to which this combination of traits actually applies to various figures within the camp of what might be called the new theoretical SPD—structuralists, poststructuralists, and deconstructionists.) At the same time, Jameson is acutely aware of the importance of the "textual revolution" and is even more concerned than other relatively "avant-garde" Marxists (for example, Terry Eagleton) to make room for its "findings" in a Marxism for our times.

It is a historical fact that the "structuralist" or textual revolution—as, mainly through Althusserianism, it has transformed a whole range of other disciplines, from political science to anthropology, and from economics to legal and juridical studies—takes as its model a kind of decipherment of which literary and textual criticism is in many ways the strong form. This "revolution," essentially antiempiricist, drives the wedge of the concept of a "text" into the traditional disciplines by extrapolating the notion of "discourse" or "writing" onto objects previously thought to be "realities" or objects in the real world, such as various levels or instances of a social formation: political power, social class, institutions, and events themselves. When properly used, the concept of the "text" does not, as in garden-variety semiotic practices today, "reduce" these realities to small and manageable written documents of one kind or another, but rather liberates us from the empirical object—whether institution, event, or individual work—by displacing our attention to its *constitution* as an object and its relationship to the other objects thus constituted. [Pp. 296–297]

But, as I have intimated, Jameson's real anxiety is provoked not by "garden-variety" semiotics but by the possibility that Marxism may prove susceptible to the more exotic imports of the French connection—from esoteric preciosity or semicomatose aporetics to less easily dismissed modes of critical self-questioning and (perhaps generative) doubt. Two structuralist-poststructuralist figures are especially important for Jameson's attempt to forge a limited "united front" between Marxism and recent critical tendencies: Louis Althusser and Jacques Lacan. Claude Lévi-Strauss is handled rather uncritically as an intermittent but authoritative guide; Jacques Derrida and Roland Barthes are in a number of ways on Jameson's suspect persons list; and Michel Foucault is accorded surprisingly little explicit treatment in Jameson's rethinking of the way history should be done. Even more surprising is the absence of any discussion of feminist thought, which has constituted a major event in recent criticism with an obvious bearing on the problem of rethinking Marxism.

ALTHUSSER

Jameson's highly selective approach centers on Althusser's conception of causation. He largely accepts Althusser's idea of the "absent cause" and, as we shall see, places it into series of his own. He also gives limited credence to two other concepts of causality that Althusser rejects: mechanical and expressive totality.

Structural causation is not causal in the mechanical sense of a given part of a system that affects other parts (the billiard-ball model) or in the sense of an "expressive totality" that identifies an inner essence in relation to which the elements of a whole are merely outer phenomenal forms of expression. Rather the cause is "absent" in that it is the structural articulation of its effects. In Althusser's own words, "the whole existence of the structure consists of its effects. . . . The structure, which is merely a specific combination of its peculiar elements, is nothing outside its effects" (quoted on pp. 24–25). "Causality" in this sense avoids older forms of economic determinism and is, by contrast, combined with a notion of the relative autonomy of various levels of society. "If therefore one wishes to characterize Althusser's Marxism as a structuralism, one must complete the characterization with the essential proviso that it is a structuralism for which only *one* structure exists: namely the mode of production itself, or the synchronic system of social relations as a whole. This is the sense in which this "structure" is an absent cause, since it is nowhere empirically present as one element, it is not part of the whole or one of the levels but rather the entire system of *relationships* among those levels" (31).

In contrast to Althusser, Jameson argues   mechanical causality is not simply a form of false conscious   error; it is a category that retains purely local validity in "(rticular fallen social reality" with its "peculiarly reified soci   l cultural life" (pp. 25–26). Thus the often shocking and sens   intervention of extraneous causes on the cultural level itself is   ptom of objective contradictions which can be overcome on   rough systemic social change. One of Jameson's favorite exam   n this respect is the way late nineteenth-century crises in pul   ng affected the inner form of the novel, for example, through   replacement of the dominant three-decker lending-library no   ith a cheaper, one-volume format—something that affected t   ructure of Gissing's novels, among others.

Jameson also rehabilitates the notion of expressive totality in relation to a totalizing narrative understanding of history. "The fullest form of what Althusser calls 'expressive totality' (and of what he calls 'historicism') will thus prove to be a vast interpretive allegory in which a sequence of historical events or texts and artifacts is rewritten in terms of some deeper, underlying and more "fundamental" narrative, of a hidden master narrative which is the allegorical key or figural content of the first sequence of empirical materials" (p. 28). To reject expressive totality is to reject the very concept of ideology as Althusser himself has explicated it. And the reason interpretation in terms of expressive totality or of allegorical master narratives remains "a constant temptation . . . is because such master narratives have inscribed themselves in the texts as well as in our thinking about them; such allegorical narrative signifieds are a persistent dimension of literary and cultural texts precisely because they reflect a fundamental dimension of our collective thinking and our collective fantasies about history and reality" (p. 34). The *telos* of this kind of interpretation is to link all phenomena to politics and history and to disclose the involvement of all cultural products in the "footnote-subtext" of specific and even local contingencies (for example, Balzac's pre-Oedipal desire to repossess a mother he felt had rejected him). To foreclose an appeal to "expressive totality" is thus to repress "the text of history and the political unconscious in our own cultural and political experience, just at the moment when increasing privatization has made that dimension so faint as to be virtually inaudible" (p. 34). One may note here that precisely those features of a Hegel or a Marx that Karl Popper found scientifically inadmissible become, from Jameson's perspective, ideologically necessary.

Yet Jameson further observes that Althusser's critique of expressive totality and his insistence upon the semiautonomy of various social levels might seem like a "scholastic quibble" if one does not see it in the light of the "attack upon Hegelian expressive causality in which all those levels are somehow 'the same'"—an attack which is itself presumably a coded battle "waged within the framework of the French Communist Party against Stalinism." Indeed "Hegel is here a secret code word for Stalin" (p. 37). Stalin's own use of the concept of expressive totality functioned to legitimate an ideology of productive forces which assured party control, precluded the need for change on other levels—for example, the labor process or culture—and diverted attention from the role of mass struggle in revolutionary social change. Within the French context (or subtext), the critique of expressive totality has a specific political function that points to the danger involved in "the importation and translation of theoretical problems which have a quite different semantic content in the national situation in which they originate" (p. 54n). In Althusser's case the semantics are for Jameson ultimately undecidable, for while the Hegel code is univocal—mere pretext for a critique of Stalin—the Stalin code is itself equivocal: Althusser's thought also harbors Stalinist elements. In France, moreover, the attack on "totalization" is bound up with opposition to extreme centralization and with the defense of decentralized, "molecular," or "punctual" politics. By contrast, in the United States, for Jameson, Hegel is not a code word and fragmentation reigns supreme. "The privileged form in which the American left can develop today must therefore necessarily be that of *alliance politics;* and such a politics is the strict practical equivalent of totalization on the theoretical level." The attack upon the concept of totality in the American framework thus means for Jameson the "undermining and the repudiation of the only realistic perspective in which a genuine left could come into being in this country" (p. 54n).

One might object here that Jameson's hermeneutic has become hyperbolic: one cannot prevent theoretical debates from migrating across contexts, and their meaning in a new context is open to debate. "Totalization" is not the only theoretical basis for an alliance politics—indeed it may undermine it. Jameson is anxious to counter the ideas of the so-called *nouveaux philosophes,* but the dubiousness of the practical conclusions they draw from the critique of totality is not sufficient reason to reject out of hand the argument that the quest for totalization functions to regenerate structures of domination. This is the type of argument that would seem to apply across a multiplicity of contexts with variations whose importance would have to be argued. Fragmentation or serialization, moreover, may well coexist with centralized forms of domination: this is in fact what Sartre among others has seen as the mechanism of bureaucratic control—a phenomenon not specific to France. And the larger question is whether the state of the left in the United States deprives Jameson of that second level which to some extent exists in the dual code of Althusser, thereby threatening to reduce his politics to the level of the academic, unrealistic, and symbolic (in the garden-variety sense). The problem is how to respond to that threat from the position one has chosen, namely, an academic one.

LACAN

The newer meaning of ideology formulated by Althusser owes much to the work of Jacques Lacan. Indeed Althusser offers his famous definition of ideology in an essay on Lacan (in *Lenin and Philosophy*): it is "the imaginary representation of the subject's relationship to his or her real conditions of existence" (quoted on p. 181). In *The Political Unconscious*, Jameson argues that psychoanalysis "may indeed lay claim to the distinction of being the only really new and original hermeneutic developed since the great patristic and medieval system of the four senses of scripture" (p. 61). And Lacan's "rewriting" of Freud is a veritable revolution within the psychoanalytic revolution—"a substantial and reflexive shift from the Freudian proposition about the dynamics of the subject (wish-fulfillment) to the interrogation of that problematic itself, foregrounding the category of the subject and studying the process whereby this psychic reality (consciousness)—as well as its buttressing ideologies and illusions (the feeling of personal identity, the myth of the ego or the self, and so forth)—become rigorous and self-imposed limitations on Freud's notion of individual wish-fulfillment" (p. 66). In other words, the Lacanian linguistic turn in psychoanalysis, with the categories it has generated to investigate the constitution and insertion of the subject in discourse, has provided a means of linking the apparently individual and private processes studied by Freud to the social and collective phenomena treated by Marx. Ideology is the means by which the subject attempts to close the gap between the privately lived and objectively collective, and Lacan's work has its place in a Marxist hermeneutic in its refinement of our understanding of the concept of ideology.

Jameson's own attempt to specify how Lacan is open to dialectical reappropriation is to be found in an essay that has achieved classical status in certain quarters and whose argument is assumed in *The Political Unconscious.* [2] It is also intended to make up for the inadequacy of the treatment of Lacan which Jameson now finds in his earlier *Prison-House of Language.* (He remains committed to his position on other figures in that book.)

The crucial conceptual contribution of Lacan is the ternary distinction among the Imaginary, the Symbolic, and the Real. It has the virtue of displacing the binary opposition between the individual and society and of revealing the latter's largely imaginary and ideological status. Yet Jameson admits the difficulty in defining the basic terms of the Lacanian lexicon, for the three "orders" are interinvolved in the experience of the adult and designate highly complex problems. Although there is no total transcendence of the Imaginary by the Symbolic and the Real, a distinction may nonetheless be drawn in terms of the developmental stages Lacan elaborates in his reconceptualization of Freud. The Imaginary reigns supreme before the child acquires language, specifically from the age of six to about eighteen months. During this period, the child, born "prematurely" with respect to the conditions of human life, lives in a pre-Oedipal world of images and part-objects. Lacan refers to this period as the "mirror stage." The little man, devoid of language and even of full motor control, seems to have mastery over

2. Fredric Jameson, "Imaginary and Symbolic in Lacan," *Yale French Studies* 55–56 (1977), 338–395. It should be noted that Jameson's approach to Lacan is one of uncritical high seriousness. Thus he does not inquire either into Lacan's foolscap strategies or into the more questionable aspects of his writing, notably its tedious petulance and willful obscurity if not obscurantism.

the other that is the specular double of himself. Emblematic in this respect is the Fort/Da game as analyzed by Freud: the image of the self which substitutes for the absent mother becomes the object of a compulsively repetitive "game" in quest of mastery over anxiety and a world which is otherwise unmanageable.

The mirror stage is a time of extreme lability and undifferentiation. Yet it is also a time of rigid binary oppositions and of narcissistic enclosure in a specular relation to the self and to images or objects that do not function as signifiers. The world of the Imaginary is thus bewilderingly mobile, univocal, and confined. But it is also for Lacan the basis for later ideas of ego-identity which unconsciously evoke the first image of a unified self available to the child. Thus what is taken by ego-psychology (Lacan's own obsessive *bête noire*) as the mature achievement of man is for Lacan indentured to the narcissistic involvements of a presymbolic, imaginary stage. (One may here note what Jameson does not: certain Lacanians, such as Jean Laplanche in *Life and Death in Psychoanalysis*, insist on the dialectical and supplementary relation between the narcissistic ego and the ego as executive agency of the mature adult—both of which were treated by Freud.)

With the entry into the symbolic order or register, there is a further alteration or "alienation" of the human being. Decisive at this point is the acquisition of language, notably language as analyzed by Saussure with his diacritical distinction between signifier and signified ($\frac{S}{s}$). The bar between S and s itself signifies for Lacan the formation of an unconscious with the entry into the symbolic order (or what anthropologists might see as a displaced variant of the passage from nature to culture). With it, objects may function as signifiers, and language has a figurative dimension in virtue of which there is a "slippage of signifieds under signifiers." Unlike the mental image or animal sign, the signifier functions in terms of multiple meanings and diacritical distinctions, but it also may resist the imaginary extremes of vertiginous lability and rigid binary opposition.

The elaborate linkage proper to the Symbolic is that conjoining a

complex series of phenomena: language, the genesis of the unconscious as "the discourse of the Other," the intervention of the
"name of the father" breaking the narcissistic complicity between
mother and child, the function of the phallus as signifier (in contrast to that of the penis as biological organ), the formation of the
Oedipus complex and castration anxiety, and the role of prohibi-
tions, norms, and laws. In a correlative way, desire is understood as
the never totally transcendable distance between biological need
and cultural demands related to recognition by the Other (initially
the parents). And one confronts the problem of the constitution and
insertion of the subject in the symbolic order given the persistent
pull of the Imaginary. I have thus far rendered Jameson's account
rather freely, glossing in the process over a number of its confusing
aspects, notably with respect to the relations among the Imaginary,
the Symbolic, binary oppositions, and undecidable lability. But let
us here turn to his own words as they refer to the relation between
the Imaginary and ethics—a relation that remains crucial to the
critique of ethics in *The Political Unconscious*:

> We may suggest that the Imaginary thought patterns persist into
> mature psychic life in the form of what are generally thought of as
> ethical judgments—those implicit or explicit valorizations or re-
> pudiations in which "good" and "bad" are simply positional descrip-
> tions of the geographical relationships of the phenomenon in ques-
> tion to my own Imaginary conception of centrality: it is a comedy we
> may also observe, not only in the world of action, but also in that of
> thought, where, in that immense proliferation of private languages
> which characterize the intellectual life of consumer capitalism, the
> private religions which emerge around thinkers like the one presently
> under consideration are matched only by their anathematization by
> the champions of rival "codes." The Imaginary sources of passions
> like ethics may always be identified by the operation of the dual in
> them, and the organization of their themes around binary opposi-
> tions; the ideological quality of such thinking must be accounted for,
> not so much by the metaphysical nature of its categories of cen-
> trality, as Derrida and Lyotard have argued, as rather by its substitu-

tion of the categories of individual relationships for those—collective—of history and of historical, transindividual phenomena.[3]

How the correlation of ethics, binary opposition, individualism, and the Imaginary itself squares with the intimate relation throughout history between evaluation and group affiliation—especially the "collective" distinction between friends and enemies—is left to the imagination of the reader. Jameson's linkage of ideology and individual relationships would seem applicable primarily to modern "privatized" contexts.

The third term—the Real—in Lacan can be approached only asymptotically through the detours of the Imaginary and the Symbolic. The Real is "what resists symbolization absolutely." Yet Jameson seems to sense the futility of a politics that does not risk a definition of the Real, however provisional and undogmatic. Indeed he goes so far as to proclaim: "it is not terribly difficult to say what is meant by the Real in Lacan. It is simply History itself."[4] In addition: "The Lacanian notion of an 'asymptotic' approach to the Real . . . maps a situation in which the action of the 'absent cause' can be understood as a term limit, as that which can be both indistinguisable from the Symbolic (or the Imaginary) and also independent of it."[5] Thus is intimated the network of associations that plays a sometimes puzzling role in *The Political Unconscious*: the Althusserian "absent cause," the Lacanian Real, and History—to which may be added totality and utopia. In fact Jameson concludes his essay on Lacan by announcing a central thesis of his book, for he asserts that the contemporary babble of interpretations can be overcome in only one way.

> The solution can only lie, it seems to me, in the renewal of Utopian thinking, of creative speculation as to the place of the subject at the

3. Ibid., 369.
4. Ibid., 384.
5. Ibid., 387–388.

other end of historical time, in a social order which has put behind it
class organization, commodity production, and the market, alienated labor, and the implacable determinism of an historical logic
beyond the control of humanity. Only thus can a third term be
imagined beyond either the "autonomous individualism" of the
bourgeoisie in its heyday or the schizoid part-objects in which the
fetishization of the subject under late Capitalism has left its trace; a
term in the light of which both of these forms of consciousness can
be placed in their proper historical perspective.

To do so, however, would require the elaboration of a properly
Marxist "ideology."[6]

One must stop and wonder over the enormity of Jameson's undertaking. Lacan, often seen as a theorist who marks the limits of
utopia and the status of desire as perennially recurrent in its over-
flowing of need and particular demands—indeed a theorist whose
thought might be taken in a more consistently institutional direction—is "rewritten" as offering a promise of the utopian realization
of desire. And his conception of the Imaginary, via Althusser, becomes the basis for a theory of ideology as that distorting but "indis-
pensable mapping fantasy or narrative by which the individual subject invents a 'lived' relationship with the collective systems which
otherwise by definition exclude him."[7] This Marxist ideology would
complement a Marxist science employing symbolism that "designates the Real without claiming to coincide with it" and offers "the
very theory of its own incapacity to signify fully as its credentials for
transcending both Imaginary and Symbolic alike."[8] What it might
conceivably mean to designate "that which resists symbolization
absolutely" is not elucidated. But what is evident is Jameson's stress
on the aspects of Lacan that are most compatible with a Hegelian
Marxism having Sartrean overtones (in contrast, for example, to
more Heideggerian tendencies which are also active in Lacan). The
Real itself is comparable to Sartre's radically other and contingent

6. Ibid., 393.
7. Ibid., 394.
8. Ibid., 389.

in-itself, and the relation between the Imaginary and the Symbolic approximates that between the lived and the conceived. Finally, the entire Lacanian thematic becomes compatible with a totalizing understanding of narrative and dialectics holding forth a utopian promise—something Lacan explicitly criticizes, especially in his later work.

ETHICS AND TOTALIZATION

In *The Political Unconscious*, Jameson continues the critique of ethics in a manner implying that the traits distinguishing ethics as Jameson defines it are indeed essential to all ethical thought— thought that can be transcended only through Marxist politics. And the subterranean connection between ethics and *ressentiment* as Nietzsche formulated it is reiterated and developed (notably in the analysis of George Gissing). Jameson ostensibly joins in the post-structuralist critique of binary oppositions and asserts that the import of Derrida's work may be found in the "unmasking and demystification of a host of unconscious or naturalized binary oppositions in contemporary and traditional thought" (p. 114). Yet what Jameson does not ask is whether certain of his own conclusions regenerate binary logic in an unguarded form. This is true not only of the inevitable positive/negative polarity whose relation to an ethics of good and evil Jameson himself remarks. It rather applies inter alia to the trenchant opposition between the private individual and the collectivity—as well as to the canonical opposition between the realm of Necessity and the realm of Freedom—binaries which are regenerated in Jameson's utopian affirmations.

One issue here is the rather unclear relation between totalization and decentering in Jameson's own approach. Jameson does not explicitly articulate a framework of inquiry in which there would be an interaction between unifying and decentering—or centripetal and centrifugal—tendencies. He asserts the primacy of totalization. Yet in practice his approach would seem to suggest a supplemented dialectical model in which the stress would fall on the problem of interaction between mutually implicated but contestatory tendencies. And certain features of his discussion of totality or totalization, when they do not culminate in confusion, would also seem to suggest such an approach.

Jameson himself notes that the older Hegelian-Lukácsian idea of expressive totality assumed the organic unity of the work and that, in reaction, the "interpretive mission" of later critics found its privileged content in exploring rifts and discontinuities in the work. Yet he insists that the poststructural emphasis on heterogeneity is only an initial moment that "requires the fragments, the incommensurable levels, the heterogeneous impulses, of the text to be once again related, but in the mode of structural differences and determinate contradictions." And he adds: "In the interpretive chapters of the following work, I have found it possible without any great inconsistency to respect both the methodological imperative implicit in the concept of totality or totalization, and the quite different attention of a 'symptomal' analysis to discontinuities, rifts, actions at a distance, within a merely apparently unified cultural text" (pp. 56–57). Yet if Jameson is indeed able to perform this feat in his concrete studies of Balzac, Gissing, and Conrad or in his discussion of the novel as a form, why he is able to do so remains mysterious on a theoretical level. In chapter 2, "Magical Narratives," for example, Jameson asserts that the novel may be read as having a "layered or marbled structure . . . according to what we will call *generic discontinuities*. The novel is thus not so much an organic unity as a symbolic act that must reunite or harmonize heterogeneous narrative paradigms which have their own specific and contradictory ideological meanings" (p. 144). Yet as Mikhail Bakhtin insisted with such kaleidoscopic brilliance: what is novel about the novel is that its narrative cannot be contained within centripetal conceptions suited to classical genres, for its consuming and heteroglot "dialectic" threatens recurrently to burst all preexisting generic boundaries. To elucidate the nature of the novel as other than a monogeneric form, Jameson himself appeals to Ernst Bloch's concept of *Ungleichzeitigkeit*, or nonsynchronous "uneven development," to indicate the interaction of genres within a textual structure. But the implications of this view of the novel are not translated into theoretical implications for the project of totalization, notably as it bears upon the problem of narrative. When Jameson does try to clarify his grounds, he resorts to the idea that his approach decenters the *individual* while simultaneously centering everything on the *collectivity*. He thereby seeks refuge in the unproblematic logic of binary oppositions.

A similar problem arises with Jameson's attempt systematically to historicize all problems by showing how conceptual antinomies or aporias may be resolved into specific historical contradictions. Perhaps his apparent unfamiliarity with influential tendencies in contemporary historiography lessens Jameson's sensitivity to the way in which excessively topical—or narrowly historicist—contextualization may function to ward off responsive, dialogical understanding in the relation between past and present. In fact, instead of attempting to specify what aspects of a phenomenon are indeed specific to a historical situation, Jameson often argues as if relativizing specification amounted to full derivation. The result is that despite the fact that he offers numerous examples of the role of repetition with variation in cultural history—for example, in his discussion of the history of genres—he does not provide a theoretical articulation of the problem of displacement with reference to his totalizing project or to the issue of interpretation in general. Such an articulation would raise the question of the interaction of continuity and discontinuity over time, and it would point to a dimension of Nietzsche's notion of recurrence not reducible to what Jameson sees as the "private and intolerable ethos of the eternal return" (p. 115). It would also help to elucidate the complex nature of Derrida's inquiry into the transferences of the metaphysical tradition in the course of history and reveal the spuriousness of attributing "priority" to ethics in the generation of binary oppositions, as Jameson attempts to do, for it would indicate how metaphysics and ethics are themselves not fully resolvable into a binary opposition that would allow one to establish any definitive order of priority.

To make the foregoing observations is to say in another way that Jameson, like Lukács and Sartre, remains by and large within the tradition of Hegelian Marxism, certain of whose difficulties he resists acknowledging—he even has a curious passage in which he marshals heterogeneous and even contradictory arguments to reach the desired conclusion that Hegel was free of any trace of "identity-theory" (pp. 50–52). For the relations between totalization and decentering, dialectics and repetition, identity and difference are recurrent problems in that tradition—with the explicit stress on the former terms in these binary pairs providing little room for the theoretical exploration of the latter terms despite their repeated invocation or use in the discourse of the theorist himself. There is a culminating moment in this tradition when differences, to the extent that they continue to have a role to play, cease to make a difference—a utopian moment in which everything fuses in the full authority of an ideally unified and uncontested discourse.

Hegelian Marxism has indeed been crucial in the twentieth century in renewing the very role of interpretation—indeed of broader philosophical concerns in general—and, concurrently, in prying loose the heavy hand of economism and Stalinism. But there is a widespread belief among contemporary Marxists that there are still only two viable options within the Marxist tradition—authentic Hegelianism and some variant of positivism (or inauthentic Stalinist Hegelianism). Jameson's effort may give new life to this belief, especially insofar as he provides more up-to-date rationales for Hegelian tendencies in Marxism and joins them to the newer Lacanian concepts in taking up again the attempt to build a bridge between Marx and Freud.

The one nodal point at which Jameson approximates confusingly "identitarian" tendencies is in his more mystifying use of the concept of an "absent cause," for in its union of various images of the radically "other," this concept seems at times to become a secular surrogate for a missing divinity, open to negative theology and other ideological investments that indicate the hoped-for presence of some ineffable "transcendental signified." This is especially the case when the "absent cause" seems to designate an empty but paradoxically crowded space wherein a number of concepts meet or even fuse with one another: the Real, History, Utopia, totality, and the "political unconscious" itself. These concepts are all discussed in the same terms—terms that appear to make them highly labile substitutes for one another. At these points, Jameson seems quite close to "identitarian" Hegelian Marxism in the "mystical" form of higher immediacy, for he furnishes a vision of a night in which all sacred cows are gray. Thus, for example:

> In some paradoxical or dialectical fashion, Lukács' conception of totality may here be seen to rejoin the Althusserian notion of History or the Real as the "absent cause." Totality is not available for representation, any more than it is accessible in the form of some ultimate truth (or moment of Absolute Spirit). . . . The "whole" is kept faith with and "represented" in its very absence. [Pp. 54–55]

In contrast to these tendencies, one might object that there is nothing short of a totally transcendental mystery that resists symbolization absolutely, just as nothing is totally amenable to symbolization—even symbols which are themselves the object of reflexive metacommentary. This is the fascinating and the disconcerting ambivalence of symbols—the fact that nothing entirely escapes their signifying power or is simply presented, grasped, or given by them. They thus subvert "realms" of pure absence (or Necessity) and pure presence (or Freedom) alike (as well as stimulate desire for these "realms"). Even the purely transcendental signified that one tries to protect from the "contamination" of signification or nomination requires taboos which may be transgressed. Indeed one feature of modern thought has been to approximate transcendence to more extreme or sacrilegious forms of transgression. Jameson's emphasis upon the radical alterity of certain "things" has the merit of underscoring the finitude of man as a symbolic animal, but this finitude is conveyed in less mystifying ways by the notion that man is implicated in a relational network of symbols and "world" in which absolute horizons or things-in-themselves are questionable limits or

zero-points. The idea of total blindness to—o   stance of—the
radically "other" is the mirror image of the ide   otal insight (or
Absolute Knowledge)—not its alternative. A "d   ical" approach
would rather seem to require a notion of re   ently displaced
"blindness" which cannot be fixated once and f   on a formal or
nominal level, even if it be in the form of a cor   of the "unconscious." In these respects, the limiting terms   ciated with the
"absent cause" are more suspect than Jameson   vs, and they do
not entirely escape the project of a critique of   ogy.

THEOLOGY AND THE MANIFOLD HERM   JTIC WAY

A rather distinctive feature of Jameson's Ma   i is the limited
attempt to rehabilitate theological hermeneutic   i more properly
scholastic sense. Reappropriated by a totalizing   lectic," the latter becomes a source for reflection on "the pro   s and dynamics
of interpretation, commentary, allegory, and   tiple meanings
. . . primarily organized around the central text   e Bible" (p. 69).
Indeed Jameson asserts that Walter Benjamin's   e of theology as
the wizened dwarf within the automaton calle   orical materialism refers implicitly not to any traditional theol   l content but to
the centrality of interpretation and, in coded f   to the tradition
of hermeneutic Marxism driven undergroun   the 1920s and
1930s by Stalinism. He also discusses Northroj   e's reinscription
of the medieval fourfold system of interpreta   in the modern
guise of archetypal myth criticism. He detects   rye's plangently
formalized romantic approach an evanescent   an explosion of
the transfigured libidinal body whose radical   ctive and social
implications are "recontained" in Frye's ultii   (anagogical) vision of a "privatized" apocalypse wedding th   nd of the individual to nature (pp. 72–74).

Jameson is wary about the relation of allego   f desire to anar-
chism (p. 68). But he also maintains that a N   an hermeneutic
cannot do without "the symbolism and the   ilse of libidinal

transformation" (p. 73). Further, in criticizing Frye's individualism, he asserts that "a social hermeneutic will, on the contrary, wish to keep faith with its medieval precursor in just this respect, and must necessarily restore a perspective in which the imagery of libidinal revolution and of bodily transfiguration once again becomes a figure for the perfected community" (p. 74). One may note that the mirage of libidinal liberation is as specific as Jameson gets about the "positive" object of utopian hope. Otherwise utopia remains a blank space in his thought—an allegory of pure and blind hope rather than a concrete source of historical possibilities. As Jameson quite bluntly states in his preface:

> The reader should not, in the first place, expect anything like that exploratory projection of what a vital and emergent political culture should be and do which Raymond Williams has rightly proposed as the most urgent task of Marxist cultural criticism. . . . The reader will . . . find an empty chair reserved for some as yet unrealized, collective, decentered cultural production of the future, beyond realism and modernism alike. [P. 11]

More specific is Jameson's elaborate proposal for a Marxist "re-writing" of the scholastic notion of phases, levels, or stages in interpretation in terms of widening horizons or concentric circles of "semantic enrichment." These are the political level in which "the individual work is grasped as a *symbolic* act" (and here Jameson invokes Lévi-Strauss's readings of myths as imaginary resolutions of real contradictions); the social level which focuses directly on "the great collective and class discourses of which a text is little more than an individual *parole* or utterance"; and "the ultimate horizon of human history as a whole" which situates the political and the social in "the whole complex sequence of the modes of production" (pp. 76–77). The movement from one phase or stage to another, Jameson announces, broadly coincides with the different but complementary methods employed in his three case studies of Balzac, Gissing, and Conrad (chapters 3–5).

Concerning the political level of text as symbolic act, Jameson argues that the traditional notion of context is blatantly inadequate. The interpretation of the interaction between text and context is

> more satisfactorily grasped as the rewriting of the literary text in such a way that the latter may itself be seen as the rewriting or restructuration of a prior historical or ideological *subtext*, it being always understood that that "subtext" is not immediately present as such, not some common-sense external reality nor even the conventional narratives of history manuals, but rather must itself always be (re)constructed after the fact. [P. 81]

The second, social horizon requires a further "rewriting" of the individual text or artifact in terms of "the antagonistic dialogue of class voices" (p. 85). Here Jameson appeals to Mikhail Bakhtin's notion of the dialogical, but it is to observe that Bakhtin's use of it is "relatively specialized" to apply to moments of carnival or festival whereas the "normal form of the dialogical is essentially an *antagonistic* one" (p. 84). Rewritten in accordance with the Marxist social code, the individual text or utterance is grasped as a symbolic move in an essentially strategic and polemical confrontation between classes. For Jameson, moreover, the cultural monuments and masterworks of tradition serve to perpetuate the voice of a hegemonic class in social dialogue, and the reconstruction of popular culture is not a question of giving "equal time" to neglected groups but one of restoring the silenced or stifled voices of opposition with their possibly polemic and subversive strategies. In his conclusion, Jameson returns to these motifs with reference to Benjamin's thesis that "there has never been a document of culture which was not at one and the same time a document of barbarism." He there dialectically reverses the thesis to elicit the ways in which documents of barbarism are also documents of civilization in their wish-fulfilling and phantasmatic appeal to utopian hope. But he nonetheless reasserts Benjamin's "hard saying," which leaves the final stress upon the ideological and hegemonic dimension of all high culture and "comes as a rebuke and a warning against the facile reappropriation of the classics as humanistic expressions of this or that historically 'progressive' force" (p. 299). Jameson does not explicitly pose the question of whether "classics" have critical and transformative dimensions that cannot be reduced either to utopian desire or to facile "humanistic" nostrums. Instead the operational upshot of his study of the social phase is the attempt to specify "ideologemes" (on the apparent model of Lévi-Strauss's "mythemes") as the minimal organizational units of class discourse—a task scarcely begun in Jameson's view and to which his study of *ressentiment* in Gissing is intended as a contribution.

The final enlargement of the analytic frame takes one to the transformation of codes with the change in modes of production in the course of history as a whole. This "problematic" of modes of production is for Jameson both "the most vital new area of Marxist theory" and also "one of the most traditional" (p. 87). Relying on the work of Nicos Poulantzas, Jameson emphasizes that "no historical society has ever 'embodied' a mode of production in any pure state. . . . What is synchronic [what Weber would have called an ideal type] is the 'concept' of the mode of production; the movement of the historical coexistence of several modes of production is not synchronic in this sense, but open to history in a dialectical way" (pp. 94–95). Recent experience leads Jameson to designate as cultural revolution the moment at which the coexistence of various modes of production becomes visibly antagonistic, and he suggests that the Enlightenment was a "bourgeois cultural revolution," while romanticism was a significant and ambivalent moment in the resistance to it (p. 96).

DECODING BALZAC

Jameson's chapters on Balzac, Gissing, and Conrad are perhaps best read as intricate, post-Lukácsian studies in realism and its problematic transformation over time. It would be incorrect to see these chapters as mere arabesques or finger exercises illustrating Jameson's hermeneutics of "phases," for the very diversity and complex-

ity of critical commentary in them both subs⸱ ⸱ ates his larger
claims and contests them in subtle ways. Jameso⸱ ⸱ 'practical criticism" is itself both historical and genealogical in ⸱ ⸱re—genealogical in the sense Jameson specifies:

> In genealogical construction, we begin with a ⸱ ⸱ olown system
> (capitalism in Marx, and in the present book, reifi⸱ ⸱ n) in terms of
> which elements of the past can "artificially" be is⸱ ⸱ d as objective
> preconditions: genealogy is not a historical *narr*⸱ ⸱ , but has the
> essential function of renewing our perception of t⸱ ⸱ nchronic sys-
> tem as in an x-ray, its diachronic perspectives se⸱ ⸱ to make per-
> ceptible the articulations of the functional elemen⸱ ⸱ a given system
> in the present. [P. 139]

(Such a definition would, by the way, eliminat⸱ ⸱ umber of common, misplaced criticisms of Nietzsche's though⸱ ⸱ ince it is out of
the question to discuss fully Jameson's three ve⸱ ⸱ s in writing the
history of the present, I would simply commen⸱ ⸱ m to the reader
and raise a few questions about the treatmen⸱ ⸱ Balzac and the
more regional historical sequences in which ⸱ ⸱ placed, for the
latter issue has become an acid test of Marxist ⸱ ⸱ ary criticsm.

The Lacanian system comes into its own ir ⸱ ⸱ analysis of the
novelist who was central in Lukács's theory of ⸱ ⸱ cal realism, for
Jameson interprets Balzac in terms of the pre-⸱ ⸱ pal mirror stage
and the precentered subject of desire and th⸱ ⸱ naginary. "The
constitutive feature of the Balzacian narrati⸱ ⸱ pparatus . . . is
something more fundamental than either auth⸱ ⸱ omniscience or
authorial intervention, something that may be ⸱ ⸱ gnated as libidinal investment or authorial wish-fulfillment, ⸱ ⸱ rm of symbolic
satisfaction in which the working distinction b⸱ ⸱ en biographical
subject, Implied Author, reader, and character ⸱ ⸱ irtually effaced"
(p. 155). It is, however, significant that Jameso⸱ ⸱ nits the narrator
from his checklist, for the role of the narrator is ⸱ ⸱ ificant in Balzac
in ways that do not negate Jameson's thesis but ⸱ ⸱ ialify it substan-
tially. In the passage Jameson quotes from *La* ⸱ ⸱ *le fille* to clinch
his interpretation, the portrait of a house pre⸱ ⸱ bly embodies a

bourgeois variant of utopian libidinal desire in a pre-Oedipal manner. Yet this effect is counteracted by the role of the narrator, who arranges the scene and enjoins or even commands the reader to perform certain functions that set the stage for ensuing events. ("On the balustrade of the terrace, imagine great blue and white pots filled with wall flowers" and so forth.) And libidinal investment is paralleled on a symbolic level by a hyperbolic use of language which (as Erich Auerbach argued in *Mimesis*) exceeds, or even overwhelms, its "real" referent to create at times monstrous imaginary objects.

Early in the book, Jameson objects to Barthes's decision in *S/Z* "to rewrite Balzac as Philippe Sollers, as sheer text and *écriture*" (p. 18). Yet Jameson's "allegorical" approach at times harbors its own mode of extreme permissiveness, which, in its quest for the strikingly new "rewriting," allows for dubious distortions. For it is just as questionable to "rewrite" Balzac as Gilles Deleuze or J.-F. Lyotard, as desiring machine and decentered *pulsion*.

For Jameson the realism of Balzac, shot through with allegories of desire, is followed by high realism, which brings penitential rigidity and fixation on principles of representation adapted to the contours of ordinary reality. Thus, in an initial moment of his analysis, Jameson seems to arrive by a parallel route at estimations strikingly similar to those of Marxist theorists such as Lukács in tracing the movement from Balzac to Flaubert and beyond. The perfected narrative apparatus of Flaubert and other "high realists" is based upon the threefold imperatives of authorial depersonalization, unity of point of view, and restriction to scenic representation. In this confining context, romance reemerges as the narrow gate of transcendence and utopian hope in an increasingly "commodified" society and "reified" art (p. 104). Flaubert's so-called *style indirect libre*, along with a Jamesian concept of point of view, is presumably a sclerotic but strategic locus "for a fully constituted or centered bourgeois subject or monadic ego" in contrast to the prepersonal decentering effected by desire in Balzac (p. 154).

Yet there are unevenly developed tendencies in Jameson's own account that contest the narrative sequence leading from Balzacian libidinal realism to Flaubertian high realism. One might, in contrast to the interpretation sketched above, argue that Flaubert's *style indirect libre* is itself inserted into a larger narrative practice involving at times abrupt and drastic shifts among multiple narrative positions in ways that have critical and even carnivalizing effects with respect to the "monadic" or centered "bourgeois" subject.9 It is, curiously, in his discussion of Conrad—itself displaced from the study of Balzac—that Jameson intimates as much.

> Point of view is not nearly so stable a part of Flaubert's practice as has been supposed, while even the uses of classical point of view in Flaubert sometimes generate a quite different problematic from what we find in James. I am thinking particularly of Jean Rousset's comment about Flaubert's art as one of transition: here there is a fundamental displacement, and what is essential to the production of the text is not, as in James, the construction of a central observational and psychic perspective within which one may for a time remain, but rather the quite different matter of inventing modulations, chromatic bridge-passages, cinematographic fadeouts or montages, which allow us to slip from one point of view to another. [Pp. 222–223]

It would, moreover, be inaccurate to present Jameson's analysis of Balzac as one-dimensional, for the emphasis upon the role of desire is overlaid by a larger Lacanian framework. By way of Lacan, Jameson effects a telling reversal of Lukács's formula that Balzac's genial insight into historical reality countermanded his own aristocratic and Royalist wishes. Lukács is right about Balzac, but for the wrong reasons. Balzac's insight into historical realities was generated by the very resistance reality posed to his own exorbitant desires and demands (pp. 183–184).

In eliciting the nature of Balzac's novels as symbolic acts with potentially subversive force, Jameson focuses upon the way "semes"

9. For an elaboration of this point, see my *"Madame Bovary" on Trial* (Ithaca, 1982).

or abstract semiotic bits in symmetrical binary relations (Greimas's semiotic rectangle is employed here) combine to generate characters in a narrative that is, in this sense, characteriologically decentered. And Jameson extends his discussion to encompass the seemingly more conventional, monadically character-laden, and "commodified" *La rabouilleuse.* The result is a structural reading that may be seen either as graphically illuminating or as illustrative of the type of computeresque dissociation and reprogramming that others might correlate with reification. Indeed what is at times most pronounced in Jameson's specific readings or "rewritings" is a structuralist flair and a fascination with combinatory models that recall Lévi-Strauss at his most flamboyantly acrostic.

THE PROBLEM OF MEDIATIONS AND AUXILIARY DISCIPLINES

This is perhaps the point to conclude with my major reservations about this impressive book—reservations that cluster around the axial "dialectical" problem of mediation itself. The critical issue here is whether Jameson's combination of metacommentary, meta-history, and utopianism provides a formula for the contemporary "recontainment" of critical and transformative thinking in a highly scholastic framework. One cannot, I think, give an unqualified and self-certain answer to such a question. And the attempt to address it readily stimulates ritualistic, even regressive, gestures that can easily be turned against oneself. But I still think that the issue must be addressed, and the assertive cast of the following comments should not conceal their tentative character.

I have already alluded to Jameson's own style of writing in the light of which mediation seems to be just another four-syllable word. His own comments on the problem of mediation reinforce the impression of an addiction to a highly hermetic approach that remains on a narrowly hermeneutic level in attempting to "break out of specialized compartments of (bourgeois) disciplines" (p. 40). A model-centered semiotics with its own proliferating lexicon of code words becomes Jameson's all-too-modern "political" answer to the problem. Indeed: "If a more modern characterization of mediation is wanted, we will say that the operation is understood as a process of *transcoding*: as the invention of a set of terms, the strategic choice of a particular code or language, such that the same terminology can be used to analyze and articulate two quite distinct types of objects or 'texts' or two very different structural levels of reality" (p. 40). Here a highly restrictive view of mediation is complemented by an abstract and exaggerated conception of the role of codes in relation to actual usage—a conception that would seem to be more formalist than Marxist in nature. And one may further note that Jameson's own style rarely conveys to the reader the sense that he is confronting committed writing, checked by self-criticism but motivated by the intensity, flashes of wit, polemical turns, and feeling of involvement that give so much force to Marx's prose. (Jameson himself refers to "the unavoidably Hegelian tone of the retrospective framework of *The Political Unconscious*" [p. 12].) Nor does Jameson broach the problem that would seem central for a socially oriented approach—especially for a democratic Marxism: the problem of working out mediations not simply between "reified" disciplines but between their technical or special languages and ordinary language. This mutual questioning between the ordinary and the "esoteric" might help to create the "space" for an effective transformation of both. In Jameson's terms, it would require an effort to convert an antinomy or aporia into a dialectical contradiction.

Jameson's own occasional *ouvriérisme* is no substitute for such an effort. Indeed, functioning as a romantic allegory, it may reinforce the tendency for self-enclosed speculation to go its own way. (See Jameson's comments, which end with the assertion that one cannot "glamorize" the tasks of intellectuals "by assimilating them to real work on the assembly line and to the experience of the resistance of matter in genuine manual labor" [p. 45].) The rather indiscriminate attempt to rehabilitate traditional narrative or vast master allegories may itself readily function as a conduit for mythologizing tendencies and as an invitation to turn away from more critical modes of discourse (including more experimental and self-critical modes of narrative). In addition, the pathos of utopianism in blindingly eschatological form may be understandable coming from members of a destitute and desperate underclass; it is suspect when it emanates from intellectuals as a kind of strained, high-altitude messianism. At the very least, it functions to divert attention from the problem of institutions. For it is the institution in the broad sense that mediates between individual and society as well as between various uses of language. (This might be termed the institution in the Durkheimian sense of a pattern of norms relating social individuals and regulating the interaction of order and excess in their lives, and it is puzzling that Jameson's own appeal to Durkheim seems to revive not this but rather Durkheim's most dubiously sociologistic and symbol-shuffling extremes.) One cannot in all fairness criticize Jameson for the highly rhetorical understanding of past or present institutions that are denoted largely in catch-phrases; the nature of the synthetic and far-ranging cultural study he undertook did not realistically allow for any other approach. But one can, I think, question the understanding of utopianism in terms which function to exclude the relevance of thought about alternative institutions— or to defer it to an empty chair to be mysteriously filled by a decentered collective production of the future. It would at least be a beginning in the attempt to decipher and contribute to an emergent political culture to recognize that the dearth of anything approximating pointed and "creative" (generative, if one prefers) institutional thought has been a primary defect of modern radical intellectuals—indeed something binding them to the Vegas-world of free-floating, "commodified" symbols in which we all live. Here one may note that whatever its limitations the work of Bakhtin, with its "dialogical" and carnivalesque "rewriting" of dialectics, as well as its stress upon the role of carnival-type phenomena over time, was more than a relatively specialized mode of cultural analysis to be contrasted with "normal" forms of class conflict; it was a critical effort to elaborate a historically and genealogically informed model that might situate the utopian element in literature and suggest institutions to come effectively to terms with the tendencies Jameson decries—one of the few such efforts that the history of modern radical thought reveals.

This somewhat rhetorical reference to Bakhtin may become substantive by permitting a more sympathetic return to the concept of the "absent cause," for Bakhtin provides an interpretation that supplements our earlier discussions of this concept and that may articulate a significant aspect of Jameson's correlation of various imagos of the radically other:

> Each utterance always has an addressee (of a different nature, different degrees of proximity, of specificity, of consciousness, and so forth), whose responsive understanding the author of the verbal work seeks and anticipates. This is the "second" (in a non-arithmetical sense). But, in addition to this addressee (the "second"), the author of an utterance imagines, more or less consciously, a superior super-addressee (a third), whose absolutely accurate responsive understanding is projected either in the metaphysical distance or in a distant historical time. (An addressee as friend-in-need.) In different epochs and in different conceptions of the world, this superaddressee and its responsive understanding (ideally accurate) receives different ideologically concrete expressions (God, absolute truth, the judgment of the impartial human consciousness, the people, the judgment of history, science, and so forth).
>
> The author can never entirely offer himself and his verbal work to the complete and definitive will of present or immediate addressees (immediate descendants can also be deceived) and he imagines . . . (more or less consciously) a sort of superior instance of responsive understanding, which may extend or recede in different directions. Each dialogue takes place, in some manner, on the basis of the responsive understanding of an invisible and present third, holding itself above all the participants of the dialogue (above the partners). . . .
>
> For discourse (and, consequently, for man) nothing is more frightful than *the absence of response*.[10]

10. Quoted by Tzvetan Todorov, *Mikhaïl Bakhtine: Le principe dialogique* (Paris, 1981), 170–171 (my translation).

The response to Jameson's venture I have offered is by no means that of the collective superaddressee which is the teleological "absent cause" whose advent Jameson would like to proclaim, but observations on the "secondary" level evoked by Bakhtin may not be altogether irrelevant to the question of the status and function of the dreamed-of utopian "third." For—to the extent that they are to the point—they are necessary discursive mediations of utopian desire, and they indicate the importance of history, commentary, and concrete institutional criticism.

[8]

Reading Marx: The Case
of *The Eighteenth Brumaire*

Driven by the contradictory demands of his situation and being at the
same time, like a conjurer, under the necessity of keeping the public
gaze fixed on himself, as Napoleon's substitute, by springing constant
surprises, that is to say, under the necessity of executing a *coup d'état
en miniature* every day, Bonaparte throws the entire bourgeois
economy into confusion, violates everything that seemed inviolable to
the Revolution of 1848, makes some tolerant of revolution, others
desirous of revolution, and produces actual anarchy in the name of
order, while at the same time stripping its halo from the entire state
machine, profanes it and makes it at once loathsome and ridiculous.
The cult of the Holy Tunic of Treves he duplicates at Paris in the
cult of the Napoleonic imperial mantle. But when the imperial
mantle finally falls on the shoulders of Louis Bonaparte, the bronze
statue of Napoleon will crash from the top of the Vendôme Column.

Marx, *The Eighteenth Brumaire of Louis Bonaparte*

The question of how to read Marx has recently been reopened.
The indubitable merit of Louis Althusser is to have initiated and
stimulated the attempt to apply to Marx's texts the sustained and
careful scrutiny that is more often found in the analysis of literary
and philosophical writing.[1] Yet the themes shaping Althusser's in-

1. See Louis Althusser, *For Marx*, tr. Ben Brewster, (London, 1979; first pub.
1965); Louis Althusser, with Etienne Balibar, *Reading Capital*, tr. Ben Brewster,
(London, 1979; first pub. 1968); *Lenin and Philosophy*, tr. Ben Brewster, (New
York, 1971); and *Essays in Self-Criticism*, tr. Grahame Lock (London, 1976).

terpretation often grate harshly with the finer mechanisms at work in his hermeneutic. To oppose the totalizing incentive of Hegelian Marxism, Althusser stressed the role of discontinuity in Marx. But at first he did so in a linear form that amounted to a simple reversal of the Hegelian emphasis. Decisive in the development of Marx's thought was not dialectical totalization but rather the role of an "epistemological break." That the location of the famous break became increasingly indeterminate as Althusser pursued it, combined with his recognition of recurrent Hegelian motifs in the later Marx, was only the most blatant sign that subtler theses were needed to guide inquiry into Marx's texts—as Althusser himself partially acknowledged. What Althusser, however, did not recognize as questionable was his stress on production as central not only to Marx's writing but to the investigation of all spheres of human activity, including a narrowly "economic" understanding of the "production" of knowledge itself. The decentering of the subject thus came accompanied by a recentering of understanding around a concept of productivity that was applied with abandon to all objects of investigation. Not subjected to critical scrutiny was the extent to which a productivist ethos in its one-sided form constituted the area wherein Marx at times implicitly shared the assumptions not only of Hegel but of the society and culture that gave rise to capitalism itself.

Jean Baudrillard attacked Marx for fashioning only the "mirror of production," and he insisted upon a more thoroughgoing critique of capitalism motivated by a notion of "symbolic exchange."[2] But Baudrillard accepted in essence the image of Marx provided by Althusser. That his acceptance premised a full-scale denial rather than an affirmation of the object is less significant perhaps than that he uncritically assimilated the dominant understanding of Marx's texts forged by his adversary. What neither Althusser nor Baudrillard formulate forcefully enough is the need to inquire into the

2. Jean Baudrillard, *The Mirror of Production*, tr. Mark Poster (St. Louis, 1975; first pub. 1973).

role of possible tensions and recurrently displaced discontinuities, even modes of internal contestation, in Marx's writings. This focus places in the foreground the importance of rhetorical and stylistic considerations in their relation to the "theses" for which Marx has become famous or infamous.

In this light, for example, *The Economic and Philosophic Manuscripts* of 1844 reacquires significance not simply as the charter of Marxist humanism—although the status of the human agent in history as a mediating force cannot be conflated with that of the imperialistic subject as uncontested center of thought and life. Rather, Marx's early attempt to "see things whole" may itself be seen as the place where one may find, both thematically and stylistically, the most forceful internal dialogue in Marx between a vision of man as Promethean producer (or hyperbolic *homo faber*) and one that stresses his nature as a receptive, sensate, suffering, and limited being. Perhaps nowhere more than in the *Paris Manuscripts* does Marx's writing inscribe this double image of man.

But if one moves to *Capital*—the *locus classicus* of the "mature" Marx for many commentators, even for those who would reinterpret it in the context of the *Grundrisse*—one has what is probably the most crying case of a canonical text in need of rereading rather than straightforward, literal reading geared to a putatively unitary authorial voice. Here the readings of both Althusser and his opponents may have been more dogmatic than Marx's writing. The issue that should, I think, guide a rereading is that of "double voicing" in the argument of *Capital*. Of the utmost pertinence would be a set of related questions circulating around Marx's indecision—at times calculated and at times seemingly blind—between a "positivistic" assertion of theses and a critical problematization of them. Among these questions would be the following: To what extent is Marx putting forth certain propositions in his own voice (for example, a labor theory of value) and to what extent does he furnish an ironic deconstruction of the system of classical economics and the capitalistic practice it subtended (including the assumption of a labor theory of value)? Does Marx himself simply have a labor theory of value or is it part and parcel of the system he is criticizing? If the labor theory presents certain difficulties, are they Marx's or are they constitutive of the modes of theory and practice he is analyzing and dismembering? Is his discovery of the role of abstract labor power both a "scientific" coup (as both he and Althusser think it is) and an insight into the mechanism of an "alienated" and destructive system? If abstract labor power is revealed by Marx as the shared essence of exchange values in terms of which they may be exchanged as equivalents, does this mean that Marx himself is straightforwardly reverting to a metaphorics or even a metaphysics of identity, or is it the case that he discloses a central component of the theoretical foundation of a system he finds absurd? Is the primary object of Marx's criticism the reduction of living labor (an important concept in the *Grundrisse*) to abstract labor power rather than the extraction of surplus value from already reduced labor in a constituted capitalistic system? Is the fact that Marx never overtly criticizes use value simply a blockage in his critique of its binary correlate, exchange value? Is it an instance of Marx succumbing to the ideological naturalization or universalization of capitalistic values of which he accused the classical economists? Is the discussion of commodity fetishism a marked change in discursive register—or even a "reversion" to the problematic of alienation—when compared with the more abstract, "scientific" delineation of concepts with which the commodity form is analyzed in the preceding sections, or is it a guide to reading those sections? Does the posing of this seeming alternative itself ignore the ironic footnotes and apparent textual asides in the earlier sections as well as the limitations in the analysis of fetishism with its reliance on a restricted strategy of reversal in decoding the secret of the fetishized commodity? ("A commodity is therefore a mysterious thing, simply because in it the social character of men's labor appears to them as an objective character stamped upon the product of that labor.") Is the "confusion" generated by *Capital*, as well as its amenability to diverse and divergent interpretations, understandable in terms of the duality of Marx's voice in it?

To address these questions would require a close reading of *Capital*, whose conditions of possibility are perhaps first becoming available today. Its demands exceed the limits of this essay. Instead, what I would like to do is to turn to a text that has since its publication been a special object of fascination for historians—*The Eighteenth Brumaire of Louis Bonaparte.*[3]

This text was written from December 1851 to March 1852, just in the wake of Louis Napoleon's coup d'état. It ends with a catalogue of mounting contradictions that typify Louis Napoleon and culminate in an ultimate, convulsive image.[4] The Napoleonic imperial mantle, itself a parodic imitation of the Holy Tunic of Treves

3. Karl Marx, *The Eighteenth Brumaire of Louis Bonáparte* (New York, 1963); all page references in the text are to this (International Publishers) edition. For a reading that is in limited ways comparable to the one I offer, see Jeffrey Mehlman, *Revolution and Repetition* (Berkeley and Los Angeles, 1977). The difficulty with Mehlman's vigorous analysis is the overly direct and at times vertiginous projection of poststructural motifs onto a rather conventional reading of *The Eighteenth Brumaire* as it presumably fits into the context formed by the rest of Marx's thought. The result is the postulation of a series of doubtful thematic equivalencies (Louis Napoleon and the "uncanny," the *lumpenproletariat* and the "pineal eye" of Georges Bataille, Bonaparte's fiscal policy and a general economy in the sense of Bataille or Derrida). I have, however, adapted other aspects of Mehlman's discussion, which I find more fruitful. Alvin Gouldner, in his *The Two Marxisms* (New York, 1980), also explores the "contradictions" and "anomalies" in Marx, focusing upon the oppositions between critical and scientific Marxism. In his discussion of *The Eighteenth Brumaire* (pp. 300ff), he underscores the emphasis placed by Marx upon the importance of the state as well as the attempt to "normalize" that emphasis in order to make it conform to Marx's standard idea of the state as the executive agency of the ruling class. There are certain broad parallels between the approach in Gouldner's book (which I read only after completing this study) and the one I try to take. The major difference is that Gouldner does not explore indications in Marx and Marxists of a critical Marxism that renders problematic both the standard notion of Hegelian dialectics and the split between science and critique. Whatever his shortcomings, Althusser, especially in his later writings, does at times touch upon this kind of critical Marxism, which does not conform to Gouldner's opposition between Hegelian critique and positivistic science. Employed in a certain way, poststructuralist strategies of textual interpretation may, I think, make a contribution to the elaboration of this dimension of Marx's writings—what might be called an open or supplemented dialectic that is self-critical and enlivened by carnivalesque forces.

4. See the epigraph to the present essay from p. 135 of *The Eighteenth Brumaire.*

(reputed to be Christ's garment), falls on the shoulders of Napoleon the Little, and the bronze statue of the first Napoleon plunges from its perch atop a column. How is one to interpret this final image? Is it a prediction attesting to the uncannily premonitory powers of Marxism as a positive science of society? (The statue of Napoleon I was indeed made to crash from the top of the Vendôme column during the reign of his nephew, Louis Napoleon, as Marx himself tells us in the preface to the second edition, 1869.) Does it embellish rhetorically the quite literal idea that Louis Napoleon is too small a figure to bear the burden of power or to withstand comparison with his illustrious uncle? Is it an actively prophetic, indeed an apocalyptic, herald of the proleterian revolution which, in the body of the text, will come to pass in spite of everything? Or is it a more or less unwitting prefiguration of generalized crisis and possible collapse? The overdetermined image that closes the text serves to reopen once more the problem of reading it by indicating the ambivalences, paradoxes, and equivocations running through its entire body.

The historian's interest naturally turns first to the unmistakable scientific dimension of the text: its close analysis of social groups and political factions related to economic interests and espousing divergent ideological perspectives. In his preface to the second edition, Marx himself tells the reader how the text should be read in this respect. He contrasts his own project with those of Victor Hugo and Pierre-Joseph Proudhon. The latter were ironic victims of texts whose workings escaped their manifest intentions.

> Victor Hugo confines himself to bitter and witty invective against the responsible publisher of the *coup d'état*. The event itself appears in his work like a bolt from the blue. He sees in it only the violent act of a single individual. He does not notice that he makes this individual great instead of little by ascribing to him a personal power of initiative such as would be without parallel in world history. Proudhon, for his part, seeks to represent the *coup d'état* as the result of an antecedent historical development. Unnoticeably, however, his historical construction of the *coup d'état* becomes a historical apologia

for its hero. Thus he falls into the error of our so-called *objective* historians. [P. 8]

Marx himself is presumably to escape the paradox of unintended consequences and its ruselike "errors" by explaining the role of Louis Napoleon through a central thesis: "I, on the contrary, demonstrate how the *class struggle* in France created circumstances and relationships that made it possible for a grotesque mediocrity to play a hero's part" (p. 8). In his preface to the third German edition in 1885, Engels goes beyond Marx in asserting his collaborator's position of total mastery in narrating events. Marx's unparalleled familiarity with French history and current affairs made it the case that "events never took him by surprise" (p. 14). In addition, Engels himself takes Marx's self-commentary in a more narrowly positivistic direction. Marx's "picture," he tells us, "was drawn with such a master hand that every fresh disclosure since made has only provided fresh proofs of how faithfully it reflected reality" (p. 14). For Engels a fully representational or documentary epistemology underwrites both a general conception of Marxist science and its specific application to conditions in France.

> The centre of feudalism in the Middle Ages, the model country of unified monarchy, resting on estates, since the Renaissance, France demolished feudalism in the Great Revolution and established the unalloyed rule of the bourgeoisie in a classical purity unequalled by any other European land. And the struggle of the upward-striving proletariat against the ruling bourgeoisie appeared here in an acute form unknown elsewhere. . . . In addition, however, there was another circumstance. It was precisely Marx who had first discovered the great law of motion of history, the law according to which all historical struggles, whether they proceed in the political, religious, philosophical or some other ideological domain, are in fact only the more or less clear expression of struggles of social classes, and that the existence and thereby the collisions, too, between these classes, are in turn conditioned by the degree of development of their economic position, by the mode of their production and of their exchange determined by it. This law, which has the same significance

274

for history as the law of the transformation of energy has for natural science—this law gave him here, too, the key to an understanding of the history of the Second French Republic. He put his law to the test on these historical events, and even after thirty-three years we must still say that it has stood the test brilliantly.   [P. 14]

It is perhaps significant that Engels's assertion of a "scientific" law, intended to cover and explain the occurrence of specific historical events, is itself textually positioned as a supplement to those events. The law, which is supposed to provide the general proposition that events merely illustrate or instantiate, is "unnoticeably" introduced as an ex post facto addition to those events. But Engels clearly intends to assert that Marxism is grounded in lawlike propositions that cover the course of history in an explanatory way. He enunciates with unguarded insouciance the "positivistic" understanding of Marxism—at times put forth by Marx himself—that seems to take the idea that economic determinism and class struggle are to be seen as symptoms of an "alienated" condition and relegate it to a prescientific stage of the history of Marxism. Engels's proleptic reading of *The Eighteenth Brumaire* raises the broader question of the position of this text in Marx's corpus. Here we return to variations of certain issues I touched upon earlier. Does *The Eighteenth Brumaire* fall squarely into a putative but elusive later "scientific" stage of Marxism interpreted either in Engels's relatively simplistic terms or in the more sophisticated formulations of Althusser? Should it by contrast be read within the context of human self-alienation elaborated in *The Economic and Philosophic Manuscripts* of 1844 and serving as the interpretative framework of Marxism as a whole? Is it in some delimited sense a transitional text? Or is the reading of this text as well as its relation to Marx's other texts a more complicated problem requiring a delineation of multiple movements within it and in the other texts—movements that further relate to one another in ways that render radically problematic any simple model of the "development" of Marx's thought?

It is probably impossible to reject the anticipatory reading in

Engels's preface as simply beside the point. At the very least one wants to know the relation of *The Eighteenth Brumaire* to the well-known theses that have coagulated into the more or less standard version of Marxism—a standard version itself based upon a selective reading of Marx's texts. It is all too easy to enumerate the basic components of this standard version: economic determinism, class struggle, the state as executive agency of the ruling class, ideology as superstructure, the progressive evolutionary development of human history, the polarization of modern society into the bourgeoisie and the proletariat, and the coming of the proletarian revolution that realizes the *telos* of history in a reign of freedom. Marx will attempt to make his analysis in *The Eighteenth Brumaire* conform to at least certain of these tenets. For example, he will propose the orthodox version of the superstructure theorem in his analysis of the Legitimist and Orleanist factions of the Royalist Party of Order:

> Was that which held these factions fast to their pretenders and kept them apart from one another nothing but lily and tricolour, House of Bourbon and House of Orleans, different shades of royalism, was it at all the confession of faith of royalism? Under the Bourbons, *big landed property* had governed, with its priests and lackeys; under the Orleans, high finance, large-scale industry, large-scale trade, that is, *capital*, with its retinue of lawyers, professors and smooth-tongued orators. The Legitimist Monarchy was merely the political expression of the hereditary rule of the lords of the soil, as the July Monarchy was only the political expression of the usurped rule of the bourgeois *parvenus*. What kept the two factions apart, therefore, was not any so-called principles, it was their material conditions of existence, two different kinds of property, it was the old contrast between town and country, the rivalry between capital and landed property. That at the same time old memories, personal enmities, fears and hopes, prejudices and illusions, sympathies and antipathies, convictions, articles of faith and principles bound them to one or the other royal house, who denies this? Upon the different forms of property, upon the social conditions of existence, rises an entire superstructure of distinct and peculiarly formed sentiments, illusions, modes of thought and views of life. The entire class creates and forms them

276

out of its material foundations and out of the corresponding social relations. [Pp. 46–47]

One may choose to interpret Marx's conception of ideology as superstructure in a heuristic way and thereby relate it to hypotheses that may, to varying degrees, be confirmed or disconfirmed by research. At times, however, it is situated in Marx's thought as the simple opposite of a metaphysical notion of full representational truth: ideology is distortion that serves invidious class interests in contradistinction to truth as a faithful reflection of reality. Truth in the full sense of totally transparent relations to nature and to other people would depend upon the realization of socialist society. In this sense, truth is further implicated in a modified Hegelian vision of the progressive and totalizing movement of history toward liberation in the form of a society entirely grounded in truth. Given this vision of history, which plays an active role in *The Eighteenth Brumaire*, seeming setbacks such as the course of events from 1848 to 1851 may be interpreted as transitory retrogressions in a more comprehensive movement.

In different but at times related ways, however, the three assumptions of ideology as superstructure, truth as full representation of reality and total transparency of relations, and history as progressive, totalizing movement toward the moment of truth, may be rendered problematic in the very same text in which they are active.

There is a curious dissymmetry, for example, between two of Marx's most important analyses of ideology. The Royalist factions in adhering to one or the other pretender to the throne presumably followed their true class interests. The peasants, however, in backing Louis Bonaparte supposedly adhered to interests that may have been "true" interests in the time of Napoleon I but were in the time of Louis Napoleon false or illusory interests. Attachment to the small holding made the peasantry fail to recognize its true interests which, in Marx's analysis, would have allied it with the proletariat. One may of course question this analysis and even invert its terms, for it is possible to argue that the Royalist factions were upholding positions that were out of touch with reality after 1848—as Marx intimates, what difference did it make whether a Bourbon or an Orleans was on the throne?—while the peasants were at least clinging to a real interest in the attachment to their land. In addition, there are grounds for arguing that large landed property and capital, which Marx affiliates with the houses of Bourbon and Orleans respectively, had at least as great an objective identity of interest as did the peasantry and the proletariat. The very existence of the Party of Order attested to a degree of political organization that did not exist either within the peasantry or between the peasantry and the proletariat. (Here one may recall the analogy Marx uses with reference to relations among the peasants—that of potatoes in a sack of potatoes.) But the basic theoretical point is that Marx provides no explanation of why certain groups ideologically disguise *real* interests while other groups are seemingly motivated in political action by *illusory* interests that correspond at best to past realities. This state of affairs might lead one to attribute more "independent" weight to so-called ideological factors and the phantasmatic investments with which they are bound up. It would also suggest a more complicated relation between real and illusory interests.

A further point is that the France of 1848 did not conform to Engels's picture of the "unalloyed rule of the bourgeoisie" struggling with the "upward-striving proletariat." In *The Eighteenth Brumaire* one does not have the two-class society projected on the basis of an extrapolation from a market "model" in *Capital*, and little seems to indicate that this society was in the offing. Of course, during the direct social conflict of the June Days, there was a temporary polarization of society. But it did not oppose an overwhelming majority of proletarians to a minority of capitalists. The working class was a minority that was relatively isolated. And, after its defeat, society returned to an extremely complicated structure. Not only was the bourgeoisie internally splintered into various groups with varying connections to the two Royalist factions of the Party of Order. The peasantry still formed the majority of the population, and there existed beneath the proletariat a *lumpenproletariat* which was not simply an industrial reserve army. It was an important social group with a potentially significant political role. In addition—a very important addition—there was the Bonapartist phenomenon with its relations to social groups, notably the peasantry and the lumpenproletariat, and, quite significantly, to the state with its bureaucracy and army. As Marx himself intimates, the state under Louis Napoleon could not plausibly be seen simply as the executive agency of the bourgeoisie, if indeed the bourgeoisie could be unequivocally presented as the ruling class in France at the time.[5] Indeed for Marx the power of Louis Napoleon derived in large part from his ability to organize the lumpenproletariat into his shock troops—the Society of December 10—and to satisfy the interests of social groups through the state bureaucracy and army, for example, the peasantry's interest in jobs for its surplus sons.

Thus many significant problems are raised for the "standard version" of Marxism by the nature of Marx's own analysis in *The Eighteenth Brumaire*. One crucial manner in which Marx tries to come to terms with these problems is through the category of parasitism. Parasitism reveals *en creux* the role in *The Eighteenth Brumaire* of one of Marx's most salient emphases—that upon productivism. The parasite is the nonproductive phenomenon par excellence, living at the expense of its host.[6] In *The Eighteenth Brumaire*, however, interesting complications arise with reference to the category of parasitism and, by implication, to the ethos of productivity. For Nietzsche, one may recall, health was measured by the number of parasites one could tolerate while still remaining healthy. While Marx never arrives at this perception, his confrontation with the parasite affects his rhetoric in rather telling ways, for the deadly image he encounters is that of a generalized parasitism with primarily destructive consequences.

Three phenomena are explicitly analyzed by Marx as unproduc-

---

5. Marx indiscriminately refers to the Party of Order (as to the July Monarchy) as bourgeois. For the general problem of the importance of nobles with landed wealth, see André-Jean Tudesq, *Les grands notables en France, 1840–1849* (Paris, 1964).

6. For a dicussion that tries to rehabilitate the role of the parasite, see J. Hillis Miller, "The Critic as Host," *Critical Inquiry* 3 (1977), 439–447.

tive parasites—the state bureaucracy, the lumpenproletariat, and Louis Napoleon himself. This categorization seems to corroborate the belief in an ultimately progressive development of history in relation to which phenomena may be seen as excrescences or merely transitory retrogressions. It also functions to shore up a model of society in terms of a productive class—the proletariat—and other classes or groups some of which are simple parasites. The notion of parasite, however, promotes the tendency not to take certain phenomena "seriously," notably as serious threats to one's own conception of society and the movement of history, for the threat posed by a massive state bureaucracy, a significant and politically manipulable underclass, and a grotesque mediocrity with a large following is that this entire complex may be a "parasite" large and powerful enough to consume or contain its putative host—not a passing retrogression but, on the contrary, the wave of the future. *The Eighteenth Brumaire* may, in other words, be most relevant to the analysis of later history in terms of what it classifies as parasites.

The threat that Marx has himself drastically misread the historical process harbors the possibility that he is not in the position of full mastery indicated in Engels's preface but instead confronted with the danger of ideological mystification and the paradox of unintended consequences. Facing the course of events, he may turn to what Althusser suggestively analyzes as an ideological recognition scene, a mirror effect whereby he focuses only on what he wants to see and casts what disturbs his vision in the marginalized role of the parasite. Yet the threat of misreading is also related, in complex fashion, to an ambivalent rhetorical dimension of Marx's text that cannot be identified with false consciousness, for his rhetoric involves an actively performative use of language that attempts to affect the course of events.[7]

7. One may note that the performative dimension of rhetorical usage has a number of significant consequences. It prevents the identification of rhetoric with the aesthetically autonomous or purely intralinguistic idea of language. It also indicates the political role of rhetoric as the specific link between theory and practice.

The Eighteenth Brumaire is highly charged writing—polemical invective of the most intense sort. Marx upbraids and belittles not only Louis Napoleon but the historical process itself from 1848 to 1851. That Marx feels he is in a position to take history itself to task is astounding, for he is led to elaborate something like an inverted or negative apostrophe to culture rather than nature. Whether or not Marx was surprised by the course of events, things clearly were not going the way he expected or wanted them to go. The historical context was at loggerheads with the desires of the narrator. And Marx responds in a complex prose style that intricately conveys his anger and sense of outrage. As Marx writes, the proletariat is no longer fighting in the streets. Indeed any such attempt would probably be doomed to failure. But Marx is still fighting with words—in forceful and compelling ways. His construction of the significance of events often borders on a hyperbolic act of will, and his determination to present the proletariat as the revolutionary subject of history accompanies an attempt to shape the future.

Marx's "nonrepresentational," highly performative invective in the face of historical "regression" enables a better appreciation of the quality of parody in *The Eighteenth Brumaire*.[8] The parodic aspect of Marx's account is of course blatantly apparent, but less apparent is its precise nature and its relation to the critique of ideology. One of the most telling features of parody in *The Eighteenth Brumaire* is its role in the critique of ideology. That critique is bound up with defensiveness attests to the apotropaic nature of certain rhetorical modes, for strong, polemical parody, with its performative, indeed carnivalesque, use of language, may be directed against a bedeviling, anxiety-producing threat, including one that involves the risk of misreading and self-mystification.

As both antidote and literary form, parody makes selective, stylizing use of some "original" text as the object of its procedures. In *The*

8. For another view of the problem of parody, see John Paul Riquelme, "*The Eighteenth Brumaire* of Karl Marx as Symbolic Action," *History and Theory* 19 (1980), 58–72.

Eighteenth Brumaire, history is interpreted as a text; it is itself already lived as a parody, hence textually. For Marx, people in 1848 are leading self-parodic lives. (This note is struck in the very opening lines of the text: "Hegel remarks somewhere that all facts and personages of great importance in world history occur, as it were, twice. He forgot to add: the first time as tragedy, the second as farce.") But any full original in the historical process is tainted with imperfection and impurity. Parodic repetition of one sort or another seems to prevail as far back as one can go in the course of history. For example, the French Revolution, on Marx's reading, was the bourgeois revolution that had a "real" content. But even it employed past forms to convey its revolutionary content. Between 1789 and 1848, however, there is a significant difference of degree, which affects the nature of parody.

> Thus the awakening of the dead in those revolutions [France in 1789 or England in 1648] served the purpose of glorifying the new struggles, not of parodying the old; of magnifying the given task in imagination, not of fleeing from its solution in reality; of finding once more the spirit of revolution, not of making its ghost walk.   [P. 17]

The events of 1848 were no more than a ghost walk of a revolution, while those of 1789 had a more truly revolutionary spirit, for in 1789 the bourgeoisie, according to Marx's interpretation, wore Roman costumes but performed "the task of unchaining and setting up modern bourgeois society" (p. 16). On several occasions in *The Eighteenth Brumaire*, Marx intimates that the proletarian revolution of the nineteenth century will be the first to transform a difference of degree into a full-fledged difference in kind—one in which there will be a total and definitive break with the past, a laying to rest of ghosts, a chance to let the dead bury their dead. The occasion seems to arise for men finally to make spirit flesh or to speak a new language without translating it back into their former mother tongue. This utopian moment is properly modernist. And it would seem to correspond to Marx's desired position as a narrator who is in the fully liberated position of master of parody—using it to demystify ideology but himself free of even the risk of mystification.

In this sense, parody as an instrument in the critique of ideology would serve to repeat the blind and unself-conscious *lived* parody of historical agents from 1848 to 1851 but in a fashion that would raise their parody to full self-consciousness, thus offering the promise of a liberation from the nightmare of history. The topsy-turvy, "fetishized" world of lived parody would be set right-side up—once and for all. Thus parody would not only be a crucial force for the critique of ideology—an antidote functioning in ways that would vary with social contexts. It would be the true miracle drug bringing the total transcendence of ideology and a definitive cure for mystification. Indeed it would seem that in the totally emancipated society which this restricted and fully mastered use of parody anticipates, there would be no further room for parody or analogous forms. With the prevalence of entirely transparent relations, there would be nothing for parody to do in either critical or constructive terms. Rhetoric would, so to speak, be rendered entirely superfluous, and the dream of transparency shared by idealists and positivists, by modern figures as seemingly diverse as Sartre, Habermas, the early Wittgenstein, and the early Althusser himself, would be realized.

The ideal of full emancipation in a revolutionary future whose utopian status is repeated in the desire of the narrator for full mastery over events does not, however, prevail in uncontested hegemony in the text of *The Eighteenth Brumaire* itself. The force of Marx's abusive invective both subverts it and at times implicates it in more problematic possibilites—possibilities that might be interpreted to indicate that, in a transformed society, parody and other carnivalizing forces would not disappear. Rather, as relations became more legitimate (but not fully transparent), their carnivalized doubles would acquire more richly ambivalent qualities as modes of praise-abuse. Indeed ambivalence would be most marked with reference to what was experienced as most legitimate.

Primarily aggressive, negative, critical abuse appears to be the dominant tone of Marx's own use of parody in *The Eighteenth Brumaire*. The very objects being parodied would seem to demand this belittling treatment. Louis Napoleon and the social groups that allow his rule are not worthy of ambivalent praise-abuse in any comprehensive sense. They constitute forces that must be overcome for both legitimate structures and their parodic counterparts to emerge in more ambivalent forms. Yet this line of argument, while having a certain plausibility, does not account for all pertinent features of Marx's use of parody in *The Eighteenth Brumaire*, for his use of parody in certain ways intimates and anticipates its potential in a transformed society. We have to delay gratification on how this point may be seen to apply, however, and look more closely at what counteracts it.

The castigation of the lumpenproletariat as the "scum of bourgeois society" (p. 26) or the "scum, offal, refuse of all classes" (p. 75) would appear to attest to Marx's commitment to the proletariat and, paradoxically, to his rather bourgeois, indeed Victorian, sense of propriety that is offended by *la bohème*. In any case, it occludes the problem of the oppression of this group or category in modern society as well as the need for radical politics to address that oppression and its implications. Marx's famous description of the lumpenproletariat combines the hyperbolic heterogeneity and massive homogeneity that generally typify perceptions of the radically "other": "Alongside decayed *roués* with dubious means of subsistence and of dubious origin, alongside ruined and adventurous offshoots of the bourgeoisie, were vagabonds, discharged soldiers, discharged jailbirds, escaped galley slaves, swindlers, mountebanks, *lazzaroni*, pickpockets, tricksters, gamblers, *maquereaux*, brothel keepers, porters, *literati*, organ-grinders, ragpickers, knife-grinders, tinkers, beggars—in short, the whole indefinite, disintegrated mass, thrown hither and thither, which the French term *la bohème*" (p. 75).

The intensity of Marx's polemical animus against the lumpenproletariat and other groups blocking revolution might be seen as a function of a concealed or even repressed fear that the proletariat itself is not the revolutionary agent Marx wishes it to be and that other groups do not hold out the transformative promise he seeks. In *The Eighteenth Brumaire*, Marx seems to be on the verge of the dilemma that would confront radical intellectuals in the twentieth century when they were to face the possibility that modern societies did not offer a more or less ready-made group analogous to the classical revolutionary subject. Marx's own account of the ease with which the proletariat was repressed in June 1848 and duped into taking to the streets in June 1849 creates suspicion concerning the proletariat's fitness to assume the heroic role in which Marx would cast it. In fact, after the proletariat is brutally driven from the stage in June 1848, its goal—the social republic—can only "haunt the subsequent acts of the drama like a ghost" (p. 118).

A similar point might be made about the two "positive" lessons Marx strives to derive from the course of events. In the 1852 edition, he writes: "When he is disappointed in the Napoleonic Restoration, the French peasant will part with his belief in his small holding, the entire state edifice erected on this small holding will fall to the ground and the proletarian revolution will obtain that chorus without which its solo song becomes the swan song in all peasant countries" (p. 148n). Marx here indicates a prerequisite of revolution in certain societies. But did not the text of *The Eighteenth Brumaire* indicate that in a country such as France, the foundation of revolutionary hope upon a worker-peasant alliance might itself herald the swan song of radical change? What were the historical chances of a worker-peasant alliance if the workers could be manipulated and if the peasantry was benighted enough to see in Louis Napoleon the spokesman for demands that themselves were, for Marx, hopelessly anachronistic? Marx does discuss the very important role of mortgage debts and taxes, which opposed peasant interests to those of "bourgeois capital" and the state (pp. 127–128). But he provides little indication of how these interests, which could be sources of radicalization in the peasantry, might serve in practice to forge the desired alliance between it and the proletariat.[9]

Marx puts the second lesson in these terms:

9. On the problem of peasant protest against the *fisc*, see Maurice Agulhon, *La République au village* (Paris, 1979).

But the revolution is thoroughgoing. It is still journeying through purgatory. It does its work methodically. By December 2, 1851, it had completed one half of its preparatory work; it is now completing the other half. First it perfected the parliamentary power, in order to overthrow it. Now that it has attained this, it perfects the *executive power*, reduces it to its purest expression, isolates it, sets it up against itself as the sole target, in order to concentrate all its forces of destruction against it. And when it has done this second half of its preliminary work, Europe will leap from its seat and exultantly exclaim: Well grubbed, old mole! [P. 121]

The displacement of peasant interests in the direction of the proletariat would thus be complemented by a condensation of inimical state power in the hands of the executive. In a convergence of *la politique du pire* and dream-work, Marx himself tries to adjust the period from 1848 and 1851 to an overriding idea of historical movement in relation to which it represents a merely transitional impediment. If it is purgatory, the promise of redemption is still at hand after the labor of expiation. And the image of the old mole tunneling underground is set off against that of the false Napoleonic eagle that is really a parasitic raven. But both the allusion to the mole and the quotation concerning the eagle are borrowed from other sources—the former from *Hamlet* and the latter from a pun by the mistress of M. de Morny, a Bonapartist deputy. And each image harbors its own equivocations. For if the soaring eagle can metamorphose into a thieving eater of carrion, the mole has its blindness. How promising, one may ask, is the concentration of state power in an enormous and ubiquitous bureaucracy if that state power is big and wily enough to render protest ineffective? In this context, is the intellectual who staunchly defends proletarian revolution in the position of an Oedipal Hamlet who remains willfully blind to problems that carry the risk of indecision?

Marx's most detailed parodic portrait (or exercise in systematic belittling) is of course that of Louis Napoleon and his crazy-quilt relations with various social groups. Of Bonaparte, Marx writes: "As a fatalist, he lives in the conviction that there are certain higher powers which man, and the soldier in particular, cannot withstand, Among these powers he counts, first and foremost, cigars and champagne, cold poultry and garlic sausage" (p. 77). Bonaparte is the voice of the inarticulate peasantry—a falsetto voice, since what he represents is a vanished reality. But Napoleon also has intricate ties to other groups which, except for the proletariat, share in his deceptions and his ability to degrade the commodity form itself by turning all exchanges into channels of false advertising and fraud. Napoleon is the crowned fool of a false and noxious carnival whereby ordinary life itself puts on garishly deceptive masks and enacts perverse inversions—a modern variant of the traditional *monde à l'envers*. The Party of Order cashes in its aristocratic pretensions to ally itself with a bogus hero and a bathetic buffoon. Through the so-called Napoleonic ideas of Louis Bonaparte, the Napoleonic legend is reduced to its pettiest and most reactionary components—unprofitably small peasant holdings, strong and unlimited government, excessive taxation, a large bureaucracy, the political rule of priests, and the domestic intervention of the army. The respectable bourgeoisie in seeking the comfort of law and order confides in a disreputable regime that institutionalizes covert operations and disorder, indeed a regime that does not hesitate to apply the club, if need be, to refractory or inconvenient bourgeois heads.

Every demand of the simplest bourgeois financial reform, of the most ordinary liberalism, of the most formal republicanism, of the most shallow democracy, is simultaneously castigated as an "attempt on society" and stigmatized as "Socialism." And, finally, the high priests of "religion and order" themselves are driven with kicks from their Pythian tripods, hurled out of their beds in the darkness of night, put in prison-vans, thrown into dungeons or sent into exile; their temple is razed to the ground, their mouths are sealed, their pens broken, their law torn to pieces in the name of religion, of property, of the family, of order. Bourgeois fanatics for order are shot down on their balconies by mobs of drunken soldiers, their domestic sanctuaries profaned, their houses bombarded for amusement—in the name of property, of the family, of religion and of order. Finally, the scum of bourgeois society forms the *holy phalanx of order* and the hero Crapulinsky installs himself in the Tuileries as the *"saviour of society."* [Pp. 25–26]

Yet the protean figure of Louis Napoleon almost takes on dimensions antipathetic to Marx's intentions in portraying him, for the "grotesque mediocrity" may combine traits in oxymoronic tension. In the carnival of dunces that is French society at the time, he is the most stupid protagonist—except for all the others! He after all begins as the carrier of Marx's own affirmed value—lucidity. He sees through the comedy that others live and is able to manipulate those who believe they can manipulate him. Only in time does he become the pathetic victim of his own illusions. This very ability to be a confidence man would seem a prerequisite of the measure of political success Louis Napoleon did attain. And the more ambivalent dimensions of the figure of Louis Napoleon in Marx's text itself would seem to derive from Marx's parodic treatment of him insofar as vigorous parody cannot be confined within the boundaries of univocal abuse or one-dimensional denigration. Hyperbolic invective magnifies the object of derision whatever may be the intentions of the author.

The almost Rabelaisian exuberance of Marx's writing is, however, itself a force that cannot be contained within one-sided interpretations. Marx never thematizes the problem of carnival as a sociocultural force, and his explicit emphasis is often upon modes of productivity that would seem anticarnivalesque in nature. But in a work such as *The Eighteenth Brumaire*, Marx deploys a powerfully carnivalized style—one that exceeds any narrowly productive or didactic project or goal. Through this use of language, Marx confronts a world in which the critic, despite the desire for full mastery, is never altogether immune from mystification—hence the necessity for antidotes (such as parody) whose effectiveness is never certain. In this world, certain "parasites" threaten to become larger and more encompassing than the hosts. The latter possibility pertains especially to the state, which as a "parasitic body acquires ubiquity" and "enmeshes, controls, superintends and tutors civil society from its most comprehensive manifestations of life to its most insignificant stirrings" (p. 62). In his analysis of the Napoleonic regime, Marx himself clearly stresses the role of the state in the surveillance and control of society—a phenomenon that renders problematic the assertion of economic determinism and that has become particularly important in the twentieth century. Indeed Marx's analysis in *The Eighteenth Brumaire* has with some justice been seen—among others, by Ernst Bloch in *Die Erbschaft dieser Zeit*—as a prescient delineation of those pseudorevolutionary, protofascist forces in modern society to which more orthodox forms of Marxism have often been blind. And the overdetermined image of the parasite itself suggests how power, while tending to become concentrated in the state, nonetheless spreads out into the pores of the body politic to operate with microscopic pervasiveness in relationships that come into increasing contact with the state. In this sense, one may look to another facet of this image and notice how it may help to renew our very concept of the political by directing attention to the "politics" of everyday life.

In terms of the considerations I have been emphasizing, I will conclude by noting that the one social force that is not beaten by the course of events as analyzed by Marx is the force of language as Marx himself uses it. In this use of language with its rhetorical power, wakelike exaltation, and insistently resurgent potency, Marx not only manages to disclose crucial dimensions of the historical process. He makes mincemeat of the *idées napoléoniennes*, the illusions of the Party of Order, the contradictory demands of bourgeois factions, and the Napoleonic legend. To a significant degree, his own use of language may prefigure a better future by giving some idea of what is meant by "living labor." (Here one is tempted to paraphrase Engels's famous comment about the Paris Commune and to declare: if you want to know what living labor is like, look at Marx's use of language in *The Eighteenth Brumaire*.) Indeed in it Marx attains heights of destructive-regenerative ambivalence that are relatively rare in the modern world. He simultaneously raises for us the issue of the relationship, in a historical account, between cognitive (or "scientific") and performative uses of language— prominently including carnivalesque uses. In *The Eighteenth Brumaire*, Marx does not simply provide an empirical reconstruction, narrative description, or analytic explanation of his object of inquiry; he also offers a robust critique of it and, through his own use of language, tries to effect a change in the larger situational context.

[9]

Bakhtin, Marxism,
and the Carnivalesque

Now and formerly. —What good is all the art of our works of art if
we lose that higher art, the art of festivals? Formerly, all works of art
adorned the great festival road of humanity, to commemorate high
and happy moments. Now one uses works of art to lure aside from
the great *via dolorosa* of humanity those who are wretched,
exhausted, and sick, and to offer them a brief lustful moment—a
little intoxication and madness.

> Nietzsche, *The Gay Science*

Labour cannot become play, as Fourier would like, although it
remains his great contribution to have expressed the suspension not of
distribution, but of the mode of production itself, in a higher form,
as the ultimate object. Free time—which is both idle time and time
for higher activity—has naturally transformed its possessor into a
different subject, and he then enters into the direct production
process as this different subject. The process is then both discipline,
as regards the human being in the process of becoming; and, at the
same time, practice [*Ausübung*], experimental science, materially
creative and objectifying science, as regards the human being who is
transformed, in whose head exists the accumulated knowledge of
society.

> Karl Marx, *Grundrisse*

Open seriousness always ready to submit to death and renewal, true
open seriousness fears neither parody, nor irony, nor any other form
of reduced laughter, for it is aware of being part of an uncompleted
whole.

> Bakhtin, *Rabelais and His World*

The professional practice of intellectual historians is to approach problems indirectly through conversations with the illustrious living or dead who, under carefully controlled conditions, may become masks for the intellectual historian himself. In keeping with this constraint of the genre, I shall focus my discussion on the role of one important context for writing as it has been explored in the texts of Mikhail Bakhtin and his circle—that of the carnivalesque or, in the more dynamic term, carnivalization. I shall also touch upon the question of contexts in which Bakhtin himself wrote, and in which he has been received, for they bear upon one's own attempt to provide a critical reading of his texts.

Until recently Bakhtin has been read—to the extent he has been read at all—largely in the context of Russian studies, specifically as the author of *Problems of Dostoevsky's Poetics*.[1] In the light of his *Rabelais and His World*, he has also been accorded a rather eccentric place in the literature on Rabelais.[2] His position in Russia itself was a difficult one, subject to the vicissitudes of the times. In the 1920s, he was the head of the so-called Bakhtin circle, a group that included figures such as V. N. Vološinov and P. N. Medvedev. The precise nature and extent of Bakhtin's contribution to books published under the names of Vološinov and Medvedev are moot, but it is evident that his role in their conception was crucial.[3] Upon the appearance of his study of Dostoevsky in 1929, Bakhtin was sent to Kazakhstan where he spent the next six years in exile as a book-keeper. From 1940 to the end of World War II, he lived in the environs of Moscow. In 1940, he submitted his dissertation on Rabelais, but its defense was delayed until after the war. It was rejected following stormy meetings among faculty, which finally led

1. Mikhail Bakhtin, *Problems of Dostoevsky's Poetics*, tr. R. W. Rotsel (Ann Arbor, 1973; first pub. 1929).
2. Mikhail Bakhtin, *Rabelais and His World*, tr. Hélène Iswolsky (Cambridge, Mass., 1968; first submitted as a dissertation in 1940.)
3. The books in question are V. N. Vološinov, *Marxism and the Philosophy of Language* (New York, 1973; first pub. 1929); V. N. Vološinov, *Freudianism: A Marxist Critique* (New York, 1976; first pub. 1927); and P. N. Medvedev, *The Formal Method in Literary Scholarship* (Baltimore, 1978; first pub. 1928).

to the intervention of the state, and was not published until 1965. Given the nature of his thought, especially with reference to the carnivalesque, one further biographical fact may be mentioned. Bakhtin contracted a bone disease in 1923, which led to the amputation of a leg in 1938. (He died in 1975 at the age of eighty.)

In the West, one early study recognizing the general importance of Bakhtin as a theorist was Julia Kristeva's "Le mot, le dialogue et le roman" of 1967.[4] His work also had some impact on historical research, for example, in the studies of Natalie Z. Davis.[5] In 1981 there appeared both a good introduction to Bakhtin's work by Tzvetan Todorov and a collection of four of Bakhtin's essays, admirably edited, translated, and introduced by Michael Holquist and Caryl Emerson.[6] These two publications confirmed Bakhtin's status as a major reference point in current critical thought. Indeed, Todorov began his study with the comment: "Without too much hesitation, one could confer two superlatives on Bakhtin in affirming that he is the most important Soviet thinker in the realm of the human sciences and the greatest theorist of literature in the twentieth century."[7] One may perhaps detect a hint of Bakhtin's own irony in these hyperbolic encomia. But the fact that a minor cult is presently forming around Bakhtin should not lead to a "backlash"

4. Julia Kristeva, "Le mot, le dialogue et le roman," in *Semeiotikè* (Paris, 1969). See also her "Une poétique ruinée," in Mikhaïl Bakhtine, *La poétique de Dostoïevski* (Paris, 1970).

5. Natalie Z. Davis, *Society and Culture in Early Modern France* (Stanford, 1975).

6. Tzvetan Todorov, *Mikhaïl Bakhtine: Le principe dialogique* (Paris, 1981); *The Dialogic Imagination*, tr. Michael Holquist and Caryl Emerson (Austin, 1981). Todorov's book also contains French translations of four shorter pieces of Bakhtin and Vološinov. Todorov downplays the importance of the question of authorship in the case of members of the Bakhtin circle given their own concept of the dialogical. He nonetheless asserts that it is "impossible not to take into account the unity of thought to which the ensemble of these publications bears witness (and which one can attribute, following diverse witnesses, to the influence of Bakhtin)" (p. 23; my translation). According to Holquist and Emerson, "ninety percent of the three books in question [*Freudianism; Marxism and the Philosophy of Language;* and *The Formal Method in Literary Scholarship*] is indeed the work of Bakhtin himself" (p. xxvi).

7. Todorov, *Mikhaïl Bakhtine*, 7 (my translation).

whereby his importance is ignored or denied. One reason for his importance is his inquiry into the role of the carnivalesque in literature and in life—a problem connected with all the significant aspects of his thought.

CARNIVAL AND CARNIVALIZATION

How does Bakhtin see the carnivalesque as a context for writing? First, one must stress that Bakhtin in many ways offers a modern intellectual's image of popular culture in general and of the carnivalesque in particular—one that is derived primarily from literary sources. Bakhtin provides scant description or analysis of social carnivals except insofar as they appear in the texts of figures such as Rabelais and Goethe.

In certain respects, his largely normative and even visionary image may be more valuable for his purposes than the empirical workings of carnival-type phenomena in past societies, for it may embody the features of carnival he stresses to a greater extent and in a more marked fashion than do empirical forms of carnival or even carnivalesque accounts in the writings of figures who are more literally "men of the people." Indeed it is significant that although he emphasizes to the point of exaggeration the relation of Rabelais's texts to popular or folk culture, he chooses Rabelais to illustrate the points he makes about carnival and carnivalization. The very choice of Rabelais rather than a figure such as the shoemaker Hans Sachs may bear witness to the particularly forceful carnivalizing role of certain complex texts.[8]

8. Bakhtin takes Lucien Febvre to task for committing the same "sin" that Febvre ascribes to other interpreters of Rabelais: the "sin" of anachronism. Febvre "hears Rabelais's laughter with the ears of the twentieth century, rather than with those of the sixteenth. . . . He misses the main point of Rabelais's laughter, its universal and philosophic character" (*Rabelais and His World*, 133). Thus Febvre misunderstands Rabelais's philosophy, especially in interpreting Rabelais with reference to official culture rather than with reference to the popular culture of folk humor. Bakhtin's criticism is quite ironic in that it is addressed to a founder of the *Annales* school, which became famous for writing history "from the bottom up." Yet, as we shall see, his criticism may be turned around, for he underplays the more erudite and humanist dimensions of Rabelais that were of concern to Febvre.

By the same token, however, Bakhtin's views must be used with caution in the empirical and analytic investigation of social carnivals. Here he furnishes a model or an ideal type—one that is also a philosophical and cultural ideal with important contestatory functions in his own and other modern societies, for however much carnivals may be argued to reinforce social structures in certain contexts, Bakhtin's image or model of carnival plays a critical role in modern societies given the state of carnival in them. Bakhtin, however, does tend to exclude or underemphasize aspects of carnivals or carnival-type phenomena that can appear only pathological from his normative and philosophical perspective—aspects such as victimization, repressive social control, and the manifestation of ordinary social grievances or conflicts. For example, charivari in early modern Europe at times worked to keep deviants in line and to punish them for unpopular behavior.[9] Emmanuel Le Roy Ladurie, in his recent study of the 1580 carnival in Romans, shows, moreover, how this carnival became a conduit for class conflict that finally erupted into violence through which the upper classes eliminated opponents in the more popular classes.[10] The nature of car-

9. See, for example, Peter Burke, *Popular Culture in Early Modern Europe* (New York, 1978), 200.
10. Emmanuel Le Roy Ladurie, *Le carnaval de Romans* (Paris, 1979). Le Roy Ladurie nonetheless observes: "Carnival is not only a dualistic, prankish, and *purely momentary* inversion of society, destined in the last analysis to justify in an 'objectively' conservative fashion the world as it is [*comme il va*]. It is rather more an instrument of satiric, lyric, epic knowledge for groups in their complexity; therefore, an instrument of action, with eventual modifying force, in the direction of social change and possible *progress*, with respect to society as a whole [*dans son ensemble*]. . . . It goes without saying, however, that an anti-Semitic Carnival (Montpellier, Rome in the modern age) can with difficulty be seen as 'progressive'! The feast and social change do not always go in one direction" (pp. 349–350; my translation). One may, however, raise a question that Le Roy Ladurie does not explore, perhaps because his book interprets carnival primarily with reference to its role as an instrument of ordinary social and political conflict. Were the craftsmen and peasants led by Paumier especially susceptible to a surprise attack by Guérin and the upper classes precisely because they did not expect direct group violence to erupt in an unmediated way during carnival? Were the upper classes under the "Machiavellian" Guérin more prone to use carnival as a mere pretext for group conflict of an altogether serious and deadly sort? What is evident from the material Le Roy Ladurie presents is that Paumier, the popular leader, did not want to resort

nival is obviously bound up with the nature of the rest of social and cultural life, and its function depends, at times in complex ways, upon the variations of that mutual relationship.[11]

Bakhtin's specific focus is of course carnivalization in literature— a genre tradition that encompasses a number of genres but is especially pronounced in certain of them, notably the novel. Its ultimate sources are lost in the night of time, for like carnival it stems from what is for Bakhtin the largest and most indestructible context for literature and life: millennial folk culture and, especially, the

---

to violence during the carnival itself, although Le Roy Ladurie credits the belief that his followers might have turned to direct violence later on. Was this simply a misguided *Realpolitik* calculation or was it evidence that, at least for certain groups or individuals, carnival at this time was experienced in a way that made ordinary social violence seem out of place or even sacrilegious—a breach of certain unwritten laws?

11. Bakhtin's model of the carnivalesque may nonetheless be seen as an alternative to René Girard's "monologic" theory of culture. For Girard, a sacrificial crisis marked by chaotic nondifferentiation and generalized "mimetic violence" is overcome by the arbitrary selection of a scapegoat or sacrificial victim on whom ambivalence is concentrated. The violent expulsion of the victim ritually limits violence and generates the clear-cut oppositions on which society and culture are presumably based, including that between the innocent community and the guilty victim. The scapegoat mechanism, which Girard often presents as the key to all culture, is itself overcome only by the apocalyptic Christian doctrine of love, which, for Girard, entails the unorthodox denial of the sacrificial nature of Christ's death. See *La violence et le sacré* (Paris, 1972) and *Des choses cachées depuis la fondation du monde* (Paris, 1978). Girard's theory is marked both by an intolerance for ambivalence and by a desire for clarity and fullness of being that eventuate in an invidious distinction between Christianity and other cultural forms. It also stimulates a defense of a logic of identity and difference that is paradoxically based on conflation and confusion. One such conflation is that between chaotic or conflictual nondifferentiation (a bizarre concept in itself) and ambivalence, whereby Girard repeats the scapegoat mechanism in his treatment of ambivalence and those who try to come to terms with it in ways differing from his own approach. By contrast, the carnivalesque as interpreted by Bakhtin is a way of relating to ambivalence that counters the violence at work in the deadly serious scapegoat mechanism. Bakhtin, however, does indulge in at times naive populism that ignores the possibility that an egalitarian community, as well as an authoritarian elite, can in fact turn to scapegoating and violence, especially when victims become victimizers. His populism is periodically grounded in a phonocentric metaphysic in which the only vehicle for authentic expression is the spoken vernacular. But, as we shall see, his populism also has other features.

culture of folk humor. In certain historical periods, carnivalization in literature exists in close and dynamic interchange with carnival in social life. But in modern times it tends to become a largely detached component of literary writing. The interaction of social carnival and literary carnivalization was in evidence in different forms in antiquity and the Middle Ages, but in many ways the Renaissance was the high point of the carnivalesque, and writers of that period did have direct and sustaining contact with carnival as a major force in social life. Emblematic of that contact for Bakhtin is the legend of Rabelais's masquerade on the threshold of death when, during his last illness, he asked to be dressed in domino and travestied a quote from Holy Scripture: "Blessed are they who die in the Lord." Of Dostoevsky, however, Bakhtin makes an observation that in one sense could be applied to Bakhtin as well: "Carnivalization influenced him, as it did the majority of other writers of the eighteenth and nineteenth centuries, primarily as a tradition of literary genre whose extra-literary source, i.e. carnival proper, he did not, perhaps, even clearly perceive."[12] The chief sources of carnivalization for the literature of the modern period were writers of the Renaissance such as Boccaccio, Rabelais, Shakespeare, and Cervantes.

What for Bakhtin were the pertinent features common to carnival in social life and carnivalization in literature—features he sometimes referred to as constitutive of a carnival attitude toward the world? Let us begin with a quotation in which he specifies some of them and then enumerate them in as complete and concise a fashion as possible.

> Carnival is an eminent attitude toward the world which belonged to the *entire folk* in bygone millennia. It is an attitude toward the world which liberates from fear, brings the world close to man and man close to his fellow man (all is drawn into the zone of liberated familiar contact) and, with its joy of change and its jolly relativity,

12. Bakhtin, *Problems of Dostoevsky's Poetics*, 131.

counteracts the gloomy, one-sided official seriousness which is born of fear, is dogmatic and inimical to evolution and change, and seeks to absolutize the given conditions of existence and the social order. The carnival attitude liberated man from precisely this sort of seriousness. But there is not a grain of nihilism in carnival, nor of course, a grain of shallow frivolity or trivially vulgar bohemian individualism.[13]

The carnival attitude generates an ambivalent interaction between all basic opposites in language and life—a "jolly [or cheerful] relativity" in which poles are taken from their pure binarism and made to touch and know one another.

> Positive and negative elements are, of course, inherent in every word of a living speech. There are no indifferent, neutral words; there can only be artificially neutralized words. In the most ancient forms of speech the merging of praise and abuse, that is a duality of tone, is characteristic. . . . It is as if words had been released from their shackles to enjoy a play period of complete freedom and establish unusual relationships among themselves. . . . Their multiple meanings and the potentialities that would not manifest themselves in normal conditions are revealed.[14]

This ambivalence, with its Freudian overtones, is not confined to the play of language. It affects all significant dimensions of existence which, in the case of the human being, are themselves bound up with signifying processes. This includes the relationship between life and death. For Bakhtin, death in carnival dress is portrayed as a comic monster, an old hag that gives birth to a child, "something that occurs 'just in passing,' without overemphasizing its importance."[15] With an alacrity that sometimes seems precipitate, Bakhtin underplays the role of anxiety in order to stress the relationship between death and renewal in carnivalesque forms.

Yet reversals that set the world topsy-turvy occur within the

13. Ibid., 133.
14. Bakhtin, *Rabelais and His World*, 432, 423.
15. Bakhtin, *The Dialogic Imagination*, 194.

broader context of ambivalence. They are not one-sided inversions that remain within the framework of a dominant hierarchy which may prevail in ordinary life. At least within the carnival setting, reversals effect, or should effect, a generalized displacement of ordinary assumptions. "Both body and meaning can do a cartwheel, and in both cases the image becomes grotesque and ambivalent."[16]

Carnival is related to a grotesque in contrast to a classical aesthetic. The latter fashions perfectly rounded-off forms in which the apertures are sealed and the protuberances flattened. A grotesque aesthetic emphasizes orifices and bulges in larger-than-life forms that make them ecstatic. The grotesque body "is not a closed, completed unit; it is unfinished, outgrows itself, trangresses its own limits."[17] It enjoys food and sex; it is always eating, drinking, defecating, or copulating either literally or figuratively. Thus Rabelais's declaration (in the prologues) that he writes only while eating and drinking is a profound expression of the grotesque and carnivalesque "truth" of table talk.[18] Insofar as it is related to the carnivalesque realm of freedom, labor itself is always punctuated by the joyous consumption of food in banquet festivity and liberality. "Food often symbolized the entire labor process."[19]

A grotesque aesthetic sheds an uncommon light on Bakhtin's conception of civil liberties, for, in his eyes, the only truly free speech is festive, carnivalized speech. "The grotesque symposium does not have to respect hierarchical distinctions; it freely blends the profane and the sacred, the lower and the higher, the spiritual and the material."[20] Carnivalesque contestation with its consecrated laughter is not, however, detached from all seriousness; it is for Bakhtin a precondition of scientific inquiry and of realistic fantasy in art. "As it draws an object to itself, laughter delivers the object into the fearless hands of investigative experiment—both scientific

---

16. Bakhtin, *Rabelais and His World*, 418.
17. Ibid., 26.
18. Ibid., 117.
19. Ibid., 281.
20. Ibid., 285–286.

and artistic—and into the hands of free experimental fantasy."[21] Here one might add the political to the scientific and the aesthetic, given the interaction between politics and the carnivalesque in such institutions as coffee houses, pubs, cafés, and cabarets.

The theme of the double plays a vital role in carnivalesque processes. "Everything serious had to have, and indeed did have, its comic double."[22] For Bakhtin, "there never was a single strictly straightforward genre, no single type of direct discourse—artistic, rhetorical, philosophical, religious, ordinary everyday—that did not have its own parodying and travestying double, its own comic-ironic contre-partie. What is more, these parodic doubles and laughing reflections of the direct word were, in some cases, just as sanctioned by tradition and just as canonized as their elevated models."[23] Precisely what was most worthy of respect called for parody and could measure up to its challenge. Here Bakhtin gives the example of the satyr play, the fourth drama, which followed the tragic cycle as its laughing counterpart. He also notes that the great tragedians were reputed to have been the authors of their own parodies and travesties. "Aeschylus, the most serious and pious of them all, an initiate into the highest Eleusinian Mysteries, was considered by the Greeks to be the greatest master of the satyr play."[24]

The importance of the mask in carnival and carnivalized literature corroborates this duality, the ability to change in ways that destabilize fixed identities and suspend ordinary rules and role differentiations. The structure of masks—"the noncoincidence with themselves and with any given situation—the surplus, the inexhaustibility of their self and the like"—indicates "the incongruity of man with himself."[25]

The mask has a special relationship to the problem of authorship. Personal authorship is for Bakhtin "a particular problem that has

21. Bakhtin, *The Dialogic Imagination*, 23.
22. Ibid., 58.
23. Ibid., 53.
24. Ibid., 54.
25. Ibid., 36–37.

arisen only recently, since 'autographed' literature is a mere drop in an ocean of anonymous folk literature."²⁶ The role or function of the author is thus specific to certain genres in given contexts. It confronts the novelist in a peculiar way. "The novelist stands in need of some essential formal and generic mask that could serve to define the position from which he views life, as well as the position from which he makes that life public."²⁷ Especially in conditions of growing privatization that render intimate what was formerly public, the novelist finds the means of disclosure in the folk masks of the clown, rogue, and fool—masks that are "linked to the folk through the fool's time-honored privilege not to participate in life, and by the time-honored bluntness of the fool's language."²⁸ The clown, the rogue, and the fool are the envoys of carnival in everyday life, and the novelist dons their masks in modern society.

The indirect, metaphorical, or allegorical nature of these masks raises the question of metamorphosis—metamorphosis in the carnivalesque mode of reversal—for the clown and the fool are displacements of the czar and the god into a dreamlike nether world. Here allegory arises in a very elemental form. With the mask that doubles or multiplies the self, man is in an "allegorical state" of being in which he has "the right not to be taken literally, not 'to be himself.'"²⁹

The public square and the streets adjoining it are the proper place for carnival. The public square brings what is marginal or borderline in ordinary life to the very center of the community. On it all ordinary opposites meet and intermingle, and in this zone of festive familiarity, there are no footlights to separate spectators from participants. In ancient times for Bakhtin, the public square was "the highest court, the whole of science, the whole of art, the entire

26. Ibid., 160. For a comparable view, see Michel Foucault, "What Is an Author?" in *Language, Counter-Memory, Practice*, ed. Donald F. Bouchard (Ithaca, 1977).
27. Bakhtin, *The Dialogic Imagination*, 161.
28. Ibid.
29. Ibid., 163.

people participated in it."[30] With the separation of official society and culture from the public square, the withdrawal of the elites from popular culture, and the emergence of a private sphere of life, literature sought surrogates for the former public meeting place. The sense of scandal in Dostoevsky's novels stems from his conversion of drawing rooms and thresholds, which are supposed to be chambers of intimacy, back into squares for carnivalesque scenes of public disclosure and uncrowning.

Especially in certain periods of history, carnival is on the unofficial side of life.

> The serious aspects of class culture are official and authoritarian; they are combined with violence, prohibitions, limitations and always contain an element of fear and intimidation. These elements prevailed in the Middle Ages. . . . In the official philosophy of the ruling classes [a] dual tone of speech is, generally speaking, impossible: hard, well-established lines are drawn between all the phenomena (and the phenomena are torn away from the contradictory world of becoming, of the whole). A monotone character of thought and style almost always prevails in the official spheres of art and ideology.[31]

By contrast, the "unofficial" is "a peculiar conception free from selfish interests, norms, and appreciations of 'this world' (that is, the established world, which it is always profitable to serve)."[32] In the unofficial world, life is "drawn out of its usual and, so to speak, legitimized rut."[33]

The dominant key of carnival is of course the key of laughter. And laughter for Bakhtin is the sole force in life that cannot be entirely coopted by official powers and made hypocritical. "Laughter remained outside official falsifications, which were coated with a

30. Ibid., 131.
31. Bakhtin, *Rabelais and His World*, 90, 433.
32. Ibid., 262.
33. Bakhtin, *Problems of Dostoevsky's Poetics*, 132.

layer of pathetic seriousness."[34] Or, as Bakhtin put it in a hidden paraphrase of one of the most quoted lines in Dostoevsky, "to holiday laughter, almost everything was permitted." Laughter placed everything in "cheerfully irreverent quotation marks" and presented the serious genres themselves "against a backdrop of a contradictory reality that cannot be confined within their narrow frames. The direct and serious word was revealed, in all its limitations and insufficiencies, only after it had become the laughing image of that word—but it was by no means discredited in the process. Thus it did not bother the Greeks to think that Homer himself wrote a parody of the Homeric style."[35] Given its profound ambivalence, morever, carnival laughter is not invidious; it includes everyone and "is directed at all and everyone, including the carnival's participants."[36]

34. Bakhtin, *The Dialogic Imagination*, 236. One may note that Christianity for Bakhtin participated in the atmosphere of "pathetic seriousness." For example, it held forth the "sacrament of new life through food and drink," but it did so with "the complete absence of laughter, and copulation has been sublimated almost beyond recognition" (p. 223). Bakhtin does not emphasize what Le Roy Ladurie sees as the insertion of carnival into Christian time: "the burial of one's pagan life by giving oneself up to an ultimate pagan debauch" before acceding to the ascetic time of the catechumen. Nor is this sequence ever for Bakhtin what it is at one point in the intricate interpretation of Le Roy Ladurie: "The essence of Lent [which] corresponds to the primordial concept of Carnival" (*Le carnaval de Romans*, 340). The "primordial concept" of carnival for Bakhtin stems from millennial folk culture that is older than Christianity. And Bakhtin is evidently involved in an attempt to rehabilitate a sin-free notion of "pagan" values that Christianity accommodated only in very restricted ways or even at times opposed root and branch. Certain values that had a place in Christianity did play a part in Bakhtin's thought, such as the nonviolent principle of reciprocity (the Golden Rule) and the importance of responsibility or answerability (in contrast to full authorship). But neither Christianity nor the Russian Orthodox form of it was the unproblematic center of his texts. This seemingly self-evident point must be made, given the tendency in certain quarters to subject Bakhtin to an extremely "monologic" interpretation—precisely the kind of interpretation he rejected with reference to Dostoevsky—on the basis of his putative adherence to Russian Orthodox religion in his early years.

35. Bakhtin, *The Dialogic Imagination*, 55–56.
36. Bakhtin, *Rabelais and His World*, 9.

It is not like the joke that has a separate butt or the satirist's mockery that assumes a position of superiority vis à vis its object.

Scattered throughout Bakhtin's writings are references to historical periods as they relate to the carnivalesque. The high points for him were late antiquity and, even more so, the Renaissance. The Middle Ages subordinated its strong penchant for carnivalesque forms to a sharp division between an authoritarian official culture and an at times barely tolerated unofficial culture. The Enlightenment was characterized by "a lack of historical sense, an abstract and rationalistic utopianism, a mechanistic conception of matter, a tendency to abstract generalization and typification on [the] one hand, and to documentation on the other"—features that ill suited Enlightenment figures such as Voltaire to appreciate the grotesque and carnivalesque in others (such as Rabelais), although they might, more or less unwittingly, make use of it in their own works. [37]

It would, however, be a mistake to overemphasize this excessively schematic—should one say "enlightened"?—typification of periods that Bakhtin himself never codifies into a comprehensive model of historical periodization. Anything approximating a classification of periods in Bakhtin is subordinated to a dialogue with the past as it bears upon the present, and it is the excessively stereotyped nature of his inherited period concepts that indicates the limits of his own attempt to think through the implications of his approach for older modes of periodization and for the status of clear-cut period concepts in general. From Bakhtin's perspective, periodization, while remaining significant, loses its centrality and tends to be displaced by the problem of a dialogical relation to the past.

Bakhtin's basic conviction was that the context of folk culture and festive popular celebration "reveal the deepest meaning of the his-

37. Ibid., 116–117. In the Enlightenment one thus had a combination of theoretical nonrecognition of the carnivalesque with the ability to employ it in practice. The obvious problem in Bakhtin is of course the combination of a theoretical recognition of the importance of the carnivalesque with a largely academic, noncarnivalized style.

toric process."[38] The festive, carnivalesque attitude shapes time to its own image as a destructive, regenerative force that opens the dialectic at both ends and supplements it with the ambivalent power of laughter. Dialectics becomes dialogic and carnivalesque. "Time itself abuses and praises, beats and decorates, kills and gives birth; this time is simultaneously ironic and gay; it is the 'playing boy' of Heraclitus, who wields supreme power in the universe."[39]

Lest the last quotation create the mistaken impression that Bakhtin simply provides yet one more variant of an aesthetic of play, it is important to note that carnival and carnivalization are for him crucial dimensions of life that must coexist and interact with other dimensions. That they are the people's "second life," as he often puts it, invalidates purely instrumental or functionalist interpretations marked by the spirit of gravity and geared exclusively to questions of political power, social hierarchy, and economic organization. Carnival is not a mere safety valve—or, when it is, it has lost much of the carnivalesque. For Bakhtin, "the feast (every feast) is an important primary form of human culture. It cannot be explained merely by the practical conditions of the community's work, and it would be even more superficial to attribute it to the physiological demand for periodic rest. The feast had always an essential, meaningful philosophical content."[40] Indeed the existential importance of festive carnival forms in certain cultures and groups might lead one to reverse standard functionalist preconceptions and to interpret "ordinary" life in terms of the way it prepares for carnival. But the fact that carnival is never a total social environment implies that it is not a self-sufficient entity either in existence or in analysis. This point is always quite clear in Bakhtin, whatever his deficiencies in exploring actual and possible variations in the larger complex formed by carnivalesque phenomena and their "ordinary" complements. When carnival goes the way it should, it

38. Ibid., 447.
39. Ibid., 435.
40. Ibid., 8.

would seem that its "function" in relation to other social structures is itself ambivalent. It tests and contests all aspects of society and culture through festive laughter: those that are questionable may be readied for change; those that are deemed legitimate may be reinforced.

A major concern of Bakhtin, one that often colors his views of the past, is what he saw as the drastic diminution of a carnivalesque component in modern social life and the concomitant restriction of carnivalization to literature where it often turned bitter or involuted for want of a sustaining social and cultural setting. With special reference to modern society, one may, however, detect an unthematized tension in Bakhtin between his seemingly naive, egalitarian populism and the sentiment that extreme democratization, in its tendency to level all structures of authority, makes carnivalesque forms weak and trivial if not otiose. One may also notice a polemical inclination to accentuate the negative features of modernity, especially in Bakhtin's restricted reading of modern texts as symptomatic of larger forces hostile to the true carnival spirit—an aspect of his thought that became more pronounced under Stalin's regime.

SEMIOTICS AND LANGUAGE

Bakhtin has an important place in the history of semiotics. A remarkable feature of his thought is the shift of attention to the problem of language as a signifying practice in society and, more specifically, to collective phenomena such as genres. The genre for Bakhtin was not simply an analytic classification of the scholar; it was a discursive institution which exercised constraint upon the writing process as well as created opportunities for it. Bakhtin stated his principal objective to be the elaboration of a stylistics of genre, of "the great and anonymous destinies of artistic discourse itself."[41]

41. Bakhtin, *The Dialogic Imagination*, 259. See also *Problems of Dostoevsky's Poetics*, 133: "We emphasize again that we are interested in the influence of the *genre tradition itself*, which was transmitted through the given authors. The tradition is reborn and renewed in each of them in [his] own unique way. It is in

In works published under the names of Vološinov and Medvedev, the objective was expressed in terms of a sociological poetics
that situated more conventional concerns in a critical light. The
problem of consciousness, for example, was translated into the
problem of signification: "Consciousness takes shape and being in
the material of signs created by an organized group in the process of
its social intercourse. If we deprive consciousness of its semiotic,
ideological content, it would have absolutely nothing left."[42] The
reality of the inner psyche (or soul) was the same reality as that of
the sign. "Outside the material of signs there is no psyche." The
psyche, moreover, could not be situated within the individual; it
was a threshold phenomenon. "By its very existential nature, the
subjective psyche is to be localized between the organism and the
outside world, on the *borderline* separating these two spheres."[43]
The intentions of communicating subjects had to pass through a
linguistic material on which other subjects had left a mark, and any
given speaker had to negotiate the traces left by other speakers and
by the anonymous discursive practices of which individual speakers
might have little awareness. "Language is not a neutral medium
that passes freely and easily into the private property of the speaker's
intentions; it is populated—overpopulated—with the intentions of
others. Expropriating it, forcing it to submit to one's own intentions
and accents, is a difficult and complicated process."[44]

A principal defect of the conventional philosophy of language—
one shared by linguists, stylistic analysts, and phenomenologists—
was the assumption of an unmediated relationship between language (or consciousness) and its object or subject matter. Indeed,
"the isolated, finished, monologic utterance, divorced from its verbal and actual context and standing open not to any possible sort of
active response but to passive understanding on the part of the

---

them that the tradition lives. To use a simile, we are interested in the word [or
discourse] of language, not in its *individual usage* in a particular *unique context*,
although, of course, the one does not exist without the other."
42. Vološinov, *Marxism and the Philosophy of Language*, 13.
43. Ibid., 26.
44. Bakhtin, *The Dialogic Imagination*, 294.

philologist—that is the ultimate *'donnée'* and starting point of linguistic thought."[45] Bakhtin insisted on the dual reference of language to its object and simultaneously to other uses of language or
discursive practices. The problems of reported speech in all its variants—from direct quotation through indirect discourse to modes of
quasi-direct or free indirect speech—were for him the crux of a
theory of language in both literature and life. Especially significant
in quasi-direct or free indirect speech was that it did "not at all
contain an 'either/or' dilemma; its *specificum* [was] precisely a matter of *both* author *and* character speaking at the same time, a matter
of a single linguistic construction within which the accents of two
differently oriented voices are maintained."[46]

The internally dialogized phenomenon of quasi-direct or free
indirect speech had more than a local significance. It revealed the
ways in which actual uses of language were already implicated in
prior or simultaneous uses. It indicated the spuriousness of transcendental axioms that postulated either an arbitrary or a necessary
relationship among language, meaning, and referents. It emphasized the need to understand language as it was used in social
interaction (including that among author, narrator, character, and
reader). And it brought to the forefront of discourse analysis problems such as the roles of stylization, parody, irony, quotation, concealed polemic, and so forth—indeed all the problems currently
associated with the notion of intertextuality.

Bakhtin's own word for what has become known as semiotics was
translinguistics. In terms of it, members of the Bakhtin circle directed against the Russian formalists a reformulation of contextual
concerns.[47]

45. Vološinov, *Marxism and the Philosophy of Language*, 74.
46. Ibid., 144.
47. See especially Medvedev, *The Formal Method in Literary Scholarship*. This
book, like those signed by Vološinov, often relies on narrowly sociologistic and
orthodox Marxist formulations. Despite his dogmatic tenor, the author does make
some attempt to work out an immanent critique of formalism that integrates its
valid aspects. Somewhat surprisingly, the author finds these more in Western than
in Russian variants. The book ends with the words: "Every young science—and

Paralleling their controversy with the formalists and often relying on similar arguments was the Bakhtin circle's critique of Ferdinand de Saussure and his disciples. Bakhtin's lifelong conviction was that linguistics, especially Saussurian linguistics, was an inadequate model for discourse analysis. The study of discourse had to focus on the way language was actually used rather than rely on an abstraction such as *langue*, which was devised under Cartesian presuppositions for the purpose of what was taken to be scientific analysis.

In *Marxism and the Philosophy of Language*, Vološinov traced two opposed tendencies in modern linguistics affiliated with the names of Saussure and Karl Vossler. Vossler's school, influential in the German-language context, emerged from the romantic tradition and from one of the strands in the thought of Wilhelm von Humboldt. It stressed the individual use of words—*parole* in Saussure's lexicon—as constitutive of the dynamic, historical life of language. Vološinov criticized the subjective, individualist premises of the Vossler school, but he saw limited value in their interest in history and their attempt to work on the border of linguistics and stylistics.

Vološinov's critique of Saussure's "abstract objectivism" was more unqualified and in certain ways more relevant to contemporary problems in semiotics. Saussure's bracketing of the problem of language as a sociohistorical ensemble (*langage*), and his binary opposition between the synchronic linguistic system (*langue*) and the use of language by individual speakers (*parole*), while having limited validity in linguistics, amounted to a misleading abstraction for discourse analysis. On Saussure's assumptions, the use of language was falsely seen as the realm of instantiation of structures inflected by individual variations that were construed as epiphenomenal contingencies, accidents, or mistakes. In riveting linguistics on the ahistorical concept of a stable synchronic system

---

Marxist literary scholarship is very young—should value a good opponent much higher than a poor ally" (p. 174). Contextualism in books signed by Bakhtin becomes more supple through the use of notions such as the carnivalesque and the dialogical. But one thing Bakhtin never fully learned from the formalists and accommodated to his own approach was the value of close reading.

made up of normatively identical forms, Saussure brought to an extreme point a perspective he shared with other linguists and philologists: the foundation of a theory of language upon assumptions suited only to the reconstitution, codification, and teaching of dead languages rather than those employed and undergoing transformation in social life and usage.

But Vološinov's solution to the dichotomy between Vossler's and Saussure's approaches harbored its own difficulties. The restricted nature of his critique, along with a suspicion of the formalists' internal method in analyzing "how a text is made," produced a significant limitation in the perspective of the Bakhtin circle itself. Vossler is seen as combining individualism with a dynamic stress on *parole*, while Saussure is said to combine collectivism with a synchronic emphasis on *langue*. The alternative Vološinov postulates relies on a simple combination of features found in Vossler and Saussure rather than on a more thorough-going critique of the assumptions subtending their opposed choices. His own alternative is a sociological poetics centered on a diachronic study of collective discourses, that is, genres.

Bakhtin never quite manages to combine a theory of discourse with a close but nonformalistic reading of texts. The nearest he comes to so doing is in his study of Dostoevsky, but even in it one has a series of brilliant analyses of scenes, fragments, and problems but never of an entire novel or story in all its complexity. *Rabelais and His World* is much more schematic in furnishing a set of prescriptions for reading Rabelais's texts in one important context; it is not an extended, subtle reading of those texts themselves. On a theoretical level, Bakhtin will at times go beyond the formulations of *Marxism and the Philosophy of Language* in indicating an awareness of the intertextual or dialogical nature of the relation between texts and discursive contexts or institutions. He then broaches an understanding of the text not as an entirely unique object or as a precipitate of structures but as a signifying event that inscribes, tests, and perhaps contests larger discursive contexts. The question then becomes that of how a text internalizes or resists multiple and at times tensely interacting contexts, for example, how Rabelais's text relates to both folk culture and "elitist" humanism—a problem Bakhtin himself never thematizes. It is, however, noteworthy that Bakhtin never enunciates as a principle of semiotics (or translinguistics) the idea that one should confine analysis to the elucidation of codes or conventions that provide the conditions of possibility or the range of options in reading texts. At most he defends an emphasis upon genres and genre traditions in terms of his own interests in research. Indeed the value-neutral, apolitical, and formalistic conception of science on which the restriction of semiotics to the level of codes, conventions, and structures often rests would be quite alien to Bakhtin.

At times Bakhtin's very understanding of genre situates it in an open interchange with texts.

> A literary genre by its very nature reflects the most stable, "eternal" tendencies in the development of literature. The underlying elements of the *archaic* are always preserved in the genre. True, these archaic elements are preserved in the genre only thanks to their constant *renewal* and, so to speak, contemporization. Genre is always the same and not the same, always old and new simultaneously. A genre is reborn and renewed at every stage in the development of literature and in every individual work of the given genre.[48]

Here, at least on the level of theoretical propositions, Bakhtin goes beyond the designation of "semiotic structuralist," which is often applied to him.[49] His notion of a more active and mutually interdependent relation of genre and significant texts becomes even more forceful in the light of three concepts closely associated with that of carnivalization: heteroglossia, dialogization, and responsive understanding. Bakhtin even asserts: "the authentic environment of an utterance . . . is dialogized heteroglossia, anonymous and social

48. Bahktin, *Problems of Dostoevsky's Poetics*, 87.
49. See, for example, the rather misleading introduction to *Rabelais and His World* by Krystyna Pomorska.

as language, but simultaneously concrete, filled with specific content and accented as an individual utterance."[50] "Heteroglossia" refers to the objective condition of language marked by a plurality of perspectives and value-laden, ideological practices that are in challenging contact with one another. "Dialogization" designates the condition of subjects as speakers or users of language who are always involved in symbolic exchanges with other speakers.[51]

The concepts of heteroglossia and dialogization enable a rearticulation of "context," including the way contexts are "always already" inside texts, for the most insistent and penetrating aspect of dialogization is internal, and it signals a dimension of language that cannot be separated out into the rounded-off speeches of a literal dialogue. In internal dialogization, there is a tense investment of a given utterance or text with different and even divergent perspectives (or "voices") that suggest alternative possibilities in formulation and evaluation. Through the interaction of perspectives within the same utterance or text, language becomes a site on which contesting and contested discourses of different periods, groups, or classes engage one another as sociolinguistic forces. Dialogized heteroglossia creates the space for critical and self-critical distance in language use, for it disrupts myth in the sense of an absolute fusion or bonding of a use of words to a concrete ideological meaning.[52]

Internal dialogization introduces alterity or otherness into the self. It renders personal identity problematic and raises the question of the constitution of the subject of discourse with relation to the word of others. Here Bakhtin parallels the reformulation of psychoanalysis in the writings of Jacques Lacan, although the Bakhtin circle had an overtly critical relation to Freud ·in part because of

50. Bakhtin, *The Dialogic Imagination*, 272.
51. "The word, directed toward its object, enters a dialogically agitated and tension-filled environment of alien words, value judgments and accents, weaves in and out of complex interrelationships, merges with some, recoils from others, intersects with yet a third group" (Bakhtin, *The Dialogic Imagination*, 276).
52. Ibid., 369.

what they perceived as his underemphasis of the problem of language. In Vološinov's *Freudianism*, however, the concept of "unofficial consciousness," with its link to the carnivalesque, was the substitute proposed for the unconscious. Since aspects of this "consciousness" might be unconscious, both in structural and in dynamic-repressed senses, and since its processes often approximated those discussed by Freud as dream-work, the differences with Freud often seemed nominal.

In terms of literary studies, Bakhtin's emphasis upon dialogization directed attention to the more ambivalent or undecidable dimensions of texts, such as the double or multiple voicing of utterances in free indirect style. The kind of literal dialogue that most resembled internal dialogization was the "interminable prose dialogue" wherein each speaker inwardly understands and is genuinely tempted by the perspective of the other—where atheism exists on the border of faith, or courage on the confines of fear. The dialogues in *The Brothers Karamazov* were paradigmatic in this respect. Dialogization highlighted the importance of the border or the threshold where seeming opposites entered into an exchange and possibly coexisted, often in tensely charged relationships. It thus inserted the public square into language use itself.

The dialogical in *Problems of Dostoevsky's Poetics* is contrasted with the monological in which the unifying force in discourse becomes intolerant or at least dominant, giving rise to a totalizing point of view. The quest for a one-voiced and fully integrated subject that speaks the uncontested truth is found in certain theologies as well as philosophies, including both Hegel's speculative dialectic and the narrow forms of instrumental rationality Hegel criticized. In Bakhtin's "Discourse in the Novel" (1934–1935)—probably the most important text in *The Dialogic Imagination*—the monological-dialogical polarity is replaced by another opposition that has a special bearing upon Bakhtin's understanding of interpretation. This is the opposition between the authoritative and the internally persuasive word. The authoritative word, such as the word of the

313

father, is hierarchically distanced. "It is given (it sounds) in lofty spheres, not those of familiar contact."[53] It allows "no play with the context framing it, no play with its borders, no gradual and flexible transitions, no spontaneously creative stylizing variants on it."[54] Internally persuasive discourse, on the contrary, makes a claim on the speaker that may carry authority but is open to questioning and modification. It demands not sterile aping or mere reportage but dialogical transmission through what Bakhtin terms "responsive understanding," and it becomes joined to one's own word. With responsive understanding, the internally persuasive word of the other

> is not so much interpreted by us as it is further, that is freely, developed, applied to new material, new conditions; it enters into interanimating relationships with new contexts. More than that, it enters into an intense interaction, a *struggle* with other internally persuasive discourses. Our ideological development is just such an intense struggle within us for hegemony among various available verbal and ideological points of view, approaches, directions and values. The semantic structure of an internally persuasive discourse is not *finite*, it is *open*; in each of the new contexts that dialogize it, this discourse is able to reveal ever new *ways to mean*.[55]

Bakhtin here reveals the workings of class struggle internal to the individual speaker (or text)—a struggle that is more intense to the extent that the speaker is open to the conflict of internally persuasive discourses.

Bakhtin, however, does not authorize the free rewriting of the discourses of the past in terms of present interests. Responsive understanding does not exclude all objectivity in attending to the words of others. "Precisely such an approach is needed, more concrete and that does not deflect discourse from its actual power to mean in real ideological life, an approach where objectivity of understanding is linked with dialogic vigor and a deeper penetration

53. Ibid., 342.
54. Ibid., 343.
55. Ibid., 346.

into discourse itself." But Bakhtin nonetheless insists that "ideological meanings . . . can only be grasped dialogically and . . . include evaluation and response. The forms in which a dialogic understanding is transmitted and interpreted may, if the understanding is deep and vigorous, even come to have significant parallels with the double-voiced representations of another's discourse that we find in verbal art."[56] Here one has an intimation that the internal dialogization and even the carnivalization of critical discourse is the horizon of responsive understanding.

It is evident that carnivalization is for Bakhtin the most creative form of dialogized heteroglossia. The absence or breakdown of carnivalization facilitates a movement toward a pure power struggle between opposed forces. In this respect, one may note an important sense in which dialogization is a broader concept than heteroglossia, for it includes the interaction between heteroglot (or disseminating) and unifying tendencies in language. Bakhtin's critique of monologism and his sensitivity to the appropriation of unifying forces for purposes of political centralization or even totalitarian control did not lead him to reject all types of unity. Language itself was a force field in which centripetal (unifying) contended with centrifugal (heteroglot) tendencies, and their "dialogue" was perhaps the most comprehensive one in culture. Unitary language for Bakhtin "makes its real presence felt as a force for overcoming this heteroglossia, imposing specific limits to it, guaranteeing a certain maximum of mutual understanding and crystalizing into a real, although relative, unity—the unity of the reigning conversational

---

56. Ibid., 352. Compare Vološinov: "Word comes into contact with word. The context of this inner speech is the locale in which another's utterance is received, comprehended, and evaluated; it is where the speaker's active orientation takes place. This active inner-speech reception proceeds in two directions: first, the received utterance is framed within the context of factual commentary (coinciding in part with what is called the apperceptive background of the words) . . . second, a reply (*Gegenrede*) is prepared. Both the preparation of the reply (*internal retort*) and the *factual commentary* are organically fused in the unity of active reception, and these can be isolated only in abstract terms" (*Marxism and the Philosophy of Language*, 118).

(everyday) and literary language, 'correct language.' "[57] The significant work of art itself requires not "mindless and unsystematic mixing of languages—often bordering on simple illiteracy" but "orchestration by means of heteroglossia."[58]

The discursive institutions of primary interest to Bakhtin—genres and genre traditions—were in part unifying forces in the history of literature. The concept of the chronotope was Bakhtin's own higher-order attempt to provide a unifying classification that intersected traditional generic categories. Chronotopes, or space-time coordinates, were "the organizing centers for the fundamental narrative events of the novel. The chronotope is the place where the knots of narrative are tied and untied."[59]

Tied and untied: even the chronotope was not a pure unifying concept, and the role of discursive contexts as dialogizing forces with both unifying and heteroglot potential was always Bakhtin's stress. He provided his own metaphoric and oxymoronic statement of the kind of unity that seemed permitted by his approach to problems in these terms: "I imagine the whole to be something like an immense novel, multi-generic, multi-styled, mercilessly critical, soberly mocking, reflecting in all its fullness the heteroglossia and multiple voices of a given culture, people and epoch."[60]

These considerations enable a clearer understanding of the privilege Bakhtin at times accorded to the novel in the history of literature or even of language in general. The novel was for him the "fullest and deepest expression" of dialogized heteroglossia.[61] It emerged from folklore and the low literary genres, developed on the "boundary line between cultures and languages," and blossomed as the carnivalesque expression of the unofficial culture of laughter against the pretension of the elevated genres.[62] "The novel took

57. Bakhtin, *The Dialogic Imagination*, 220.
58. Ibid., 366.
59. Ibid., 250.
60. Ibid., 60.
61. Ibid., 275.
62. Ibid., 50.

shape precisely at the point when epic distance was disintegrating, when both the world and man were assuming a degree of comic familiarity, when the object of artistic representation was being degraded to the level of a contemporary reality that was inconclusive and fluid. . . . A lengthy battle for the novelization of the other genres began, a battle to drag them into the zone of contact with reality."[63]

The classical genres for Bakhtin "express the centralizing tendencies in language," while the novel "is associated with the eternally living element of unofficial language and unofficial thought (holiday forms, familiar speech, profanations)."[64] With the novel, the closure assumed in the epic (and sought on another level in Hegelian dialectics) becomes impossible. "The temporal model of the world changes radically: it becomes a world where there is no first word (no ideal word), and the final word has not yet been spoken."[65] Throughout the history of the novel, "its intimate interaction (both peaceful and hostile) with living rhetorical genres (journalistic, moral, philosophical and others) has never ceased."[66] As a result of "novelization," the other genres "become more free and flexible, their language renews itself by incorporating extraliterary heteroglossia and the 'novelistic' layers of literary language, they become dialogized, permeated with laughter, irony, humor, elements of self-parody and finally—this is the most important thing—the novel inserts into these other genres an indeterminacy, a certain semantic openendedness, a living contact, with unfinished, still-evolving contemporary reality."[67]

Thus the novel arises when language goes on holiday, and it exerts a fascination over other genres. But Bakhtin is at times aware of the fact that he is trading in models or ideal types and that the features he attributes to the novel, often in stark opposition to other

63. Ibid., 39.
64. Ibid., 67, 20.
65. Ibid., 30.
66. Ibid., 269.
67. Ibid., 7.

genres (notably poetry), may vary greatly with specific texts, especially in the modern period. Indeed what is striking about his entire discussion of the novel is that he does not even mention what is for other theorists its defining characteristic: the specific role of fiction in it. Bakhtin is in fact always concerned with aspects the novel shares with other genres to a greater or lesser degree. His notion of the "novelization" of other genres seems to assume a unilateral causal or mimetic influence that he does little to document. But what is apposite in his view is the idea that other genres, including critical discourse or even philosophy, may take on features he sees epitomized in the novel. Where, for example, could one find a more powerful case of an internally dialogized, carnivalesque style than in Nietzsche's *gaya scienza* where all the phenomena discussed by Bakhtin are not simply commented upon but energetically dramatized and played out? Indeed "novelization" as Bakhtin uses it becomes virtually synonymous with dialogization and carnivalization. This expanded usage and the seeming privilege it extends to the novel might well be seen as a strategic move which is justified by the traditionally subordinate place the novel has occupied in the hierarchy of genres—a subversive move analogous to that made by another strikingly carnivalesque and many-styled writer, Jacques Derrida, when he shifts the notion of *écriture* (writing) from its position as opposite of speech to make it the synonym not only of language but also of the "instituted trace" in general. In social theory, Marx himself stands out as a writer who made telling use of carnivalesque procedures in criticism, from subtle double-voicing to almost cannibalistic irony. The uncrowning of German ideology, the heated praise-abuse of Hegel, the ironic deconstruction of classical economics, and the appeal to parody in the critique of ideology are only the most blatant instances of a highly carnivalized style. In *Rabelais and His World*, Bakhtin weaves into his own discourse a number of explicit and hidden quotations from Marx, including this one from Marx's *Contribution to the Critique of Hegel's Philosophy of Right*: "History acts fundamentally and goes through many phases when it carries obsolete forms of life into the grave. The last phase of the universal historic form is its comedy. . . . Why such a march of history? This is necessary in order that mankind could say a gay farewell to its past."[68]

MARX AND MARXISM

Bakhtin is generally not discussed in the context of the history of Marxist thought. For example, his name does not even appear in David McClellan's panoramic survey, *Marxism after Marx*.[69] More surprisingly, he is mentioned only in passing in Rosalind Coward and John Ellis's *Language and Materialism*[70] and in Fredric Jameson's *The Political Unconscious*[71] despite the relevance of his concerns to the problems treated in these two books. Indeed when Bakhtin is compared with theorists attempting to relate Marxism and semiotics—including Jürgen Habermas—the distinctiveness of his emphases becomes apparent. One is tempted to conclude that what is needed is more of a "dialogue" between other Marxists and Bakhtin, whose concerns have relatively little place in Marxist literature.

68. Quoted in Bakhtin, *Rabelais and His World*, 435.
69. David McClellan, *Marxism after Marx* (Boston, 1979).
70. Rosalind Coward and John Ellis, *Language and Materialism* (London, 1977).
71. Fredric Jameson, *The Political Unconscious* (Ithaca, 1981). But see Tony Bennett, *Formalism and Marxism* (London, 1979). Bennett does accord importance to the work of Vološinov-Bakhtin in the rethinking of Marxism. One may note, moreover, that Bakhtin never mentioned the work of Georg Lukács—an omission so glaring for someone thoroughly versed in German-language scholarship that it is difficult not to see it as intentional. Especially in his later work, Bakhtin seemed to share Lukács's view of most modern literature as a "decadent" symptom of its context, but he did not explicitly restrict this limited view to Western "bourgeois" literature. In addition, Bakhtin was not a Hegelian Marxist stressing the role of concepts such as "totalization," and his emphasis upon carnivalization takes Marxist aesthetics and Marxism in general in directions quite different from those pursued by figures such as Lukács, Sartre, and Jameson. In a word, Bakhtin—while contrasting the epic and the novel in ideal-typical terms reminiscent of those employed by Lukács—saw the novel itself as the image of culture in general and did not join the quest for displaced epic totality through apocalyptic, revolutionary politics.

What is the changing position of Marxism in the texts of the Bakhtin circle, and how may one portray Bakhtin's overall attempt to rewrite a materialist dialectic? Texts such as *Marxism and the Philosophy of Language* and *The Formal Method in Literary Scholarship* are militantly Marxist in rather orthodox ways, for example, in making obeisance to the determinative role of the economic base "in the last analysis." But they also introduce the problem of language into Marxism by presenting language use itself as a locus of class and group conflict. And the entire issue of ideology is reformulated in a larger semiotic framework. The sign itself is seen as having a dual ideological significance as a necessity of consciousness or of communication and as a mutable, refracting, distorting medium. The very problem of a critique of ideology is thus shifted from the simple classical opposition between universal truth and self-serving falsehood to the question of the nature, limits, and functions of various kinds of "distortion" in the use of language in society—a shift that is related to Bakhtin's later inquiry into carnivalization and its "mystifications."

The role of Marxism is harder to detect in *Problems of Dostoevsky's Poetics*. One obvious analogy to Marx's thought is the conception of capitalism as an equivocal phenomenon—one both destructive of the social order and creative in bringing into contact forces that remained separate in earlier society. (Indeed in its role as "panderer" among different perspectives, capitalism might even be said to have a position analogous to that of Socrates in Athens.) Dostoevsky's works are interpreted as owing much to the rapid emergence of capitalism in Russia for their genesis, and as being critical of the newer social system in their implications. But the concepts of the carnivalesque and the dialogical are not directly related to Marxist themes and problems as they will be in *Rabelais and His World*. *Problems of Dostoevsky's Poetics* has much of the experimental daring and bravado of the 1920s in Russia, although it was published as this period was drawing to a close. In its lack of concern with making connections between its analyses and rather obvious possibilities in social criticism, it might seen to be liable to certain of the criticisms addressed to the formalists in *The Formal Method in Literary Scholarship*. It also emphasizes the creative dimension of modern literature to the point of presenting Dostoevsky's "polyphonic" novel as the high point in the history of the genre.

I have observed that in Bakhtin's later studies modern literature tends to be seen in a largely negative light. Indeed it is astounding that Dostoevsky is barely mentioned in *Rabelais and His World*, where the high point of the novel is shifted back into the Renaissance. And the sole, guardedly qualified reference to creative developments in the genre of the grotesque and carnivalesque is to "complex and contradictory" developments in the "modernist" line represented by Alfred Jarry and in the "realist grotesque" line of Thomas Mann, Bertolt Brecht, and Pablo Neruda.[72] (No mention is made of Joyce, for example, and the way he carnivalizes Homer in *Ulysses*.) The one concern that spans Bakhtin's masterworks on Dostoevsky and on Rabelais is that in the modern period the carnivalesque survives primarily as a literary tradition cut off from interaction with vital and important social institutions such as carnival itself.

In the study of Rabelais, however, there are a number of explicit and highly positive references to the works of Marx. They point, at times obliquely, to the ways the book is a profound rethinking of Marxism in terms unorthodox enough to help account for Bakhtin's reticence in spelling them out. With respect to its more immediate context, *Rabelais and His World* can be read as a hidden polemic directed against Stalinist uses of Marxism in the Soviet regime of the 1930s and 1940s. This reading does much to explain why the dissertation caused such controversy and finally led to state intervention. It also provides one rationale for Bakhtin's seemingly naive but perhaps strategic populism, which stressed those aspects of Marx's thought that were brutally betrayed under Stalinism. It also clarifies the otherwise curious tendency to insist that popular culture is *the*

72. Bakhtin, *Rabelais and His World*, 46.

context for Rabelais's work despite the fact that Bakhtin was well aware of the erudite and humanist dimensions of Rabelais. The fight to make Rabelais a man of the people is a fight to make Marx a man of the people, for the "new sober seriousness" Rabelais heralds can be seen as that of Marx. And Rabelais tends to become a *narodnik* in good part as a protest against Stalinism. In this respect, it is striking that the last powerful image in the book is a scene from *Boris Godunov*, where "Pushkin lets the people have the last word."[73] The pretender to the throne, a false ruler and a "people-eater," has a nightmare in which he is uncrowned by the laughing people of the marketplace.

> The people swarmed on the public square
> And pointed laughing at me,
> And I was filled with shame and fear.[74]

The more general point is that the people as a laughing chorus in a society where carnival is the necessary complement and counter-point to workaday, productive existence is also essential for Bakhtin's rethinking of Marxism. Carnival becomes the reign of freedom, the realistic utopia that has been approximated in the past and can be recreated in the future. In his insistence upon the significance and value of carnivalesque phenomena, Bakhtin introduces into a materialist dialectic forces that often appear as alien to it as they do to bourgeois society. Foremost among them are language, the body, and laughter in the multiple dimensions I have already touched upon. From Bakhtin's perspective, materialism refers to the material body and especially to the grotesque lower stratum that unseats both abstract idealism and the one-sided, productivist ethos Marx himself at times seemed to share with bourgeois society. Economic determinism becomes more manifestly what it sometimes is in Marx: a symptom of an "alienated" society. And language

73. Ibid., 474.
74. Quoted in ibid., 474.

emerges as a signifying practice related to other signifying practices in a world that is both material and cultural. What Bakhtin said of Rabelais could be applied to Bakhtin himself with special reference to the problem of a Marxist philosophy of language: "He wants to return both a language and a meaning to the body, return to it the idealized quality it had in ancient times, and simultaneously return a reality, a materiality to language and to meaning."[75] Bakhtin's dialogical and carnivalizing rendition of dialectics provides an alternative to the totalizing incentive of speculative dialectics, and it substitutes a Rabelaisian for a Hegelian Marx. It also provides some intimation of the needs of social reconstruction in the modern period.

POLITICS AND INSTITUTIONS

For Bakhtin, modern culture is characterized by a split between carnivalization in literature and the dominant tenor of social life. This split is in his view detrimental to both literature and social life, for it deprives literature of a sustaining context with which it might viably interact, and it signals the repression, trivialization, or noxious disfigurement of a crucial dimension of social existence itself. Bakhtin's stature as a social theorist is diminished by the fact that he devotes little attention to the workaday institutions and settings with which carnivalesque phenomena must interact in the larger rhythm of social life. A fortiori, he does not extend his vision to encompass alternative institutions suitable to modern conditions and germane to any attempt to regenerate carnivalesque forms. But he clearly recognizes the need for these institutions in any larger social context.

In addition, Bakhtin provides a notion of utopia in terms not of a total social environment but of a vital dimension of social and cultural life. Utopia in this sense becomes an "experimental fantasy" that has to some extent been approximated in institutions of

75. Bakhtin, *The Dialogic Imagination*, 171.

the past and that tests and contests existing conditions to open possibilities of historical transformation.

For a variety of reasons, the Marxist heritage has shared with those it criticizes a dearth of creative institutional thinking addressed to the problem of alternative social contexts. In Marx this lack of alternatives may be explained by a combination of factors: the suspicion of utopianism, the commitment to immanent critique, and a faith in the role of the proletariat as the revolutionary subject of history. More recently, the realization that faith in the proletariat is problematic at best, and the recognition that even immanent critique requires alternative goals, have often led either to an admission that modern conditions do not permit a bond between theory and practice or to a turn toward utopianism of a completely wishful and contentless sort. The great refusal and pure messianic desire are themselves less genuine alternatives than desperate complements. In this context, the value of Bakhtin is his attempt to furnish a critical vision of society and culture in which the utopian dimension is a transfiguration of historical phenomena that keeps a viable connection with the requirements of institutionally structured social life.[76]

76. This essay cannot end without at least a reference to Georges Bataille, whose writings would merit extensive comparison with those of Bakhtin. Bataille explored the carnivalesque and the festive with greater attentiveness than Bakhtin to the problematic relation between life and death in ambivalent phenomena. On Bataille, see Jacques Derrida, "From a Restricted to a General Economy: A Hegelianism without Reserve," *Writing and Difference* (Chicago, 1978; first pub. 1967), 251–277. I am indebted to Martin Jay for pointing out that Henri Lefebvre is one important Marxist who escapes the generalization that Marxists have tended to neglect the issues Bakhtin deemed important. Yet the resonance of this dimension of Lefebvre's work has of course been limited.

[10]

Marxism and
Intellectual History

There was only one Christian and he died on the cross.
Nietzsche, *The Antichrist*

The historian of tomorrow will be a computer programmer or nothing at all.
Emmanuel Le Roy Ladurie, *Le territoire de l'historien*

In this concluding essay, I shall discuss the problem of interpreting or reading Marx as it bears upon, or leads up to, general issues in intellectual history. My approach to Marx will not provide even a sketch for a comprehensive interpretation of his thought, because it will not include the important questions of his relation to social contexts of his own time or the use and abuse of him in social and political movements over time. Instead I shall focus upon the interpretation of his writings on a more circumscribed, intellectual level—but one that is not entirely divorced from social and political issues. On this level, one may distinguish between two ways of understanding Marx's texts that represent not mutually exclusive choices but significantly different emphases.

One way is to see Marx as providing a theory, method, or set of "ideas" that may be applied in the explanation of other texts and the historical process in general. Here Marx might be said to furnish a code that is a key to other codes and practices. One may also try to

325

integrate it with, or graft it onto, other codes, for example, existentialism, psychoanalysis, structuralism, or deconstruction. This recurrent activity of modern intellectuals on the left confronts as its initial problem the definition of the privileged Marxist code.

Since the time of Marx, there have been at least two principal options in the last respect. The first is that presented by positivism or, more accurately, by varieties of positivism. The variant elaborated by theorists of the Second International and then institutionalized under Stalin was a relatively narrow "economism." Recently a more sophisticated scientific Marxism—often interpreted as a variant of "structuralism"—emerged in the works of Louis Althusser. In time, Althusser himself came to view structuralism as an ideology, and he tried to distance his own approach from "positivism."

In his early collection of essays entitled *For Marx* (1965), Althusser insisted upon the role of an "epistemological break" [*coupure épistémologique*] in Marx which created a radical discontinuity between his early humanistic, somewhat Hegelian works and his later mature, scientific ones. Althusser's application of the notion of "epistemological break" enabled him to identify a "true Marx" whose identity underwrote that of Marxism-Leninism. Althusser's theoretical and political desire to stress the difference between Marxism and earlier "bourgeois ideologies" led him to continue to insist upon the validity of the notion of a "break" in Marx. But, in 1972, he could nonetheless problematize the notion in these terms: "Every recognized science not only has emerged from its own prehistory, but continues endlessly to do so (its prehistory remains always contemporary: something like its *Alter Ego*) by *rejecting* what it considers to be *error*, according to the process which Bachelard called 'the epistemological break.'"[1] To indicate his own criticism of what he came to see as the "theoreticist" bias of *For Marx*, Althusser now used the term "*rupture*" instead of "*coupure*" to signify the famous break.

---

1. Louis Althusser, *Essays in Self-Criticism* (London, 1976), p. 114. The quote dates from 1972.

Althusser had already provided a more nuanced schematization or periodization of Marx's works in his substantial contribution to *Reading Capital* (1968). Here he distinguished among the early Marx, the texts of the transition (including *The Eighteenth Brumaire* and *The German Ideology*, earlier believed to have marked the decisive break), and the writings of the mature Marx such as *Capital*. Althusser recognized elements of Hegel in the mature Marx, but he insisted that they represented mere vestiges or residues of the past in a decisively different problematic. This was not quite the same as his later view of a science's past as its Alter Ego.

Althusser's views influenced literary and cultural critics such as Fredric Jameson, who followed Althusser's self-understanding in locating "Marx's great theoretical revolution" in the principle of structural causation.[2] But they had relatively little impact upon the practice of professional historians. E. P. Thompson took it upon himself to write a vitriolic polemic against Althusser which tried to show that the implementation of his principles would lead to the writing of very bad history.[3] The object of Thompson's polemic may well have been Perry Anderson even more than Althusser, for Anderson did see value in Althusserian theory and tried to write long-term histories at least somewhat informed by it.[4]

Most practicing historians looking to Marx tend to be heuristic positivists with a suspicion of general theory more or less akin to E. P. Thompson's. They often interpret Marx in a limited, even narrow, manner by extracting from his texts theses or hypotheses that can be applied and tested in empirical research. Thus, for example, they may take the ideas of class struggle and ideological superstructure or the thesis concerning the French Revolution as a "bourgeois" revolution and subject them to standard procedures of critical examination to see whether or to what extent they hold up. Specifically Marxist historians may of course combine heuristic positivism

2. Fredric Jameson, *The Political Unconscious: Narrative as a Socially Symbolic Act* (Ithaca, 1981).

3. E. P. Thompson, *The Poverty of Theory* (New York, 1978).

4. See Perry Anderson, *Lineages of the Absolutist State* (London, 1974) and *Considerations on Western Marxism* (London, 1976).

with a more or less revolutionary ideology, but they often try to keep the two as separate as possible. Indeed they may overcompensate for the radicality of their ideology by being more orthodox in their methodologies and research practices than the ordinary bourgeois historian. Hence they may try to furnish two footnotes for every one of the bourgeois adversary's or indulge a "my footnote is bigger than yours" mentality. (Here of course one touches upon a general problem of ideologically marginal approaches, at least once they begin to acquire a measure of professional legitimation.) Relatively rare is the blend of solid research, challenging hypothesis, and moral pathos that characterizes the work of E. P. Thompson even when his specific conclusions or his aversion to theory are open to question.

A second principal option when Marx is seen as providing a master code to history is Hegelian Marxism. It presents the early Marx as the key to all Marxism. This key unlocks the story of self-alienation and its *Aufhebung*. One finds this option in scholarly form in Shlomo Avineri, where Marx's later thought is interpreted as a corollary to his early critique of Hegel.[5] In a more dynamic, Lukácsian vein, it is also active in Istvan Meszaros's *Marx's Theory of Alienation* as well as in his later study of Sartre.[6] Sartre himself of course furnished an influential formulation of the existential variant of Hegelian Marxism wherein the totalizing dialectic becomes the center of theoretical concern.[7] In this perspective, the problem of mediations and the attempt to relate future-oriented projects to past conditions (for example, in the family) further define the nature of a totalizing method. Explicitly contrasting himself with Hegel, however, Sartre stressed the role of the concrete and of individual agents as the specific contribution of existentialism to Marxism. He also insisted upon the openness of a dialectic that would never reach the closure anticipated in Hegel's concept of Absolute Knowledge. Why

---

5. Shlomo Avineri, *The Social and Political Thought of Karl Marx* (Cambridge, England, 1968).

6. Istvan Meszaros, *Marx's Theory of Alienation* (London, 1970) and *The Work of Sartre* (Atlantic Highlands, N.J., 1979).

7. Jean-Paul Sartre, *Search for a Method*, tr. Hazel E. Barnes (New York, 1963; first pub. 1960).

328

this closure was impossible was never fully explicated by Sartre, but his otherwise vacuous notion of a "reign of freedom" seemed to exclude it by definition or by ontological fiat.[8]

The second option in the first way of seeing Marx has often been interpreted as more "critical" in its implications than the first option.[9] But I would like to contrast both options that I have included

---

8. Fredric Jameson tries to amalgamate Althusser's structural Marxism with Sartre's existential variant of Hegelian Marxism. A different amalgam is offered by Michael Ryan in his *Marxism and Deconstruction* (Baltimore, 1982). The dream of *l'histoire totale* of course captured the imagination of the earlier generation of the *Annales* school that combined a neo-Durkheimian social metaphysic with a methodological (but ideologically anti-Marxist) idea of the totalizing dialectic of history. Fernand Braudel recognized that Sartre's attempt to trace the relation between "concrete example" and "deep structural context" paralleled his own and that their views would coincide even more if Sartre paid greater attention to the "journey . . . from the event to the structure, then from the structures and models to the event" ("Time, History, and the Social Sciences" in Fritz Stern, ed., *The Varieties of History* [New York, 1972], p. 427). It might, however, be observed that Sartre was more sensitive to the dialectic of temporality than members of the *Annales* school, who often seemed to construe change over time in terms of the succession of synchronic structures or cross-sectional types. Recently, the entire project of a total history has been severely questioned by younger exponents of the *Annales* tradition. (See, for example, Roger Chartier, "Intellectual History or Sociocultural History? The French Trajectories" in Dominick LaCapra and Steven L. Kaplan, eds., *Modern European Intellectual History: Reappraisals and New Perspectives*, [Ithaca, 1982], pp. 13–46.) But some followers of the *Annales* school in this country still seem to be guided by the light of an exploded sun. (Observe the almost Platonic dream of a quasi-Marxist historiography as a "moving synthesis across time," enunciated in the "Concluding Observations" of Harold T. Parker to the volume he edits with Georg G. Iggers, *International Handbook of Historical Studies* [Westport, Conn.], 1979, pp. 419–431.) The problem remains: what are the possibilities and limits of "synthesis" in view of problems—including textual problems—of which social historians are themselves becoming aware.

9. This is noted by Alvin Gouldner in his *The Two Marxisms* (New York, 1980). But Gouldner observes that scientific Marxism can also return to Hegel to avoid the narrowness of specialization and to restore the sense of a comprehensive system. For a powerful critique of Althusser, see John O'Neill, *For Marx Against Althusser* (Washington, 1982). O'Neill defends Hegelian Marxism but in a form that brings out the complexities of Hegel and the convergences between his thought and Marx's. O'Neill argues, for example, that Hegel did not simply conflate objectification and alienation and that certain uses of Hegel by Marxists fail to do justice to his thought. It should further be observed that my own references to Hegel are by and large restricted to an influential stratum of his texts and are in no sense offered as a comprehensive interpretation of them.

in the first way to a second general way of seeing Marx. Instead of providing a master code for the rewriting of all history, Marx's writings—seen in this second way—become a set of nonsacred texts that are marked by various and at times internally divergent, even self-contestatory, tendencies. Given their heterogeneity, there is no simple model that covers their relation to one another, to the past, or to political practice. The most general apprehension of them is approximated by a complex model of recurrence and change and itself has relevance for the interpretation of historical processes at large. In this light, Marx's texts have had—and can still have— various uses and abuses, some of which they invite more than others. The problem they pose is that of their selective use in theory and practice. Yet the texts of Marx can still be argued to be worthy of emulation in the attempt to understand history and in the writing of texts that come to terms with it. Their worth is in a sense broader and more critical than that intimated in the work of heuristic positivists, for Marx's texts combine documented knowledge—or "science"—with performative and dialogical uses of language. They do things with words in an exchange with the past that may affect the present and future. History as written by Marx is bound up with rhetorical, stylistic, and existential problems that implicate the historian in an intricate interaction with his or her object of study. Indeed, when comparing Marx with his successors, one is tempted to give in to hyperbole and to paraphrase Nietzsche: stylistically, there was only one Marxist, and he was buried at Highgate. And, with reference to prominent tendencies in "professional" historiography, one is led to contrast Marx's sense of significant problems with the rather abstract motivation for research provided by the desire to fill a gap in the record or to rehabilitate some putatively underestimated event or figure. [10]

10. Even such a fine social historian as Maurice Agulhon can give this professionally commonplace and anodyne reason for research into the revolution of 1848: "Why in fact should one speak of '48 today? . . . 1848 seems to us to be a forgotten revolution, or one depreciated by the great majority of our contemporaries, and it seemed to us that there was an injustice, a slope that needed to be climbed again, or a reputation to reinstate" (*Les quarante-huitards* [Paris 1975], 9–10; my translation).

One may further note that the two aspects of Marx's texts selected by structural and Hegelian Marxists are not the only ones in Marx. Indeed a moot issue is how even these two aspects relate to one another. As Althusser at times seemed to intimate, a one-dimensional concept of an epistemological break may be rather misleading in the attempt to account for the obvious differences between Marx's early texts and his later ones. The question is how to interpret the significance of these differences as well as their connection to recurrent problems in Marx. There is no extensive and detailed analysis and critique of the capitalist system in the early Marx to compare with that in *Capital*. But Marx's relation to Hegel (and, in certain respects, to the classical economists) undergoes more subtle transformations over time and, occasionally, in one and the same text. It is most fruitful, I think, to see Marx's relation to Hegel as one of internal dialogue involving both receptivity and variable struggle. The early Marx internalizes the Hegelian "problematic," and the latter recurs and is "rewritten" with notable variations throughout Marx's career. Or, to change the metaphor, Marx is always wrestling with Hegel, and the two combatants are in different positions at different points in their encounter. Often Marx is deeply ambivalent about Hegel, reacting to his opponent with praise-abuse. And a seeming "break" in one text (such as *The German Ideology*, where the very questions posed by the "German ideologists" are said to harbor mystification) does not obviate a return to Hegel in other texts (such as the *Grundrisse*) or even in other segments or arguments of the same text (such as the reliance on the concept of "world-historical" being in *The German Ideology*).

While Marx's relation to Hegel was a real intellectual affair or even a romantic marriage, it is not the key to all of Marx. The inadequacy of interpreting Marx only in terms of a Hegelian—or, by contrast, a positivistic-structural—"problematic" is indicated by the active role in Marx of other tendencies. Without any pretense of being inclusive and exhaustive, I would simply note three such tendencies (the first is explicitly articulated by Marx, while the other two remain implicit in his "practice" or very use of language). (1)

On a certain level of analysis, Marx will problematize the notion of stages or periods of development by formulating a notion of interaction among elements in a relational network (as Althusser himself indicates in his concept of structural causation). This view may not be identified with a purely static synchronism, however, for variations in the relations among elements are coordinated with change over time. This is the sense in which Marx discusses the relation between production and other aspects of the economic process in the introduction to the *Grundrisse* and the relation between "moments" of social activity (or between forces and relations of production) in *The German Ideology*. (2) Quite striking in Marx is the use of "carnivalized" language as a mode of critique, for example, in a text such as *The Eighteenth Brumaire*. Indeed his many-sided use of parody and irony, which may at times go to uproarious extremes, is what most distinguishes his style from the often leaden satire and polemic of many later Marxists. (3) Marx sometimes employs a "model" of repetition with variation in his understanding of the historical process (as well as in his own use of language). This "model" further specifies the workings of a relational network and its bearing upon the problem of temporality or "historicity." It also provides insight into "carnivalized" language use as an especially potent mode of repetition-variation.

An illustration of the third point will serve to raise the entire question of how to read *Capital*. It may even broach the issue of how to "triangulate" Marxism, psychoanalysis, and poststructuralism.[11] Here a fictionalized reconstruction of the "phenomenology" of reading *Capital* may serve a heuristic function. Marx himself claimed that the initial sections of *Capital* were the most difficult. In a sense, the way one reads them prefigures the way one reads the entire text.

11. Hans Kellner discusses this problem in terms of the "anxiety" it provokes in intellectual historians, but he seems to offer little hope of addressing it in a critical and constructive manner. See "Triangular Anxieties: The Present State of European Intellectual History" in LaCapra and Kaplan, eds., *Modern European Intellectual History*, 111–136.

Reading these opening sections for the first time, one is struck by the seemingly abstract delineation of concepts to analyze the commodity form (use value, exchange value, abstract labor power, and so on). Marx seems to conform to the image of the pure scientist, indeed the theorist who, in the afterword to the second German edition, seems to invert Hegel by collapsing positivism and the dialectic into a purely objectivist notion of the laws of motion of the capitalist economy. A positivistic dialectic appears to be revealed as "the rational kernel within the mystical shell." The first three sections of the principal text also seem to fall neatly within this "problematic." But then the section on commodity fetishism seems to erupt as an almost traumatic reminder of the past—a repetition of the theory of alienation that causes a rupture in the text and disorients one's expectations about it. One is led to reread the earlier sections in its light and to notice the evidence of "double-voicing" or of "internal dialogization" operating to disfigure their seemingly placid positivistic facade. Bizarre footnotes on Benjamin Franklin and on the problem of human identity appear to cast an ironic light on the concept of abstract labor power as the essence or "quiddity" of exchange values. An ironic countervoice even surfaces in the principal text to strike dissonant notes with respect to the seemingly dominant positivistic voice. ("The fact that [linen] is [exchange] value, is made manifest by its equality with the coat, just as the sheep's nature of a Christian is shown in his resemblance to the Lamb of God.") The reader begins to wonder whether he should take the concepts of abstract labor power and exchange value altogether at face value. Is their value (like that of the concepts of the classical economists of which they are more expanded elaborations) provisional? Are they "scientific" articulations of an "alienated" system whose fundamental fault is the reduction of "living labor" to "abstract labor power" in the first place?

A certain reading of the section on commodity fetishism would seem to imply a simple affirmative answer to these questions. But difficulties in that section itself indicate that the answer is not that simple. It contains diverse and even divergent lines of analysis that

333

disclose problems in the conception of "alienation" and its over-coming. One line of critical analysis explains the commodity fetish through a simple principle of inversion or reversal. ("A commodity is therefore a mysterious thing, simply because in it the social char-acter of men's labour appears to them as an objective character stamped upon the product of that labour.") Marx seems to fall back on a Feuerbachian "transformative criticism," which is not terribly transformative in that it remains within the criticized "problematic" and simply inverts its terms or lexicon. This inversion or reversal may have an initial critical force in that it upsets a dominant hier-archy; it attributes to human labor what in the established capitalis-tic system was hypostatized or naturalized in the product of labor. And it draws an analogy with the putative human creation of gods in "the religious world" to reveal how "a definite social relation be-tween men . . . assumes, in their eyes, the fantastic form of a rela-tion between things." But the reversal, by remaining within the same "problematic" (or retaining the same syntax while inverting the terms of the lexicon), now appears to attribute to men the "fantastic" powers or unproblematic position of generative cen-trality that was formerly ascribed to gods—or to commodities.

Another aspect of the section on commodity fetishism invites a different view of the "social hieroglyphic" constitutive of the fetishized commodity. Fetishism is construed in the light of a secu-lar *displacement* of "mystifying" religious values—a movement that threatens Marx's own seemingly dominant "decoding" of the com-modity fetish itself. But there is also a sense in which the moment of fetishization is located in the *fixation* of a series of exchanged sub-stitutes and a *projection* of meaning entirely stripped from the labor process onto a reified product or "symbol." One might extrapolate from this aspect of the analysis to argue that abstract labor power is itself a primary mode of fixation of "living labor" and that its over-coming, while never entirely free of the risk of "mystification," requires a network of relations among humans and between hu-mans and nature in which work is not reduced to a purely or predominantly instrumental value in the production of other val-

334

ues. The problem posed in this respect is not one of simple reversal (the reign of use value or the repossession of surplus value) but of generalized displacement and rearticulation of a given frame of reference. The dimension of the early *Economic and Philosophic Manuscripts* that is most helpful here is not its one-sided productivist or Promethean impetus but rather its counteracting stresses upon human action and receptivity in a double or dual image of the human being. It is significant that it is only in this text, where Marx emphasizes the limited, sensate, suffering, and passionate sides of man, that he also asserts the need for a history of the senses and posits the relation between the sexes as the criterion of social development.

This brief discussion of commodity fetishism might be extended to encompass the question of the Marx-Freud relation as it bears upon the interpretation of the historical process and the chances of significant change in it. The attempt to "build a bridge" between Marx and Freud has of course become a mainstay of modern thought, especially on the left. Theorists attempting to link the two have, however, often been content to manipulate set pieces, that is, to adjust existing concepts or disciplines such as psychology and sociology. Even Fredric Jameson relies on the staid formula that Freud is to the private individual as Marx is to the collectivity, and the concept of ideology becomes the predictable cement for the "bridge" between the two.

The more profound and far-reaching attempt to connect Freud and Marx, which draws on the work of "poststructuralists," would rather invite a basic rethinking of the historical process and the very concept of temporality. The standard dichotomy upon which historians still tend to rely returns to Aristotle's opposition between the universal, as the realm of philosophy, and the particular, as the realm of history. History is commonly identified with the study of the particular, indeed the unique, in contrast to the study of the universal, the intemporal, human nature, general psychology, and so forth. A mediation between the universal and the particular is at times sought in the sociological concept of the type, but the epis-

335

temological status of typology is often left in doubt or identified in ahistorical fashion with the static or synchronic definition of a structure.[12]

The very notion of the type may itself be temporalized in terms of the process of repetition with change that Freud approached through the concepts of displacement and transference. The "universal" represents pure repetition to the idealized point of intemporal identity. The "particular" represents pure change to the idealized point of isolated uniqueness. The problem, as Heidegger indicated, is to "think" repetition and change together rather than in abstract, ahistorical isolation. The historical process may be understood, following Derrida's lead, in terms of iteration with alteration—a process for which language provides one important model. This understanding relativizes the concept of stages or periods, for the latter now refer to distinctive variations that are judged to be particularly significant without entailing total dissociation or the impossibility of all communication across period lines. But major discontinuities or breaks across time are still possible. Freud, it may be recalled, saw the trauma itself as a decisive rupture or breakdown in experience brought about by the repetition of an early scene, which the child did not have the capacity to comprehend at the time of its occurrence (indeed, which may never have occurred in the form in which it was remembered), in a later and more intelligible scene. The trauma could not be localized in either the early or the later scene in isolation but was brought about by the relational process of repetition itself. Without repetition, the early scene was like an untranslated foreign text in the unconscious. The transference in Freud was another repetition of a childhood scene in the relation of

12. Fernand Braudel's influential distinction among event, medium-term time span (*la conjoncture*), and long-term, relatively permanent structure (*la longue durée*) is often conceptualized as a modulated refinement of the traditional opposition between particular event and intemporal structure. It should, I think, be rethought along the lines of a model of variable articulations of repetition with change, which its actual usage would seem to imply, for the virtue of Braudel's distinction is to reveal the fictional status of the concepts of purely unique event and purely intemporal structure.

patient and therapist, and the problem of analysis was how to work through the transference in a way that would make it less destructive and convert it into a force for more responsible adult interaction.

The Freudian notions of displacement and transference have, I think, great analogical value for articulating more implicit tendencies in Marx and for interpreting the historical process in general. Displacement signifies repetition with variation over time, and its historical use would require detailed and well-documented investigation of processes where it might be argued to pertain—for example, in the relation of religious to secular phenomena. Historiography itself has often had the quasi-liturgical function of preserving and commemorating the collective heritage, and the critique of this displacement has often led to a more parochial variation whereby historiography becomes the handmaiden of the professional conscience of historians themselves. In any event, the turn to Freud may bring into prominence the role of transference as it affects the historicity of the historian in entering into an exchange with the past, for, despite the importance of critical distance, the historian is never in a position of total mastery over the object studied, and the concerns agitating figures in the past may find their analogues in the work of the historian himself. What is especially perplexing in this respect is that self-proclaimed psychoanalytic or psychobiographical historians will often not employ Freud to rethink the historical process and their own implication in it but simply abstract from Freud certain concepts and more or less reductive strategies of interpretation that are inserted into the most conventional and self-certain models of research. In this they tend to resemble certain Marxist historians who treat Marx's texts in an analogous manner.

The notion of displacement as repetition-change also helps one to problematize the concept of anachronism. Anachronism was used by James Harvey Robinson in a "progressivist" sense to attack reactionary vestiges of the past that blocked reform in the present. It is used by Quentin Skinner and those akin to him in castigating the insertion of present concerns into the study of the past—a usage that at times approaches antiquarianism in its insistence upon knowing the past in its own terms and for its own sake. But what underlies the concept of anachronism in both these uses is the idea that a radical divide separates periods and times and that the only alternative to an abstract concept of difference over time is an equally abstract concept of intemporal universality (or human nature). There is also an overly ready willingness to postulate what was or was not possible for people to think or to imagine at a given time—a postulation that is itself often identified with the "historical sense."

I would suggest that the concept of anachronism is much more open to question than these views allow. Anachronism denies the significance of difference or change in the historical process, but it is difficult to control for difference or change in abstraction from processes of recurrence that implicate the historian in problems comparable to the ones he or she studies. And the historical process cannot be identified in a carte blanche manner with the aspect of difference or change alone. In addition, it takes a great deal of presumption to assert what was or was not "possible" at a given time. At the very least, one must entertain the question of whether what seems "impossible" was avoided or repressed—or at least constituted an elaboration of possibilities that entailed the overcoming of too many blockages or resistances to be plausible. In any event, the concepts of historical possibility and impossibility are much more flexible than appears to be the case in the works of those who invoke them. The most basic point is that the concept of anachronism, whatever its limited usefulness, must not itself become a bar to a dialogue across time that is itself respectful of differences and distances—a dialogue that even those relying greatly on the concept of anachronism acknowledge in practice, albeit in a rather curtailed form.

Given the approach taken in this essay, one of the most crucial questions at the juncture of Marxism and intellectual history is that of the nature of a "political" reading of texts. Precisely what constitutes a "political" reading is of course highly debatable. Even more subject to debate is the very question of what it means to be a Marxist in North America at the present time, especially in the absence of any viable political organization to serve as the social correlate for an intellectual stance.

I shall not pretend to answer this question. Instead I shall intentionally displace the general issue of a political reading onto the smaller, less charged, and more manageable issue of the reading of texts in professional historiography. This relatively inconspicuous issue is itself, however, not entirely divorced from the problem of a dialogue with the past having practical, political implications for the present and future. The university itself is a strategically located place in modern society where people learn to read in ways that may affect the manner in which they come to terms with problems in general.

In a sense, historians are professionally trained not to read. Instead they are trained to use texts in rather narrow, utilitarian ways—to "strip mine" or "gut" them for documentary information. Indeed, historians tend to appreciate texts to the extent that they provide factual information about given times and places. That the general reading public has recently shown a preference for historical texts providing information—or for fiction simulating the historical text—is one index of the manner in which the reading proclivities of historians are attuned to the demands of contemporary society.

A restricted documentary reading when ringed with the appropriate disclaimers and caveats may have a certain validity in social history. (Here I would note that one important function of structuralism has been to reprocess phenomena in terms that allow them to be coded and fed into computers, especially with respect to information reduced to binary oppositions.) But a documentary reading always threatens to reduce significant texts to a redundant or merely suggestive status—redundant when factual propositions derived from them must be checked against more strictly documentary sources and merely suggestive when the latter process proves impossible. A restricted documentary reading obviously is most justified for manifestly documentary texts and for "weak" or second-rate fictional and theoretical texts that tend to illustrate or reflect popular stereotypes. But even in these cases, such a reading may blind one

339

to the textual dimensions of documents or the ways they are not simply transparent representations of reality. It may also obscure the manner in which even diaries or memoirs rely on *topoi* or literary conventions in conveying information about life, which can never be taken altogether at face value. Even pamphlet literature addressed to immediate political interests and demands employs rhetorical devices that repay close analysis. And how many writers of diaries or autobiographies have been motivated by the desire to be or not to be like Rousseau?

The general problem facing the "human sciences" is to arrive at a differential understanding of the relation between documentary and other than merely documentary components of various texts and types of text. Although there are referential uses of language and although historiography may to some extent investigate all uses of language from a referential perspective, no artifact is a mere representation or reflection of "reality," and different artifacts have differential relations to what is classified as "ordinary" reality. The most stereotypical, cliché-ridden text affects what it represents, just as the mirror in ordinary life is always more than a neutral medium of reflection for the person who gazes into it. The fact that the mirror itself is in any real situation or context never an innocent source of representations could be taken to indicate that there are no purely documentary texts. All texts must be read in one way or another, and the historian's passage to the past is always through texts or other "textualized" traces—traces that are textualized in that they have always been subjected to prior interpretations and uses. But if there is a working distinction between first-rate (or "classical") and second-rate texts, it is that the latter tend less to rework their stereotypes and clichés in explicitly critical and transformative fashion. Their problems and ambivalences are typically blind and must be observed by the critic. The first-rate text—and this point is of course to some extent definitional—will often highlight problems and explore ambivalences, for example, by "internally dialogizing" the stereotype and parodically citing or ironically framing it. In this sense, it may serve as a "model" for the critic who reads it well. The difficulty is that historians tend to read all texts as if they were documentary (if not second-rate) in an unproblematic sense. And the prevalence of a narrowly documentary idea of understanding may inhibit them in learning how to read and in accounting for their own rhetoric.

Not only does the language used by the historian affect the realities it represents. The artifacts through which we approach historical reality are themselves historical realities whose interest for the historian is not exhausted by their representational relation to some privileged reality such as "society" or "ordinary life." What happens in these artifacts constitutes a historical process worthy of study, and the relation between this process and reconstructed "ordinary" reality—which is often privileged in the accounts of historians—must itself be posed as a problem. Indeed the assumption that there is a privileged reality in relation to which artifacts are simply representations rests not on a historical but on a metaphysical foundation—one no less metaphysical for being assimilated to a notion of "common sense." There may be good reasons for this metaphysic, and within limits I would assent to them, but the way the metaphysic functions is at times highly dubious.

The commonsense metaphysic that privileges ordinary life or social reality has a long lineage. Marx himself indulged it to deflate the pretensions of German idealism. (One may recall Marx's litany to the "real" and the "empirical" in *The German Ideology*.) But a social metaphysic of everyday or ordinary life was more broadly part of the mystique of social history and sociology. (Here Durkheim is superior to more empirically minded and discreet social scientists precisely because he made overt the metaphysic that is often implicit in research strategies, interpretative protocols, and professional decisions.) In earlier variants of social history and sociocentric interpretation, a social metaphysic was frequently bound up with an ideology of the common man or with populist and egalitarian sentiments in general. James Harvey Robinson, one of the founders of social and of intellectual history, relied on such an ideology in affirming the very bond between social and intellectual

341

history, indeed in insisting that one should interpret the texts of "high culture" only insofar as they were intelligible to, and thereby had an impact upon, the common man of a given period. The attempt to interpret the most difficult and demanding texts exclusively from a perspective that coincided with the preexisting capacities of the common man (or the "generally educated person") became in certain quarters an institutionalized limitation of intellectual history fixated at a popularizing and introductory level of analysis.

At this point, one is tempted to put forth the dictum that in the "human sciences" everything begins in ideology and ends in methodology, for, at present, the perspective and techniques of social history (or of sociocentric interpretation in general) may be pursued and refined for purely methodological reasons and, in the process, carried in computerized directions that escape the comprehension of the "common man." Those pursuing this kind of research may even have elitist ideas about their own position in the historical profession or in the society at large. Indeed the methodological imperatives of advanced social research may be either positivistic in nature or infused with a rather conservative ideology (an especially convenient one when the object of inquiry is premodern). In any event, the methodology of social history often leads to the privileging of certain documents (such as wills, parish registers, police reports, or diaries) on questionable grounds—questionable to the extent that they induce the exclusion or the homogenization of other texts and documents such as novels, philosophical works, or the writings of someone like Marx. One of the hallmarks of a restricted documentary perspective, after all, is the reduction of all artifacts to a unitary body of information putatively reflecting social reality.

The insistence upon the importance of reading certain texts does not imply the denigration of social history. It may prompt the defense of qualitative distinctions between kinds of texts but *not* between those who study one or another kind of text. (Thus Marx may be judged to be more worth reading, at least from the perspective of intellectual history, than various pre-Marxists, Marxists, or post-

Marxists, but the investigation of the latter is pertinent to the reconstruction of the various discursive contexts necessary for the understanding of Marx and even for the judgment of Marx's relative value.) In addition, the argument in this essay need not lead to a rigidly elitist social or political position. Rather it bases itself both on the necessary and possibly creative tension between common and expert knowledge and on the desirability of enabling the "common man" (including the "common man" in oneself) to develop a more critical perspective, in part through the reading of demanding texts. For certain texts, including those of Marx, may in their work and play provide a model worthy of emulation in social life as well as a stimulant to creativity in popular culture, which is threatened by assimilation into an often mindless "mass" culture. At the very least, the "conversation" with these texts may be an educational force not only in the use of language but in the manifold activities with which language is intimately connected.

Do the foregoing considerations mean that one is now faced with the indiscriminate problem of "reading" and that no disciplinary distinctions can be drawn even on pragmatic grounds? I think that distinctions can still be drawn, but they need not be taken to the extreme of total dichotomies. [13]

The difference between social and intellectual history is primarily

13. Marx's notion of alienation becomes misleading when it is taken to imply that everything cultural derives from some originally unitary source that is to be reattained on a higher level through the speculative "dialectic" of history. Used in this way, the notion lends itself to a "humanism" that is excessively indentured to a religious creationism (itself displaced in Hegel's concept of *Geist*). But the notion retains its value insofar as it is distinguished from objectification, difference, and otherness in general. Then it is no longer a direct derivative of a "logocentric" metaphysic, and it may be specified to apply to pure dichotomies and the rigid hierarchies that accompany them. The latter are what Marx attacked in his critique of multiple extreme divisions in humans, including class conflict and capitalistic exploitation. But, in its specific form, alienation may not be identified with, or entirely derived from, the capitalistic system, for it may include other oppressive modes. Indeed it is a recurrent threat in any social system. In addition, the goal of overcoming alienation, while it may never be achieved once and for all in some condition of total mastery, may nonetheless be argued to imply types of social relation and a measure of control over the economy that are significantly—even qualitatively—different from those prevailing in the system Marx criticized.

one concerning the direction of interest. Social history uses texts to reconstruct a context or a past social reality. It becomes questionable from the perspective of intellectual history when it fosters assertions that reduce certain texts to representative, illustrative, or symptomatic functions. Conversely, it provides the only techniques with which to check the claims concerning the representativeness or influence of texts that intellectual historians at times make in impressionistic ways.

Literary critics and philosophers in their distinctive modes are especially interested in elaborating "good" or "competent" readings. Prompted at times by revulsion against the crudeness of narrowly documentary readings, they may confine themselves to micrological scrutiny of texts or textual fragments, with little concern for the broader historical contexts or implications of their textual strategies (except in extremely allegorical ways). At present, more experimental forms of literary criticism, when they do not replace older types of formal or "new" criticism, threaten to remain on the level of delicate miniatures that are like verbal analogues of the paintings of the Dutch school. "History" itself may be invoked as an extremely abstract, indeed intemporal, category either to defend or to reproach more formal and micrological methods of criticism. Or the "contexts" that are called upon to flesh out an interpretation may be the outgrowth of wild speculation rather than careful research.

Intellectual historians should, I think, try to provide good, close readings. In attempting to transcend the rough, homespun interpretations often characteristic of their subdiscipline, they have much to learn from literary critics and philosophers. But their dialogue with the past requires an effort to situate texts with respect to their multiple, interacting contexts of creation and reception. They should also render explicit the relation of close readings to larger historical problems, including the reconceptualization of the historical process itself. When literary critics or philosophers make such attempts, their work joins that of intellectual historians. Perhaps the most essential point that can be made in this respect is that the role of specific characteristics in defining disciplines or subdisciplines should not be given exclusive importance or made to obscure the vital need for interaction in addressing problems of reading and interpretation. Within the discipline of history, polemics may be necessary to defend the importance of reading difficult texts insofar as a textual perspective threatens to be submerged by other perspectives or at best marginalized with the rise to dominance of other methods in intellectual history itself. But a practitioner of a discipline should not seek to avoid the professional anxiety generated by the unavailability of an analytically pure object of study that defines his or her field with clear and distinct precision. Instead the necessary anxiety inherent in any mode of cultural or social study should be converted as much as possible into a source of tension that stimulates work whose import cannot be safely confined within disciplinary walls.

By now, my perorating discussion may seem to have displaced the problem of "political" and, even more so, of Marxist reading so far as to be irrelevant to their concerns. But the issue of how to read and the limits of narrowly documentary reading are highly pertinent to the Marxist tradition. If Marxism is to be reformulated as a protocol of interpretation having practical implications, it will have to come to terms with problems of "reading" in their modern forms. It will have to recognize texts—including the texts of Marx—as significant historical events worthy of careful study and related to other events in ways we are still attempting to fathom. It is not a sign of elitist prejudice to assert that certain texts have a special status: they are special not because they are the sacred pillars of a canon or the preserves of a mandarin class but because the processes they engage are among the highest and the best in our culture and still have broadly educational value. This value may become most evident and accessible when texts of the canon are reopened through more or less noncanonical, contestatory readings—readings that explicitly explore their own relations to larger historical processes and possibilities. I do not think that it is an exaggeration to say that intellectual history, in the form I have tried to present it, is at present an endangered species within the historical profession. In fact the question may not be what direction intellectual history will take but whether it will be allowed to die a graceful death as its exponents are not replaced in departments of history. The importance of reading the texts of "high culture" and of attempting to interpret them with reference to their various contexts does not depend upon any world-historical, anti-Marxist theory about the causal role of "ideas" in history. It does depend upon the argument that an informed reading of certain texts has a vital place in the formation of cultured historians and in the education of a public able to raise critical questions. We should of course make every effort to discover all the mute, inglorious Menocchios we can. [14] But we should not do so at the expense of texts that are readily available and that repay renewed investigation in good part because they provide instances of the critical and transformative activity Marx referred to as "living labor." Neither social history nor social practice is well served by the methodological scapegoating of critical intellectuals and their texts by either excluding them from the historical record as "unrepresentative" or reducing them to merely symptomatic tokens of collective discourse. In stressing the importance of a close reading of texts and a careful investigation of their relations to discursive contexts, one enables a mutually challenging interaction between social and intellectual history on what should be a matter of mutual concern: a better understanding of the actual relations between "elite" and "popular" culture in the past and a better standpoint for judging their desirable relations in the present and future.

14. The reference is to the miller whose "world view" is pieced together from testimony in inquisition registers by Carlo Ginzburg, *The Cheese and the Worms* (Baltimore, 1980).

Index

Library of Congress Cataloging in Publication Data

LaCapra, Dominick, 1939–
   Rethinking intellectual history.

   Includes index.
      1. Philosophy—Addresses, essays, lectures.
   2. Philosophy, Marxist—Addresses, essays, lectures.
   I. Title.
   B29.L24   1983   190   83-7218
   ISBN 0-8014-1587-X
   ISBN 0-8014-9886-4 (pbk.)